*Mistress of Herself*

# Mistress of Herself

## SPEECHES AND
## LETTERS OF
## ERNESTINE L. ROSE
## EARLY WOMEN'S
## RIGHTS LEADER

Edited and with a Preface and Introduction
by Paula Doress-Worters

Foreword by Ellen Carol DuBois

The Feminist Press
at the City University of New York
New York

Published in 2008 by The Feminist Press at the City University of New York
The Graduate Center
365 Fifth Avenue, Ste 5406
New York, NY 10016

Preface and Acknowledgments, Introduction, and headnotes copyright © 2007 by Paula Doress-Worters
Foreword copyright © 2007 by Ellen Carol DuBois

Library of Congress Cataloging-in-Publication Data

Rose, Ernestine L. (Ernestine Louise), 1810-1892.
  Mistress of herself : speeches and letters of Ernestine L. Rose, early women's rights leader / edited and with an introduction by Paula Doress-Worters; Foreword by Ellen Carol DuBois
      p. cm.
  ISBN-13: 978-1-55861-544-1 (lib. bdg.)
  ISBN-10: 1-55861-544-X (lib. bdg.)
  ISBN-13: 978-1-55861-543-4 (pbk.)
  ISBN-10: 1-55861-543-1 (pbk.)
  1.  Rose, Ernestine L. (Ernestine Louise), 1810-1892--Correspondence.
2.  Feminists--United States--Correspondence. 3.  Women's rights. 4.  Speeches, addresses, etc., American. I. Doress-Worters, Paula B. (Paula Brown) II. Title.
  HQ1413.R6A34 2007
  305.4209'034--dc22
                          2007021434


Cover Art: Image of Ernestine L. Rose—The Schlesinger Library, Radcliffe Institute, Harvard University. Handwriting of Ernestine L. Rose—Supplied by the National Co-operative Archive, UK (http://archive.co-op.ac.uk). Rose to Robert Owen, folio 1344, December 1844, decrying Fourierism. All inquiries should be directed to archive@co-op.ac.uk.

Text and cover design by Lisa Force
Printed in Canada

13  12  11  10  09  08    5  4  3  2  1

**To Allen J. Worters, my beloved late husband,** often my brainstorming partner and always my first reader of drafts, who gave lovingly and generously of his skills and time to this project and looked forward to the publication of this volume with great enthusiasm.

**To my dear friends and coauthors of *Our Bodies Ourselves*.** For more than thirty years I have enjoyed the support and friendship of this unique group of women who have become my closest friends and extended family. The activism of the Women's Liberation Movement that we were a part of in the 1970s, and critique of medical institutions and advocacy for universal health care in the decades that followed provided the core experiential basis for my investigation into the life and work of Ernestine L. Rose and her sister reformers.

**To all who commit themselves to the advancement of human society**. In this sentiment, I cannot improve upon the words of Ernestine L. Rose in her toast to reformers: "Let us by honoring the memory of reformers in the past, and by aiding the efforts of those in the present, encourage the rise of others in future time."

"*For here lies the corner stone of all the injustices done woman, the wrong idea from which all other wrongs proceed. She is not acknowledged as mistress of herself. From her cradle to her grave she is another's. We do indeed need and demand the other rights of which I have spoke, but let us first obtain OURSELVES.*"—Ernestine L. Rose, first day's speech at the National Woman's Rights Convention in Cleveland, Ohio, October 1853

# CONTENTS

*Unless otherwise indicated, all texts are by Ernestine L. Rose*

## 1856-1860

## 1861-1867

THE CHAMPIONS OF WOMAN'S SUFFRAGE.

# FOREWORD

There are many great women in the early history of the American women's rights movement, but not all continue to invite a kind of personal connection over history and across time. Ernestine L. Rose is one of these few. Paula Doress-Worters characterizes Rose as ahead of her time, meaning that her words, ideas, and life speak to us in modern times, even more perhaps than to her own contemporaries. Indeed, Rose saw the position of her sex from an angle different from other thoughtful women of her own time. Her speeches and writings, her life and experiences, offer oblique yet illuminating insights into the past and on the present.

Paula Doress-Worters has chosen to let Rose's words speak largely for her, providing, for the first time, virtually a complete record of Rose's public life, her speeches and writings, and the reactions of friends and critics to her words. By combining Rose's own words with the acute biographical and critical observations of the modern editor, *Mistress of Herself* brings to mind a similarly innovative volume published thirty years ago, also by The Feminist Press, Bell Gale Chevigny's *The Woman and the Myth: Margaret Fuller's Life and Writings* (1976). Although Fuller was a contemporary of Rose, the only place they met was inside the first volume of the *History of Woman Suffrage*, in which Elizabeth Cady Stanton paid tribute to them as forerunners of the women's rights movement (1881). Rose and Fuller are similarly intriguing historical figures. Like Fuller, Rose's life, combined with her insights and writings, remain so inviting and multifaceted that each generation of biographers, feminists, and general readers has found something unique, some new lesson about a woman's effort to make sense of, live through, dissent from, and change history.

Ernestine Rose offers the feminist historian a compelling combination of an heroic, path-breaking life dedicated to the well-being of all humanity, made palpable through an action-packed life of social commitment. Doress-Worters' Introduction provides an account of the limited information available about her early life. Here let me note elements which conform to the not uncommon romance of the rebellious daughter, who appears often in the history of women's rights. There is also the motherless child of a stern father, who educates his girl child because he has no son on whom to lavish his love of learning. This is much like the story that Fuller told of herself, and to some degree, Stanton's as well. There is also the loveless marriage arranged by the father, a particular element in the history of young women fleeing from traditional society into modernity. Somehow the young woman finds the strength to break away from a confining patriarchal society to search for a personal freedom that she knows exists for her somewhere. This is the story that Emma Goldman and Ayaan Hirsi Ali have told of themselves. The girl that would become the woman named Ernestine Rose found herself in these feminist autobiographical traditions.

Rather than remain a reproach to more conventional lives, however, Rose turned the freedom of action she won for herself toward the pursuit of greater freedom for all. Why did she choose social action and the pursuit of justice—rather than, for instance, cosmopolitan living or literary distinction—as the purpose of the life she had secured through her individual acts of courage and vision? One answer may be that in so doing she could seek a community of other visionaries and boundary-breakers like herself. To break free of one's inherited social restraints often secures broader vistas at the considerable cost of loneliness and alienation. Rose sought to escape such consequences within a series of alternative communities: of Owenite socialists, Paine's freethinkers, and women's rights feminists. In these contexts, she took the impulses which had led her to forge her own unconventional life, and joined them with others who also wanted to change social conditions and political possibilities for all. Ultimately, as Rose's life testifies, freedom of belief and action should not require outstanding individual heroics. Individual freedom should be the condition of all, not only of those forced by irresistible internal discontent to seek it.

The breadth of Rose's vision for radical social change is important to emphasize. She believed in women's rights and she believed in other causes as well. Popular and scholarly judgment too often miscasts feminism as an exclusive political tradition, in which dedication to women's advancement crowds out all other aspects of social change, inevitably becoming a "single-issue movement." This flies in the face of considerable evidence from many historical periods, none more insistently than the antebellum years in which the American women's rights movement came into being. Despite an increasing concern with women's rights, Rose neither turned away from her determination to overcome religious superstitions, abolish economic inequality, and banish human slavery; nor did she allow her determination to advance women's equality to be set aside in favor of these other commitments. To me, this is the repeated pattern of feminism, its reinvention through the extension of broad social justice claims to women; and the rediscovery, virtually in each generation, that women need their own champions, that change will not occur in their favor of its own accord, that finding a secure place for women's equality in a radically different social order is always a struggle, and that this struggle must always be made by women themselves.

Even in alternative communities dedicated to radical social change, Rose often found herself on the margins. Within the history of the American women's rights movement, Rose is an especially interesting figure precisely because she differed from her sister activists along several crucial dimensions. Her presence alone forbids us from describing this early movement as exclusively "white middle class." She was an immigrant among the native born and of Jewish origins in a society in which even the religious dissidents worked from thoroughly Protestant premises. She and her husband earned their living through their own labors. Among other women who linked their efforts to the national promise of American democracy, she was an internationalist. She was a socialist, by virtue of her knowledge of British Owenite communitarianism. Each of these dimensions means that once we insist on Rose's proper place among the leaders of American feminism's first generation, our sense of who and what fueled the earliest phases of that movement must be considerably enlarged.

I am particularly interested in Rose's Jewish origins. To point to Rose's Jewishness needs some clarification, in light of her strenuous repudiation of all religious superstition. In what ways then is there any point to linking this self-declared materialist and atheist to a religious tradition that she herself had abandoned, at great personal cost? Although Rose was a freethinker, she was never a Christian, despite every sort of pressure to become one. "I have not abandoned the trunk in order to attach myself to the branches," was how she explained it. By this, she meant, "If my reason prevents me from being Jewish, it cannot allow me to become Christian." Conversion, and only conversion, could have removed the taint of Jewishness under which she labored and this she would not do. Her Jewishness was thus not something from which, ultimately, she was willing to remove herself.

My point here is not a parochial one. I do not want to claim, through the mysterious alchemy of identity politics, this long-ago figure as continuous with myself. Rather I want to point to the way that Rose's irreducible non-Christianity helps us to clarify exactly what "religion" meant in antebellum United States, both to those who held fast to it and those who declared war on it. "Religion" was the hegemonic Protestantism of that time, not the diverse forms of spiritual belief and practice that we now mean by the term. Insisting on this distinction is part of the work of reconstructing those aspects of antebellum women's rights activism that are foreign to us now, all the more important given the counter-move encouraged above of linking our present to their past. Doress-Worters makes this point by emphasizing Rose's disagreements with the great antislavery leader of her time, William Lloyd Garrison, whose perfectionist Christianity fueled his driving vision for radical social change. Proper appreciation for Rose's Jewishness, I believe, is invaluable in clarifying the gap between that time and ours. Ironically, she can help us to see how crucial Protestantism was to antebellum women's rights, while at the same time making it clear that non-Christian as well as Christian impulses gave birth to that tradition.

Paula Doress-Worters links Rose's Jewishness and her own in a different way. Her labor on Rose's behalf, beginning with the memorial stone that she and her husband placed in 2002 on the unmarked grave of Ernestine and William Rose in Highgate Cemetery, London, has been a kind of religious obligation on her own part. "In Jewish ethics, it is the highest form of giving to do for the dying and dead because they cannot reciprocate," she writes. In modern Jewish belief, the dead live on in the hearts of those who cherish their memory, as long as they are remembered and honored by the living. This is also the obligation of historical reconstruction, and the act out of which ongoing traditions, political as well as religious, are made.

Rose remembered Tom Paine, who was in danger of being forgotten for his radical hopes for the American Revolution. In a similar spirit, we remember Rose, in honor of those aspects of her vision of a free womanhood that have not yet been realized and that continue to inspire. To remember our ancestors is an act on our own behalf as well as theirs.

Ellen Carol DuBois
Los Angeles, California
July 2007

# PREFACE AND ACKNOWLEDGMENTS

Ernestine's story has been calling to me since I began teaching women's studies courses in the mid-1970s. My interest in Ernestine L. Rose was first piqued by several mentions of her in Eleanor Flexner's *Century of Struggle* (1973 [1959]), which I used as a text for a course I taught on the history of women in the United States. Rose's name appeared six times, most often in a short list of important women's rights reformers. One reference that was unique to Rose described her circulation of the first petition for a Married Women's Property Law while she herself was still a new immigrant, and her distinction as the first to attempt to improve women's status through legislation (Flexner 1973, 65). I wondered why I had never heard of Ernestine Rose and, as a first-generation American, was particularly intrigued that she was an immigrant and a Jew, not a background shared by any of the women's rights reformers that I had included on my syllabus.

A search for more of Rose's story led me to the only book-length biography at the time, Yuri Suhl's *Ernestine Rose and the Battle for Human Rights* (1959), which provided a rich and lively picture of Rose's life and accomplishments. Suhl, a popular writer on secular Jewish subjects, had gathered a tremendous amount of material and had provided an extensive bibliography, but did not provide citations linking the facts to particular sources. As a feminist, I puzzled over why there was such a detailed telling of Rose's idealization of her father and her later break with him, and so little mention of her mother.

Decades passed before I, as a working mother, had the time and resources to investigate these questions. In 1998, I won an appointment as a Women's Studies Scholar at Brandeis University to pursue my interest in Rose. By then a new search led me to Carol A. Kolmerten, who was about to publish *The American Life of Ernestine L. Rose* (1999). She generously provided me with a copy of the galleys so that I could begin my project conversant with the most recent work on Rose. I was so impressed with Kolmerten's searching questions, the thoroughness of her research over some ten years, and the clarity of her presentation that I determined another biography was not needed so soon after Kolmerten had published such an excellent one.

Researching and writing about Ernestine Rose was a challenge to her twentieth-century biographers because of the absence of any repository or archive of her collected speeches, personal letters, diaries, or journals. In 1869, Rose left the United States to return to England; important papers may well have been discarded or lost at that point. At the time of her death in 1892, she had been widowed for ten years and had no living descendants who might have kept her papers. Yet the absence of journals or letters also heightened the aura of mystery surrounding the inner motivations behind Rose's life and work. For a time that mystery led me to work on a novel based on Rose's life. By combining educated hunches with creative imagination based on my own identification with Rose, I hoped to create a fictional narrative of her personal reflections as she moved through her public life of lectures and reform conventions. Chapters of that novel still sit in a box in my study, waiting for me perhaps to return to them.

The more I learned about Ernestine L. Rose, the more I felt drawn to understand what it was about her character and circumstances that enabled her extraordinary sense of agency—her ability, at the age of seventeen, to break with her destined life as a rabbi's daughter and strike out on her own to create the life she wanted to live. By leaving Poland for Berlin on her own in 1827, a time when women of any age rarely traveled without a male escort, Ernestine literally carved out her own path, one that brought her to Germany to study; to England where she embraced socialism; and then to the United States, where she broke new ground for radical women's rights reform. She was so successful in defining her life's path that, through her activism, she helped shape progress toward the egalitarian society in which she wanted to live.

My quest for Ernestine's voice and ideas led me, through unearthing her speeches and letters, to create this documentary history. Though the time was not right for another biography, I could capture Rose's voice through a compilation of her words. Rose was considered one of the foremost reformers and orators of her day, and her public life, it turned out, has been amply documented, but in many different places. Ernestine Rose spoke at every national woman's rights convention from 1850 to 1869, and those speeches were recorded in convention proceedings, most of which are extant. Other speeches and letters to the editor were preserved in reform newspapers such as the abolitionist *Liberator* and the freethought *Boston Investigator*, as well as in mainstream newspapers. The challenge was to find them. The detective work involved following clues laid down by her contemporaries, Stanton, Anthony, and Gage, who were determined to recognize and preserve her contribution to the movement. They excerpted many of her important women's rights speeches in their *History of Woman Suffrage* (1881–1886). The task was to find the original source and the complete speech. Other clues were provided by her twentieth-century biographers, Suhl (1990), who printed longer excerpts of some of her major speeches, and especially Kolmerten (1999), who tracked Rose's whereabouts during her lecture tours and cited many venues and dates of her speeches.

Reading through Rose's speeches and letters highlighted the contradictions contained within her personality and her thought. She was a socialist who fought for women's property rights; an atheist who could not simply be indifferent to religion, but remained engaged with it by struggling against its hegemonic control. Rose was an internationalist who had lived in four different countries before she became "an American by my own choice" (Yale 1931) as she declared after moving back to England in 1869. While in the United States, she devoted herself to the values of the Declaration of Independence, and to making those ideals a reality through a universal rights interpretation that included white women and all African Americans. Despite her admiration for the United States' founding documents, Rose did not herself become a U.S. citizen until three weeks before she left to return to England, although William had done so in 1845, nine years after they arrived in New York (Kolmerten 1999, 70, n1). Perhaps Ernestine Rose had been waiting for a time when women could vote and citizenship for her would be more meaningful.

The similarities between my background and that of Ernestine L. Rose are numerous, but so are the differences between us. I was not an immigrant as Rose was. Traveling and book tours aside, I have lived my whole life in and around Boston, Massachusetts. However, as the child of Polish-Jewish immigrants, I felt that Rose and I emerged from a common culture. My parents and many of my immigrant relatives, like Ernestine Rose, spoke four or five languages, and I grew up learning to recognize the differences in a person's accent and choice of words, in both English and Yiddish, depending on their country of origin. Like Rose, I became active at the dawn of a new movement. In retrospect I can see that my interest in Rose was fueled by a mid-life reappraisal of my own life as a social activist, first in the peace and civil rights movements of the 1960s and then in the second wave of the feminist movement.

In the summer of 1998, my husband, Allen Worters and I traveled to England. Included in our vacation trip was time for research on Ernestine's early years in England at the British Library in London, in Robert Owen's correspondence at the National Cooperative Archive in Manchester, and at Highgate Cemetery, where we thought we would easily find the graves of Ernestine and William Rose by following the instructions verbally "mapped out" by Yuri Suhl in his 1959 biography of Rose. Suhl took the grave of Karl Marx as his starting point in describing the location of the Roses' gravesite, perhaps wishing to link Rose's socialism and human rights activism with that of Marx. As we learned after searching with no success, scrambling over brambles and vines that had overgrown many of the headstones, Marx's grave and marker had been moved at the behest of some of his followers, perhaps believing that a liberator of the proletariat required a massive monument visible from the main road through the cemetery. Thus, Marx's marker and remains were removed to the new megamonument, and Suhl's instructions were thus a dead letter, so to speak.

On leaving Highgate, we discussed our problem with docent-administrator Dawn Squires, who offered us help. She took down the information we had with us, and later located the joint grave of the Roses by its plot number. She then sent us photographs of the site with a space where the marker should have been. We were stunned and devastated. That Ernestine L. Rose, who had devoted her life to advancing human progress and the rights of women in particular, should lie buried with her beloved and supportive husband in an unmarked grave was simply unacceptable to us. Later, when we began discussions with cemetery staff, their conjecture was that the roots of a large tree had encroached on the burial site and caused the Roses' modest stone to crumble over the years.

I determined, as part of my work to revive Rose's legacy, to raise the money needed to replace the missing marker. One concern at first gave me pause. Would Ernestine L. Rose, with her innate diffidence about personal recognition, her lifelong focus on the cause rather than the individual, have wanted money spent on such a project? Urging me forward was Rose's own heartfelt statement on the importance to progressive social change of honoring reformers of the past, supporting reformers in the present, and fostering those of the future, a sentiment that I found so persuasive that I have used Rose's words as part of the dedication to this book. She saluted Robert Owen and Frances Wright whenever there was an opportunity to do so. Indeed, Rose spoke annually for some three decades at the Thomas Paine Celebrations to revive and maintain Paine's legacy as a fighter for liberty. Others in the freethought movement also honored their forebears, some in ways similar to the mission we were now pursuing: Gilbert Vale of New York, a leading freethinker and a contemporary of Rose, undertook the repurchase of Thomas Paine's farm at New Rochelle, New York, and restoration of his burial site (Jacoby 2004, 64).

In 1963, the Emma Lazarus Federation honored Ernestine L. Rose by reprinting the proceedings of a convention where she had spoken a hundred years earlier. They included a statement from Daisy Bates, a heroine of the Civil Rights Movement in Arkansas as mentor to the Little Rock Nine, the students who integrated the city's schools. Thus they honored a reformer of the past and an activist of their own period. In doing so, they preserved a document that would otherwise not have been available to include in the present volume and made it accessible to students, scholars, and potential reformers in the future. Poet and novelist Alice Walker (1983, 93–116) wrote "Looking for Zora," a moving account of her quest to find and restore the grave of African American folklorist and novelist Zora Neale Hurston.

Finally, this project was important to me as part of the religio-cultural tradition that I shared with Rose. In Jewish ethics, it is the highest form of giving to do for the dying and dead because they cannot reciprocate. Thus one does not act out of self-interest but simply out of a desire to do the right thing. There were many reasons to go forward.

Soon after I began my residency at the Women's Studies Research Center at Brandeis University, I founded the Ernestine Rose Society with the mission of reviving Rose's legacy. The Society's first project was raising money to restore the Roses' grave marker at Highgate Cemetery. Within less than two years, the Society had nearly one hundred members and had raised enough money to purchase and engrave the stone and have it set in place. It was particularly rewarding to me that the marker was funded primarily by American women and men, those who had benefited the most from Rose's life of committed activism.

On August 4, 2002, on the 110th anniversary of the death of Ernestine L. Rose, Allen and I, with members of the Rose Society, joined with members of the Susan B. Anthony House in Rochester, New York, to hold a commemorative symposium at the Woman's Library in London, followed by a ceremony at the restored gravesite at Highgate (photographs of the event and a scripted memorial service may be found on the web site of the Ernestine Rose Society: www.brandeis.edu/centers/wsrc/Ernestine_Rose_website/ERhomepage.html).

We live in a time when the efforts to effect social change may seem ephemeral, even futile. Those who try to move society in a progressive direction may question whether they leave much of a footprint. If Ernestine Rose ever wondered about her effectiveness, she left no record of having such doubts. The story of her life is one of constant travel to carry her reform message through twenty-three of the then twenty-five states, as well as some that were still territories. She was eloquent not only about the reforms she advocated, but about the *value* of bringing the issues before the public, of debating questions at conventions and other gatherings. She also insisted upon the importance of women's voices at a time when women lacked even the power of the vote.

With this book, I hope to help preserve Rose's legacy, primarily through documents that contain her speeches, and some of her written words, along with a few key documents about her by her contemporaries. Her eloquent formulation of women's rights issues provided a new language that was key to understanding the inherent fallacy of the conventional wisdom that women lived (and must continue to live) in a "separate sphere" of domesticity. This idea had been at the core of an ideology that kept women marginal and disempowered, until Rose and her sister women's rights reformers began to chip away at it. Today, women are active in every sphere, and our task is to bring our insight, knowledge, and ability to question authority and work for change wherever our own life paths take us.

At the dawn of the twenty-first century, Rose's words exhort us to raise our voices once more to redeem the vote for which preceding generations of women fought so valiantly and with so much hope. Today, we, especially women in the United States, must wrest our elections from the control of moneyed interests that Rose alluded to in her great Voices for Votes speech of 1867. We must reclaim our right as a nation of voters to self-determination through fair and honest elections. As Ernestine Rose so cogently argued, we must live up to the promise of the Declaration of Independence for universal rights, and in our time, resist the exclusion of new groups. Finally, as Rose insisted, we must return to that core principle of our founding documents, the separation of church and state.


## ACKNOWLEDGMENTS

This work is testimony to the generosity of feminist historians, biographers, and other scholars who welcomed me into their circle and encouraged my work on Ernestine Rose, demonstrating that the alleged divide between academic and community feminists has been highly overstated.

Ellen Carol DuBois welcomed my contribution to reviving Rose's legacy by acknowledging me for my research on Rose and the founding of the Rose Society from the podium on October 27, 2001, at the conference, "Sisterhood and Slavery: Transatlantic Antislavery and Women's Rights" at the Gilder Lehrman Center of Yale University. This was not only a generous gesture, but contributed to the origins of this volume. For it was at that conference that I met Livia Tenzer, then an editor at The Feminist Press who invited me to submit a proposal for a book of

Ernestine Rose documents. Further, DuBois's books and articles on the woman's suffrage movement were invaluable to my understanding of the Proceedings where I found many of Rose's speeches. DuBois also continued to provide information and support, read an early draft of this work, and provided incisive comments and suggestions. Thanks are also due to historian June Namias for her support, and for referring me to DuBois.

My deep appreciation to Carol A. Kolmerten. Thanks to Bonnie S. Anderson, Rosalyn F. Baxandall, DuBois, and Kolmerten for their whole-hearted and scholarly contributions to a panel on the Life and Legacy of Ernestine L. Rose that I proposed and moderated at the 2002 Berkshire Conference on the History of Women. Thanks to Keri Bodensteiner, professor of speech and rhetoric at Truman State University, whose dissertation on Ernestine Rose provided a perspective on Rose as a public speaker and reassured me that I hadn't missed any major speeches or letters.

Thanks to Shulamit Reinharz, director of the Women's Studies Research Center at Brandeis University, for seeing the potential of my research on Ernestine Rose and providing a supportive context for me to reinvent myself as a scholar of women's history. Thanks to my sister scholars at the WSRC for their unfailing support, and in particular to my writing groups: Writing Women's Lives/ Memoir I, and The Biography Group for providing a collegial environment, and incisive comments and suggestions. And many thanks to WSRC scholars Susan Porter and Sherri Broder for reviewing drafts from the perspective of historians.

My thanks to the Hadassah-Brandeis Institute for a generous grant in support of this work. I am also grateful to the Student-Scholar Partner program at the WSRC for providing me with intrepid and intellectually curious student assistants, Carla Hostetter, Ying Hua Huang, Vered Blonstein and Rita Trivedi.

Thanks to the community of friends, independent scholars, and editors who helped in a variety of ways.

Denise Bergman helped editorially with style and language issues. I first met Denise, when she served as a coeditor of the 1998 edition of *Our Bodies, Ourselves,* and I was her editorial board contact. When we introduced ourselves and discovered that we were each writing about the life of a woman whose history had been lost, she as poet-biographer of Annie Sullivan, the conclusion of our work meeting turned into a visit of discovery that continued throughout that afternoon, and in some sense continued over years as we met to discuss and critique one another's work.

Laurie Carter Noble, biographer of the Reverend Olympia Brown, was another independent scholar with whom I met regularly as we each researched the life of a forgotten suffragist. Carter Noble was a bracing-goals partner as we kept each other on track with our projects.

My thanks to cousin and friend, Frieda Forman, translator and editor of Yiddish women writers, for advice and resources on the language and culture of Rose's Eastern European Jewish origins and on German-Jewish research as well. Thanks to Lisa Samelson who provided me, through her family, with links to the survivors of Piotrkow, Poland, Rose's birthplace, and referred me also to Ben Giladi, editor of *A Tale of One City* which contains a detailed and comprehensive timeline and history of Piotrkow (1991).

For help with the period of Rose's self-education in Berlin, I am grateful to Sabine von Mering, Assistant Professor of German in the Department of German, Russian, and Asian Languages and Literatures and Executive Director of the Center for German and European Studies. It was a privilege to audit her provocative and eye-opening seminar, "Jewish-German Woman Writers," and to have the benefit of her informed comments on my writing about Rose's Berlin years. Thanks to Marvin Shulman, Professor Emeritus of German at Barnard College who generously emptied out his library and shared his deep knowledge of German culture to acquaint me with Berlin of the 1820s when Rose lived there.

For information on the Owenite socialist movement in England, I am grateful to Edward (Ted) Royle of York University for sharing his scholarship on Robert Owen and the Owenites, and to Kolmerten for referring me to him, and for her work on that movement. My deep appreciation to Barbara Taylor for her startlingly original work on the women of the Owenite movement. Thanks to Gillian Lonergan at the Cooperative College in Manchester, UK, for welcoming me to the National Cooperative Archive and for access to documents from the Robert Owen Correspondence.

Many, many librarians helped with the search for Rose's speeches and letters. My deepest gratitude goes to the dedicated librarians at the Schlesinger Library on the History of Women at Harvard University, especially Sarah Hutcheon, who demonstrated a special gift for locating Proceedings of women's rights conventions and other women's rights documents that were especially hard to find. Thanks to Eric Robinson and Jan Hilley of the New-York Historical Society for finding, copying, and sending pages of Proceedings, as requested, to staff at the Sophia Smith Collection at Smith College, and to Alex Rankin at the Howard Gottlieb Archival Research Center at Boston University for assistance with the Yuri Suhl papers.

Because the Freethought movement has been so little studied, finding information on its history was challenging. Dennis Laurie was most helpful and welcoming during my research at The American Antiquarian Society in Worcester, Massachusetts, a beautiful historic building with computer hookups that holds an unparallelled collection of early American newspapers. It was there that I tracked Rose's path in the Freethought movement through the pages of the *Boston Investigator*. The AAS holds a comprehensive collection of that newspaper that spans the nineteenth century, perhaps the only such collection on the east coast. Archivists at the Isaac and Amy Post Family Papers web page helped me find the Proceedings of the Hartford Bible Convention of 1853. Thanks to Martha Smalley at Yale Divinity School Library who kindly provided copies of Rose's two speeches at the HBC.

To the team at The Feminist Press, Florence Howe, editor and publisher, whose thoughtful, incisive, and critical comments and suggestions helped me pare and improve the manuscript. Jean Casella, the most engaged copy editor imaginable, one who knew so much about feminism in the nineteenth century. It was a pleasure to work with Anjoli Roy, a smart and highly responsive assistant editor.

How can I ever adequately acknowledge the many roles played in creating this volume by my late husband, Allen J. Worters, to whom this volume is dedicated? He was a willing and eager research assistant, technical assistant for public presentations, creator of the web site for the Ernestine Rose Society, and coeditor for graphics and layout of the Society's annual newsletter. It was one of his web searches that turned up the Isaac and Amy Post Family web page.

Despite this outpouring of support from so many family members, friends, and colleagues, some errors may have crept in during the execution of this project, and these, of course, are my own responsibility.

Paula Doress-Worters
Brandeis University, Massachusetts
August 2006

Photograph copyright © 2002 by Nigel Sutton, taken on August 4, 2002, of the Highgate Cemetery ceremony to dedicate the new grave marker for Ernestine and William Rose, including a delegation of five members of the Susan B. Anthony (SBA) House in Rochester, New York. From left to right: Jean Fushi, Chicago; Anna Davin, Middlesex University, United Kingdom, and SUNY, Binghamton; Sue Gaffney, SBA; Barbara Blaisdell, SBA; Teresa Froncek, SBA; Paula Doress-Worters, founder of Ernestine Rose Society, Brandeis University; Colleen Hurst, historian at SBA; Lorraine Cappellino, SBA; Carol A. Kolmerten, author of *The American Life of Ernestine L. Rose*; and Allen J. Worters, webmaster and member of Ernestine Rose Society.

# INTRODUCTION

On May 14, 1836,[1] Ernestine L. Rose and her husband, William E. Rose, disembarked at the Port of New York as immigrants from England to the United States. Within months of their arrival, a new voice resonated from the reform platforms of the northeastern states. It was a strong, fervent, melodic voice, praising, in foreign-accented English, the Declaration of Independence, and protesting the exclusion of white women and all African Americans from its promise of universal justice. The voice was that of the petite, twenty-six-year-old, Polish-Jewish Ernestine L. Rose.

Rose captivated her audiences with the passion and audacity of her women's rights reform message, her freethought ideas, and her utter lack of self-consciousness. As she walked about the platform, her clear brown eyes conveyed sincerity of feeling, while her orator's gestures added emphasis and fervor to her eloquent arguments. Her caustic humor provided a defense against hecklers, and served to entertain and win over her audiences.

Simply appearing before mixed audiences flouted the accepted customs of her adopted land, where the public platform was still off-limits to women. But Rose was a visually striking figure as well. Unlike most married women of her day, she did not cover her head in a gesture of modesty or piety, and her black curls cascaded over her shoulders. Rose dressed with European sophistication and simplicity, in black or gray with white lace at her throat and cuffs and ever-present leather gloves. To accentuate the simplicity of her outfit, she wore a single piece of jewelry, either a cameo pin or a watch on a chain. Both pieces may have been crafted by her husband, a jeweler and watchmaker, from whom she was separated during her frequent and often lengthy lecture tours.

## EUROPEAN ROOTS OF ROSE'S LIFE AND IDEAS

The women's rights activist known in the United States as Ernestine L. Rose was born on January 13, 1810, in Piotrkow, Poland. Her biographers have noted that Ernestine Louise was not a likely name to be given to a Jewish child in Poland. It is certainly possible that she took those names, popular among German-Jewish women during the 1820s, while living in Berlin in her late teens. However, Jews in the West, in addition

1

to Hebrew and Yiddish names, often give their children names adapted to the countries in which they live. Piotrkow was under Prussian rule prior to the time of Ernestine's birth, so she might well have been given German names. Of perhaps greater significance is her use of two last names prior to her marriage, when she called herself Ernestine Susmond Potowski. Suhl (1959;1990) refers to her father as Rabbi Potowski, but d'Héricourt (1856, in Doress-Worters 2003) refers to Ernestine as Mlle. Susmond, perhaps a family name from her mother's side.

Rose described her father to Jenny P. d'Héricourt, her first biographer, as "one of the principal rabbis of the city," respected for "his science, his virtue, and to some degree for his wealth" (1856, in Doress-Worters 2003, 190). D'Héricourt discusses Ernestine's relationship with her father in great detail but does not discuss Ernestine's mother's role in her upbringing.

A significant part of Ernestine's socialization as a Jewish child, typically imparted by both parents, would have been the Judaic ethic of repairing and restoring the world through acts of charity. Rose did not specifically refer to Jewish ethical precepts, preferring to speak of "human progress," but the ideal of repairing the world was one that she exemplified in her actions throughout her life.[2]

It was not usual in Jewish communities of Poland during Ernestine's childhood to educate girls beyond the elementary level. Yet her father, a scholarly rabbi whom she revered, taught her, at her own demand, to read Torah in Hebrew so that she could discuss the original texts with him. Ernestine may also have learned the Talmudic style of scholarship—how to look beneath the surface of a text, to raise questions, and to argue her case. She would have learned thereby to *value* argument as part of a mutual search for understanding, rather than to avoid argument as an expression of rudeness, aggression, or hostility. This would have set her apart from most women of her generation, in Jewish and especially in Christian society (Kolmerten 1999, 117).

However, young Ernestine's rationalist turn of mind and intellectual precocity led her to ask questions that pushed the limits of her father's and her community's religious tolerance. Neighbors began to gossip that she was a heretic; her father became alarmed, informing her that a young girl's place was not to understand the reasons for the laws, but simply to obey them (d'Héricourt 1856, in Doress-Worters 2003, 191).

Ernestine's modern ideas may have stemmed from the influence of the Haskalah, the Yiddish literary movement that brought the rationalist ideas of the Enlightenment to the Jewish communities of Eastern Europe. Some rabbis declared the movement's books trafe, or forbidden. Despite these efforts to keep modern, secular ideas out of traditional Jewish communities, such books continued to circulate clandestinely in reading groups and even sewing circles (Kellman 1997, 18–21; Parush 1994, 1–23).

When Ernestine was fifteen, her mother died suddenly. Fearing that without his wife's help he would lose all ability to rein in Ernestine's rebelliousness, her father, just one year later, arranged a marriage for Ernestine to a man closer to his own age than to hers. While it was customary at the time for young women in Polish-Jewish communities to marry in their mid-teens, the ages of their husbands could vary enormously, since romantic love was not a priority in making matches. In an extraordinarily courageous move for her time and station in life, Ernestine refused the match, telling her father she would agree to marry only for love with an equal partner, not a master who would take control of her life. Threatened with forfeiture of her inheritance from her mother—which had been promised as dowry in the marriage contract her father had signed, and could be claimed as damages if the contract were not carried out—young Ernestine took another unprecedented action. She traveled, in winter by sleigh, to appeal to the secular court in Kalisz, where she argued her own case, and won. No one has yet authenticated Rose's story by finding the record of her successful appeal at the court at Kalisz, to retain her inheritance, which apparently took place about 1826, but she provided an account of it in her own testimony to d'Héricourt (1856, in Doress-Worters 2003, 192). It is not known where she learned the skills required to win a legal case. Perhaps her early training in Talmudic argument was a factor. That victory may well have been a defining moment for Ernestine—the moment when she recognized her own powers as a speaker, and realized that if she could successfully fight injustice for herself, perhaps she could do so for others as well.

When she returned home, she turned over most of the recovered money to her father. Fearing that unearned wealth would corrupt her, she kept only enough money to live on until she could find work to support herself. At seventeen, Ernestine Louise Susmond Potowski left home for Berlin, a city she admired as a center of Enlightenment thought, never to return to her family or community in Poland.

When Susmond Potowski (Rose) arrived at the gates of Berlin, she found that the laws were not as enlightened as the ideas she had associated with that city. Jews were restricted from settling in Berlin unless they brought with them a significant amount of capital. Rose told d'Héricourt that she appealed first to a police chief at the city gate, then to a magistrate, who in turn conducted her to a minister of Frederick William III, King of Prussia. The king proposed that admission to Berlin would be simplified if Ernestine would only adopt Christianity. If she agreed to be baptized, he himself would be her godfather. She replied, "I thank you, Sire . . . but I have not abandoned the trunk in order to attach myself to the branches. If my reason prevents me from being Jewish, it cannot allow me to become Christian" (d'Héricourt 1856, in Doress-Worters 2003, 193). D'Héricourt reports that the king, who fancied himself an enlightened monarch, provided Ernestine with a residence permit despite her refusal of baptism.

Could such an incident as meeting the king of Prussia ever have happened? Monarchs, especially "enlightened" ones, as well as U.S. presidents of that period, sometimes held open sessions to meet people and hear their ideas and grievances. Even in her youth, Ernestine chose to make her voice heard. Ever resourceful, she supported herself for the next year and a half in Berlin, at first by tutoring and then by marketing a product of her own invention that dispelled unpleasant odors, something considered highly desirable by new residents of the rapidly growing tenements of Berlin. These room-perfuming papers turned out to be profitable enough to allow Ernestine to give up tutoring in order to study and to explore Berlin and its surroundings. From 1827 to 1829, therefore, Ernestine Susmond Potowski lived in a modest rented room and studied "the laws of men and society." Yuri Suhl describes her transformation from a "ghetto provincial" to "a much traveled, well-informed young lady" who spoke perfect German (Suhl 1990, 24). These two years were, in a sense, her university education.

Women were not admitted to German universities until the 1890s, and Jewish students were kept to a very limited quota, so Susmond Potowski could not possibly have attended as a regular student. Yet, senior professors were known to hold advanced seminars in their own homes, and a determined young woman could prevail upon a male student to take her along to such a class.[3] Newspaper reading rooms were another source of education, especially about politics and current events. In addition, they offered the possibility of meeting others with similar political concerns and opinions.

Susmond Potowski could also have attended salons where intellectuals gathered to discuss arts and ideas; by the turn of the 19th century, more than half the salons in Berlin were hosted by German-Jewish women, such as Rahel Varnhagen and Dorothea Schlegel (Hertz 1995, 184–85). The Jewish background they shared with Ernestine would have increased the likelihood of having acquaintances in common, and Ernestine's interests in Enlightenment thought and social change would have fit well with topics discussed at many salons. Many of the *salonnières* were converts to Christianity, often out of a desire for social acceptance more than religious conviction, and some later wrote of regretting their choice. The German poet Heinrich Heine noted, with regard to his own conversion to Christianity, that baptism for Jews was "a ticket of admission to European culture" (Heine 1995, 258–59). Perhaps observation of the effects of such social inequality was part of what prompted Susmond Potowski to characterize Berlin, upon leaving that city on June 6, 1829, as a place of "public and private misfortunes" (d'Héricourt 1856, in Doress-Worters 2003, 193).

## ENGLAND AND OWENISM

At the age of twenty, having visited France for over a year and Holland briefly (and having lost many of her belongings in a shipwreck), Ernestine Louise Susmond Potowski arrived in London in 1830. Knowing not a word of English, she purchased a dictionary in order to describe her home-perfuming invention to pharmacists, whom she persuaded to market her product on consignment. To augment her income until her products began to sell, she obtained employment tutoring the four daughters of a duke in Hebrew and German (d'Héricourt 1856, in Doress-Worters 2003, 193). Ever eager to find others who shared her views and ideals, she continued her study of "men and laws," attending lectures and tours by prominent reformers.

The reformer who most impressed her was Robert Owen (1771–1858), a wealthy industrialist turned social reformer often described as the father of British socialism. Owen put his communitarian ideology into practice by founding cooperative communities in conjunction with his mills and factories. At New Lanark in Scotland, for example, children under ten were educated at the expense of the community and were forbidden to labor in factories, as was the practice almost everywhere else where industrialization was under way. Among other reforms, Owen advocated national, publicly supported education for children and succeeded in convincing the king of Prussia to start one of the first public school systems in the world. Owen would become Ernestine's mentor in social theory and public speaking, and later her colleague as a social reformer. Robert Owen believed that individuals should not be blamed for crimes and misdeeds; instead they were to be educated, preferably in planned communal settings. In contrast to most of the ideologies of the time, which emphasized sin as the cause of vice and misery, Owen taught that people are shaped by the kinds of communities in which they are reared. Therefore, to improve individual character, it was necessary to improve the social environment.

In the 1820s, Robert Owen, together with his son, Robert Dale Owen, founded a community in Indiana called New Harmony. Like many experiments in communal living, especially the secular ones (Kanter 1972), New Harmony failed in less than a decade,[4] and the senior Owen returned to England in 1829, at a time when there was a resurgence of interest in his social theories (Suhl 1990, 31).

It was during this second wave of Owenite socialism that twenty-year-old Ernestine Susmond Potowski arrived in England. Exploring the various sects and groups meeting in 1830s London, seeking broader knowledge and understanding of the interplay of individual and society, she was deeply impressed by the generosity and humanity of Owen's social philosophy.

Carol A. Kolmerten discovered a letter in the *New Moral World*, an Owenite newspaper, that she "would like to believe" was written by Ernestine Louise Susmond Potowski (Kolmerten 1999, 19, n22). Published on November 29, 1834, the letter, addressed to Robert Owen and signed "E.L.," conveys the sense of revelation that Ernestine seems to have found in Owenite ideas.

> No words can possibly express the joy and delight I feel in looking over the different plans proposed by you to terminate the irrational existence of moral evil, and to enter upon that of moral good. I have just been perusing the last number of the *New Moral World*, I may add, with great pleasure and a solid satisfaction. Every number that comes out appears to me so big with truth, that almost all the other periodical publications sink into nothingness in comparison with this. (Quoted in Kolmerten 1999, 19, n22)

Kolmerten suspects that Susmond Potowski is the author of the letter because it reflects the "ardor" for Owen's ideas that Rose continued to express throughout her life. I find the language and style similar to Rose's later letters and speeches but with the added glow of her youthful enthusiasm. And the publication of the letter in 1834 is consistent with the dating of other events, including Susmond Potowski's arrival in London and the beginning of her involvement in the Owenite movement.[5]

Soon after her arrival, Ernestine Susmond Potowski began to speak at Owenite events, some of which she also organized and staffed—including, as she later told d'Héricourt, washing the cups and saucers. As in many utopian movements, women often continued to do the domestic work, though in groups rather than isolated at home (Kolmerten 1999,

10–18). Nonetheless, a most appealing feature of Owenism for a young woman in search of gender justice must have been the active feminist wing of the movement, which included such impressive speakers and writers as Anna Wheeler, Emma Martin, and Frances Wright (Taylor 1993). In the Owenite movement Susmond Potowski honed her English language, public speaking, and convention-leading skills. She contributed to an important conference called the Association of All Classes and All Nations (AACAN) held in 1835, when the Owenites moved from a focus on trade unionism to a vision of unity across all social groups and classes. Throughout her life, Rose was proud of the progressive nature of the resolutions passed at AACAN, and often cited them in her subsequent years in the United States. The text of the resolutions reveal, among other things, the Owenite perspective that socialism is inextricably linked with opposition to organized religion, and clearly in keeping with Susmond Potowski Rose's freethought beliefs.

> The religion of the New Moral World consists in the unceasing practice of promoting the happiness of every man, woman, and child, to the greatest extent in our power, without regard to their class, sect, party, country or color.
>
> There will therefore be no worship—no forms or ceremonies— no temples—no prayers—no gloom—no mortification of the flesh or spirit—no anger on account of religious differences—no persecutions, but friendship, kindness and charity for the Jew and Gentile. All that will be required by man for the Glory of God, will be to make himself and all the other living things, as happy as possible.
>
> In the New Moral World to produce happiness with others will be the only religion of man, and the worship of God will consist in the practice of useful industry, in the acquisition of knowledge; in uniformly speaking the truth; and in the expression of joyous feelings which a life in accordance with nature and truth will be sure to produce. (Quoted in Suhl 1990, 33)

In addition to meeting politically congenial comrades, Ernestine found her life companion in the Owenite movement. She married William Ella Rose, a silversmith and jeweler three years her junior, who became her confidant and the loving supporter of her reform activities. In keeping with a shared belief in avoiding religious ceremonies, Ernestine married William in a civil ceremony conducted by a notary in her rented room.

Very soon thereafter, in 1836, Ernestine and William Rose sailed to New York. They were part of an Owenite emigrant group of thirty-six persons, who were planning the establishment of Socialland, an Owenite community (Kolmerten, 1999, 19–20). During the crossing, Rose observed that members of the group did not seem to be prepared for the mutuality required by communal life. Instead of settling with the Owenite colony, Ernestine and William chose to live and work in New York City. J.B. Hatrat, a contemporary writer on emigration recommended settlement in large cities among people who shared their values and customs (Kolmerten 1999, 20). The Roses may have read his work and followed his advice by establishing themselves on the Lower East Side of Manhattan among a community of immigrant freethinkers. Once they settled in New York, William opened a silversmith shop, and Ernestine offered for sale European-style colognes of her own manufacture.

While Owenite thought advocated planned rural communities that would serve as models of the "New Moral World," it also offered another path. Individuals could serve Owenite goals by working for broadscale social change in the larger society—advocating against child labor, for free public education, for women's economic and legal rights and divorce reform, among other human rights. This was the path that Rose ultimately chose.

## BEGINNING A CONVERSATION ON WOMEN'S RIGHTS

Almost as soon as she set foot on American shores, Rose began speaking in public on a variety of reforms, but whatever her topic, she always linked it to women's rights (Kolmerten 1999, 37-68). Rose's model for bringing reform issues before the public was Frances Wright, a Scotswoman who shared with Rose a commitment to the socialist philosophy of Robert Owen. Wright had come to the United States in the 1820s to lecture on a variety of issues, including freethought, women's rights, and opposition to slavery. Rose credited Frances Wright for being the first to break up "the time-hardened soil" of conservatism and propriety. Many years later, Rose visited Wright's burial place in Cincinnati following a women's convention there, and reflected upon Wright's legacy in her letter of November 20, 1855. Eventually, severe criticism and notoriety diminished Wright's influence, and personal tragedies, including a bad marriage, depleted her energies. While Wright was long remembered as an inspiring author and orator, her work did not lead to continuing efforts toward women's rights.[6]

When Ernestine Rose arrived in the United States nearly two decades after Frances Wright, there was still no organized women's rights movement. Eager to raise the issue, Rose toured as an itinerant lecturer, speaking on women's rights in a republic, a lecture known as her "Science of Government" speech.[7] She toured in twenty-three of the twenty-five states then in existence. Rose's primary goal as a visionary activist was always to "agitate the issues," with the intention of reaching as many people as possible with her speeches and petitions. She did so by combining factual information and laws as well as women's personal experiences. Intellectual honesty was an important value for Rose. As a freethinker, she urged her audiences to rely upon their own reason rather than religious authority or custom to decide what was right. She believed that debate was an important way to discover "the truth," that in the free exchange of ideas the best ideas would win out. Her desire to speak was so strong that she was away from home nearly six months of each year, speaking wherever she could. Ernestine L. Rose practiced what she preached to other reformers—a life of generous and deep commitment to human rights and human progress.

> Throughout the 1840s, Rose spoke on a variety of platforms: Paine freethought celebrations, Owenite community-building conferences and social reform conventions, and abolitionist rallies. Rose's activities in the 1840s illustrate how literally and figuratively multilingual she was. Her many activities—their variety plus the fact that she appeared on stages with so many different people, speaking for so many different causes—helped create a political and cultural climate that accepted women as part of a reformist agenda. Rose's experience rousing audiences at conventions during the 1840s provided an invaluable grounding for the women's rights movement that would fully emerge in the 1850s. (Kolmerten 1999, 40)

Rose was not alone in building a platform for women's rights through involvement in other reform movements of the time. Many of the Quaker women who would become central to the women's rights movement, including Lucretia Mott, and Sarah and Angelina Grimké, found their voices while speaking out against slavery as unjust and contradictory to Christianity (Lerner 1971; Sklar 2000, 21–24). Like Rose, the Grimké sisters traveled and spoke as itinerant lecturers in the mid-1830s, so it is possible that they and Rose met or at least knew each other. If they met during this early period, such a meeting remains undocumented. It is also possible that they met later at women's rights or antislavery meetings or through mutual friends, most likely among the Philadelphia Quakers.

Nevertheless, we can imagine Rose's joy when she learned of activist abolitionist women, such as Sarah and Angelina Grimké and Lucretia Mott, already lecturing in public and thus demonstrating the equality of women as fighters for justice. Together with these women, Rose began to build a movement for women's rights.

In those early days prior to women's rights conventions, Rose presented her talks as an itinerant lecturer throughout New York State, Pennsylvania, and by 1845 as far west as Indiana and "several settlements in the backwoods of Ohio" (*1877 January*). Rose traveled by train when she could but often had to resort to traveling in uncomfortable stagecoaches and sleighs, even walking part of the way. According to her friend Joseph Barker, to reach less accessible destinations, Rose often had to walk along riverbeds and swamps "exposed to the deadly vapors of unhealthy regions" (Kolmerten 1999, 158).

Traveling to the Midwest in a time of primitive transportation and hardscrabble pioneer homesteads may have put a strain on Rose's already fragile health. As she headed home from Ohio in 1845, Rose became ill with "the ague," as malaria was then commonly called, with symptoms including fever, shaking, and chills. By the time she reached Buffalo, New York, a state of delirium had developed which prevented her continuing on her journey. A Quaker family in Buffalo took her in and cared for her with the help of a friend who traveled from Syracuse (Suhl 1990, 88–89). William Rose traveled to Ernestine's bedside to comfort her and assure himself that she was receiving the best care. He then returned to New York City and wrote to Robert Owen and the freethought community to report on Ernestine's health (*1845 September*).

Within a year of being dangerously ill, Rose was once again on the road. She addressed committees of state legislatures, including those of New York and Massachusetts, as early as 1846 (Kolmerten 1999, 56–57). She brought the ideas and energy of the nascent women's movement to the young state of Michigan, twice addressing its legislature and speaking in Detroit, Lansing, and Ann Arbor (57). Indeed, Rose may have attended the follow-up convention later that summer in Rochester, as implied in her letter on the thirty-year anniversary of the National Woman Suffrage Convention (*1878 July*).

Rose was the first in the United States to petition a state legislature for women's rights and to seek legislation as a remedy for women's lack of rights (Flexner 1973, 65), all the more remarkable considering her status as a newly arrived immigrant. Within six months of arriving in the United States, she began collecting signatures urging passage in New York State of the first married women's property rights legislation in the nation. The bill had been introduced by Thomas Herttell, a New York City judge elected to the New York State Assembly as the candidate of the Working-man's Party (Kolmerten 1999, 31).[8] It took courage to take on the power structure of her newly adopted country, yet Rose's ability to launch a peti-tion campaign may have stemmed from her six-year sojourn in England (1830–1836) where a number of radical movements were in progress in addition to that of the Owenite Socialists. She may have observed the power of petitions, especially to improve the lot of those without a vote, from the success of British women who successfully petitioned in 1834 for the abolition of slavery in the British colonies (Midgley 1992).

The Chartist Movement, based on "the People's Charter," was anoth-er British political movement that made the collection of signatures a central political strategy to attain their objectives. In 1839 the Char-tists collected one million and a quarter signatures to present to Parlia-ment, and by 1842 they had collected over three million. The Charter's six demands, universal (male) suffrage, equal representation, abolition of the requirement that elected representatives be property owners, payment for those who serve in Parliament (so that the nonwealthy could serve), annual general elections, and the secret ballot were considered radical, verging on subversive at the time. In retrospect, the Chartist's demands formed the underpinning of representative democracy as we understand it today (see Glenn Everett's "Chartism or the Chartist Movement" 1987). Yet, even the British Chartists, the most radical democratizing movement in the oldest parliamentary democracy in Western Europe, refused to include women in their demands for the expansion of democratic rights for all adults (Offen 2000, 110).

Rose, according to her account, started the petition campaign on her own in New York City in "the winter of 1836–37" (*1877 January*).[9] It did not, however, remain a one-woman movement for long: Within a year or two, Paulina Wright (Davis) was collecting signatures in west-ern New York. In 1840, Elizabeth Cady Stanton and other women across New York State began to collect ever more signatures, until thousands of women had signed the petitions. Rose addressed the New York State leg-islature numerous times during the 1840s, and Stanton eventually did so as well, in 1848. Stanton enjoyed the credibility of being the daughter of Judge Cady, a member of the State Assembly. Unable to talk Stanton out of her support of new rights for women, Judge Cady coached her in how to appeal to the Assembly and threw his support behind the new legisla-tion. The groundbreaking law was passed in April 1848, three months before the convention in Seneca Falls that has been widely credited as the birth of the women's rights movement.

The first Married Women's Property Act was limited in its scope. It covered only married women and protected only those who had brought assets into a marriage. Married women needed many more reforms to make them equals in marriage, but passage of the first such bill provided women's rights reformers with an early victory even as they were mobilizing for their first women's rights convention. As Stanton notes in her memoir, its passage by an all-male legislative assembly served as an incentive to women to ask for more (Stanton 1997, 150).

Many waves of petition campaigns followed, with speeches on legal and economic issues, Rose's specialty areas, woven into the agendas of state and national conventions. These campaigns included demands that married women control their wages (which could be legally taken directly from their employers by their husbands); that inheritance rights for widows and widowers be equalized; that mothers have equal control over child custody (a father could board a child out to work or school without the mother's permission). Gaining the right to the custody of children within marriage increased women's chances of obtaining custody after divorce; the father's presumptive right to custody had in the past served as a deterrent to women seeking to get out of abusive marriages. After years of debate, these aims would finally be achieved in New York State in 1860, inspiring a wave of such laws in other states (*1860 March*).

## CREATING A MOVEMENT: THE NATIONAL WOMEN'S RIGHTS CONVENTIONS

The Seneca Falls Convention of 1848 has been highlighted by many historians as the birth of the U.S. women's rights movement. As Eleanor Flexner observes in her groundbreaking work, *Century of Struggle*, however, birth is only one moment in a longer process of gestation. Consciousness about women's wrongs and women's rights had been building for half a century (1973, 77).

The convention was a local, or at best a regional event for women and men who came from a radius of 50 miles in response to a single advertisement in the *Seneca Courier*. Undoubtedly there was also a great deal of word-of-mouth promotion on the part of the women who had planned the gathering. Elizabeth Cady Stanton and Lucretia Mott had longed to hold such a meeting ever since they first met in London in 1840 when women delegates were refused their seats at a World Anti-Slavery Convention. The opportunity presented itself when the Motts were traveling to attend a Quaker conference in the Seneca Falls area to which the Stantons had recently relocated. Together with Mott's sister, Martha Coffin

Wright, Jane Hunt, and Mary Ann McClintock, they planned a public meeting. Under Stanton's leadership, they drafted a Declaration of Sentiments concerning women's rights modeled on the Declaration of Independence.

Ernestine L. Rose was not present at this historic meeting, and her biographers have wondered why not. Various theories have been proposed, but we do not have the documentation to answer the question and can only speculate. Had Stanton, who knew her from the campaign for the married Women's Property Act, not thought to invite her? Was the Convention too much a local affair in the minds of the organizers even to consider inviting participants from outside the immediate area? Had Rose been invited, but declined due to illness? Rose was often ill with the ague during the 1840s and may have wished to avoid the swampy Seneca Falls/Genesee area. On the other hand, Rose, who lived in New York City, and who had been traveling extensively in the late 1840s as far away as Massachusetts, Indiana, Michigan, and South Carolina, may have been traveling at the time of the 1848 Convention.

By the 1850s, Rose was in the thick of an organized women's rights movement in the United States, with annual national conventions and local and regional meetings in many areas. After years of traveling from town to town in relative obscurity, activist reformers gained from these annual conventions the opportunity to address hundreds of women all gathered in one place, all avid to hear them, and all eager to participate in debates and discussions. The participants, whose numbers grew each year, were often sent home with petitions and literature to circulate in their hometowns, further expanding the national network of women's rights reformers.

The first two *national* women's rights conventions were convened at Worcester, Massachusetts, not only home to a lively community of activist women, but also a railroad hub to which women from all over the United States could readily travel. In addition to improved transportation, the invention of the telegraph also contributed to the effectiveness of reformers in planning and conducting meetings and conventions.[10] It was a fortuitous turn of events for the women's rights movement that telegraph lines reached Rochester, New York, by 1848 (Goldsmith 1999, 33).[11] In those years between the Seneca Falls Convention and the beginning of national women's rights conventions in 1850, the availability of telegraphing increased exponentially, thus expanding the speed and ease of communication among reformers, including confirmation that prominent speakers would be available on projected convention dates, and also allowing newspapers to report on conventions promptly and widely.

From that first national women's rights convention in 1850 through the next two decades, Rose served as a featured speaker, a committee member, and a framer and debater of resolutions. The Business Committee, her committee of choice, was the one responsible for drafting resolutions to be debated at the conventions, a skill Rose had learned in the Owenite movement in England. Rose thrived on participation in the debates. She had a firm grasp on her ideas and was deft at speaking extemporaneously as well as in prepared speeches. She often gave a prepared speech in the evening, an honor reserved to the best and most entertaining of the speakers. As a particularly well-known and well-regarded orator and debater, she also attracted newspaper coverage to the cause (Kolmerten 1999, 100–01). The text of Rose's speech at the first national convention survives, for example, only because it was reported in the *New York Tribune*, since it was omitted from the proceedings (*1850 October*). She achieved additional coverage for the movement by writing letters to newspapers, though the mainstream papers rarely printed them. Over the years, Rose developed a pattern of writing letters to the editor at the *Boston Investigator*, a weekly freethought paper, and also sending along the letters that the *New York Times* and *Tribune* had chosen not to print.

The mid-1850s were the heyday of visionary women's rights reformers, who rode a wave of excitement that kept them in constant motion. In addition to the conventions, Rose continued her practice of lecture tours, speaking on women's rights and a variety of other reforms. Kolmerten identifies 1853 as Rose's most crucial year as an activist (1999, 102); Yuri Suhl, in an earlier biography, names 1855 as her busiest one (1990, 167–69). Certainly the years 1853 to 1855 represented the zenith of her fame as a public figure. For example, in 1854, Rose traveled with Susan B. Anthony to the border states region including Washington, D.C., Baltimore, Maryland, and Alexandria, Virginia, "to bring women's rights to the South." Despite such efforts, it remained a movement based in the northeast and closely linked with the antislavery movement. Rose was drawn into controversy for discussing slavery when the issue came up, for she could not, in conscience, hold back from doing so even when speaking in states where slavery was legal. Rose and Anthony were refused the use of a hall at the U.S. Capitol and another in Alexandria on grounds of Rose's lack of affiliation with any religious society, and instead Rose spoke at Carusi's Saloon, an elegant restaurant and ballroom in Washington, D.C. (Kolmerten 1999, 141–45). Following the southern tour, Rose and Anthony toured New York State together with the Reverend Antoinette Brown (Blackwell), addressing many local and regional conventions along the way (Kolmerten 1999, 140–54, 164–70).

Rose often spoke on four major components of women's rights reform: education, occupation, legal rights (especially after women married), and political rights. In her women's rights speeches she sometimes focused on one of these topics and sometimes ranged over all four—as she did in one of her most highly praised speeches, at the second national women's rights convention in Worcester in October 1851, where she incorporated a variety of situations, laws, and anecdotes. Rose gave this speech numerous times on the road and later she published a version with a slightly different introduction. She had perhaps learned from her experience at the first national convention, when her remarks during the debates were not included in the published proceedings. She prepared her 1851 speech in advance, had it printed, and arranged to have it circulated as a pamphlet (Rose 1851).

## BUILDING BRIDGES: FREETHOUGHT AND WOMEN'S RIGHTS

Throughout this period of heightened women's rights activism, Rose continued her equally fervent advocacy for the cause of freethought. Because of Rose's multiple affiliations, she was able to disseminate the ideas of each of her causes more widely, bringing women's rights and antislavery to freethought events and freethought ideas to women's conventions.

At an Owenite social reform convention in Boston in 1844, Rose had already spoken on secularism and on socialism when, on the third day, she took the opportunity to recognize and address the women present, identifying them as a constituency. In her speech, she exhorted women to take action for the poor and dispossessed, but also on their own behalf. Rose urged women to withdraw support from churches *and* government, since both institutions oppressed women. At this phase of Rose's involvement with Owenite socialism, the movement in New York seemed to have temporarily taken an anarchistic turn under the leadership of John Collins, rejecting law and government as well as the influence of religious institutions. Where, she asked, would the churches be without women's labor? As for government, she had "a word to say to her sisters" about voting: "She need not advise them to stay away from the polls. This was a vice with which their lords would not allow them to meddle, though they were willing to deluge the land in blood, to secure this privilege for themselves" (*1844 May*). Rose's observation that women lacked even the right to refuse to vote demonstrated that government ruled over women without their consent. This reference to women as nonvoters was the first public expression of woman's aspiration for the vote by a woman who would soon become a major activist in the movement to enfranchise women.

Between the Social Reform Convention of 1844 and the beginning of the national women's rights conventions in 1850, Rose continued to speak at freethought events such as the occasional Owenite and "Infidel" Conventions, and more regularly at the annual Thomas Paine Celebrations in New York City[12] which included speeches, toasts, a dinner, and a dance. This in itself was a groundbreaking achievement. Prior to 1840, only men were speakers at the annual celebrations, while women observed from a balcony until invited to come down for the dance. In 1840, with Ernestine L. Rose taking the lead, women began to participate in the toasts at the New York Paine Celebration. However, judging by reports of the celebrations each year in the *Boston Investigator*, progress toward full female participation seems to have waned until 1846, when once more women participated in the toasts.

At first, those who planned the annual celebrations may have been reluctant to make a place for a speaker on women's rights, preferring to focus on freethought issues and their hero, Thomas Paine. In the 1840s, perhaps to avoid shocking public opinion, Rose's addresses had to appear to be spontaneous responses to comments or toasts by scheduled male speakers.

At the Thomas Paine Celebration of January 29, 1848, Rose responded to a toast "to Woman" and expressed pleasure that so many women were present. She spoke on freethought while including some brief comments about women's rights in the context of women's "enslavement" by the churches, and declared: "Knowledge will make them free." At the following year's celebration in 1849, once again rising in response to a toast "to Woman," Rose spoke more directly to the need for women's rights, devoting much of her talk to women's participation in the struggles for democratic government in many nations of Europe during the prior year. She asserted that equality of women was key to human progress. With the emergence of women's rights as a significant reform objective in its own right, and Rose's growing fame as one of the movement's best orators and spokespersons, she was increasingly sought after as a speaker. Her ever greater ability to attract news coverage to her causes made her an especially attractive speaker within her own community of freethinkers.

At the 1850 Thomas Paine Celebration, Ernestine L. Rose was actually toasted by name. This suggests that a speech by her, which would naturally come in response to such a toast, was planned or at least expected by those managing the event. In response, she presented an eloquent and informed speech on international human rights, ending with a call to women to take an active part in the fight for human freedom by freeing themselves (*1850 January*). After 1850, Rose continued her annual speeches to the Thomas Paine Celebrations until the early 1860s, addressing a variety of topics. From 1850 on, as the women's rights movement grew stronger, her comments focused more and more on the attainment of women's rights, rather than on the ways women could contribute to other causes.

In 1853, when Rose was at the height of her fame, she was elected president of the Paine celebration, given the honor of chairing the event in addition to presenting her talk. This represented official recognition for women's rights reform within the freethought community. That same year, Rose also presided at two Robert Owen birthday celebrations, one in Philadelphia and one in New York. Women's right pioneer Lucy Stone attended the latter, and congratulated the gathering on demonstrating the truth of her toast to women's "co-equality with man" by electing Rose as their president (Kolmerten 1999, 102–04).

Over the years, Rose used her platform to urge her freethought colleagues to consider women's rights and the abolition of slavery in the United States as equally important international human rights issues. At the same time, she brought freethought ideas and an insistence upon secularism to the devout Protestants in the women's rights and abolitionist movements with whom she had made common cause. Rose argued her freethought position at the women's rights conventions, where she often debated Antoinette Brown (Blackwell), the first woman ordained as a minister in a mainstream denomination. The two women were feminist colleagues who differed on religion. Rose respected Brown as a feminist who could use biblical arguments in favor of women's rights to beat the antiwoman male ministers at their own game. It was Rose's commitment to freethought and secularism that informed her challenge to Brown at the women's rights convention of 1852 in Syracuse, New York, where she opposed Brown's resolution providing biblical justification for women's equality: "We have met here for nobler purposes than to discuss Theology; we need no such authority; our claims are on the broad basis of human rights, irrespective of what Moses, Paul or Peter may say" (*1852 September 9, "Debate"*). In this and other debates, Rose insisted that biblical arguments could be found to support or oppose almost anything. She warned that if women's rights advocates were to adopt religious arguments, women's conventions would be taken over by theological disputation and precious time would be lost which could be better used to debate issues more germane to women's rights. Rose demanded that arguments for women's rights reform be grounded in natural rights, with human reason as the highest authority.

## "TRUE MARRIAGE"

After her early involvement with the trailblazing Married Women's Property Act in New York State, passed in 1848, Rose continued to advocate for the legal and economic rights of married women. She became well-versed in the marriage laws of her home state. Rose always preferred to do her own legal research for her lectures rather than consult lawyers; she was, in effect, an independent legal scholar. She also kept up with the progress of such laws in other states and internationally. And she spoke often on the subject at state and local conventions (*1853 September*).

Rose and her colleagues demanded passage of an expanded law, one that would benefit not only those women who brought inherited property into a marriage. Such a law would give women control over their own earnings, equal rights to child custody in marriage and after divorce, and equal inheritance rights between spouses so that widows would not be left impoverished. Although Rose herself had no surviving children, she empathized with the situation of mothers who risked losing custody in the event of divorce. In 1851, at the Second National Women's Rights Convention, for example, she said:

> In case of separation, why should the children be taken from the protecting care of the mother? Who has a better right to them than she? How much do fathers generally do toward bringing them up? . . .Whether from nature, habit, or both, the mother is much more capable of administering to their health and comfort than the father and therefore she has the best right to them. And where there is property, it ought to be divided equally between them, with an additional provision from the father toward the maintenance and education of the children. (*1851 October*)

Writing with a sense of hard-won triumph after twelve years of petitions, testimony before legislative committees, and the passage of a bill followed by rescission of key provisions in the mid-1850s, Rose at last was able to report, in the spring of 1860, a new victory on property rights for women in New York State. To spread the news, Rose sent to the *Boston Investigator* the full text of the new Married Women's Property Act. The new law included joint guardianship rights to children during marriage and continuing after the death of one of the spouses, equal inheritance rights, and other rights that had not been included in the 1848 law. Divorce is not explicitly mentioned, but the granting of joint guardianship to both parents during marriage would limit a father's right to contract a child's labor away from home, and also increase women's chances of obtaining custody *following* separation or divorce. Loss of custody was a threat that severely curtailed women's option to end a marriage, and thus reduced women's equality within marriage. At the conclusion of her letter introducing the new law, Rose gives her scathing assessment of the ineffectual role of the press in educating the public.

In every reform the press has to pass three stages: 1st. Opposition and abuse, 2d. Slander and ridicule; 3d. Silence, standing on the fence—outgrown the former cowardly weapons, and still fearing to speak in favor except of what has already been achieved. In the Woman's Rights movement, the whole press (I mean in the free States) has passed the first two stages. They are now in the third, and when they next find their voices, it will be to advocate and to praise. Indeed, since the Legislature passed the above law, the papers speak of it as a very just movement, and it would not much surprise me if they claim the merit of it as their own achievement! Let them; they are welcome to it, as long as it is done. (*1860 March*)

Although Ernestine Rose focused considerable energy on the legal and economic side of marriage, she most certainly did not view marriage solely as a business partnership. To the contrary, for Rose legal and economic equality in marriage served as a necessary precondition for love and affection to exist freely between equal partners, undisturbed by issues of power and control. In addition, joint ownership of property, Rose believed, would build a community of interest between husband and wife that would strengthen marriages.

In Rose's view, love and "true marriage" must be voluntary as well as equal. She believed all woman and men must have the freedom to marry the person of their choice and the freedom to leave a marriage that was no longer a loving relationship. Rose could be blistering in her attacks on hypocritical moralizing men who restricted women's lives while allowing free rein for their own desires. In two letters to the *Boston Investigator*, for example, she expressed her outrage over proposed legislation in England in which different remarriage standards were proposed for women and men after divorce. In the second letter, Rose is furious that the *Book of Common Prayer* is being seriously proposed as a standard for forming and dissolving civil marriages in England (*1857 October; 1857 December*). Rose's Jewish roots in a culture that had permitted divorce for over one thousand years, combined with her longstanding political affiliation with the Owenites, who advocated liberalized divorce laws, inclined her to view marriage as a contract, a human institution soluble by humans.

Although Rose believed strongly in the right to divorce, Kolmerten writes that, like many other women's rights reformers, she was not sure she wanted to see this issue surface at the women's rights conventions, where it might prove divisive. She did speak on the subject at the 1853 National Women's Rights Convention in Cleveland, Ohio, but she may have been ambivalent about the wisdom of holding such a discussion at a time when an updated women's rights bill was before the New York legislature. However, when Elizabeth Cady Stanton introduced a divorce reform resolution at the Tenth National Women's Rights Convention and Antoinette Brown Blackwell opposed it on the grounds of the sacramental nature of marriage in Christian theology, Rose felt honor-bound to be true to her principled belief in civil divorce and speak in support of Stanton's resolution. She took the floor and made an impassioned plea for the freedom to dissolve bad marriages so that "true marriage" could flourish (*1860 May 11*).

What did Rose mean by "true marriage"? The available evidence suggests that her own marriage was an example of such a bond. According to accounts of their contemporaries, Ernestine and William Rose enjoyed a happy and harmonious marriage. Both were skilled craftspersons, a class that figured prominently among the followers of Robert Owen. From early on in their marriage, they shared the responsibility of earning money for their household. Once settled in New York City, William established a silversmith and jewelry repair business, and developed a successful specialty in creating mountings for cameos (Voorsanger and Howat 2000, 504)[13] and fashionable silver handles for gentlemen's walking sticks called cane mountings (Soeffing 1999). A photograph of a cameo mounting by William Rose of a bust of Andrew Jackson inscribed "THE UNION IT MUST AND SHALL BE PRESERVED" appears in Voorsanger and Howat (2000, 504). Ernestine "manufactured Cologne and other German waters" according to an article in the *New York Beacon*, a local freethought paper, that announced their respective offerings of goods and services from the shop (and residence) they shared "at 9 Frankfurt Street near Tammany Hall" on the Lower East Side. In this 1838 article, William's wares were mentioned almost as an aside, while Ernestine was identified as someone known to the community for her role in public meetings—perhaps an effort to attract business from the freethought community (Suhl 1990, 73–74).

William won praise from other reformers for his support of Ernestine's advocacy work. It seems clear that William's great respect for Ernestine was predicated on her autonomy of spirit and her dedication to reform causes, and there are no signs that he was bothered by her fame. Martha Wright wrote to her sister, Lucretia Mott, that Susan B. Anthony had told her that Mrs. Rose had a husband who "idolized" her (Kolmerten 1999, 173). Further, both were Owenites, a movement that encouraged women's leadership. Though it was unconventional for women to travel alone, William Rose did not exercise his legal right to forbid Ernestine to travel away from home as did some other husbands of reformers.[14] For example, the husband of Paulina Wright Davis supported her lecturing only in the town where they lived, and did not permit her to travel to New York to study anatomy at a medical school. Some of Rose's freedom to travel may also have been due to the fact that the couple had no children who survived infancy.[15]

On the public platform, Ernestine Rose rarely spoke of her personal life. On one occasion in 1858, at a freewheeling gathering of reformers ranging from abolitionists to spiritualists to free love advocates held in Rutland, Vermont, however, Rose made it abundantly clear that her advocacy on behalf of married women did not stem from complaints about her own marriage:

> I am a married woman: have been married over twenty years; have a husband, and, as far as individual rights are concerned, I have as many as I ought to have. But I do not thank the laws for it. And why? Because it happens that my husband is "a law unto himself,"[16] there is no need of any other law; and, therefore, we might say, Abolish all laws, because there is one who is a law unto himself. But what are laws made for? Not for my husband, nor for myself either; but for those who recognize no law but their own passions and lusts, and their own rights, at the expense and sacrifice of the rights of everyone else. (Quoted in Kolmerten 1999, 206)

Rose believed in, and exemplified in her own marriage, a voluntary, monogamous commitment between two people solemnized in a nonreligious civil ceremony. Her marriage to William was a model of "true marriage" that she envisioned would become the norm in an egalitarian future.

Although Ernestine Rose believed that love must be a freely chosen relationship between equals, she did not believe in "free love" as interpreted by the opponents of women's rights. "Free love" was a hot-button phrase used to conjure images of ever-changing short-term relationships, which we might today call "serial monogamy," but would have been seen as promiscuity in the culture wars of the nineteenth century. Indeed, almost any new right for women was likely to be interpreted by the opposition as giving free rein to lust.

While she had little respect for the free love movement, Ernestine Rose did not shrink from raising an equally controversial issue: the grossly unequal consequences of unconventional sexual behavior for men and for women. She spoke on this subject at the 1853 National Women's Rights Convention in Cleveland: "It is time to consider, whether, what is wrong in one sex, can be right in the other?" (*1853 October*). Her courage in speaking out was rewarded with praise in the media coverage of the convention. The *Cleveland Plain Dealer* reported:

> [Ernestine L. Rose is] the master spirit of the convention. . . . [She is] a Polish lady of great beauty being known in this country as an earnest advocate of human liberty. Though a slight foreign accent is perceptible, her delivery is effective. She spoke with great animation. The impression made by her address was favorable both to the speaker and the cause. (Stanton, Anthony, and Gage 1881–1886, 1,145)

Rose's philosophy of gender was outspokenly egalitarian. Unlike many of her sister reformers, who often appealed to male legislators for rights on the premise that women would bring virtue and purity into government, Rose's argument for women's rights was based on a deep belief that women and men were more similar than different. At the same time, she had the mental flexibility to incorporate ideas about women's "special nature" as part of the egalitarian rationale. In an 1867 speech, she creates an especially clever argument, showing that either interpretation of women's nature demands that women be given the right to govern themselves.

> Are we the same that man is? Then we have the same rights that he has. Are we not the same that he is? Then what right has he to judge us? How can he plead for us? How can he understand the motives of a being so entirely different from himself? There is no justice in it. (*1867 May*)

## POLITICAL RIGHTS: THE VOTE IS THE KEY

Rose's early speeches on government, starting in the mid-1830s, broke ground on a path that led directly to the Woman Suffrage movement. Following her arrival in 1836, Rose consistently argued for women's rights based upon the founding documents of the United States, especially the Declaration of Independence. This was a feature of many of Rose's addresses to state legislatures, sometimes labeled her "Science of Government" speeches (Kolmerten 1999, 42). Perhaps she used this title to lend her social theories some scientific respectability, in the manner that Robert Owen used the term "the Science of Society" to describe his approach to Social Reform (Royle 2003).[17] Adapting her Owenite politics to the American political environment, Rose demonstrated the gap between the values of the nation's founding documents and the discriminatory granting of citizenship rights solely to white men, who owned property.

As early as 1844, in her first known speech on women's rights in the United States, Rose called for the enfranchisement of women. Because of her belief that sex was merely "an animal distinction," which need not influence thought or behavior or political rights, Rose was certain that, when the founders of the Republic wrote "all men" were entitled to life, liberty, and the pursuit of happiness, they meant, or should have meant, all humankind, including all African American men and all women (*1844 May*). More than a decade later, at a national women's rights convention, Rose declared that the Declaration of Independence "does not mean the oldest, biggest, strongest, wisest, or the most cunning only, is endowed with natural rights, but 'all,' and by all, 'all' are meant" (*1856 November*). In one of her resolutions to the National Women's Rights Convention of 1852, Rose boldly demanded that legislators in Congress acknowledge women's true Constitutional rights or present a case to disprove her points:

[W]e call upon the law-makers and law-breakers of the nation, to defend themselves for violating the fundamental principles of the Republic, or disprove their validity. Yes! They stand arrayed before the bar, not only of injured womanhood, but before the bar of moral consistency. . . .(*1852 September 9*, "Debate")

"No taxation without representation" was another founding principle that somehow did not extend in practice to white women and African Americans. It was a principle for which the patriots were willing to risk their lives "turning Boston Harbor into a teapot," as Rose wittily described the dumping of the unfairly taxed tea. Yet women and African Americans were taxed for their property, and held accountable when they broke laws not of their making, since they were not represented in government or on juries. To Rose, consent of the governed was "the argument of arguments . . . the broad ground of human rights . . ." (1854 October 18).

Rose at first believed that the right to vote was just one of an array of women's rights, but eventually, she became convinced that the vote was the key that would protect women's right to choices in other areas of life. She declared in 1856:

> The ballot-box is the focus of all other rights, it is the pivot upon which all others hang; the legal rights are embraced in it, for if once possessed of the right to the ballot-box, to self-representation, she will see to it that the laws shall be just, and protect her person and her property, as well as that of man. Until she has political rights she is not secure in any she may possess. (*1856 November*)

By the mid-1860s, the women's rights movement focused increasingly on suffrage. The challenge faced by nineteenth-century women, a constituency lacking both the political and the economic power to influence elected representatives, was enormous. Rose addressed this challenge in her talk at the 1867 American Equal Rights Association. Rose made an observation which has only become more true in our own time, of the link between dollars and political clout, a link that we have learned is not easily remedied even with the vote. As women in her time had neither dollars nor votes, she urged them to use their voices to change public opinion and thereby influence male voters and legislators. To bursts of laughter and applause, she said:

> Give us one million of dollars, and we will have the elective franchise at the very next session of our Legislature. But as we have not got a million of dollars, we want a million of voices. There are always two ways of obtaining an object. If we had had the money, we could have bought the Legislature and the elective franchise long before now. But as we have not, we must create a public opinion, and for that we must have voices. (*1867 May*)

As Rose envisioned as early as her great speech of 1851, with the winning of the vote, women could achieve her proper place in many walks of life including, as a slogan of second wave feminists would put it, "in the House . . . and in the Senate."

> [H]ow much more beneficial would be woman's influence, if, as the equal with man, she should take her stand by his side, to cheer, counsel, and aid him through the drama of life, in the Legislative halls, in the Senate chamber, in the Judge's chair, in the jury box, in the Forum, in the Laboratory of the arts and sciences, and wherever duty would call her for the benefit of herself, her country, her race. . . . (*1851 October*)

## A VISIONARY LEADER

Throughout her life, Ernestine L. Rose was often the first to take aim at established "truisms"—a characteristic of activists in the visionary phase of social movements. Rose's vision of women's rights was radical, or "ultra" to use the word of her time, demanding nothing less than a complete and thorough change in the status and opportunities available to women in every area of life. She demonstrated the courage of her convictions, living her life as if her ideal of complete sex equality had already come into being. Her oratory emphasized the connection of ideas to action, of moving from individual thoughts and beliefs to influencing public opinion to forming a constituency that becomes a social movement. Her vision posed a challenge to the nineteenth-century notion of "separate spheres" of activity for women and men, based on women's supposed special qualities, with women confined to the domestic sphere and barred from participation in public life.[18] Visionaries such as Rose are sometimes criticized for failure to adopt approaches that are strategic or politically practical. Though Rose was uncompromising on principle, she did not resist incremental change. Once she drew the attention of lawmakers to any of the reforms she sought, Rose was willing to accept—until the next battle—a gradualist strategy. In a letter on the 1860 Married Women's Property Act, for example, she wrote:

> In 1855, while speaking before the Legislature, I told them we claimed perfect equality of rights; we ask for no more, we can be satisfied with no less; we will accept as much as you are prepared to accede, and then claim the rest; and now, having obtained this much, we can 'wait a little longer'[19] not in silence and inaction, but in the faith which springs from work. (*1860 March*)

While she flourished during the visionary stage of the women's rights movement, Rose resisted moving to what some felt was the next stage. She may have been temperamentally unsuited to the "implementation stage" of a social movement, when debating ideas gives way to the creation of organizations, and when opening minds may take second place to devising strategies to influence politicians. As early as 1852, Rose, along with other early-stage reformers, including Angelina Grimké, opposed a proposal to create a national women's organization; Rose spoke on the subject at the National Women's Rights Convention in Syracuse that year on September 10 (text not included in this volume). These women viewed organizations as stultifying, as limiting the exploration of ideas, rather than as potentially empowering. They may well have been correct in their assessment that creation of one major organization for women's rights at that early date would have been premature.

As a visionary, Rose's chief contribution to women's rights reform was to emphasize the importance of ideas and principles, to remind her sister reformers not to compromise the core values and goals that had brought them together in the first place. She spoke of human rights as cutting across national boundaries and linked women's rights to human rights movements at home and abroad. She vigorously opposed discrimination based on race, religion, immigration status, and sex, a singularly progressive stance for her time.

## ANTISLAVERY

Ernestine L. Rose firmly opposed racism and was an early and committed advocate for the abolition of slavery. Her dual activism in both women's rights and abolition was typical of the first generation of women activists. Many of Rose's colleagues in the antebellum women's rights movement were also abolitionists. Indeed, a considerable body of literature documents the overlapping activity between these two movements. Kathryn Kish Sklar's *Women's Rights Emerges Within the Antislavery Movement: 1830–1870* provides considerable evidence for the emergence of women's rights from women's activism in the abolition movement. The two movements, for example, often held their conventions in tandem so that women reformers could attend both (Sklar 2000). Many women's rights activists began their public advocacy speaking out against slavery. Sarah and Angelina Grimké were contemporaries with Rose, but they did not begin speaking publicly to change the status of women. Drawing upon their deeply felt religious convictions, the Grimké sisters and other abolitionist women grew into their feminism through shedding the social constraints placed on them as women in order to engage in public discourse against slavery.

While Rose shared the antislavery politics of her abolitionist colleagues, her commitment was based not on religion but on the secular "natural rights" philosophy of the Enlightenment and on Owenite socialist theory. In contrast to women who began their public activism fighting for the rights of others in a religiously inspired mode of feminine piety and compassion, Rose began her activism out of a core belief in human rights for *all* human beings, a perspective that always included women (Kolmerten 1999, 24).

Few of Rose's earliest speeches on abolition have been preserved, though more may yet be found. As Rose herself noted in her 1877 letter

to Susan B. Anthony, "Thirty or forty years ago, the press was not sufficiently educated in the rights of women, even to notice, much less to
report [women's] speeches as it does now." Women's words became news-
worthy once the national women's rights conventions began in the 1850s
and women became a constituency that commanded the attention of the
press. While Rose's women's rights speeches from 1850 onward can be
found in proceedings of the women's conventions (and her contributions
to secularism found in freethought publications), her early antislavery lectures were apparently not reported in the abolitionist press until 1853,
when Rose became well-known as a reformer.

Nonetheless, persuasive evidence exists that Rose had been speaking out on the issue of slavery at least since the late 1840s, bringing a
freethought perspective to a movement that had declared a Christian
"holy war" on slavery (Kolmerten 1999, 58–59). Over that decade, Rose
traveled and lectured throughout New York State and in Philadelphia,
where she met many abolitionists, including Lucretia Mott, Abby Kelley
(Foster), Stephen Foster, Frederick Douglass, and William Lloyd Garrison (Kolmerten 1999, 58–59). Embedded in Rose's first documented
antislavery speech is her report of an altercation with a young lawyer who
baited her about her abolitionist views during a trip to South Carolina six
years earlier, perhaps in 1847. The detail and fervency with which Rose
recounts her response to his challenge suggests that this was not the first
time she had spoken on the subject of slavery. Rose recounts the conversation as part of her talk at an abolitionist rally in 1853, where her satiric
view of slave owners, according to the transcript, provoked laughter and
applause throughout.

> I said: "The only civilization you have exists among your slaves:
> for if industry and the mechanical arts are the great criterion of
> civilization (and I believe they are), then certainly the slaves are
> the only civilized ones among you, because they do all the work."
> In Charleston and Columbia, S.C., the slaves are painters, gla-
> ziers, carpenters and masons; in fact, all the trades are filled with
> slaves. The owners cannot do any kind of manual labor. . . . Said
> he, " . . . when we catch a good Abolitionist, we give him a coat of
> tar and feathers." (Laughter.) I then told him that, as for me, I was
> an Abolitionist in the fullest sense of the word and be I a woman
> or not, said I, you are so exceedingly lazy and inactive here that
> it would be an act of charity to give you something to do, were it
> even to give me a coat of tar and feathers. (*1853 August*)

Rose deserves credit for her courage in daring to bring women's rights and abolition to the Deep South, however briefly. She may have been the only reformer to do so. Even South Carolina–born abolitionists Sarah and Angelina Grimké, arguably the first women to speak in public on any subject (Lerner 1971), left the South and spoke against slavery primarily in the North.

In 1849, Rose was part of a lecture tour of eastern New York State organized by abolitionists Abby Kelley and her future husband, Stephen Foster. Kelley credited Ernestine Rose and Lucretia Mott as "the only lecturers who aided them" in that four-month-long tour. Kelley described Rose as an abolitionist and women's rights advocate but "not a Garrisonian," and as one who "made very acceptable speeches [that were] not as useful as remarks from a person who sympathizes fully with us would have been." Mott, by contrast, was praised as one who "did great service. . . . Her labors here are invaluable" (Sterling 1991, 253). Kelley implied that Rose was less than fully committed to abolition, perhaps because of her refusal to use the rhetoric of the Christian crusade. Rose, as a Jew and as a secular freethinker, was unique among active abolitionist women. While they shared the same goal, often they did not agree on theory or strategy, and certainly not on the place of religion in the antislavery reform movement.

Rose is, nonetheless, uncompromising on the issue of slavery, as one can see in her speeches on the subject. Her 1853 "Address at the Anniversary of West Indian Emancipation," presented at an outdoor rally in Flushing, New York, justly stands as one of her most famous utterances on slavery and freedom, admirable for its lively mode of expression and its idealism about the values of the Declaration of Independence. Expressing her reverence for the founding documents of the United States, Rose insists that the practice of the nation must match its declared values and offer universal liberty to all its citizens, including all women and all African American men. It is a tribute to Rose's skills and modernity as an orator that, in addition to nineteenth-century oratorical techniques, she employs a modern rhetorical technique of engaging the audience as participants by asking them to imagine, if they could, what it would feel like to be a slave. "It is utterly impossible for us, as finite beings, with the utmost stretch of the imagination, to conceive the depth and immensity of the horrors of slavery. I would that, instead of speaking and listening today, we could all sit down in perfect silence, and each and every one of us ask ourselves what is it to be a slave?" (*1853 August*).

Rose preferred to address the abolition of slavery as part of an overarching ideal of human liberation, rather than as a single issue in isolation from others. It may have been Rose's socialism that most set her apart from the majority of her fellow antislavery reformers. Yet Rose was certainly conscious of the difference between slavery and other forms of oppression, as she demonstrates in her poignant characterization of the most dehumanizing feature of slavery: "To work hard, to fare ill, to suffer hardship, that is not slavery; for many of us white men and women have to work hard, have to fare ill, have to suffer hardship, and yet we are not slaves. Slavery is not to belong to yourself—to be robbed of yourself. There is nothing that I so much abhor as that single thing—to be robbed of one's self." Unlike some abolitionists, who questioned whether freed African Americans could live as equals in U.S. society or whether they had the capacity to be self-governing, Rose insists upon viewing African Americans as fully equal, demonstrating the fallacy of racist attitudes by pointing to the skills of African Americans in the South and the accomplishments of free Africans practicing self-government in the Caribbean.

Though the focus of the rally and Rose's speech was on abolition, in her signature fashion, Rose broadened her lens to universal human rights and made several references in her speech to women's rights. For example, she asserted, "The same right to life, liberty, and the pursuit of happiness, that pertains to man, pertains to woman also," and concluded with her enunciation of the Owenite ideal: "I go for the recognition of human rights, without distinction of sect, party, sex, or color."

Appearing at the rally with William Lloyd Garrison, leader of the radical wing of the abolition movement, Rose was introduced by the chair as "a speaker from that portion of mankind not always represented on occasions like this by their own orators." Indeed, Ernestine L. Rose was the only woman on the platform. Though a small but growing number of women reformers were speaking in public, few female orators were sufficiently skilled in projecting their voices to be heard at an outdoor gathering such as this one.

Significantly, Maurice Schappes, reintroducing this same oration in 1949, notes Rose's other differences from most of the speakers, as reported by the New York press. The *New York Tribune* noted she was Jewish. The *New York Herald* mentioned that she was Polish, and "sneered at her good looks and mocked her foreign accent." The *New York Times* "chose to be faintly mysterious," making reference to the warm applause she received as being due to the audience's familiarity with "her public antecedents." Schappes believes this last comment refers not only to her growing renown as a woman's rights reformer, but to her widely reported appearance earlier that summer at a freethought convention (Schappes 1949, 346), where Rose defiantly attacked conventional religion and the Bible itself (*1853 June 4*).

As a woman, a Jew, an immigrant, and an atheist, Rose was in many ways different from the American-born Protestant men, both white and black, with whom she shared the platform—and she acknowledged these difference in her speech. "Not being a native of this country," Rose told her audience, "I have probably had some different ideas with regard to the working of slavery from what many abolitionists have. I do not belong to any abolition Society." Rose then audaciously tweaks Garrison, joking that, "as my friend by my side said, he was compelled to belong to the Garrisonian[20] Society," implying that just as Garrison had his own ideas about abolition, she has *her* own ideas—ideas based on natural rights and Owenite socialism rather than Christianity.

The Garrisonian approach demanded an immediate end to slavery, not through legal or military means, but through noncooperation with unjust laws. He also eventually embraced what was called a "come-outer" position, urging withdrawal from those Christian churches that were complicit in slavery by refusing to denounce it. Though Garrison criticized the churches and ministers who justified or ignored slavery, he never renounced Christianity, nor did he ask his followers to do so. Indeed, Christian theology was at the heart of the Garrisonian critique of the churches, as well as of slavery itself. Despite their doctrinal differences, Rose and Garrison were allies and friends. Rose lauded Garrison at the 1853 rally, "with my whole heart, mind and soul, I bless him for having been the great and noble voice of humanity to this country for emancipation" (*1853 August*).

In April of 1854, just two years after their first documented meeting at the 1852 National Women's Rights Convention (Kolmerten 1999, 94), Rose and Susan B. Anthony together undertook their joint tour for the purpose of bringing women's rights issues to the South, lecturing in Washington, D.C., Baltimore, Maryland, and Alexandria, Virginia (Kolmerten 1999, 140–54, 164–70). On this tour, Rose was the well-known orator, while Anthony, still relatively new at public speaking, excelled as planner and organizer. While on the tour, Anthony, a former abolitionist agent, wrote a letter to Garrison's *Liberator* in which she endorsed Rose as an "out and out abolitionist" who resisted pressure from local conveners of meetings to avoid the topic of slavery should it arise. In an effort to set the record straight for the abolitionist press, Anthony took issue with the *Washington Globe*, which had reported Rose's lecture on the Nebraska Question, but misstated her antislavery views as proslavery, characterizing Rose's summation of the South's position as if it were her own. Public and congressional debate on "the Nebraska Question" concerned the proposed Kansas-Nebraska Act, whereby each territory applying for statehood would vote itself slave-holding or free. This law would effectively dismantle the Missouri Compromise of 1820, whereby all land north of the Louisiana Purchase was to remain free of slavery. When the act was passed later in 1854, it was an unexpected victory for the slave states, enraging the North and abolitionists in particular.

It is easy to see why Rose's position could have been confusing. Few people, even at that time, understood that radical abolitionists were among the first to propose "Disunion," or separation of the North from the South. Rose, like many radical reformers, identified with the Disunionist position, not for the reasons that the South later gave for secession, but because efforts to keep the South in the Union gave them too much power and influence over the values and politics of the nation as a whole. The Fugitive Slave Act of 1850, for example, mandated that persons who escaped from slavery, if captured under the jurisdiction of the United States, even if they succeeded in reaching free states where slavery was not permitted, must be returned to their legal owners (Kolmerten 1999, 69, 77, 85). Passage by Congress of the Fugitive Slave Act as part of the Compromise of 1850 demonstrated that slavery was no longer confined to the South, but now extended its evil reach over the nation as a whole. At the New England Anti-Slavery Convention in Boston in 1855, Rose elaborated further on antislavery reasons for Disunion, and deplored the existence of legally sanctioned slavery in a republic that claimed to be an exemplar of human liberty. She compared this national hypocrisy with serfdom in Russia, which, she observed sardonically, was at least consistent with the Czar's despotic mode of government.[21]

In both the 1853 and 1855 speeches, perhaps inspired by the personal testimony of formerly enslaved people, Rose departs from her customary appeals to reason and describes her own feelings and experiences. In the 1855 speech, she includes her emotional response to the testimony of Anthony Burns, an escaped slave who had been aided by abolitionists. She asks her listeners to imagine what he might have achieved and contributed had he not been enslaved in his formative years. She goes on to excoriate "scientists" who used their credentials to disseminate racist ideas, a practice that extends to the present day, but was particularly influential in Rose's time. Rose adapts the paradigm that she often used for women's rights, that humanity recognizes no differences on the basis of gender, and applied it to race: "I will say of the slave, as I often say when claiming the rights of woman—humanity recognizes no color, mind recognizes no color; pleasure or pain, happiness or misery, life or death, recognizes no color. . . ." (*1855 May*). Why, Rose asked, should a person's color or the "geographical position" of someone's birth justify enslavement? Here she echoes the language of her speech at the 1852 National Women's Rights

Convention, where she argues for the universality of women's rights across national boundaries (*1852 September 9*, "A Child of Israel").

Garrison praised Rose's speech at the 1855 convention as "lucid and able." He expressed his admiration in the pages of the *Liberator*, observing that Rose

> spoke for nearly two hours without notes or references to any manuscript, with the great vigor of appeal, powers of reasoning, and masterly ability, keeping the unbroken attention of her audience to the end, and eliciting frequent expression of approbation. Mrs. Rose is one of the most natural, dignified, intelligent and effective speakers, and for one born and educated in Poland, speaks our language with astonishing precision and accuracy. (*Liberator*, 1855 June, quoted in Kolmerten 1999, 170)

Rose continued to support the Garrisonian position of "no compromise with slavery," not only at abolitionist and women's rights gatherings, but also at freethought meetings, bringing abolition to a secular and internationalist audience. For example, in her speech at the annual Thomas Paine Celebration on the eve of the Civil War, Rose framed abolition as a human rights issue similar to the democracy struggles in Europe, and pressed the radical abolitionist argument for no further compromise with the slave states (*1861 January*).

With the documentation available,[22] only a preliminary assessment of Rose's effectiveness as an abolitionist is possible. Rose had friends and colleagues in the antislavery movement and was an active speaker on the issue, yet it appears that she did not "belong" to it in the same way that she did to the women's rights and freethought movements.

Rose was unique among women reformers in bringing antislavery discourse to the Border States and briefly to the deep South. Rose's contribution to the abolitionist movement was generally not in conflict with her work for women's rights. In the antebellum period, her participation in each movement probably strengthened her influence in the other, as most of the women's rights reformers of the time were also abolitionists. The two allied reform movements, however, would soon come into conflict.

## THE CIVIL WAR AND WOMEN'S RIGHTS REFORM

In a gesture of solidarity with the Union side, no national women's rights conventions were held during the years of the U.S. Civil War (1861–1865). Instead, some women organized and worked locally in "loyal leagues" to support the war effort and the Union soldiers. By the mid-point of the war, however, reformers became concerned that by suspending women's rights conventions and limiting antislavery activism, they were losing momentum gained in the 1850s toward rights for women and for African Americans.

In 1863, immediately after President Lincoln issued the Emancipation Proclamation freeing enslaved people in the Confederate states, women's rights reformers Stanton, Anthony, Rose, Lucy Stone, and others convened a national meeting in New York City, called the National Convention of the Loyal Women of the Republic. Their purpose was to demand that the president broaden the goal of the war beyond simple preservation of the Union to the abolition of all slavery in the United States, including the border states—slave states that had not seceded from the Union. One thousand women attended from all over the country, where there was great dissension about the goals of the meeting. Some of the women present maintained that wartime contingencies called for an emphasis on women's support for the troops and the war effort. While nearly all supported the emancipation of enslaved African Americans, many viewed bringing up women's rights as diversionary. Rose entered into this debate, arguing that women's rights were an essential element of the broader goal of universal rights. In a debate on the subject, she employed her flair for withering sarcasm, observing, "It is exceedingly amusing to hear persons talk about throwing out Woman's Rights, when, if it had not been for Woman's Rights, that lady would not have had the courage to stand here and say what she did" (*1863 May*, "Debate"). That evening, Rose gave her formal address, "War for the Utter Extinction of Slavery," in which she called attention to the importance of ending slavery at once in the border states that were under the control of the federal government.

> Let the Administration give evidence that they too are for justice to all, without exception, without distinction, and I, for one, had I ten thousand lives, would gladly lay them down to secure this boon of freedom to humanity. (Applause.) But without this certainty, I am not unconditionally loyal to the Administration. We women need not be, for the law has never yet recognized us. (Laughter) (*1863 May*)[23]

Although Rose sometimes spoke of an ideal of world peace that would prevail once women gained power, in this speech she advocates enforcing emancipation through military action:

This rebellion and this war have cost too dear. The money spent, the vast stores destroyed, the tears shed, the lives sacrificed, the hearts broken are too high a price to be paid for the mere name of Union. . . . A true Union is based upon principles of mutual interest, of mutual respect and reciprocity, none of which ever existed between the North and South. (*1863 May*)

For Rose, the principle of universal rights and liberties was more important than preserving a Union flawed by compromise. It was not consistent with her nature or her political commitments to compromise on the liberty and freedom of any group for the sake of peace.

## WOMEN'S RIGHTS REFORM AFTER THE CIVIL WAR

"The defeat of slavery was like an earthquake in American political life, and moved abolitionists much closer to the center of national political power," writes historian Ellen Carol DuBois (1978, 54). After a Union victory brought emancipation of all enslaved people in the United States, political support grew in the North for enfranchising the freedmen. Freedmen is indeed the appropriate term here, for the campaign of radical Republicans and abolitionists would grant the vote only to African American men and not to African American women or white women. Women's rights reformers expected votes for women to be included in postwar legislation, but they lacked support in Congress and even from their former allies. Shocked and disappointed at being abandoned, women's rights advocates were particularly angry and horrified that the Fourteenth Amendment, in conferring civil rights on African Americans, introduced the word "male" into the Constitution for the first time. Passage of the proposed Fifteenth Amendment, which said that the right to vote could not be denied on the basis of "race, color, or previous condition of servitude," would only confirm the exclusion of women.

Abolitionists argued that recently emancipated African American men needed the vote more urgently than did white or African American women, to protect themselves and their families in a South still hostile to their new status. The controversy drove a wedge between the two long-allied human rights movements. Rose, along with a solid core of women's rights reformers, including Stanton, Anthony, Mott, Martha Wright, and Olympia Brown, opposed pitting two excluded groups against one another and held to a vision of human rights for all. They continued to argue that the only correct course of action was to work for an amendment that mandated universal adult suffrage.

After the war, women's rights reformers began to call themselves "the women's suffrage movement." As votes for women became the main focus of the women's movement, the rationale for women's rights gradually shifted from the universal justice argument to a strategy of expediency in order to gain the support of male legislators and voters. Such arguments sometimes made use of racist and anti-immigrant rhetoric to promote the franchise for educated native-born women, on the grounds that this would increase the power of the "better classes" on voting rolls and weaken the influence of immigrants in the North and blacks in the South (Kraditor 1981, 38–63). This was a far cry from the natural rights argument advanced by Ernestine Rose and others who had insisted that the Declaration of Independence, correctly interpreted, mandated universal adult suffrage. Despite setbacks, Rose struggled to maintain a discourse of universal rights in which the rights of one group did not take precedence over the rights of other groups.

Creation of the Equal Rights Association in 1866 was part of an effort by women's rights advocates to merge their cause with that of African Americans, to defeat the Fifteenth Amendment, and to attain universal citizenship and votes simultaneously for African American men and all women (DuBois 1978, 66–67). The test of public support for enfranchisement of these formerly excluded groups occurred in Kansas, where two separate referenda were held in 1867, one on votes for black men, and one on votes for women. The defeat of both referenda in Kansas was a political debacle that, for the near future, put an end to the dream of universal suffrage (79–104).

Women's rights advocates, led by Stanton and Anthony, were determined to carry on the fight. They chose to make votes for women their primary focus and founded the National Woman Suffrage Association in 1869 with Rose moving to adopt the new name. Reformers who could not bring themselves to oppose the Fifteenth Amendment after decades of working on behalf of African Americans included Lucy Stone, Abby Kelley Foster, and most of the male supporters of women's rights reform, who formed the American Woman Suffrage Association the same year. Thus the first wave of feminism split into two competing organizations, a rift that lasted for twenty years (Flexner 1973, 153). Not until 1890 would the two groups join forces in the National American Woman Suffrage Association, and not until 1920 would women win the vote with ratification of the Nineteenth Amendment.

## ERNESTINE ROSE AND WOMEN'S RIGHTS

Rose's departure from the United States in 1869 followed within three weeks of the 1869 convention in which women's rights advocates split into two opposing camps. Except for an occasional letter, and the memories of those who had heard her speak, Rose's intensity and commitment to human progress disappeared from the movement. Perhaps Rose could not muster enthusiasm for this stage of the movement, which required more compromise of principle than she could accept.

## RADICAL FREETHOUGHT: THE FOUNDATION OF ROSE'S BELIEFS

When Ernestine Rose arrived in the United States in 1836 prepared to follow in the footsteps of Owen and Wright as a proponent of freethought. As early as 1837, Rose attracted the attention of the *Beacon*, a freethought paper, albeit as an unnamed "Polish lady" noteworthy for winning a series of debates against defenders of orthodox religion at a forum sponsored by the Society for Moral Philanthropists in New York City (Kolmerten 1999, 33–34).[24] At an Owenite social reform convention in 1844, Rose debated a speaker opposed to the very idea of reform on the grounds that "finite" humans should not be so arrogant as to question an infinite God's plan by attempting to change social arrangements. Rose responded that precisely *because* we are finite beings, we need not concern ourselves with metaphysical questions, the answers to which are unknowable. Rather, it is more important and morally urgent for us to address human needs and how to meet them.

It must have sometimes seemed to Rose and her fellow freethinkers that it was up to them to defend the secularism of the United States and its founding documents. The public culture and discourse of the nineteenth century was increasingly that of conservative Christianity, inspired by the second Great Awakening, with itinerant ministers whipping up popular religious fervor at campfire meetings. In this climate of evangelical religiosity, freethinkers worried about a potential threat to the secular nature of American society.

The core issue of the freethought movement was the right to "mental freedom," or what we today call intellectual freedom. Though protected by Constitutional safeguards, intellectual freedom in the early days of the Republic frequently came into conflict with established churches, which required belief in a specified church doctrine or creed. Orthodox Christians sometimes tried to reach for power by establishing their beliefs as a condition for those running for state or even federal office (Jacoby 2004, 29–30). Or state governors linked Christianity to a government-sponsored activity, for example, by issuing Thanksgiving Day proclamations mentioning Jesus Christ or some other aspect of Christian belief (Schappes 1971, 235–46).[25] During the antebellum period, people who spoke of mental freedom were widely assumed to be "infidels" who rejected the Bible, organized religion, and belief in a Supreme Being. Most freethinkers did reject fundamentalist interpretations of the Bible, and many were atheists and agnostics. Yet many freethinkers were Deists who believed in a Creator but did not believe in a God who was concerned in human affairs in a daily or personal way. Other freethinkers were primarily secularists, concerned about separation of church and state but not necessarily opposed to religion.

Thomas Paine, an icon of the freethought movement, was vilified by orthodox Christians as an atheist and libertine and, despite his contributions to the American Revolution, he was dropped from its pantheon of heroes. In fact, Paine had written, in *The Age of Reason* (1794), "I believe in one God, and no more; and I hope for happiness beyond this life." It was *institutionalized* religion that Paine opposed: "I do not believe in the creed professed by the Jewish church, by the Roman church, by the Greek church, by the Turkish church, by the Protestant church, nor by any church that I know of. My own mind is my own church." To Paine, "infidelity" was not unfaithfulness to the creed of a church, but failure to uphold one's own beliefs.[26]

Like Thomas Paine, Rose placed a high value in being true to her own beliefs. That commitment explains why she devoted so much of her reform efforts to the freethought movement, despite the risk to her reputation. She truly believed that religion confined people's thinking and particularly oppressed women.

When Rose left Piotrkow, Poland, for Berlin, she broke her ties with her father and the Jewish community and became a freethinker. However, as the daughter of a rabbi who had studied the Torah and its commentaries, Rose could not simply be indifferent to religion. Instead, she was among the first to embrace and lecture on the controversial "Higher Criticism" of the Bible, a critique originating in the universities of the German states, which questioned the divine inspiration of the Bible. Though now widely accepted by liberal Christian and Jewish denominations, it was considered quite controversial in the nineteenth century. Rose's critique of the Bible set her apart as an enemy of all religion. Though she came to consider herself an atheist, she continued to be engaged with religion—with winning people *away* from religion through reason, and through debating with "the Bibles," as Infidels called the religiously orthodox. Believing as she did that religion was harmful and dangerous, especially to women, Ernestine embraced freethought and atheism with the zeal of a convert.

Rose felt so strongly that the Bible and religion undermined people's belief in their own reason that she expressed vociferous antichurch and anti-Bible beliefs at an 1853 convention called by freethinkers and other reformers to debate the validity of the Bible. With remarkable courage, but a breathtaking lack of caution about giving offense to believers, Rose exhorted women, "if they wish to be free, to trample the Bible under their feet" (*1853 June 4*). Because of disruptions throughout by rowdy theology students who came to defend the Bible against the Infidels, the convention was widely covered in the press. It was the reporting of this speech, perhaps more than any other, which led to denunciations of Rose by clergy and even by conservative women's rights reformers, who did not want her to be a spokesperson for their movement. This event may have damaged Rose's effectiveness as a reformer for social causes such as women's rights and the abolition of slavery. Yet Rose continued to be a spokesperson for both those movements, and for freethought as well.

In her 1861 lecture, "A Defence of Atheism," Rose unambiguously disavowed belief in a Supreme Being, and maintained that atheism was a superior ethical system because the atheist is moral out of a desire to contribute to human happiness and receives his reward from "well-doing" itself, rather than the promise of an afterlife. Rose was avid in seeking out new scientific knowledge. She was able to cite advances in geology, for example, to argue against the biblical version of creation in her 1861 lecture. Rose's discourse continued in an adversarial mode, pitting scientific knowledge *against* religion, for it was a debate that continued to engage her.

Once again, Rose was ahead of her time. In the decade following publication, in 1859, of Darwin's *Origin of Species*, a gradual change in public discourse on religion took place. By the end of the 1860s, most liberal religious believers accepted the new science, while reserving matters of faith to the clergy, their churches, and private conscience (Warren 1966, 228–29). Among more orthodox believers, of course, these issues— the relationship of religion, and its place in secular institutions—continue to stir acrimonious debate, and many of Rose's observations still ring true today—including a statement made at the 1860 Infidel Convention: "Only let a man holding Infidel principles be nominated for office, and immediately he would be attacked by all the papers and denounced as unfit because he is an Infidel" (Infidel Convention 1860).

Rose was, of course, not only a freethinker, but also an Owenite. The Owenites took their freethought a step further than Thomas Paine, toward outright opposition to religious practice and institutions. Not all socialists in the United States were freethinkers, though most were, and only a minority of freethinkers were socialists. Radical freethinkers were those who believed that once minds were free, all other freedoms would follow, while socialists placed primary emphasis on social and economic change and were less eager to challenge the deeply held religious beliefs of those whom they wished to influence (Warren 1966, 135–36). Along with other radical freethinkers, Rose believed that mental freedom was the underpinning of freedom in every other realm. Yet Rose differed from freethinkers who were not willing to engage in immediate struggles for human equality, and instead merely waited for that great day when reason rather than superstition should rule the world.[27] Rose raised her voice for these struggles in her freethought community, lecturing frequently on the rights of women and the abolition of slavery. She pointedly remarked that physical enslavement was not consistent with mental freedom (*1861 January; 1862 January*).

## THE INFLUENCE OF ROSE'S JEWISH ORIGINS ON HER CAREER AS A REFORMER

An important source of Rose's concern about separation of religion and social policy was her background as a European Jew. In much of mid-nineteenth-century Europe, Jews were still not allowed to vote, as civil rights were often tied to professing allegiance to a national church or some form of Christianity. As a Jew who came of age in Europe under the anti-Semitic policies of Russian-controlled Poland, Rose then faced a religious barrier against Jews that almost prevented her from entering Berlin after she left Poland. She knew firsthand the consequences of privileging one religion over others—a fact that must have affected her fierce attachment to the vision of a secular democratic republic that had drawn her to the United States in the first place.

While many ambiguities surround Rose's self-identification as a Jew, on one aspect she was abundantly clear. As a freethinker, and indeed one who took a public role in the radical freethought movement, Rose was openly critical of all religion and expressly disavowed all religious belief and affiliation, including Judaism. Yet she continued to describe her life's journey in terms of her origins in a world that was culturally and religiously Jewish. The most specific reference by Rose to her Jewish origins is found in her "Child of Israel" comments, reframing the chair's introduction of her as "a Polish lady of the Jewish faith" at the 1852 National Women's Rights Convention.[28]

It is of very little importance in what geographical position a person is born, but it is important whether his ideas are based upon facts that can stand the test of reason, and his acts are conducive to the happiness of society. . . . Yes, I am an example of the universality of our claims; for not American women only, but a daughter of poor, crushed Poland, and the down-trodden and persecuted people called the Jews, "a child of Israel," pleads for the equal rights of her sex. (*1852 September 9*)

Though Rose's opening sentence seems to diminish the influence of cultural origins on values and ideas, she does, over the years, continue to describe herself in those terms.

Yet Rose did not hesitate to refer to her Jewish background in her public reform work. For example, she retold many times the story of defying her rabbi father and leaving her community of origin in order to avoid an arranged marriage. If we accept Rose's story as told to d'Héricourt (1856) as substantially accurate, we may still question what was the rhetorical value to Rose as a reformer and advocate, of this particular narrative with its focus on her Jewish roots? As a woman's rights reformer, Rose may have wanted to give personal testimony for the right of a woman to choose her own husband and to marry for love. Her appeal to a secular court defending her right to keep her maternal inheritance demonstrated the importance of a woman fighting for her own economic and legal rights, ideal credentials for carrying on the fight she later led for Married Women's Property legislation in New York State. It also demonstrates reliance on a secular rather than a religious authority. At the same time, the story grounds Rose as emerging from Jewish culture, with its valuing of education and critical argument—perhaps contributing to her persona as a successful orator and debater, but also publicizing her Jewish roots.

Another event that suggests Rose was attached to her Jewish roots is her rejection of conversion to Christianity as a means of gaining entry to Berlin. Her refusal of conversion is even more remarkable when one considers the numbers of considerably better-established Berlin Jews who converted to Christianity during the 1820s in order to more easily participate in civic and social life (Hertz 1995). Rose's story can be viewed as a parable of resistance to Christian hegemony—whether motivated by loyalty to the Jewish community or by fidelity to her freethinker beliefs, we cannot know.

Through this story of her youth and young adulthood, Rose created a life narrative in which a young woman takes a stand against religious authority and reinvents herself as a freethinker—a vivid portrait of personal empowerment. Using her younger self as the protagonist, Rose's coming-of-age story demonstrates how one of the least powerful members of society, someone young and female, can stand up against religious control and claim her own power.

## ERNESTINE L. ROSE AND THE COMMUNITY OF JEWS IN THE UNITED STATES

Did Ernestine Rose, who arrived in the United States prior to the major emigrations of Ashkenazi Jews, miss being part of a community of Jews who shared similar life experiences? As a committed freethinker, it is unlikely that she missed the religious rites of Judaism. But she may have missed cultural celebrations associated with being Jewish and the opportunities those events provided to gather together with other Jews.

Ellen Carol DuBois, eminent historian of the Woman Suffrage movement, presents an interesting hypothesis in commenting on Rose's report of a visit she made "for her health" to Charleston and Columbia, South Carolina, in 1847. DuBois astutely observes that South Carolina would have been an odd place to go for one's health, especially if one were known as a notorious abolitionist. Indeed, Rose was threatened with tar and feathers for her antislavery statements there. DuBois suggests a possible motive for Rose's trip south.

> South Carolina may have had other attractions for her. Charleston was home to the first Jewish U.S. congregation to follow the modern, rationalized, Reform order of service pioneered in Germany. In 1846, Columbia Jews followed with their own congregation. The Columbia Jews had links to Philadelphia, where Rose had strong ties with radical Quakers and I wondered if she could have learned about the South Carolina Reform Jews through them. I remain quite attached to this hypothesis, although I have found no other evidence to support it. (DuBois 2001, 6–7)

DuBois's hypothesis that the abolitionists were somehow involved in suggesting that Rose travel to South Carolina is certainly provocative, and if true, it suggests to me that Rose's motivation to travel there had more to do with finding support for antislavery and women's rights reform than with any specifically religious interest in Reform Judaism.

Thus, her motivation may have been to find a community of Jews who embraced a progressive social agenda similar to her own and with whom she would have felt a bond of community and commitment.

In almost any large European city, Rose would have had access to a community of Jewish people including liberal and secular Jews. In New York City, there were very few Jews prior to 1848, when German Jews began to arrive in larger numbers, many of them refugees from the failed revolutions in their homeland.

References to Jewish consciousness and loyalty appear throughout

Rose's work. In her review of Horace Mann's lectures on the education of women Rose retorts with sarcasm to his gratuitous slur against Jewish mothers, "[U]nmerciful and stiff-necked as the Jews are, they still are the authors and originators of his religion, and a Jewish woman was the mother of his Redeemer" (*1852 February*).

Taking the separation of church and state as her topic at the Thomas Paine Celebration of 1859, Rose deplores the kidnapping of seven-year-old Edgardo Mortara, a Jewish child living in Bologna, by the authorities of the Papal States after being baptized by a servant in the family's home: "[I]n the name of religion and of God, bands of ecclesiastical marauders break in at the dead of night to rob parents of their children—as in the case of Mortara—where the 'glad tidings of the gospel' are enforced by the light of the dungeon, the rack and the stake" (*1859 January*). As a European Jew, Rose may have identified with the Mortara family, and this identification may have given her speech more emotional resonance. Judging by the resounding applause of the audience, the entire freethinker community seemed to be following this case. The *Boston Investigator* (February 16, 1859; see *1859 January*) reported that the reverberations of the applause caused the crockery to "fairly dance with approbation."

Rose's Jewish identity may also have affected her positions in more subtle ways. In the Divorce Reform debate at the 1860 National Women's Rights Convention, for example, Rose supported Stanton's resolutions against the religious objections of Antoinette Brown Blackwell (*1860 May 11*). Judaism, unlike Christianity, viewed marriage as a contract between individuals rather than a religious sacrament. Divorce reform was an issue where Rose's freethought and Owenite convictions were not in conflict with her Judaic background, and both likely influenced her decision to support divorce reform.

## THE ROSE-SEAVER DEBATE ON JEWS AND JUDAISM

More germane to the question of Rose's Jewish identity is her extended debate, in writing, with Horace Seaver, editor of the radical freethought weekly the *Boston Investigator* (*1863 October–1864 April*). If Rose no longer identified as a Jew, how does one understand her spirited, dramatic, and tenacious "defense of the Jews" against Seaver's attack? Did she simply defend the Jews as she would any group facing bigotry and oppression, or did the vehemence of her defense suggest that she felt personally attacked as a Jew? And finally, what do we make of her defending Judaism as a religion, after explicitly disavowing all religion? The "debate on the Jews" between Ernestine L. Rose and Horace Seaver was triggered by an editorial published by Seaver on October 28, 1863, in the *Boston Investigator*. Rose wrote a letter of rebuttal in January 1864, published on February 10 and 17 of that year. One wonders why she waited until January to write. Was she on the road and not aware of the editorial until she returned? Or did she want to see whether other freethinkers would respond to Seaver's bigotry?

Seaver begins his editorial with demeaning comments on the Jews and Judaism after bemoaning the sale of a Universalist church building in Boston to a new Jewish congregation. He then goes on to deplore the warlike behavior of the biblical Israelites, concluding that the Jews were the worst people ever. Rose admonishes Seaver that the rational discourse of the freethinker community required that he keep principles and persons distinct. She calls him to account for his bigotry in confusing modern Jews with the ancient Israelites of the Bible, and for his wish that the Jews would not "spread" in the United States. Rose also chides Seaver for behaving as a "religionist" in his advocacy for one religion over another. As a self-proclaimed infidel and editor of a major freethought newspaper, Rose observes, Seaver might reasonably be expected to be equally opposed to all religions. Instead he praises Universalism as modern and progressive, and criticizes Judaism and Jews for the behavior of the biblical Israelites.

In her responses to Horace Seaver's editorial and subsequent remarks, Rose appeals to her freethought constituency by characterizing Jewish monotheism as akin to Unitarianism and to the Deism of Thomas Paine and Thomas Jefferson. She dismisses Seaver's critique of the "superstitious ritual practices of Jews" as simply a "distinguishing characteristic of the sect," similar to the bonnets worn by Quakers.[29] Aside from exchanges about religion, Rose focuses her responses to Seaver chiefly on modern Jews. In this aspect of the debate she hews closely to arguments to be expected of a human rights advocate fighting irrational prejudice against any maligned and demonized group.

However, as the debate continued, Seaver's comments grew even more pejorative toward Jews, and Rose, in a fury, responded in kind. At some points she seems to be doing just what she criticizes in Seaver—arguing for one religion over another. She cannot resist pointing out that if the ancient Jews were so barbaric as to worship a warlike and destructive God, as Seaver alleged, were not the Christians, who later accepted the God of the Hebrew Bible, equally barbaric?

As atheists, both Rose and Seaver consider whether believers were likely to abandon their faiths. Rose asserts that Judaism is preferable because it is better to have only one God than three to disavow.[30] Seaver points out that Universalists do not believe in the trinity and asserts that many more Universalists than Jews become atheists. Rose responds that many former Jews can be found among freethinkers.[31] Though Seaver states that he personally knows two former Universalists among the freethinkers, he claims he was not aware of Rose's Jewish origins—this despite their long friendship.

Speech and language expert Keri Bodensteiner has observed that Rose's argument in this exchange displays rhetorical inconsistencies. Rose claims to defend all victimized people, yet her defense of the Jews seems to elevate Judaism above other religions (Bodensteiner 2000). Though her point is well taken, Bodensteiner conflates Rose's elevation of Judaism over other religions with her defense of Jews as targets of discrimination. She overlooks the fact that Seaver begins his editorial critique of biblical Judaism by attacking modern Jews, without understanding the cultural, historical, and religious differences between the ancient Israelites and modern Jews. Though Rose challenges Seaver to note those differences, it becomes difficult for her to keep Jews and Judaism as separate in her arguments as they were in her life.

Berkowitz and Lewis (1998) analyzed the Rose-Seaver debate in its historical context. They note that Seaver published his editorials during the Civil War, attacking Jews and Judaism in a time of rising anti-Semitism, which made Seaver's slurs against contemporary Jews all the more dangerous. Seaver played on two anti-Jewish prejudices prevalent during the Civil War years: that Jews were more likely to buy their way out of the draft than non-Jews; and that they were profiteers. These prejudices were widely held and had real consequences. Based on this canard, for example, General Ulysses S. Grant barred Jews from certain war zones. Combining these dual prejudices into one sentence, Seaver further compounded his offense by mocking the accents of immigrant Jews in rendering the word percent as "per shent" (1864 February 17; see *1863 October–1864 April*).

Given the anti-Semitism and anti-immigrant prejudices of the period, Seaver's attack on the Jews constitutes an egregious lapse on the part of a supposedly progressive reformer. It is not surprising that his words angered Rose. Indeed, she may have felt personally threatened as a Jew, and a foreign one at that. While the Universalists were by then under no particular threat,[32] Rose seems to have violated her own stated principles in criticizing one of the two religions under discussion and not the other. But, she may have felt obliged to do so in order to defend Judaism, since Seaver criticized Judaism but not Universalism.

Viewed through a twenty-first-century lens, Rose's and Seaver's behavior toward one another seems to demonstrate a general lack of civility and respect. Though they were purportedly united in a movement to advance the cause of reason and human progress, they treat one another as "religionists" rather than as fellow infidels united in a quest for truth. While they did not behave appropriately as freethinkers, they were not totally out of keeping with the standards of their time on religious debate. In *Freethinkers: A History of American Secularism*, Susan Jacoby points out that in the nineteenth century, freedom of religion "did not mean that particular religious beliefs were exempt from public criticism or even from public ridicule" (2004, 172). Indeed, many religious debates of the period were notable for a lack of respect and tolerance.

When Rose outspokenly criticized religion and the Bible, as she often did at freethought or infidel gatherings, she did not focus specifically on Judaism either in attack or defense, but applied her antireligious critique to all religions, religious texts, and clergy. In her view, all religions led to the subordination of women; all blocked the progress of humanity toward the rule of reason and enlightenment. Thus it is reasonable to infer that Rose did not believe in or practice Judaism. But she was as concerned about the human rights of Jews as she was about the human rights of all people. On the other hand, given the atmosphere of anti-Semitism, and her own life experiences as a Jew, it is not surprising that Rose became angry and emotional as she responded to Seaver.

While Seaver outspokenly advocated for the progressive nature of Universalism, he confidently regarded himself as a freethinker (DuBois 2001, 16). Yet when Rose defended the Jews, he accused her of "turning Jew." It is not surprising that Rose's Jewish affinities would be aroused when anti-Semitic remarks were made, whether in the freethought or suffrage movements (Baxandall 2002). In the view of Jean-Paul Sartre, the French existentialist philosopher writing after World War II, it is not only one's self-identification that counts. To Sartre, "The Jew is one whom other men consider a Jew. . . . Because he lives in the midst of a society that takes him for a Jew" (Sartre 1995 [1946], 13, 143). Rose's situation can best be described as *Judenschmerz*, literally Jewish pain, a word coined in German to describe the experience of Jews who had left the Jewish religion and community but remained unable to gain a foothold in the larger community (DuBois 2001, 13). Thus even if Rose wished to carry on a discourse about atheism, the anti-Semitism of her fellow atheists cast her in the role of defender of the Jews and Judaism.


## JEWISH AND PROTESTANT PERCEPTIONS OF THE ANCIENT ROOTS OF JEWISH CULTURE

The debate between Rose and Seaver illuminates the diverse perspectives of a Jew and a Protestant on the meaning of an "old" religion or culture.

Jews often take pride in the ancient origin of their civilization, believing that aspects of Judaic law and ethics advanced social organization, a significant step beyond the taking of law into one's own hands. For his part, Seaver, coming from a Protestant background, regarded Judaism's ancient origins as merely demonstrating its "barbarism." While Judaism continued to adapt over the centuries through study and commentary by rabbis and religious scholars, Christianity tended to view Judaism as ossified in the part of the Hebrew Bible they renamed the "Old Testament," and stigmatized as obsolete, unable to change, and thus not as progressive as newer religions. In this debate, Seaver showed his disdain for an ancient religion over a modern one when he dubbed Moses "the barbarian" at least one out of every three times he mentioned him, beyond calling him several more times "old Moses."

Remember, by way of contrast, young Ernestine Susmond Potowski's response, at age seventeen, to the offer of admission to Berlin in the 1820s in exchange for conversion to Christianity: "Why should I leave the tree to join a branch?" Her almost offhand retort demonstrates that, even in the process of courting admission to Berlin and cutting her ties to Judaism, she still took pride in the ancient origins of her heritage, especially when compared to the younger religion of Christianity. The editor of the *Jewish Record* observed, on February 19, 1864, in praising Rose "for her fighting stand" in the debate with Seaver, that although she had abandoned her religion she still possessed "some of the old leaven of the Jewish spirit . . ." (quoted in Suhl 1990, 224). Viewed within the European context of her birth, Rose represents modernity, embracing rationality and enlightenment over traditional, communal ways of thinking, believing, and living. Rose was among the first wave of secular Jews who contributed to social reform in Europe and the United States. Although she was critical of Judaism, as she was of religion in general, she embodied in her life of social action the Judaic ethic of *tikkun olam*, the commandment to heal, repair, and renew the world, that is a prominent aspect of modern liberal Judaism. As an Owenite socialist, Rose devoted her life to a mission she described in wholly secular terms as contributing to human progress or "progression's train." Yet this Owenite vision may have captured not only her mind, but also her heart, because of her early inculcation with ethical aspects of Judaism. Despite a confluence of Judaic ethics with social reform, however, there is little evidence that Rose ever resolved her own conflicted relationship with Judaism and with being Jewish.

## ROSE'S INTERNATIONALISM

While living in the United States as an "American by choice" (Yale 1931), Rose always kept in touch with radicals from abroad. The year 1848 was a time when rising aspirations for freedom brought a series of rebellions that swept across Europe from France to Poland and Hungary to Germany. It was the year that Karl Marx published the *Communist Manifesto*; and in the United States it was the year of the first known women's rights convention at Seneca Falls. During and after the European uprisings of 1848, Rose championed the causes of European nationalist leaders trying to establish modern democracies, often looking to the United States as their model. And for those whose rebellions failed, Rose wished to welcome them to the land whose Declaration of Independence had inspired them. Rose liked to remind Americans that their country benefited from the idealism of such "foreigners" as Paine, Lafayette, and Kosciusko, who had aided the cause of the American Revolution. "If this country wishes to deserve the name as the place of refuge for the martyrs of freedom," she asserts that Americans should be willing to repay the debt by helping those who were fighting for freedom and fleeing repression abroad.

> Every sympathy, encouragement, and means of help ought to be extended towards . . . [those who] seek shelter in this land of Liberty. Our arms ought to ascend wide to receive and cherish them . . . to compensate them for all they sacrificed; for none but those who feel it, can tell the trials and sufferings of those who, for the cause of Freedom—the cause of Truth—have to sacrifice home, wealth, friends, all that makes life desirable, and become strangers and wanderers in a foreign land. (*1850 January*)

From the earliest women's conventions, Rose also fostered an international consciousness within the women's rights movement and envisioned women's rights in a very contemporary way, as a global movement. At the first National Women's Rights Convention, she declared: "We are not contending here for the rights of the women of New England or of old England, but of the world" (*New York Tribune* 1850).

The following year, at the second national women's rights convention, Rose read a letter of support from imprisoned French feminist reformers Jeanne Deroine, who had dared to stand for election to the French National Assembly, and Pauline Roland, who twice attempted to vote. She responded by opening her own speech linking women's rights in France and in the United States (*1851 October*). Rose maintained friendships with women in and from Europe, such as Jenny P. d'Héricourt of

France and Mathilde Anneke of Germany (*1853 September*), both of whom eventually relocated to the United States and continued to work for women's rights.

In May of 1856, Ernestine and William Rose made their first trip back to Europe. They traveled to England, France, Germany, and Italy, returning to the United States in November of that year. Following her trip to Europe, Rose's speeches were infused with her excitement about the political activity of women she had met during her travels. Directly upon her return, she twice addressed the National Women's Rights Convention. In her first speech, she praises of the growing consciousness of women's rights among the women and girls of England, and expresses her concern about the repression of free expression in France. In her second speech she compares the progress toward women's rights in the United States and England (*1856 November*).

In 1857, she wrote two letters to the *Boston Investigator* criticizing proposed laws on divorce and remarriage in England. In 1860, in her heartfelt speech on political activism, Rose expounds upon the internationalism of the women's rights movement, saying: "effects of this movement . . . [are] springing up here and there, yes, all over the world." Taking pride that "Our movement is cosmopolitan," Rose points to political efforts in France and Germany and women entering new occupations in England.

Rose herself was cosmopolitan in the sense that she was an international reform figure. In one of her travel letters from Europe in 1856, Rose reports "being found out" and asked to speak. Rose had probably been recognized due to coverage in the European press. Further research will undoubtedly reveal more references to Rose like this excerpt from an 1858 article by Ottilie Assing, a foreign correspondent living in the United States while reporting for a liberal German newspaper.

> More attractive, more outstanding, and more to my liking than any of those [women's rights reformers] I have mentioned so far is Ernestine Rose. . . . Her opinions are based on a clear, liberal conception of all things and are not hemmed in by tradition. The speeches she has given at women's meetings and other occasions reveal a broadly educated, independent and lucid mind; nothing is murky, nebulous, or illogical. Her knowledge of two continents has broadened her horizon; experience and understanding have matured her opinions. . . . (Quoted in Lohmann 1999, 114)

## THE RETURN TO ENGLAND

In Rose's empathic speech about the displaced freedom fighters, we can perhaps hear a poignant echo of the loneliness Rose may have felt for family and friends she left behind each time she moved on to a new land. Yet in 1869, she moved on one last time. Her primary motive in leaving the United States and returning to England is unknown.

It is also provocative that Rose applied for and received United States citizenship prior to her departure (Kolmerten 1999, 257). Was she hoping to return one day, or was this simply a gesture to underline her oft-stated preference for citizenship in a democratic republic rather than a monarchy?

She was no doubt deeply disappointed by the divisions within the reform movements after the Civil War, particularly the split within the women's movement. She may have realized, with her canny sense of politics, that the goal of votes for women would not be achievable in the United States within her lifetime, and thus she would deploy her remaining energies elsewhere. Currents within the freethought movement, Rose's other political base and William Rose's base as well, may also have been influential, especially the anti-Semitism expressed by Seaver in the pages of the *Boston Investigator*. In England, disenfranchised Jews may have been drawn to the freethought movement's efforts to extend citizenship to them and other non-Protestants. Furthermore, from England Rose could participate more easily in international conferences held in continental Europe.

Speculations about politics aside, the Roses' reasons for relocating may have been largely personal and practical. The amount of time they devoted to such restorative pursuits as spas and water cures suggest that concerns about their health were also likely factors. Ernestine's health had always been problematic, but she had heretofore had the resilience to overcome bouts of "ague" and lung problems. As she aged, rheumatism may have challenged further her peripatetic lifestyle as a lecturer. The economics of retirement were certainly a factor as well, as suggested by her letters from England in which Rose refers to the lower prices of rooms in England and the low cost of beef and mutton (Kolmerten 1999, 258–59).

Still, Ernestine Rose continued to be involved in reform activity. She met with international peace activists in France in 1870, and spoke at a meeting in Bath, England, in 1871, where female property owners were allowed to vote in local elections. Rose attracted notice in the local newspaper when she introduced herself and William as "women's rights people" and declared the foundations of Bath would not be shaken even if women cast votes for members of Parliament (Kolmerten 1999, 260).

In 1871, they moved on to London, where they had more politically congenial friends. Rose "reentered public life" by speaking at a Woman's Suffrage Conference on April 28, and addressing a crowd of over a thousand people on women's rights at the centenary of Robert Owen in May. Two London newspapers reported that hers was "*the* speech of the evening" (Kolmerten 1999, 261). Rose continued speaking on women's rights and freethought, even traveling in winter to Edinburgh to support the bill of a progressive member of Parliament "to remove the electoral disabilities of women" (Kolmerten 1999, 262).

Rose returned once to the United States, in 1874, and attended the annual National Woman's Suffrage Association Convention that year in New York, where she declared her retirement from public life. According to the New York newspapers, she gave a rousing speech summing up the wonderful progress made in building a major social movement for women's rights since she had first begun to give itinerant lectures nearly forty years earlier (Kolmerten 1999, 264). Upon returning to England, Rose continued, until 1880, to write letters to be read to the conventions.

Retiring to England cannot have improved Rose's chances of being remembered in American women's history. Until recently, there were few efforts to integrate the reformers of other nations into the history of progress and human rights in the United States. Today, with a modern global understanding of women's rights and human rights (Anderson 2002; Offen 2002); we can better appreciate the legacy of Ernestine L. Rose, who never failed to link these issues.


## THE LAST YEARS AND LEGACY OF ERNESTINE L. ROSE

In 1882, after William's sudden death, Ernestine, in failing health, implored her closest friends among the English freethinkers to protect her, should she become vulnerable to overzealous religionists seeking to publicize deathbed conversions of famous atheists. She died peacefully, undisturbed by proselytizers, on August 4, 1892, and was eulogized on both sides of the Atlantic. At Highgate Cemetery in England, George Jacob Holyoake, successor to Robert Owen as leader of the Owenite freethought movement, presented a graveside eulogy (*1892 August*), glowing with praise for Rose as a freethinker and antislavery activist, but curiously omitted recognition of her work on behalf of women's rights. The following year, at the annual women's rights convention, Elizabeth Cady Stanton spoke in praise of Rose's outstanding and early contribution to the women's rights movement (*1893 January*).

Perhaps the best commentary on Rose's life is her own. Regretting that in her eighties she could no longer "be useful," according to her own high standard of contributing to social change, she nonetheless declared with satisfaction, looking back on a lifetime of dedicated activism, "I have lived" (Kolmerten 1999, 270).

As an immigrant, a Jew, and an atheist, Rose was in many ways a social outsider in the reform movements to which she devoted her life. Her marginal status gave her freedom to advocate for reform causes previously outside of mainstream discourse. She exerted great influence due to her skills as a social thinker, an orator, and debater. She influenced her own generation and those that followed, carrying on the fight for women's rights after she left the United States in 1869. Stanton and Anthony preserved Rose's legacy through recording her contributions from her earliest days in the United States in their *History of Woman Suffrage* (1881–1886).

Rose was celebrated as "Queen of the Platform," considered the best of the female orators (Suhl 1990, 154–55). Because of her fame and drawing power, she was often featured as a speaker and nearly always signed the "calls" or public invitations to the conventions. All the women who signed the calls took a risk, for women's rights reformers were vilified by conservative clergy and ridiculed by the press. As a freethinker, Rose was a frequent target, especially of the clergy. She defended herself and her cause with her twin weapons of logic and humor. By creating early momentum toward reform, and through her decades-long commitment to the process of "agitating the issues" at annual conventions and on the lecture circuit, Rose influenced other women reformers and made a unique contribution as a "founding mother" of the movement for women's rights and woman suffrage.

But Rose was a founding mother in another sense, as well—through beliefs that linked her directly to the so-called founding fathers. Rose based her demands for women's rights on the ideal of universal justice, based on natural, inalienable rights, expressed in the Declaration of Independence, rather than on women's supposedly special qualities of virtue, caring, and compassion espoused by some women's rights reformers. Rose's philosophy linked the struggle for women's rights to the foundational values of the United States. Rose argued that the principle of consent of the governed, which was the basis of the founding of the United States, meant women deserved to have the vote (*1854 October*). Rose's insistence on the secular nature of civic life also links her to the founding fathers. She consistently fought for the principle that religious arguments must be kept out of government, and out of the conventions of reform movements (*1852 September 9*, "Debate").

When Ernestine Rose arrived in the United States in 1836, women were regarded as belonging in a separate sphere of domesticity. Even the most minimal participation in nondomestic life, such as attending a mixed university class, was regarded as boldness verging on indecency. By the time Rose left in 1869, women were being admitted to universities, working in a variety of occupations and professions, and mobilizing to win the vote. Rose described the magnitude of change in her own words, in one of her last letters to Susan B. Anthony, which Rose asked to have read at the thirtieth anniversary of women's rights.

> Speak of the wonderful change that has taken place in regard to woman. Compare her present position in society with the one she occupied forty years ago, when I undertook to emancipate her from not only barbarous laws, but from what was even worse, a barbarous public opinion. No one can appreciate the wonderful change in the social and moral condition of woman, except by looking back and comparing the past with the present. . . . Say to the friends. Go on, go on, halt not and rest not. Remember that "eternal vigilance is the price of liberty" and of right. Much has been achieved; but the main, the vital thing, has yet to come. The suffrage is the magic key to the statute—the insignia of citizenship in a republic. (*1878 July 19*)

Rose's colleagues and protégés became better known than she, but her vision continued to inspire them, and at the dawn of the twenty-first century, she inspires us still.

NOTES

1. The Roses' arrival date was symbolically important as the birthday of Robert Owen, Ernestine's mentor in public speaking and social activism.

2. The phrase *tikkun olam*, Hebrew for repair of the world, may not have been commonly used among Ashkenazi Jews as it has been since the social change movements of the 1960s, since it arose from the Kabbalistic movement started by Sephardic Jews in Israel after the expulsion from Spain in the fifteenth century. Yet the concept embedded in Judaic ethics may have influenced the freethought movement. In Rose's earliest years in the United States, she began her public speaking career debating at a freethinker forum, the Society for Moral Philathropists, run by Benjamin Offen, another British emigrant, who appears in a portrait holding a book embossed with the words "Renovating the World." Benjamin Offen, Lecturer of the Society of Moral Philantropists/ Benjamin Offen/ This plate is humbly Dedicated to the trustees and members of the said society by the Publisher/Printer and Published by H.R. Robinson, 48 and 53 Cortland St. New York. Entered according to the Act of Congress in the Year 1836 by H.R. Robinson, in the Clerk's Office of the District of the United States of the Southern District of New York.

3. I am indebted for this piece of lore about nineteenth-century Prussian university life to Professor Sabine von Mering of the Germanic and Slavic Languages Department at Brandeis University.

4. Despite the failure of the New Harmony community, the Owenites brought a legacy of progressive politics to Indiana. Robert Dale Owen was subsequently elected to the U.S. Congress, where he championed women's rights reform. He also wrote a tract on birth control, published in England, that was quite advanced for its time.

5. Furthermore, the initials "E.L.," presumably for Ernestine Louise, would be consistent with the letter having been written prior to her marriage to William Rose, which probably did not take place until late 1835 or early 1836 just before they emigrated together to the United States. If Susmond Potowski as a young, single woman did choose to sign her initials rather than her full name, it was the only instance of such caution of which I am aware. Her first documented letter published in the United States in 1847 is signed with her full name, Ernestine L. Rose, as are all the others.

6. While in the United States, Frances Wright conceived and carried out an intervention to oppose slavery—the creation of Nashoba, an interracial community near Memphis, Tennessee. Wright's community purchased a number of enslaved persons, with the intention that through their labor they would purchase their own freedom. Though innovative, aspects of this venture were ill-conceived, beginning with the purchase of enslaved persons so that they were legally still chattel, and ultimately the failure of the community to protect African American women from the very real power imbalances between them and white members of the community (Morris 1992, 108–40).

7. In *Victory: How Women Won It* (1940), celebrating the twentieth anniversary of the enfranchisement of women, the National American Woman Suffrage Association noted Ernestine L. Rose's 1836 lectures on government in an appendix of "Interesting Events in the Woman's Rights Movement," a list that began with Anne Hutchinson's woman-led prayer meetings in 1636 and extended to the ratification of the Nineteenth Amendment for woman suffrage in the United States in 1920.

8. The Workingman's Parties were part of a democratizing movement to extend the franchise beyond the propertied classes to all (white) men. By the Jacksonian era, this goal had been largely accomplished, and Herttell turned his attention to women's rights (Post, 1943, 129).

9. Elizabeth Cady Stanton corroborated Rose's account in her memoir. When she first met Rose in 1840, Rose had been circulating petitions and testifying before legislature committees "for years before" passage in New York State of the first Married Women's Property Act in 1848 (Stanton 1971 [1898], 150).

10. On May 24, 1844, Samuel Morse sent the first telegraphed message using the system and code he developed in the 1830s. A recent work on the invention and implementation of the telegraph, *The Victorian Internet* (Standage 1998), is so titled to highlight the revolution in communications that the telegraph brought about.

11. Goldsmith writes, "Members of [a group of radical Quakers]. . . . had carried to an extreme the Quaker principle that God's laws were written in every human soul . . . that 'an unbroken chain of communications exists between the Infinite and all beings.' This conviction seems, to be confirmed in the year 1848, when telegraph lines finally reached the Rochester area, making it possible to send messages by means of a little understood electrical force. The concept formulated by Isaac Post that one could utilize a 'Spiritual Telegraph' to establish a line of communication to those who had 'passed over' was no more difficult for these people to accept than the telegraph itself."

12. Freethinkers of Rose's time maintained that Thomas Paine was among the first to utter the word *independence*. He had given enormous support to George Washington and contributed money for the revolutionary army, yet he had been removed from prominence as a founding father because of popular hostility to his religious views and because of slanderous allegations about his way of life. To keep his memory alive, the community of

freethinkers in many large cities in the Northeast and Midwest, and even in some territories such as Indiana, organized annual Thomas Paine Celebrations on his birthday.

13. George W. Jamison created the cameo bust of Andrew Jackson. The inscribed, gold frame is the only extant example of William Rose's work.

14. Women who left home without permission could be forcibly returned by the police.

15. Héricourt reports that Rose told her of the loss of two children in infancy. Kolmerten searched for, but could not find, a record of their births or deaths in New York, but did note Ernestine's reduced travel schedule during the probable years of the births (d'Héricourt 1856; Kolmerten 1999).

16. The expression "a law unto himself" is often used to mean someone who recognizes no law but his or her own desires. Here, Rose uses the phrase to characterize William as someone who is governed by his own ethical standard and consideration for his spouse. Perhaps this was the usage at the time, or possibly Rose misused the phrase.

17. For Robert Owen, "Government in a political sense was but an extension of . . . the management of people through an understanding of the effect of circumstances on human character." The usual phrase adopted by Owen and his followers for this was the "Science of Society" (Royle 2003).

18. For a thoroughgoing analysis of the issue of "separate spheres," see "The Radicalism of the Woman Suffrage Movement" (DuBois 1998).

19. "Wait a little longer" is a line from the song, "There's a Good Time Coming," set to music and sung by the Hutchinson Family Singers at antislavery rallies and women's rights conventions. See Kolmerten (1999, 113n).

20. Many of the woman reformers called themselves Garrisonian abolitionists in honor of Garrison's support of women's right to serve as delegates at the World Anti-Slavery Convention of 1840 in London, and for his consistent support of women's rights in the years following.

21. Rose seized every opportunity to criticize Czarist Russia, having experienced in her youth its tyrannical control over her Polish homeland.

22. More research is needed to discover whether Rose attended and spoke at other antislavery conventions in addition to those in 1850 (where she was shouted down) and 1855.

23. This speech by Rose in 1863 was reprinted in 1963 as part of the reproduction of the proceedings of that convention. It was published by the Emma Lazarus Federation, a radical Jewish women's organization, with a Preface by Daisy Bates, civil rights activist and mentor to the Little Rock Nine in the integration battles of the 1960s.

24. Kolmerton quotes reports in the *Beacon* of October 14, 1837, and January 26, 1839.

25. Schappes (1971) reproduces, as document # 92, "Non-sectarian Thanksgiving. Correspondence between the Jews of Charleston, S.C. and the Governor of South Carolina, and other documents, November, 1844."

26. As John M. Robertson, a historian of freethought over the centuries, argued, "[the claim to mental freedom is] an important element of forward movement in history." Indeed, the importance of expressing one's real beliefs is not only important for the psychological well-being of the individual, but is an advantage to society as a whole. Modern freethought draws upon the "capacity of man to doubt, to reason, to improve on past thinking, to assert his personality as against even sacrosanct and menacing authority" (1957, 5–6).

27. See Warren for discussion of the differences between radical freethinkers, for whom infidelism is the primary issue, and socialist freethinkers, who put social reforms ahead of freethought doctrine (1966, 135–55).

28. By way of context, there were many references to religion and nationality at the 1852 women's rights convention due to an upsurge of nativist sentiment and religious bigotry engendered by the American Party, commonly called the Know-Nothing Party, which was growing in influence. Rose complained to Susan B. Anthony a year and a half later about the antiforeigner comments of some prominent reformers at that convention, a conversation recorded by Anthony in her diary (*1854 March–April*).

29. Here Rose seems to anticipate Reconstructionist Judaism, founded in the early twentieth century, in which ancient rituals are retained as links with cultural tradition, while embracing a liberal theology consistent with a modern scientific understanding of the world.

30. The one god vs. three gods argument calls to mind the court debates between Jews and Christians mandated by Christian rulers dating from medieval times, which Rose, as a European Jew, would probably have known. Some of the frequently used Jewish arguments may have been taught to her as part of her religious or political education. She may, indeed, have known them so well that she could hardly restrain herself from using them.

31. This comment by Rose on Jews in the freethought movement, along with her subsequent interview with the Jewish periodical, *The Hebrew Leader* (1869), suggests that by the 1860s, she did have Jewish friends and acquaintances in the United States.

32. The Universalists may have been under some threat a generation earlier. Jacoby cites an instance during debates on ratification of the U.S. Constitution when concern was expressed that without a religious oath "a Turk, a Jew, a Roman Catholic, and what is worse than all, a Universalist may be President of the United States" (2004, 29).

## EDITOR'S NOTE

Reporting speeches was not as precise an art in the nineteenth century as it is today, perhaps due to lack of sophisticated technology for transcription. Consequently, in some of these documents, taken from both Proceedings of conventions as well as newspaper accounts of speeches, the reporter or transcriber starts off presumably in the mode of direct quote in the first person account, then shifts into summary mode in third person, perhaps having lost some words, then shifts back again. When the document is an example of a type of speech we might not otherwise have, or a particularly early one, or expresses ideas that would otherwise be excluded, I have included such texts as Ernestine's speech and invite the reader to judge how precisely her language has been represented.

For ease of reading, spelling errors in the original sources, including the letters and other documents herein, have been corrected at the request of the publisher. However, wherever possible, the original punctuation has been retained.

1840-1850

# TOASTS AT THE THOMAS PAINE CELEBRATION

*By Ernestine L. Rose, William E. Rose, and Others*
January 29, 1840
New York, New York

For the freethought community of New York, celebration of Thomas Paine's birthday on January 29 was a secular winter "holiday," but with an undercurrent of serious intent. It was an annual event since 1827, that was similarly celebrated by freethinkers in many states and some territories. The purpose was to honor Thomas Paine, who freethinkers believed had been denied his place in history as a founding father because of his radical beliefs and his alleged "libertine" behavior. This document affords an early glimpse of Ernestine L. Rose as a public personality. It is also the only recorded instance of William E. Rose, here speaking (or perhaps singing) in public. The toasts, often presented as songs, expressed deeply held beliefs on religion and politics. It was noteworthy that women participated at all in the toasts and speeches at the 1840 celebration. Rose spoke three times, perhaps to encourage other women to participate, and she was one of three women who offered toasts. Over the next few years the Thomas Paine Celebrations in New York reverted to being largely male events (except for the dance held after the speeches, when the women were invited to join in). By the late 1840s, with the rise of the women's rights movement, women's participation increased, and Rose became an annual speaker.

The following report is excerpted from the radical freethought weekly the *Boston Investigator*, February 19, 1840, under the headline "Celebration of Paine's Birthday in New York." The report refers to an extemporaneous speech by Ernestine Rose, regrettably not recorded.

⁓&⁓

The philanthropist Thomas Paine was commemorated on his birthday, January 29, 1840 in Union Hall by the Society of Socialists in New York city, who advocate the principles of the National Community Friendly Society of Rational Religionists founded by Robert Owen. The Chair was filled by Mr. Alex. Bennet, and assisted by Mrs. Ernestine Rose, and Mr. Lewis Masquerier. The company, consisting of ladies and gentlemen, met about 7 o'clock, and in a social and agreeable manner gave up to the entertainment of the occasion. They discarded that stiffness and reserve too prevalent in many of the fashionable meetings for amusement. The object of the Socialists, is to introduce reform in every thing—having learned that startling truth to the mass of mankind, that the whole system of society, the present moral world, and even great nature itself, are yet susceptible of a very improved organization. At 8 o'clock both ladies and gentlemen sat down together to supper, where lemonade was substituted for all ardent spirits. After the repast, the President called to order with preparatory remarks: when Mrs. E. Rose, a Polish lady, and disciple of Robert Owen, addressed the meeting in a ready, extemporaneous and eloquent manner. After whom L. Masquirier and others gave addresses. Numerous toasts were then given and drank [to] with applause, interspersed with songs, speeches and recitations, &c. The music then summoned the hour for dancing, when all so inclined partook of that agreeable exercise until 12 o'clock, when all retired to their homes, had their usual sleep, and awoke the next morning with no other *pain* than that of Thomas Paine in their heads.

## REGULAR TOASTS.

Thomas Paine—whose birthday we now celebrate. May his doctrines of toleration pluck the sting of slander from the tongues of Christians, as they have already snatched the sword of persecution from their hands.

Song, by Mr. McArthur.

Our Country—While we give it our patriotic support, let it not be at the sacrifice of that philanthropy and justice due to all mankind as brethren.

Song, by Mr. W. E. Rose.

Free Enquiry—May it continue to search with the penetrating quality of lightning, every dogma and prejudice, and electerise [electrify] with positive knowledge the negative state of the human mind.

Song, by Mrs. E. Rose.

The People—They bear all the burdens of society, they produce the wealth of the aristocracy by the sweat of their brow, and then defend it by shedding their blood.

Recitation, by Mr. J. Walker.

. . . . . . . . .

Life, Liberty, Property and Happiness—they can only be equalized, secured and perpetuated by a new organization of society upon cooperative principles; whereby all can be made producers as well as consumers of property.

Recitation, by Miss E. Munn.

The English Charterists [Chartists ] May they perceive that they can effect more good by the peaceable exercise of their reason, than by physical violence.

Song, by Mr. J. Crowel.

Women—As much as men oppress each other, they oppress the fair sex still more; may many Woolstencrafts [*sic*] and Darusmonts [refers to

Frances Wright], arise in defense of the rights of woman.

Song, by the President.

## VOLUNTEER TOASTS

*By L. K. Coonley.* The works of Thomas Paine—Though "these are the times which try men's souls," if we have but "Common Sense," to discern the "Crisis," and to understand the "Rights of Man," we will be prepared to usher in the "Age of Reason."

*By Mrs. E. Rose.* The march of improvement in the past and present—May all see in it a proof that it must still progress, and learn how to choose the good and to avoid the evil in the future.

. . . . . . . .

*By W. E. Rose.* "Health to the sick; honor to the brave; success to the lover; and freedom to the slave."

. . . . . . . .

*By Mrs. E. Rose.* Robert Owen—the author of the formation of Character—May his principles soon be so successful as to form many such characters as he is himself.

*By J. Hickman.* The Social Missionaries—May their success in the establishment of the Social System [planned communities] in England, soon be extended in every nation, and prove to them that the true Messiah has come to all, and not to a small portion of the earth.

*By Mrs. E. Rose.* Reformers—Let us by honoring the memory of reformers in the past, and by aiding the efforts of those in the present, encourage the rise of others in future time.

. . . . . . . .

*By Mrs. Donnelly.* Education—Educate the nurses of children and you will reform the world.

. . . . . . . .

*By W.E. Rose.*
The philosophic Thomas Paine,
Who wrote his "Common Sense" so plain,
His "Crisis" in a trying time,
His "Rights of Man" 'gainst royal crime
His "Age of Reason" 'gainst the priest,
Has thus Columbias's sons released.

# SPEECH AT THE NEW ENGLAND
## SOCIAL REFORM SOCIETY CONVENTION:
### "A WORD TO MY SISTERS"
May 30, 1844
Boston, Massachusetts

The New England Social Reform Society was created to discuss and compare the many utopian communities springing up in New York and New England, and to attract support in particular for Community Place (1843 to 1846) at Mottville, New York, a suburb of Skaneateles. Community Place was created on the Owenite model, and Ernestine Rose and John Collins often spoke on its behalf, while William Rose raised funds for the community. Though they were active on behalf of the Community, the Roses never actually lived there.

This may be Rose's first recorded speech on women—one that ties her ideas on women's enforced dependency and lack of rights to her Owenite socialist principles. She had spoken earlier at this convention of the New England Social Reform Society, on freethought and on socialism, and was ready to talk about women.

John Collins, who issued the call to the convention, had been a prominent abolitionist agent in New York State. He became so convinced of the primacy of "the property question" that he turned his attention to the creation and development of this Owenite community. However, as Rose mentions in the next document, his leadership style created controversy which frequently roiled the community. One example of a conflict where Rose and Collins disagreed was the wisdom of registering their deed to the community's land. Collins preferred not to acknowledge property rights under the auspices of the state, but Rose insisted that they do so. Thus when the community failed within three years, the members were able to salvage their investment along with a small profit due to a rise in property values.

∾

Mrs. Rose . . . had a word to say to her sisters.—She need not advise them to stay away from the polls. This was a vice with which their lords would not allow them to meddle, though they were willing to deluge the land in blood, to secure this privilege for themselves.

But women did give their influence in favor of this, the tyrant's weapon.—She besought them not only to discourage and discountenance forceful governments in every shape, form and manner, that they might be presented, but, also, to use every moral and virtuous means in their power to bring into odium, to break down this popular religion which was absorbing the people's sympathy, time and means; which directed their hopes and attractions from earth to heaven, and from the present to a future life. The clergy and the church don't recognize your right, my sisters, continued Mrs. R., to speak publicly or in the church. Speak, then, not in their favor. They say, that in your appropriate sphere—in the nursery and private circle, you have an all powerful influence—exercise it for their destruction, and for your own elevation, and for that of the race. What rights have women? Are they not the merest slaves on earth? What of freedom have they? In government they are not known, but to be punished for breaking laws in which they have no voice in making. All avenues to enterprise and honor are closed against them. If poor, they must drudge for a mere pittance—If of the wealthy classes, they must be dressed dolls of fashion—parlor puppets,—female things. When single, they must be dependent on their parents or brothers, and when married, swallowed up in their husbands. Nothing of nobleness, dignity and eleva-tion is allowed to exist in the female. All such traits in her are indelicate and unbecoming. A few are allowed to thrum the keys in a piano—to smatter a little French or Italian—to do cunning needlework—to study the combined colors of the rainbow—but then how masculine, indelicate, and unwomanlike for her to pry into the heavier sciences—into the false-ly—so-called sciences of politics and religion. She may lean upon a gen-tleman's arm, but to travel alone would be immodest and vulgar. This state of society does not recognize woman's equality. Her living is in the hands of man. My sisters, speak out for yourselves. Tyrants never will willingly relinquish their grasp. All that the lords of creation will yield will be what they are forced to by public sentiment.

> "Know ye not, who would be free
> Himself must strike the blow."

This property system, while he [*sic*] is allowed to continue, will, with the rest of the race, particularly oppress you. It must be destroyed. Spend one-tenth part of the time, strength and devotion, in spreading informa-tion upon this question, that you do in the Ministerial, Church, Bible, Tract, Mission, and other religious causes, and the work will be accom-plished. In all these movements, is not woman the stay and the staff? What could the church and clergy do without woman? I call upon you, then, as you venerate truth and reason, as ye love yourselves, your children and the race, never to enter a *church* again. Countenance them not. They oppress you. They prevent progression. They are opposed to reason.

This appeal burst upon a listening throng like a thunderbolt, and they were instantly lashed into the wildest excitement of fury and applause.

The door and passage-way were crammed with spectators, most of them the devotees of the church, and the speaker was assailed with a shower of hisses as fierce as though Pandemonium had let loose its metamorphosed angels upon a single woman! Mrs. R. waited calmly until the tumult had subsided, when she again repeated the injunction, and again the tumult rose still higher; and the repetition and uproar went on until the excited multitude, unable longer to keep up the din, were compelled, through exhaustion, to hear the daring heresy in silence.

# LETTER TO ROBERT OWEN
December 1844
New York, New York

This is the earliest extant example of Rose's writing, and shows that in 1844 she still struggled, as do many immigrants, with written English, especially spelling and style. Rose wrote apparently in reply to Robert Owen, her mentor in public speaking and socialism, while he visited his son Robert Dale Owen at the Owenite community they founded at New Harmony, Indiana. She addresses Owen in both letters as "Respected Father," and demonstrates her loyalty to him in a variety of other ways. Especially telling is her request to Owen that he carve out some work for her to do in the event that she and William move south for her health. At this point in her life, Rose still looked to Owen for political direction.

Yet Rose did not shrink from letting Owen know *her* views on his words and actions. Rose enclosed with her letter an article from the *Phalanx*, a newspaper published by American followers of the French socialist philosopher François Marie Charles Fourier, who had founded a community in New Jersey. Rose criticizes the article for its bias in favoring Fourierism over Owenism, and chides Owen for allowing himself to be quoted praising Fourierism, rather than strictly promoting his own purer form of socialism.

Madam. D'Arusmond was the marriage name of Frances Wright, an Owenite feminist who spoke in the United States in the 1820s. Rose often praised Wright in public lectures as the first women to speak out in the United States on women's rights and as an inspirational role model who shared her Owenite views. Thus her negative comments here are puzzling. It is likely she is simply expressing sympathy for Owen's position in being thrown together with Wright when there was personal tension between them. The issue, according to George Jacob Holyoake, was that Wright had hoped to marry Robert Dale Owen, but his parents disapproved (see Holyoake 1904, Part II of "Unpublished Correspondence of the Robert Owen Family" 17, 465).

This letter, dated only "December 1844," is one of three—two from Ernestine L. Rose, and one from William E. Rose—found in the Robert Owen Correspondence Collection at the National Co-operative Archive, Co-operative College, Manchester, UK. All are being published for the first time in this volume.

⤦

New York, December 1844

Respected Father

I received your kind letter from Newharmony and was very happy to hear that you arrived safe at your family. I would have answered it immediately but at the time I received it my health was very bad and there was some new difficulty in the community of Skaneateles whose issue I waited so as to have something certain to communicate to you on the subject, but they are in as unsettled a condition as ever. Mr. Collins is not the man for so great an undertaking. He has too much ambition and policy, and so little straightforward honesty to retain the confidence of his friends. Nor has he a knowledge of the practice necessary to carry the object out. Some of the other members do not understand the first rudiments of the social science, and the rest are moral cowards though good men and thus become the tools of the more designing.

I regretted to hear that Madam. D'Arusmond came on the same boat that you was [sic]. I know it must have been unpleasant to you, she has an inveterate spite amounting almost to vengeance against you and your family. She is now here engaged in writing out some plans which she keeps quite secret. Her great object is to get someone in Washington to invite her to lecture in the House. I think she is a woman of a good deal of book learning but of very small mind. I received your kind letter from Washington and was very glad to hear that you arrived safe and well. I have some hope to have the pleasure of seeing you soon. My health since you left us has not been good. I had several quite severe attacks of depression of mind. Mr. Rose wishes me to go to Washington. He and our friends think that the change of climate and scenery and society will be beneficial to me likewise to see something about the south as we have some idea of going south if it agrees with me so my dear father if you could cut out some work for me so as to make me useful while there I would be very happy to do all in my power to dispel error and disseminate Truth. I think of going sometime in January and would be glad to know your opinion on it. I saw a letter of yours in the *Phalanx* with some comments of the Editor which I send you. Some parts of it I regretted to see as it appears to me to be an error. Whatever Fourier's views were, his system as advocated here is certainly not calculated to benefit Mankind, even if it could be carried into practice, which I believe cannot be done, for it combines all the destructive elements of the present state of society with just enough of Truth to ignite by its radiant light the combustible materials thus brought into close contact and blow it all to destruction. Nor would that system in any way prepare the mind for a better state. Men brought together in a close connection upon false Principles, isolated interest, and without a knowledge of the formation of character cannot fail to call forth and continuously excite the very worst faculties of their nature and thus become worse than ever. No, while isolated interest exists, let men be separated as they now are. Truth and Error are antagonisms that can never be brought into a harmonious relation, the one must destroy the other. Nor is Fourierism any easier commenced though it holds out false and deceptive promises to Rich and Poor. Their principles have not sufficient intrinsic value to take hold of the better part of men's nature. I am well aware of the difficulties in commencing the rational system, but it can be overcome, all that is wanted is a few well intentioned honest intelligent men that understand the Principles in all their bearings with clear vision and practical minds, and such that understand the quality of the materials requisite for commencing. And then believe me my dear Father that Robert Owen's system would be much easier commenced and carried out than any other. I speak not as an enthusiast from the little experience I have of the people here I am convinced that by a persevering attempt measured means could easily be obtained. You will see from the remarks of the Editor of the *Phalanx* that they want to make capital of the remarks you made in favor of Fourierism. I saw your address to the world in the *Herald* with some good remarks of his which I send you. We received two numbers [issues] of the *New Moral World* of September which I send to you with a *Tribune*. I saw Mr. Readfield. Your book will be out next month. Please give my best respects to Robert Dale [Owen]. I am very much obliged to him for his kind note. I hope to have the pleasure of seeing him soon. I thank you for forwarding me the letter of my friend the late Mrs. Hunter. Mr. Rose sends his kind respects to you and your son. Wishing you health and happiness, I remain my dear Father,

Affectionately your Daughter,
Ernestine L. Rose

# LETTER TO ROBERT OWEN
April 14, 1845
New York, New York

In this second, brief letter from Ernestine Rose to Robert Owen, sent while she was on tour in Philadelphia, Rose reports her successes and asks for his support as one might of a respected teacher or mentor. However, unlike the earlier letter, where she asks Owen's advice, this time it is clear that she has made her plans and will continue to carry them out. Both letters refer to small "commissions" or tasks that the Roses performed for Robert Owen and his son Robert Dale Owen. Possibly the Roses functioned as corresponding secretaries, receiving mail and literature from the Owenites in England and mailing them on to Owenite groups in the Untited States.

❧

New York, April 14, 1845

My dear and respected Father

I received your mail and perceived with pleasure that you were well. I am surprised that your letter to Philadelphia did not reach its destination as it was positively put in the Post-Office. Have you seen the gentleman to whom it was directed? The little Commission I received of Robert D. Owen from Philadelphia last week I promptly executed. Should you write to him, please to mention it. I hope he had a pleasant journey and found all the family well. The Socialists requested me last week to address them on Sunday evening, which I did to a large and respectable audience, and I hope to some satisfaction. They advertised in the papers that I would speak in the afternoon, which gave some dissatisfaction to the audience on finding they were disappointed, it also was noticed in the *Tribune* that you would speak in their Hall on Sunday. My dear Father if you think proper you might mention to some of the Friends there about my intended journey west, and that I would be in Philadelphia in the middle of May, but I leave it entirely to your consideration. My health is tolerable well, considering the changes in the weather. We sent you a letter last week that arrived here from England, hope you received it. Mr. Rose is very well and sends his best respects to you. With the best wishes that Health and Success may attend all your undertakings, I remain your Affectionate disciple.

Ernestine Louise Rose

# SPEECH AT THE INFIDEL CONVENTION
## May 4, 1845
## New York, New York

At the close of this convention, Rose publicly disagreed with Owen and the Convention Committee about the naming of the convention, and urged an identity-affirming approach that was well ahead of its time. She called for the convention to proudly claim the name of "Infidel," with which the freethinkers had been tarred. They should seek to make a name given in derision respectable, she said, through living up to their principles (Suhl 1990, 87). She was so persuasive that this and subsequent Owenite freethought conventions were known as Infidel conventions. This particular convention was called to coincide with a visit by Robert Owen to New York City. Owen made brief opening remarks, urging support for those in Europe who were just beginning to fight for an ideal of liberty modeled upon the "true brotherhood" found in the United States, and Rose followed, speaking in praise of Owen and his remarks. Rose's second speech at the convention, included here, is one of the clearest statements of her socialist beliefs, identifying "isolation of interest" and the misallocation of resources as the root cause of poverty.

The *Boston Investigator* reported the convention proceedings in its May 14, 1845, edition, where this excerpt appeared, and continued its report in the May 28 edition.

⟨❧⟩

My Friends: After what you have heard from our dear and venerable father, Robert Owen, I could wish that nothing more should be said. He has truly remarked that the evils of society are caused by ignorance and unkindness, and that the reform of those evils is to be brought about by the diffusion of knowledge and universal charity. There are many reforms; this is an age of reform; every one acknowledges that society is in a wrong state, and ought to be reformed. What makes man act wrong? Is it his desire to do it? We have been and are yet told that the heart of man is wicked, and in accordance with this, such arrangements have been made in society as to fulfill the prophecy, and make him bad indeed. It is the greatest libel that has ever been put upon nature. Every human being has a tendency to do good, but the fundamental error, that man forms his own opinions, feelings, and acts, has made him bad. He was considered as a being independent of every man around him; hence followed the isolated condition of society. These two fundamental errors are the cause of all evil; they make every man an enemy to his neighbor. Tell me, my friends, will the preaching "thou shalt love thy neighbor as thyself," as long as isolated interests exist, avail us anything? So long as the precept exists, Every one for himself, and some supernatural power for us all—how much can you love your neighbor? There is a great deal of poverty in the world; but is there any necessity for poverty? Is there any collective poverty? There is no such thing as poverty; there is ten times more in the world than would maintain all in yet unknown luxury. Yet how much misery there is in our midst; not because there is not enough, but owing to the misdirection of it. Those who create the most, get the least; those who build the largest castles, often have not where to lay their heads: and then we say that man is bad by nature, because if he has not a crumb to eat, he will take some from his neighbor. Why is it man has never been placed in a position to make himself happy? Isolation of interest is the cause— the contrary is the remedy. I have thrown out these few hints for you to reflect on. We must inquire what sort of beings we are, and are we rightly situated? Ponder over these questions. The welfare of the race depends upon them, and the application of the remedy is the reversion of the present arrangements of society. Ignorance is the evil—knowledge will be the remedy. Knowledge not of what sort of beings we shall be hereafter, or what is beyond the skies, but a knowledge pertaining to *terra firma*, and we may have here all the power, goodness and love that we have been taught belongs to God himself.

# LETTER TO ROBERT OWEN
### By *William E. Rose*
### September 31 [*sic*], 1845
### Buffalo, New York

This letter from William E. Rose to Robert Owen is included as the only extant letter in William's words and handwriting. The letter testifies to William's concern for Ernestine, noting that he has traveled from New York City to Buffalo to be with her and make sure she was recovering and being well cared for after she fell ill on her way home from a speaking tour. William wrote to let Robert Owen know about Ernestine's illness and also sent a copy of his letter to be reprinted in the *Boston Investigator*, which was published on October 8, 1845, so that others in the freethought community might send well wishes to cheer Ernestine. He also expresses gratitude toward and trust in the members of the freethought community for providing for her care.

❧

Buffalo, Sept. 31 [sic], 1845

Dear and Respected Father,

I arrived here on Friday morning and I found My Dear Ernestine, was very low with the remittent of Brain fever, but since then she has been better, and then worse again. I think now she is somewhat better and the Doctor thinks the fever is broken, but which is uncertain and she is very feeble and great care has to be taken with her. I think I shall be able to return to New York in a few days, as she is with very good and kind friends that do all they can for her. If you please you might give the *Boston Investigator* an intimation of it, so that the friends may know how she is. I delayed writing till I knew how the fever would turn. My Dear Ernestine sends her love to you and regrets that she is not able to attend the convention. She wishes very much to hear from you. Address. Mrs. Rose, Care of Charles Howland, Buffalo, NY.

Yours very respectfully & affectionately,<br>W.E. Rose

# SPEECH AT THE THOMAS PAINE CELEBRATION: THE 1848 REVOLUTIONS IN EUROPE
## January 29, 1849
## New York, New York

Ernestine Rose spoke fervently of the revolutions that swept across Europe in 1848, bringing hope for a new age of "Liberty, Equality, and Fraternity"—which she here toasts as "the trinity of humanity." Following the ceremonial annual praise of Thomas Paine and the *Rights of Man*, she reminds the audience that the task of their generation is to achieve the Rights of Women, without which the Rights of Man cannot truly exist. The speech was published on February 21, 1849, in the *Boston Investigator*, which introduced it by saying: "The 10th Regular Toast—'Woman'—was eloquently responded to by Mrs. Ernestine L. Rose, who has kindly furnished us with a copy of her remarks:—"

❧

. . . My Friends—Since last we met, we have passed through a year full of the most interesting, startling, and important events—events which, though they were the effects of tyranny and oppression, will become the causes of an entire change in the political and social affairs of Europe, perhaps the world. It is a terrible but a glorious strife for a nation to struggle for liberty. The task is more than Herculean for a people who have for many years been crushed to the earth, to rise and shake off the yoke that oppresses them; and the longer they silently submit to a tyrannical government, the less able they become to emancipate themselves from its thralldom. This holds good with all governments, for even the best of them, as at present constituted, press like an incubus on the energies and vitality of the people; and in one great particular all governments are alike—namely, in the usurpation of power. The more you give them, the more they claim, until they have deprived you of the power of resistance.

Among the many suffering nations of Europe, look at poor, downtrodden Ireland! That people once had energies; they had once power to act. What are they now? The combined powers of a corrupt government and a false and debasing religion have crushed all their energies, and deprived them of all their courage, until they have become so enervated and spiritless that they have lost the strength, physically and morally, to work out their deliverance. Even that ennobling feeling, the desire of freedom, they no longer retain; it has been crushed or starved out of them, for if they had had it strongly burning within their breasts, they never would have allowed the few brave and noble spirits who manfully stood up for their rights, to be sacrificed on the altar of corruption. I am no advocate of war or violence, but the heart sickens in contemplating the scenes of horror that have been perpetrated on poor humanity. And why all this? Because man claimed his birthright, liberty.

But a bright star is beaming in the moral horizon, that speaks to us with a prophetic voice of the future destiny of man. Its effulgent light has already eclipsed the diadems in the crowns of Europe. "Liberty, Equality, and Fraternity," that glorious trinity that requires no miraculous power to understand it, no priest nor prophet to interpret it, makes itself understood by its own power, for already has it caused thrones to shake, scepters to bow down, and miters to be crushed. Kings and priests tremble before this new-born messenger of peace, for well they know, that if it generally rules, "Othello's occupation's gone." But until Humanity assumes her reign, nations like individual man will have to struggle for life and liberty, for liberty cannot exist without equality of rights—and as long as we have the favored few, must we also have the injured many, and under such a state of things, liberty is only an empty sound. But whenever liberty shall be based on equality, the only sound basis upon which a true republic can rest, then man will find that there are stronger and far more beautiful bonds between man and man, than those which mere conventionality or commercial intercourse has forced upon him. His mind and feelings will become expanded until he will recognize in every man a brother, and in every woman a sister.

But to hasten this glorious period, we my Sisters, must not remain idle. While we gratefully remember all that Thomas Paine has done for the *rights of man*, we must also remember that to us is left to achieve that greater task—the rights of woman!—without which, even the works of Thomas Paine, I greatly fear, will be useless, for man can never be truly free until woman has her rights as his equal, until she becomes elevated as an intellectual, independent, moral being. Let us, therefore, endeavor to convince man practically that the mind of woman can be cultivated as well as her sympathies; that while she is the guardian angel of infancy and the consoler of old age, she may be equally efficient in giving counsel to manhood; that while she can feel strongly, she can think rightly and act promptly. Then the time, I trust, will not be far distant—

"When, as the equal to man, each woman will think,
    And burst all the fetters that bind her,
At the fountain of knowledge she will freely drink,

And be what fair Nature designed her;
Then science will shine like the bright orb of day,
    Diffusing its influence o'er all,
And they who now turn from her teaching away,
    Will be proud to attend to her call."
And now, my friends, if it is not asking too much, I will solicit your
particular understanding for my toast—

*The Trinity of Humanity—*
"Liberty, Equality, and Fraternity."

# SPEECH AT THE THOMAS PAINE CELEBRATION: WOMEN IN INTERNATIONAL FREEDOM FIGHTS

January 29, 1850
New York, New York

At the 1850 Thomas Paine Celebration, Ernestine L. Rose was introduced by name, not simply with a toast "to Woman" as in prior years. She was toasted with a literally "flowery" introduction: "Mrs. Rose—She was the Morning Glory of Poland; the Lily of England; and she is the Rose of America." In her speech, Rose reveals a knowledge of American history and an awareness about contemporary events in Europe. As an immigrant, she speaks with feeling about a yearning for freedom that crosses national boundaries. She names heroes from other lands—including Paine, Lafayette, and Kosciusko—who came to the United States to support the American dream of liberty. Referencing the 1848 uprisings in Europe, she calls upon Americans to return the favor by supporting freedom fighters abroad.

Rose exhorts women not to be idle spectators at struggles for freedom, not to let themselves be limited by notions of women's "sphere." Although her subject—international human rights combined with women's rights—is similar to her talk at the prior year's celebration, her emphasis seems to have shifted, so that here she allows more weight to women's rights as ends in themselves.

According to the *Boston Investigator*, Rose spoke with great passion to the eight hundred people who were reported present. Her talk was received with "tremendous applause," and followed by an acknowledgment from a male speaker, who praised women's abilities and welcomed the prospect of more women speakers at future events—suggesting here that Rose broke ground for other women in the freethought movement. The text published here appeared in the *Boston Investigator* on March 6, 1850. The speech was first reported in the issue of February 13, 1850, but was reprinted at Rose's request in order to correct errors.

⤳

My Friends—It is with feelings of gratitude, and emotions too deep for utterance, that I rise to respond to the kind sentiment of the President.

I thank him from my heart for remembering my poor unhappy country, which has been prostrated, but I hope not lost. She will, I trust, yet arise like the Phoenix out of her ashes. But this is not the time to speak of my country, as there are subjects more important to you on this interesting occasion.

I am happy to see so many assembled for the purpose of paying a tribute of gratitude—of lifting our united hearts and voices in one grand anthem of thanks and praise to departed genius and worth; and while we enjoy this gratification, let us endeavor to emulate him, in honor to whose memory we have assembled—catch a spark of the fire that burned in his bosom, when at the sacrifice of home, friends, interest, reputation, liberty, and the risk of life, he devoted himself to the rights of man. (Applause.)

I hope every one present is acquainted with the life and character of Thomas Paine—with his disinterested devotion to the cause of Liberty—the signal services he rendered this country in her struggle under a foreign yoke—and with the fact, that it was his mind that first conceived, his heart quickened, and his lips brought forth the talismanic word, which, when first uttered, though in the ears of the wisest and best of America's patriots, made them tremble lest the walls should have ears to hear, and tongues to repeat, and they should be sacrificed for its utterance. Yes! When in the secret council with Washington, Franklin, Rush, and Adams, Thomas Paine first spoke the magic word Independence, the four sages looked with amazement at the audacity of giving utterance to a term, which even their minds were unprepared to grasp or realize. But it was done!—the walls had ears and tongues!—the charmed word was echoed and re-echoed, and through the length and breadth of this country, Independence became the watchword! (Tremendous applause.)—Thus the offspring of obscurity gathered strength and power, and by the fostering care of Thomas Paine grew into maturity, the fruits of which we enjoy this evening. (Continued applause.)

Had he done no more than this, this nation ought to send forth one universal shout of gratitude!—the ringing of bells and the thundering of cannon ought to usher in the 29th of January as the day that gave a champion to Liberty! and to this country a most efficient aid in time of need. But he has done far more. He not only labored for the independence of one nation from the power of another, but for the independence of man from his worst foes, Priestcraft and Superstition—the serpents that, while you nurse them at your bosom, will draw the vitality and sting you to death He wished to crush the hydra-headed monster and free the human mind. and for this heroic devotion to the noblest of all causes—the emancipation of mind from worse than Egyptian darkness—he was persecuted while alive and slandered after his death, and all in the name of Religion. Well might we exclaim: "Religion! What dark and atrocious deeds have not been perpetrated in thy name"—Every tyrant, when he sets his iron heel on the necks of his victims pacifies his obedient slaves with the right divine to crush Humanity. Russia, to inspire her slaves with additional ferocity, made use of the same dark, mysterious influence. Under its banner, as the apostle of religion, she went forth to crush young Freedom in Europe, and her success is upheld as a mark of divine favor. After immolating every noble spirit she can crush, *Te Deum* is sung in the churches, and thanks given to God for the victory! The silly despot of Austria, in committing outrages that make Humanity shudder, in sparing neither age nor sex. but sacrificing every thing that comes within his pestilential atmosphere, has, like the Pope, the pretext of power from above, and in the name of religion perpetrates cruelties that would shame the darkest ages of human existence. But it will not. it cannot remain thus much longer. Though Freedom's champions have been defeated, outraged, and down-trodden, Humanity will assert her rights. The soil on which the blood of her noblest children has been shed, will re-produce an abundant harvest of the sons of freedom, who will sweep superstition and tyranny from the face of the earth! (Cries of "hear! hear!" mixed with cheers and applause.)

While we assemble to honor the memory of Thomas Paine, it would be well to remember that Paine, Lafayette, Kosciusko, and many other noble minds who enlisted in the cause of right over might, were foreigners; and that, in addition to the plea of humanity, this country owes a debt of gratitude which now is the time to pay. (Sensation.) Every sympathy, encouragement, and means of help ought to be extended towards those brave and faithful men who have taken the field against the insolence of kings and priests, from whose oppressive power they seek shelter in this land of Liberty. (Applause.) Our arms ought to ascend wide to receive and cherish them, not only while they are a novelty to gaze at, but to place them in a position to compensate them in some degree for all they sacrificed; for none but those who feel it, can tell the trials and sufferings of those who, for the cause of Freedom—the cause of Truth—have to sacrifice home, wealth, friends, all that makes life desirable, and become strangers and wanderers in foreign lands. Let Congress appropriate a portion of man's rightful inheritance—the earth. Let them give a tract of land and means enough to enable the Hungarian patriots, now in our city, with the noble Governor of Comorn [possibly a Hungarian title] at their head, to form a home for Kossuth, Bem, Mazzini, and all other brave and devoted men, whom the tempest of despotism may drift to these shores.

But I am told that Congress has no power to do so. If, among its many unrighteous deeds, Congress requires additional power to do one good act, then let the people, the sovereigns of our Republic, empower them by petitions to that effect, signed by every man, ay! and woman in the States. Let it be our task, my friends, to start it in this city, and others will follow the good example. This will be a practical demonstration in favor of European freedom that will have its good effect.

The despots of Europe will see. that if the Republic of America can give no practical aid to struggling Humanity, she can provide an asylum for her children, not indeed to make them forget, but to feed and nourish the flame of freedom, until the lava of righteous indignation will burst forth like a volcano, that shall hurl tyranny and oppression into one grand avalanche of forgetfulness.

If this country wishes to deserve the name as the place of refuge for the martyrs of freedom, let them contend for the adoption of Kossuth, Bem, and Mazzini. It is said that seven ancient cities contended for Homer dead; let us contend for living heroes, that have done what Homer wrote. Let public demonstration be made against the fiendish cruelties with which Russia and Austria hunt their victims down like beasts of prey; and in so doing will we indeed honor the memory of Thomas Paine, of Jefferson, and of Washington.

And now allow me to ask you, my sisters, shall we remain idle spectators at the death struggle of Freedom because an ignorant and degrading opinion prevails, that participating in a noble act is out of the sphere of woman? Do you want precedents and examples where woman has burst her fetters, and stood up in defense of Humanity? We need not search the pages of ancient history: there are enough in our day. One of them, whom I am proud to call my country-woman, is now in this city. Look to Poland, Rome, and Hungary, and you will see that in the hour of need, in the contest between freedom and despotism, woman, delicately brought up woman, gave her aid to the cause of Liberty! Some as ministering angels of mercy, to pour balm into the wounds of the sick, and give comfort to the dying; and others, as the avenging angels of retribution, faced Freedom's foes on the field of battle. Each in accordance with her abilities and powers—all for the good of Humanity. Were they out of their sphere? Let Freedom, let Humanity answer! (Profound sensation.)

The most cowardly usurper of her rights dare not say that the heroic and devoted women of Rome, and Mademoiselle Jagella, who bravely fought by the side of the Hungarian heroes, were out of their sphere. I mention this not, my friends, because I would wish to see woman thus engaged; for I deplore the necessity for it alike in man or woman. To my mind the whole state of things is wrong. Society is based on falsehood, force, and fraud, instead of truth, kindness, and a well directed union of men; and I trust that the time will come, when the causes that transform our fair earth into one great battle-field and charnel house, will be removed—when the present state of slavery and violence will be superseded by freedom based on human rights, without distinction of sex, class, party, country, or color. (Applause.)

But I wished to show that woman is wanting neither in strength of mind, courage, nor perseverance, and if her capacities and powers were to decide her sphere of action (and nothing else ought to do it), methinks not a few of our legislators, would, with credit to themselves and benefit to the country, have to change places with woman. (Laughter and applause.) But she must do something to break the chains that ignorance and superstition have woven around her, and tied into a Gordian knot. She must untie it with the sharp points of reason, dissolve the links by the light of knowledge, and thus, bursting the unholy fetters, she must claim her rights equal with man, and then indeed will she be a woman. Her rights, and an education to develop all her powers, will strengthen her affections, purify her sympathies, refine her feelings, mature her judgment, and fit her for the vicissitudes of life as a companion to an intellectual man—a mother to train her children to become such—and above all, an honorable and useful member of society.

Finally, let me say to all: Deserve the name of friends to Thomas Paine. The admirers of his moral courage, we must like him be true to our convictions; like him fearlessly oppose error wherever we find it, in church or state; never encourage in word or deed those things that are obstacles to human progression; never sacrifice principle for popularity, for it is unworthy of an honest and noble mind; court truth only, for it is the noblest impulse to all our actions; and with truth as our guide, let us work on for the emancipation of man, not only from his physical but mental bondage, and hasten the glorious time when tyranny and oppression will cease, and union, directed by knowledge and affection, will allow man to dwell in harmony, security, and peace. (Tremendous applause.)

# RESOLUTION AND SPEECH AT THE FIRST NATIONAL WOMAN'S RIGHTS CONVENTION: "WOMAN'S SPHERE"

October 23, 1850
Worcester, Massachusetts

At the first national convention on women's rights, five hundred women and men were in the audience (Kolmerten 1999, 79) and 267 delegates had signed in, most from the northeast, but eleven from as far away as California (Worcester Women's History Project). Though Ernestine Rose was the author of at least one important resolution and spoke in its behalf, the proceedings summarized Rose's comments in one line, simply stating that she was active on the Business Committee, the committee in charge of framing the debates. In fact, she was chair of that committee, which included such distinguished members as Elizabeth Cady Stanton (who was not present at the convention), William Lloyd Garrison, Abby Kelley Foster, Lucy Stone, and Wendell Phillips. Rose's speeches were nowhere included in the proceedings. Perhaps because of the women's inexperience in running and transcribing conventions, they did not attempt to record the debates on the resolutions, but limited themselves to reproducing prepared speeches. At the following year's convention, Rose gave a scheduled speech and had copies made in advance.

The source of the following document is the *New York Tribune* on October 25, 1850. Rose's resolution is presumably reproduced verbatim, but the report of Rose's remarks in support is apparently a mix of direct quotation and paraphrased summaries (and includes an erroneous reference to her "French accent"). In her statement in support of her resolution, Rose argued eloquently for women's capacity for and natural right to an education that allowed her to support herself and to realize her potential. Only when access to self-development is available to women, she observed, could there reasonably be any discussion of men's and women's spheres. The last paragraph of this text provides an appreciative summary of her evening speech with a brief quote from it.

It was research done by Carol A. Kolmerten, Rose's biographer, that led to my discovery of the most complete account available of a convention speech by Rose which had been left out of the Proceedings of the First National Women's Rights Convention (Kolmerten 1999, 79).

⤙

Rev. Wm. H. Channing, from the Committee on Business, read the following resolution, prepared by Mrs. Ernestine Rose of N.Y.:

*Whereas.* The very contracted sphere of action prescribed for woman, arising from an unjust view of her nature, capacities, and powers, and from the infringement of her just rights as an equal with man,—is highly injurious to her physical, mental, and moral development. Therefore

*Resolved*, That we will not cease our earnest endeavors to secure for her political, legal, and social equality with man, until her proper sphere is determined, by what alone should determine it, her Powers and Capacities, strengthened and refined by an education in accordance with her nature.

. . . . . .

Mrs. Ernestine Rose of New York, spoke with great eloquence on the subject of the resolution. Her French accent and extemporaneous manner, added quite a charm to her animated and forcible style. Woman, she asked, who is she? She is the mother, the wife, and the sister of man. Is she not coequal with man? Has she not like powers of mind, like sentiments, faculties and affections given her for culture and improvement? Why, in the name of common sense, she would ask, is she not equal in the enjoyment of life, liberty and the pursuit of happiness? But she is not equal before the law. During her minority she is the property of her parents, and when she attains her majority, and enters the relation of marriage, she is transferred from the parent to the husband. If she had her rights and was properly educated, marriage would be the union of two hearts from real affections, bound in the bonds of the purest affections, instead of being as it now too frequently is, an artificial bond producing often more misery than happiness. She said a just indignation was felt by the community on account of the law which delivers up the fugitive slave to oppression. But it was no more unjust than some of the laws are towards women. If a woman is compelled by the tyranny and ill treatment of her husband, to leave him and seek a refuge among her friends, the law will deliver her up into his hands. He may compel her return. She did not propose to examine the laws that bear so unequally upon woman. What she claimed was that the laws should be made equally for both.

She said, when a father and mother have a son born to them, what do they ask themselves? They sit down and consult together about his education; how he should be trained and fitted for usefulness in life. If they have a daughter, what do they ask? Nothing. Girls are educated with one single aim, she felt ashamed to say it. And what is that aim? It is to catch a husband. She is educated in accordance with man's desires, wishes and aims, and it is no wonder she has not risen to the true level of her womanhood. Woman has never yet received an education for the higher purposes of life. Why should she not be made acquainted with the arts, the sciences, and the philosophies of life? With all the obstacles that exist to her elevation, there are brilliant instances of her success in all that has adorned and rendered great the character and fame of man. She has even acquired distinction of the field of battle. She trusted that if ever woman touched the sword, it would be to sheathe it in its scabbard forever.

She maintained that woman could study successfully any of the professions. Is perseverance necessary? She possesses it. Look at her by the bed of sickness, where toil and sacrifice are needed. Who is it that holds out to the last? It is feeble woman! Look at man when he is ready to give up with despair. Who is that upholds and strengthens him? It is feeble woman. It is the being whom Society assigns an inferior rank and position in life. She mentioned that woman was as heroic as man, and often exhibited a higher heroism, with which that displayed in the battlefield is cowardice [*sic*]. She contended for woman's rights, not so much for her benefit as for the benefit of the world. She pointed out the evils of society under its present organization and made a strong appeal to the reason and moral sense of her audience, to give their influence to the cause.

Her speech was received with applause by a large and intelligent audience, as were also the speeches of Mrs. Mott, Mrs. Price, and Mr. Channing. The hall was very crowded and the audience seemed to have caught the spirit of the speakers.

. . . . . .

[During the evening session, Rose and others spoke again. Rose's remarks were summarized in the *Tribune* article as follows:]

Mrs. Rose of New York, made another of her effective and eloquent speeches, in which she alluded to our Pilgrim *Fathers*, and the pride and reverence with which they are often referred to. But said she, "Who has heard of the Pilgrim Mothers? Did they not endure as many perils, and encounter as many hardships, and do as much to form and fashion the institutions of New England, as the Pilgrim Fathers? Yet, they are hardly remembered."

1851-1855

# LETTER TO THE EDITOR:
## SKETCHES OF LECTURING
September 4, 1851
New York State

Rose occasionally communicated with her friends in the freethought community about her lectures on that subject, using the forum of the letters to the editor column in the *Boston Investigator*, a publication she could expect most of them to read. It is interesting to note that, although she speaks in opposition to religion, she is sometimes allowed to speak at churches. When she refers to "priests," it is in the Owenite sense of clergy of all faiths, and does not refer solely to Catholic or Episcopal priests. This letter to the editor was published under the title "Sketches of Lecturing" in the October 1, 1851, issue of the *Boston Investigator*; it was written on September 4. The date tells us that only six weeks before Rose was to give her great speech on women's rights in Worcester, she was on the road in upstate New York, lecturing on freethought issues, and invited at one church to stay and lecture on women's rights in the evening. Rose managed to be an influential advocate for all of her reform issues simultaneously.

Mr. Editor:—I had a very interesting visit in the western part of New York, about 13 miles south of Rochester, and while there I was requested to speak in public; and as it ever gives me the greatest pleasure to contribute my mite towards the general stock of knowledge and happiness, I willingly accepted the proposal. We had seven meetings in the vicinity. In the village of Rush I spoke twice in the Baptist church, on the formation of character and on woman's rights. The meetings were well attended. The Methodist minister of the place and a brother minister from Lyma College called to see me. We had a very interesting conversation on the nature and merit of belief. The minister from Rush of course deemed it very meritorious to believe in his *ism*, but wrong and wicked to believe in any other; still he was quite polite and gentlemanly. Since I left there he has taken up my lectures to preach from. I am glad he did so; it will do good, for as gold is purified and refined when passed through the fiery furnace, so does Truth come out clearer and more beautiful from under severe criticism.

At Honeyday, I spoke in the Christian Church, on the present social evils. The meeting was well attended, and at the close of it a minister made some remarks in reference to what I said concerning the clerical profession. He considered clergymen the most self-sacrificing class of people in society, and, as an evidence, he gave the fact that he had been for some years minister in that place and was not worth a dollar. In my reply I told him that when he hears that the ministers receive calls to leave large and wealthy congregations to go to some poor ones because they stand more in need of their instruction, to let me know it, and I would take back what I said. The next day, Sunday, in the afternoon, I spoke in the Universalist Church in Smithtown. The house was very much crowded, some could not obtain even standing room. After the meeting I was requested to speak there in the evening on the rights of woman. The meeting was well attended and kept up till quite a late hour. What convinced me most of the progress in intelligence and liberality in the part of the country, was the profound attention with which they listened to these lectures, and the marked interest manifested during and after the meetings. They created quite an excitement, and I received many invitations to visit and lecture in the vicinity.

The last two lectures I gave in Rochester, but owing to a want of time to give proper notice, and to the influence of the priests on the people, were not so well attended. But without wishing to burden you with a lengthy detail, I must say that much good could be done there to awaken the slumbering faculties of the people. The country around Rochester is inhabited by a fine, industrious, intelligent class of men. The land is beautiful, the fields teeming with the fruit from Nature's bountiful store-house, and if we only had more laborers in the mental and moral fields, we could reap a plentiful harvest of the glorious fruit of knowledge and truth,—a harvest not only for the present, but for generations to come.

These last two weeks I spent on a visit to Dutchess County, N.Y. A good deal of enquiry is awakened in that part of the country. I spoke in Washington Hollow, and in Dover. The family I visited as well as many others in the neighborhood, are characterized for intelligence, kindness, and the spirit of enquiry and reform; but the mass of the people are yet so deeply rooted in ignorance and sectarianism, that it would require much active energetic labor to break the hard stubborn soil of superstition and intolerance, for the admission of the light of reason and the genial rays of charity and kindness. I have prolonged this letter far beyond my expectation. If you think it would be of any interest to your readers in showing them the progressive movement in various parts of the country, please to publish it.

Very sincerely, your friend,
Ernestine L. Rose
New York, Sept. 4th, 1851

# LETTER FROM TWO FRENCH WOMEN'S RIGHTS REFORMERS

*By Pauline Roland and Jeanne Deroine*

June 15, 1851 (Read on October 15, 1851)

St. Lazare Prison, Paris

Two Frenchwomen, Pauline Roland and Jeanne Deroine, imprisoned at St. Lazare in Paris for their activism on behalf of women's rights, were inspired to write to the women's rights activists in the United States. The demands of French women for equal rights with men dated back to the French Revolution, and following the European revolutions of 1848, Parisian women once again demanded inclusion as citizens. Roland had attempted to vote in 1848, while Deroine had offered herself as a candidate for the Legislative Assembly the following year. The two women were sentenced to six months in prison for their courageous political acts, with the justification that they had been involved with an outlawed socialist organization, the Central Committee of Associative Unions (on the French feminists see Offen [2000, 19, 33, 110–14, 119] and Schneir [1994, 90–91]).

The complete text of their stirring letter (including the footnotes that accompanied the original translation) appears below, preceding the speech by Rose, who heard it read aloud and responded directly to it in her opening lines.

Offen (2000, 111) notes that when Victor Considérant, cited in note 2, a deputy influenced by Fourierism, proposed granting the vote to single adult women, he was "laughed off the floor" by the all-male National Assembly. This episode was noted by then MP Benjamin Disraeli in the British House of Commons, who defeated Considérant and the idea of parliamentary suffrage for women.

The Central Committee, referenced in note 4, was for the Fraternal Associations what the Constituent Assembly was for the French Republic in 1848. The text that follows is from records of the convention that once belonged to Lucy Stone, and now reside in the Library of Congress, in the Votes for Women: Selections from the National American Woman Suffrage Association Collection, 1848–1921.

❧

## LETTER FROM IMPRISONED FRENCH FEMINISTS, READ OCTOBER 15

Dear Sisters:—Your courageous declaration of Woman's Rights has resounded even to our prison, and has filled our souls with inexpressible joy.

In France, the Re-action has suppressed the cry of Liberty of the Women of the future, deprived, like their brothers of the Democracy, of the right to civil and political equality; and the fiscal laws, which trammel the liberty of the press, hinder the propagation of those eternal truths which must regenerate humanity.

87

They wish also—the Women of France—to found a hospitable tribunal, which shall receive the cry of the oppressed and suffering, and vindicate, in the name of human solidarity, the social right for both sexes equally; and where Woman, the Mother of Humanity, may claim in the name of her children, mutilated by tyranny, her right to true liberty, to the complete development and free exercise of all her faculties, and reveal that half of truth which is in her, and without which no social work can be complete.

The darkness of the Re-action has obscured the Sun of 1848, which seemed to rise so radiantly. Why? Because the revolutionary tempest, in overturning at the same time the Throne and the Scaffold, in breaking the chain of the black slave, forgot to break the chain of the most oppressed of all—of Woman, the Pariah of humanity.

1. "There shall be no more slaves," said our brethren. "We proclaim universal suffrage. All shall have the right to elect the agents who will carry out that Constitution which should be based on the principles of Liberty, Equality, and Fraternity. Let each one come and deposit his vote; the barrier of privilege is overturned before the electoral urn; there are no more oppressed, no more masters and slaves."

Woman, in listening to this appeal, rises and approaches the liberating urn to exercise her right of suffrage as a member of society.[1] But the barrier of privilege rises also before her. "You must wait," they say! But by this claim alone, Woman affirms the right, not yet recognized, of the half of humanity—the right of Women to Liberty, Equality, and Fraternity. She obliges man to verify the fatal attack which he makes on the integrity of his principles.

And soon, in fact, during the wonderful days of June, 1848, Liberty glides from her pedestal in the flood of the victims of the Re-action;—based on the right of the strongest, she falls, overturned in the name of "the right of the strongest."

The Assembly kept silence in regard to the right of one half of humanity—for which only one of its members[2] raised his voice, but in vain; no mention was made of the right of Woman, in a Constitution framed in the name of Liberty, Equality, and Fraternity.

2. It is in the name of these principles, that Woman comes to claim her right to make part in the Legislative Assembly, and to help form the laws which must govern society, of which she is a member.

She comes to demand of the electors the consecration of the principle of equality by the election of a Woman; and by this act[3] she obliges man to prove that the fundamental law which he has formed in the sole name of Liberty, Equality and Fraternity, is still based upon privilege. And soon privilege triumphs over this phantom of universal suffrage, which, being but the half of itself, sinks on the 31st of May, 1850.

3. But while those elected by the half of the people, by men alone, evoke force to stifle liberty, and forge restrictive laws to establish order by compression, Woman, guided by fraternity—foreseeing incessant struggles, and in hope of putting an end to them—makes an appeal to the Laborer to found Liberty and Equality on fraternal solidarity. The participation of Woman gave to this work of enfranchisement an eminently pacific character, and the laborer recognizes the right of Woman, his companion in labor.

The delegates of a hundred and four associations, united without distinction of sex, elected two Women[4] with several of their brethren, to participate equally with them in the administration of the interests of labor, and in the organization of the work of solidarity.

Fraternal associations were formed with the object of enfranchising the laborer from the yoke of spoilage and patronage; but, isolated in the midst of the Old World, their efforts could only produce a feeble amelioration for themselves.

The union of associations based on fraternal solidarity had for its end the Organization of Labor, that is to say, an equable division of labor, of instruments, and of the products of labor.

The means were, the union of labor and of credit among the workers of all professions, in order to acquire the instruments of labor, and the necessary materials, and to form a mutual guarantee for the education of their children, and to provide for the needs of the old, the sick, and the infirm.

In this organization all the workers, without distinction of sex or profession, having an equal right to election, and being eligible for all functions, and all having equally the initiative and the sovereign decision in the acts of common interests—they laid the foundations of a new society based on Liberty, Equality, and Fraternity.

4. It is in the name of law framed by Man only—by those elected by privilege—that the Old World, wishing to stifle in the germ the holy work of pacific enfranchisement, has shut up within the walls of a prison those who had founded it, those elected by the laborers.

But the impulse has been given—a grand act has been accomplished. The right of Woman has been recognized by the laborers, and they have consecrated that right by the election of those who had claimed it in vain for both sexes, before the electoral urn and before the electoral committees. They have received the true civil baptism; elected by the laborers to accomplish the mission of enfranchisement, after having shared their rights and their duties, they share to-day their captivity.

It is from the depths of their prison that they address to you the relation of these facts, which contain in themselves high instruction. It is by labor, it is by entering resolutely into the ranks of the working people, that Women will conquer the civil and political equality on which depends the happiness of the world. As to moral equality, has she not conquered it by the power of sentiment? It is, therefore, by the sentiment of the love of humanity that the Mother of humanity will find power to accomplish her high mission. It is when she shall have well comprehended the holy law of solidarity,—which is not an obscure and mysterious dogma, but a living providential fact,—that the kingdom of God promised by Jesus, and which is no other than the kingdom of Equality and Justice, shall be realized on earth.

Sisters of America! your socialist sisters of France are united with you in the vindication of the right of Woman to civil and political equality. We have, moreover, the profound conviction that only by the power of association, based on solidarity,—by the union of the working classes of both sexes to organize labor,—can be acquired completely and pacifically the Civil and Political Equality of Woman, and the Social Right for All.

It is in this confidence, that from the depths of the jail which still imprisons our bodies without reaching our hearts, we cry to you—Faith, Love, Hope; and send to you our sisterly salutations.

(Signed) Jeanne Deroine,
Pauline Roland
Paris, Prison of St. Lazare, June 15, 1851

## NOTES

1. The 27th of Feb, 1848, Pauline Roland presented herself before the electoral re-union, to claim the right of nominating the Mayor of the city where she lived. Having been refused, she claimed in April, the same year, the right to take part in the elections for the Constituent Assembly, and was again refused.

2. Victor Considérant.

3. In April, 1840, Jeanne Deroine claimed for Woman the right of eligibility, by presenting herself as a candidate for the Legislative Assembly, and she sustained this right before the preparatory electoral reunions of Paris.

4. The 3d of Oct., 1849, Pauline Roland and Jeanne Deroine, delegates from the Fraternal Associations, were elected members of the Central Committee of the Associative Unions.

# SPEECHES AT THE SECOND NATIONAL WOMAN'S RIGHTS CONVENTION

*By Ernestine L. Rose and Others*
October 15 and 16, 1851
Worcester, Massachusetts

The Second National Women's Rights Convention in Worcester, Massachusetts, was considerably better attended than the first, with more than eight hundred signing in, and over one thousand in attendance (Worcester WHP). It was also the site of Ernestine L. Rose's most famous speech. In this groundbreaking speech, Ernestine L. Rose presented her analysis of women's rights reform as comprising a broad array of rights, opportunities, and obligations, including socialization and education, access to professional training, choice of occupation, equal legal rights with men, and political rights, including suffrage. Employing a combination of facts, anecdotes, logic, and satire, Rose brought all of these women's rights issues together in one powerful argument that touched the heads and hearts of all who heard it. In this speech we find the first record of Rose's concise expression of her core egalitarian belief, "Humanity recognizes no sex—virtue recognizes no sex—mind recognizes no sex. . . ." In her talk at the twentieth anniversary in 1870 of the first National Women's Rights Convention, *History of the National Woman's Rights Movement for twenty years*, Paulina Wright Davis said: "Mrs. Ernestine L. Rose made an address of an hour in length, which has never been surpassed. She printed it at her own expense, and circulated it extensively" (1871, 27, quoted in Kolmerten 1999, 84, n13).

In addition to her "unsurpassed" main speech, Rose made a statement at the conclusion of the convention, also included below, urging men to use their greater rights and privileges to behave responsibly by supporting social equality between women and men. Following the convention, Rose continued to give versions of her main speech. Another version was published as a pamphlet, "An Address on Woman's Rights Delivered Before the People's Sunday Meeting, on Oct. 19th, 1851 in Cochituate Hall" (Rose 1851); it differs from the text published here only in omitting the opening reference to the letter from the French feminists. The texts that follow are from records of the convention that once belonged to Lucy Stone, and now reside in the Library of Congress, in the Votes for Women: Selections from the National American Woman Suffrage Association Collection, 1848–1921.

⟿

## "UNSURPASSED" SPEECH, OCTOBER 15

After having heard the letter read from our poor incarcerated sisters of France, well might we exclaim, Alas! poor France! where is thy glory? Where the glory of the Revolution of 1848, in which shone forth the pure and magnanimous spirit of an oppressed nation, struggling for Freedom? Where the fruits of that victory that gave to the world the motto, Liberty, Equality, and Fraternity? A motto destined to hurl the tyranny of kings and priests into the dust, and give freedom to the enslaved millions of the earth. Where, I again ask, is the result of these noble achievements, when Woman, ay, one half of the nation, is deprived of her rights? Has Woman then been idle during the contest between Right and Might? Has she been wanting in ardor and enthusiasm? Has she not mingled her blood with that of her husband, son, and sire? Or has she been recreant in hailing the motto of Liberty floating on your banners as an omen of justice, peace, and freedom to man, that at the first step she takes practically to claim the recognition of her Rights, she is rewarded with the doom of a martyr? But Right has not yet asserted her prerogative, for Might rules the day; and as every good cause must have its martyrs, why should Woman not be a martyr for her cause? But need we wonder that France, governed as she is by Russian and Austrian despotism, does not recognize the rights of humanity in the recognition of the Rights of Woman, when even here, in this far-famed land of freedom, under a Republic that has inscribed on its banner the great truth that all men are created free and equal, and endowed with inalienable rights to life, liberty, and the pursuit of happiness,—a declaration borne, like the vision of hope, on wings of light to the remotest parts of the earth, an omen of freedom to the oppressed and downtrodden children of man,—when, even here, in the very face of this eternal truth, woman, the mockingly so called "better half" of man, has yet to plead for her rights, nay, for her life; for what is life without liberty, and what is liberty without equality of rights? And as for the pursuit of happiness, she is not allowed to pursue any line of life that might promote it; she has only thankfully to accept what man in his magnanimity decides is best for her to do, and this is what he does not choose to do himself. Is she then not included in that declaration?

Answer, ye wise men of the nation, and answer truly; add not hypocrisy to oppression! Say that she is not created free and equal, and therefore (for the sequence follows on the premises) that she is not entitled to life, liberty, and the pursuit of happiness. But with all the audacity arising from an assumed superiority, you dare not so libel and insult humanity as to say, that she is not included in that declaration; and if she is, then what right has man, except that of might, to deprive woman of the rights and privileges he claims for himself? And why, in the name of reason and justice, why should she not have the same rights? Because she is woman?

Humanity recognizes no sex—virtue recognizes no sex—mind recognizes no sex—life and death, pleasure and pain, happiness and misery recognize no sex. Like man, woman comes involuntarily into existence; like him she possesses physical and mental and moral powers, on the proper cultivation of which depends her happiness; like him she is subject to all the vicissitudes of life; like him she has to pay the penalty for disobeying nature's laws, and far greater penalties has she to suffer from ignorance of her far more complicated nature than he; like him she enjoys or suffers with her country. Yet she is not recognized as his equal! In the laws of the land she has no rights, in government she has no voice. And in spite of another principle, recognized in this Republic, namely, that "taxation without representation is tyranny," yet she is taxed without being represented. Her property may be consumed by taxes to defray the expenses of that unholy, unrighteous custom called war, yet she has no power to give her veto against it.

From the cradle to the grave she is subject to the power and control of man. Father, guardian, or husband, one conveys her like some piece of merchandise over to the other. At marriage she loses her entire identity, and her being is said to have become merged in her husband. Has nature thus merged it? Has she ceased to exist and feel pleasure and pain? When she violates the laws of her being, does her husband pay the penalty? When she breaks the moral laws, does he suffer the punishment? When he supplies his wants, is it enough to satisfy her nature? And when at his nightly orgies, in the grog-shop and the oyster cellar, or at the gaming-table, he squanders the means she helped by her cooperation and economy to accumulate, and she awakens to penury and destitution, will it supply the wants of her children to tell them, that owing to the superiority of man she had no redress by law; and that as her being was merged in his, so also ought theirs to be? What an inconsistency, that from the moment she enters that compact, in which she assumes the high responsibility of wife and mother, she ceases legally to exist, and becomes a purely submissive being. Blind submission in woman is considered a virtue, while submission to wrong is itself wrong, and resistance to wrong is virtue alike in woman as in man.

But it will be said that the husband provides for the wife, or in other words, he feeds, clothes, and shelters her! I wish I had the power to make every one before me fully realize the degradation contained in that idea. Yes! he keeps her, and so he does a favorite horse; by law they are both considered his property. Both may, when the cruelty of the owner compels them to run away, be brought back by the strong arm of the law, and according to a still extant law of England both may be led by the halter to the market-place and sold. This is humiliating indeed, but nevertheless true; and the sooner these things are known and understood, the better for humanity. It is no fancy sketch. I know that some endeavor to throw the mantle of romance over the subject, and treat woman like some ideal existence, not liable to the ills of life. Let such deal in fancy, that have nothing better to deal in; we have to do with sober, sad realities, with stubborn facts.

Again, I shall be told that the law presumes the husband to be kind, affectionate, and ready to provide for and protect his wife. But what right, I ask, has the law to presume at all on the subject? What right has the law to entrust the interest and happiness of one being into the hands of another? And if the merging of the interest of one being into the other is a necessary consequence on marriage, why should woman always remain on the losing side? Turn the tables. Let the identity and interest of the husband be merged in the wife. Think you she would act less generously towards him, than he towards her? Think you she is not capable of as much justice, disinterested devotion, and abiding affection, as he is? Oh, how grossly you misunderstand and wrong her nature! But we desire no such undue power over man; it would be as wrong in her to exercise it as it now is in him. All we claim is an equal legal and social position. We have nothing to do with individual man, be he good or bad, but with the laws that oppress woman. We know that bad and unjust laws must in the nature of things make man so too. If he is kind, affectionate, and consistent, it is because the kindlier feelings, instilled by a mother, kept warm by a sister, and cherished by a wife, will not allow him to carry out those barbarous laws against woman.

But the estimation she is generally held in, is as degrading as it is foolish. Man forgets that woman cannot be degraded without its re-acting on himself. The impress of her mind is stamped on him by nature, and the early education of the mother which no after-training can entirely efface; and therefore, the estimation she is held in falls back with double force upon him. Yet, from the force of prejudice against her, he knows it not. Not long ago, I saw an account of two offenders, brought before a Justice of New York. One was charged with stealing a pair of boots, for which offense he was sentenced to six months' imprisonment; the other crime was assault and battery upon his wife: he was let off with a reprimand from the judge! With my principles, I am entirely opposed to punishment, and hold, that to reform the erring and remove the causes of evil is much more efficient, as well as just, than to punish. But the judge showed us the comparative value which he set on these two kinds of property. But then you must remember that the boots were taken by a stranger, while the wife was insulted by her legal owner! Here it will be said, that such degrading cases are but few. For the sake of humanity, I hope they are.

But as long as woman shall be oppressed by unequal laws, so long will she be degraded by man.

We have hardly an adequate idea how all-powerful law is in forming public opinion, in giving tone and character to the mass of society. To illustrate my point, look at that infamous, detestable law, which was written in human blood, and signed and sealed with life and liberty, that eternal stain on the statute book of this country, the Fugitive Slave Law. Think you that before its passage, you could have found any in the free States—except a few politicians in the market—base enough to desire such a law? No! no! Even those who took no interest in the slave question, would have shrunk from so barbarous a thing. But no sooner was it passed, than the ignorant mass, the rabble of the self-styled Union Safety Committee, found out that we were a law-loving, law-abiding people! Such is the magic power of Law. Hence the necessity to guard against bad ones. Hence also the reason why we call on the nation to remove the legal shackles from woman, and it will have a beneficial effect on that still greater tyrant she has to contend with, Public Opinion.

Carry out the republican principle of universal suffrage, or strike it from your banners and substitute "Freedom and Power to one half of society, and submission and slavery to the other." Give woman the elective franchise. Let married women have the same right to property that their husbands have; for whatever the difference in their respective occupations, the duties of the wife are as indispensable and far more arduous than the husband's. Why then should the wife, at the death of her husband, not be his heir to the same extent that he is heir to her? In this inequality there is involved another wrong. When the wife dies, the husband is left in the undisturbed possession of all there is, and the children are left with him; no change is made, no stranger intrudes on his home and his affliction. But when the husband dies, not only is the widow, as too often is the case, deprived of all, and at best receives but a mere pittance, while strangers assume authority denied to the wife. The sanctuary of affliction must be desecrated by executors; everything must be ransacked and assessed, lest she should steal something out of her own house; and to cap the climax, the children must be placed under guardians. When the husband dies poor, to be sure, no guardian is required, and the children are left for the mother to care and toil for them, as best she may. But when anything is left for their maintenance, then it must be placed in the hands of strangers for safe keeping! The bringing up and safety of the children is left with the mother, and safe they are in her hands. But a few hundred or thousand dollars cannot be entrusted with her! But, say they, "in case of a second marriage, the children must be protected in their possession."

Does that reason not hold as good in the case of the husband as in that of the wife? Oh, no! When he marries again, he still retains his identity and power to act; but she becomes merged once more into a mere nonentity; and therefore the first husband must rob her to prevent the second from doing so! Make the laws then, (if any are required,) regulating property between husband and wife, equal for both, and all these difficulties would be removed.

According to a late act, the wife has a right to the property she brings at marriage, or receives in any way after marriage. Here is some provision for the favored few; but for the laboring many, there is none. The mass of the people commence life with no other capital than the union of heads, hearts and hands. To the benefit of this best of capital, the wife has no right. If they are unsuccessful in married life, who suffers more the bitter consequences of poverty than the wife? But if successful, she cannot call a dollar her own. The husband may will away every dollar of the personal property, and leave her destitute and penniless, and she has no redress by law. And even where real estate is left, she receives but a life-interest in a third part of it, and at her death, she cannot leave it to any one belonging to her, it falls back even to the remotest of his relatives. This is law, but where is the justice of it?

Well might we say that laws were made to prevent, not to promote, the ends of justice. Or, in case of separation, why should the children be taken from the protecting care of the mother? Who has a better right to them than she? How much do fathers generally do towards the bringing of them up? When he comes home from business, and the child is in good humor and handsome trim, he takes the little darling on his knee and plays with it. But when the wife, with the care of the whole household on her shoulders, with little or no help, is not able to put them in the best order or trim, how much does he do towards it? Oh, no! Fathers like to have children good-natured, well-behaved, and comfortable, but how to put them in that desirable condition is out of their philosophy. Children always depend more on the tender, watchful care of the mother, than of the father. Whether from nature, habit, or both, the mother is much more capable of administering to their health and comfort than the father, and therefore she has the best right to them.

And where there is property, it ought to be divided equally between them, with an additional provision from the father towards the maintenance and education of the children. Much is said about the burdens and responsibilities of married men. Responsibilities indeed there are, if they but felt them; but as to burdens, what are they? The sole province of man seems to be centered in that one thing, attending to some business. I grant that owing to the present unjust and unequal reward for labor, many have to work too hard for a subsistence; but whatever his vocation, he has to attend as much to it before as after marriage. Look at your bachelors, and see if they do not strive as much for wealth, and attend as steadily to business, as married men. No! the husband has little or no increase of burden, and every increase of comfort after marriage; while most of the burdens, cares, pains, and penalties of married life fall on the wife. How unjust and cruel, then, to have all the laws in his favor! If any difference should be made, by law, between husband and wife, reason, justice, and humanity—if their voices were heard—would dictate that it should be in her favor.

It is high time to denounce such gross injustice, to compel man by the might of right to give to woman her political, legal, and social rights. Open to her all the avenues of emolument, distinction, and greatness; give her an object for which to cultivate her powers, and a fair chance to do so, and there will be no need to speculate as to her proper sphere. She will find her own sphere in accordance with her capacities, powers, and tastes; and yet she will be woman still. Her rights will not change, but strengthen, develop, and elevate her nature. Away, then, with that folly and absurdity, that a possession of her rights would be detrimental to her character; that if she is recognized as the equal to man, she would cease to be woman. Have his rights as citizen of a republic, the elective franchise with all its advantages, so changed man's nature, that he has ceased to be man? Oh, no! But woman could not bear such a degree of power; what has ben efited him, would injure her; what has strengthen him, would weaken her; what has prompted him to the performance of his duties, would make her neglect hers! Such is the superficial mode of reasoning—if it deserves that name—which is brought against the doctrine of woman's equality with man. It reminds me of two reasons given by a minister of Milton, on the North River. Having heard that I had spoken on the Rights of Woman, he took the subject up on the following Sunday; and in order to prove that woman should not have equal rights with man, he argued, first, that Adam was created before Eve, and secondly, that man was compared to the fore wheels, and woman to the hind wheels of a wagon. These reasons are about as philosophical as any that can be brought against the views we advocate.

But here is another difficulty. In point of principle, some say it is true that woman ought to have the same rights as man; but in carrying out this principle in practice, would you expose her to the contact of rough, rude, drinking, swearing, fighting men at the ballot-box? What a humiliating confession lies in this plea for keeping woman in the background!

Is the brutality of some men, then, a reason why woman should be kept from her rights? If man, in his superior wisdom, cannot devise means to enable woman to deposit her vote without having her finer sensibilities shocked by such disgraceful conduct, then there is an additional reason, as well as necessity, why she should be there to civilize, refine, and purify him, even at the ballot-box. Yes, in addition to the principle of right, this is one of the reasons, drawn from expediency, why woman should participate in all the important duties of life; for, with all due respect to the other sex, she is the true civilizer of man. With all my heart do I pity the man who has grown up and lives without the benign influence of woman. Even now, in spite of being considered the inferior, she exerts a most beneficial influence on man. Look at your annual festivities where woman is excluded, and you will find more or less drunkenness, disorder, vulgarity, and excess, to be the order of the day. Compare them with festive scenes where woman is the equal participant with man, and there you will see rational, social enjoyment and general decorum prevailing. If this is the case now—and who can deny it?—how much more beneficial would be woman's influence, if, as the equal with man, she should take her stand by his side, to cheer, counsel, and aid him through the drama of life, in the Legislative halls, in the Senate chamber, in the Judge's chair, in the jury box, in the Forum, in the Laboratory of the arts and sciences, and wherever duty would call her for the benefit of herself, her country, her race. For at every step she would carry with her a humanizing influence.

Oh! blind and misguided man! you know not what you do in opposing this great reform. It is not a partial affair confined to class, sect, or party. Nations have ever struggled against nations, people against despotic governments; from the times of absolute despotism to the present hour of comparative freedom, the weak have had to struggle against the strong, and right against might. But a new sign has appeared in our social zodiac, prophetic of the most important changes, pregnant with the most beneficial results, that have ever taken place in the annals of human history. We have before us a novel spectacle, an hitherto unheard-of undertaking, in comparison to which all others fall into insignificance, the grandest step in the onward progress of humanity. One half of the race stands up against the injustice and oppression of the other, and demands the recognition of its existence, and of its rights. Most sincerely do I pity those who have not advanced far enough to aid in this noble undertaking; for the attainment of woman's coequality with man is in itself not the end, but the most efficient means ever at the command of mankind towards a higher state of human elevation, without which the race can never attain it. Why should one half of the race keep the other half in subjugation? In this country it is considered wrong for one nation to enact laws and force them upon another. Does the same wrong not hold good of the sexes? Is woman a being like man? Then she is entitled to the same rights, is she not? How can he legislate rightfully for a being whose nature he cannot understand, whose motives he cannot appreciate, and whose feelings he cannot realize? How can he sit in judgment and pronounce a verdict against a being so entirely different from himself?

No! there is no reason against woman's elevation, but there are deep-rooted, hoary-headed prejudices. The main cause of them is, a pernicious falsehood propagated against her being, namely, that she is inferior by her nature. Inferior in what? What has man ever done, that woman, under the same advantages, could not do? In morals, bad as she is, she is generally considered his superior. In the intellectual sphere, give her a fair chance before you pronounce a verdict against her. Cultivate the frontal portion of her brain as much as that of man is cultivated, and she will stand his equal at least. Even now, where her mind has been called out at all, her intellect is as bright, as capacious, and as powerful as his. Will you tell us, that women have no Newtons, Shakespeares, and Byrons? Greater natural powers than even these possessed may have been destroyed in woman for want of proper culture, a just appreciation, reward for merit as an incentive to exertion, and freedom of action, without which, mind becomes cramped and stifled, for it cannot expand under bolts and bars; and yet, amid all blighting, crushing circumstances—confined within the narrowest possible limits, trampled upon by prejudice and injustice, from her education and position forced to occupy herself almost exclusively with the most trivial affairs—in spite of all these difficulties, her intellect is as good as his. The few bright meteors in man's intellectual horizon could well be matched by woman, were she allowed to occupy the same elevated position.

There is no need of naming the De Stahls, the Rolands, the Somervilles, the Wollstonecrafts, the Sigourneys, the Wrights, the Martineaus, the Hemanses, the Fullers, Jagellas, and many more of modern as well as ancient times, to prove her mental powers, her patriotism, her self-sacrificing devotion to the cause of humanity, and the eloquence that gushes from her pen, or from her tongue. These things are too well known to require repetition. And do you ask for fortitude, energy, and perseverance? Then look at woman under suffering, reverse of fortune, and affliction, when the strength and power of man have sunk to the lowest ebb, when his mind is overwhelmed by the dark waters of despair. She, like the tender ivy plant, bent yet unbroken by the storms of life, not only upholds her own hopeful courage, but clings around the tempest-fallen oak, to speak hope to his faltering spirit, and shelter him from the returning blast of the storm.

Wherein then, again I ask, is man so much woman's superior, that he must for ever remain her master? In physical strength? Allow me to say, that therein the inmates of the forest are his superior. But even on this point, why is she the feeble, sickly, suffering being we behold her? Look to her most defective and irrational education, and you will find a solution of the problem. Is the girl allowed to expand her limbs and chest in healthful exercise in the fresh breezes of heaven? Is she allowed to inflate her lungs and make the welkin ring with her cheerful voice like the boy? Who ever heard of a girl committing such improprieties? A robust development in a girl is unfashionable, a healthy, sound voice is vulgar, a ruddy glow on the cheek is coarse; and when vitality is so strong within her as to show itself in spite of bolts and bars, then she has to undergo a bleaching process, eat lemons, drink vinegar, and keep in the shade.

And do you know why these irrationalities are practiced? Because man wishes them to be delicate; for whatever he admires in woman will she possess. That is the influence man has over woman, for she has been made to believe that she was created for his benefit only. "It was not well for man to be alone," therefore she was made as a plaything to pass away an idle hour, or as a drudge to do his bidding; and until this falsehood is eradicated from her mind, until she feels that the necessities, services, and obligations of the sexes are mutual, that she is as independent of him as he is of her, that she is formed for the same aims and ends in life that he is—until, in fact, she has all rights equal with man, there will be no other object in her education, except to get married, and what will best promote that desirable end will be cultivated in her. Do you not yet understand what has made woman what she is? Then see what the sickly taste and perverted judgment of man now admires in woman. Not physical and mental vigor, but a pale, delicate face; hands too small to grasp a broom, for that were treason in a lady; a voice so sentimental and depressed, that what she says can be learned only by the moving of her half parted lips; and above all, that nervous sensibility which sees a ghost in every passing shadow, that beautiful diffidence which dares not take a step without the protecting arm of man to support her tender frame, and that shrinking mock-modesty that faints at the mention of a leg of a table. I know there are many noble exceptions, who see and deplore these irrationalities; but as a general thing, the facts are as I state, or else why that hue and cry of "mannish," "unfeminine," "out of her sphere," etc., whenever woman evinces any strength of body or mind, and takes interest in anything deserving of a rational being? Oh! the crying injustice towards woman.

She is crushed at every step, and then insulted for being what a most pernicious education and corrupt public sentiment have made her. But there is no confidence in her powers, nor principles.

After last year's Woman's Convention, I saw an article in the *Christian Inquirer*, a Unitarian paper, edited by the Rev. Mr. Bellows, of New York, where, in reply to a correspondent on the subject of woman's rights, in which he strenuously opposed her taking part in anything in public, he said: "Place woman unbonneted and unshawled before the public gaze, and what becomes of her modesty and her virtue?" In his benighted mind, the modesty and virtue of woman is of so fragile a nature, that when it is in contact with the atmosphere, it evaporates like chloroform. But I refrain to comment on such a sentiment. It carries with it its own deep condemnation. When I read the article, I earnestly wished I had the ladies of the writer's congregation before me, to see whether they could realize the estimation their pastor held them in. Yet I hardly know which sentiment was strongest in me, contempt for such foolish opinions, or pity for a man that has so degrading an opinion of woman—of the being that gave him life, that sustained his helpless infancy with her ever watchful care, and laid the very foundation for the little mind he may possess—of the being he took to his bosom as the partner of his joys and sorrows—the one whom, when he strove to win her affection, he courted, as all such men court woman, like some divinity. Such a man deserves our pity; for I cannot realize that a man purposely and willfully degrades his Mother, Sister, Wife, and Daughter. No! my better nature, my best knowledge and conviction forbid me to believe it.

It is from ignorance, not malice, that man acts towards woman as he does. In ignorance of her nature, and the interest and happiness of both sexes, he conceived ideas, laid down rules, and enacted laws concerning her destiny and rights. The same ignorance, strengthened by age, sanctified by superstition, engrafted into his being by habit, makes him carry these convictions out to the detriment of his own as well as her happiness; for is he not the loser by his injustice? Oh! how severely he suffers. Who can fathom the depth of misery and suffering to society from the subjugation and injury inflicted on woman? The race is elevated in excellence and power, or kept back in progression, in accordance with the scale of woman's position in society. But so firmly has prejudice closed the eyes of man to the light of truth, that though he feels the evils, he knows not their cause. Those men who have their eyes already open to these facts, earnestly desire the restoration of woman's rights, as the means of enabling her to take her proper position in the scale of humanity. If all men could see the truth, all would desire to aid this reform, as they desire their own happiness; for the interest and happiness of the sexes cannot be divided. Nature has too closely united them to permit one to oppress the other with impunity.

I cast no more blame or reproach on man, however, than on woman, for she, from habit based on the same errors, is as much opposed to her interest and happiness as he is. How long is it, indeed, since any of us have come out of the darkness into the light of day? how long since any of us have advocated this righteous cause? The longest period is but, as it were, yesterday. And why has this been? From the same reason that so many of both sexes are opposed to it yet—ignorance. Both men and women have to be roused from that deathly lethargy in which they slumber. That worse than Egyptian darkness must be dispelled from their minds before the pure rays of the sun can penetrate them. And therefore, while I feel it my duty, ay, a painful duty, to point out the wrong done to woman and its consequences, and would do all in my power to aid in her deliverance, I can have no more ill feelings towards man than, for the same error, I have towards her. Both are the victims of error and ignorance, both suffer.

Hence the necessity for active, earnest endeavors to enlighten their minds; hence the necessity for this, and many more Conventions, to protest against the wrong and claim our rights. And in so acting, we must not heed the taunts, ridicule, and stigmas cast upon us. We must remember that we have a crusade before us, far holier and more righteous than led warriors to Palestine—a crusade, not to deprive any one of his rights, but to claim our own. And as our cause is a nobler one, so also should be the means to achieve it. We therefore must put on the armor of charity, carry before us the banner of truth, and defend ourselves with the shield of right against the invaders of our liberty. And yet, like the knight of old, we must enlist in this holy cause with a disinterested devotion, energy, and determination never to turn back until we have conquered, not, indeed, by driving the Turk from his possession, but by claiming our rightful inheritance, for his benefit as well as for our own.

To achieve this glorious victory of right over might, woman has much to do. Man may remove her legal shackles, and recognize her as his equal, which will greatly aid in her elevation; but the law cannot compel her to cultivate her mind and take an independent stand as a free being. She must cast off that mountain weight, that intimidating cowardly question, which like a nightmare presses down all her energies, namely, "What will people say? what will Mrs. Grundy say?" Away with such slavish fears! Woman must think for herself, and use for herself that greatest of all prerogatives—judgment of right and wrong. And next she must act according to her best convictions, irrespective of any other voice than that of right and duty. The time, I trust, will come, though slowly, yet surely, when woman will occupy that high and lofty position, for which nature has so eminently fitted her, in the destinies of humanity.

## CLOSING STATEMENT, OCTOBER 16

My friends, much has been said this evening on almost all points, and I hope the truths that have been spoken will be deeply impressed upon the minds of all. Yet I wish to say a few words on the subject, or rather the origin, of Duty. Much indeed might be said to impress upon all the importance faithfully to perform the various duties devolved upon us, even if in so doing we might clash with the opinions and prejudices of others; to act fearlessly consistent with our principles and convictions, though through it we incur the risk of being unpopular. And we cannot show our desire to promote this great cause more earnestly then, not only by endeavoring to correct political and civil errors, but wherever they are found, even in the midst of us. We were told that if woman would only do her duty, she would have all her rights, implying that our rights spring from our duties.

If we reflect a moment on the subject, we will find this is an error, a very prevalent error, and therefore the more necessary to be corrected. Our duties spring from our rights, our rights from our wants. The child, when it comes into existence, possesses rights arising from its necessities, but as yet it owes no duty to any one; while the parents having exercised certain rights and privileges, they owe certain duties to the child, which, when grown up to understand the relation it sustains to its parents and to society then, owes in return duties in accordance with the rights and privileges it enjoys. The more rights we enjoy, the greater the duties we owe. And he who enjoys most rights, owes in return the most duties. And therefore we say to society, you, who enjoy all the rights, are in duty bound to protect every individual member in his rights. But as it is, while man enjoys all the rights, he preaches all the duties to woman. And hence we say to man—not in the spirit of censure, but charity and kindness, yet firmly do we say to him, that, instead of writing and preaching so much about the duties of woman, it is high time, as the elder brother, to set us the example in the performance of your duties. And in no way can you better evince your earnest desire to do so, than by giving woman her rights. And depend upon it she will not fail in the performance of her duties, not only as wife and mother, but also as a free, enlightened, rational member of the great family of man, highly conducive to the elevation and happiness of all.

# LETTER TO THE EDITOR: THE *TRIBUNE* AND THE GREAT ACCIDENT
November 29, 1851
New York, New York

When forty-four children and their teachers fell to their deaths after a railing and staircase broke at their school, a report in the *New York Tribune* suggested that such events took place "in subservience to lofty and benign purposes." Rose responded to the *Tribune* in a letter to the editor of another newspaper, the *Boston Investigator*, calling attention to the human errors and malfeasance responsible for these deaths. Often when Rose's letters to mainstream newspapers were not published, she used the tactic of writing to the freethought *Boston Investigator*, which was happy to publish letters critical of religion. Her reference to Margaret Fuller, the transcendentalist intellectual of the women's movement, is filled with sadness because of Fuller's recent death. Fuller with her infant son drowned just yards from shore in 1850 when her ship, returning from Italy, ran aground. Rose's anger burns at the unfair characterization by a Jesuit journal of Fuller's death as due to her heretical views as a Unitarian, or perhaps her "sin" of bearing a child out of wedlock. Rose takes aim at a similar view expressed by the *Tribune*. Rose courageously blames public officials who failed in their duty to protect the safety of the public.

Rose's letter, written on November 29, 1851, and published in the *Boston Investigator*, under the heading "The *Tribune* and the Great Accident," on December 10.

⤙

Mr. Editor:—You have, I presume, before now read of the dreadful and heart-rending calamity that took place in New York on the 20th of November in the public school No. 26, in the Ninth Ward, by which forty-four children and some of the teachers lost their lives, and many were severely injured. The cause of the lives lost, and injuries received, is said to be the inferior way in which the staircase and banisters were built, being entirely unfit for such a purpose, not capable of sustaining any pressure; and a well-hole badly protected by a light wooden railing, into which the poor children fell.

On the culpable neglect or ignorance of the school commissioners, under whose supervision the building was erected, and the still more criminal indifference of those authorities to whom complaints were made on the unsafety of that part of the building, I cannot comment, for I have no language adequate to express my feelings on the subject. Yet harrowing and painful in the extreme as is the reading of the account of so disastrous a catastrophe by which so many dear little ones in the very morning of their existence, in the buoyancy and elasticity of their youthful spirits were cut off from life, and destroyed the hopes and bereaved the hearts of all those that loved them, it ought to be read as a warning to all to beware into whose hands the important office of school commissioners or trustees is placed. I send you a short paragraph from the *Tribune*. You will see its moralizing on the subject. The last part of it is such a heartless, hypocritical mockery, that it must have been written by a Jesuit, as no one else could hardly be guilty at such a time of such an outrage on truth and common sense. It reminds me of that Jesuitical article in the (falsely so called) *Freeman's* Journal, edited by Bishop Hughes, after the death of Margaret Fuller.—The *Tribune* says "Cowardice is Atheism—is Infidelity," etc. Were these poor children Atheists and Infidels? Did they not as implicitly trust in Providence as any one can trust in any thing he knows nothing about? Aye, far more than the propagators of the falsehood do, for the young have less knowledge and more sincerity on the subject; and were they not brought up in the belief in a Providence?—for if the parents were too rational to fill the minds of their children with such chimeras, it is inculcated into them in the schools by the reading of the Bible. If they had been Atheists and Infidels, their lives might indeed have been saved, for reason and a knowledge of cause and effect, which is diametrically opposed to the belief in such superstitions, is the only thing to enable man under all circumstances to preserve presence of mind, while a blind faith in things unseen and unknown prevents the cultivation of reason and judgment, necessary to presence of mind. It may sometimes give a reckless audacity, but it never can give true courage; and however much the believers in a Providence may boast of their reliance in him while they are safe, who among them trusts implicitly in that chimera when in any danger?

It is a well-known fact, that in any danger the most religious are the greatest cowards that ever disgraced the name of man. I have seen professed believers in a storm at sea and other dangerous positions, and the most disgraceful, silly cowardice was always exhibited by the greatest believers in this "Divine Providence by which no sparrow's fall is unnoticed." Did he then not know of this calamity? Or, if he did, could he not by one wish, look, word, or act, save the lives of those innocent helpless beings from an untimely death? Or did he wish to do so and had not the power? Which is it, Mr. *Tribune*? But I need not ask, for the same questions must have been in the writer's mind when he penned the article, and hence the miserable subterfuge of the last part to hide his own sceptical doubts on the subject, viz., "And no seeming calamity permitted save in subservience to lofty and benign purposes." No seeming calamity!—Ye bereaved and heart-broken parents, who have in one fell swoop been deprived of those dearer to you than life, dry your tears, bid your throbbing heart be still, complain not of the ignorance or recklessness of those into whose hands you trusted your children, for it is all owing to the children's believing in Providence that he would not help them; but thank Providence for permitting this seeming calamity for some lofty and benign purpose! The Temples of Christian idolatry were open on the 27th, where the *Tribune* might have rendered thanks for it by the command of the Governor.

If I could attach any rational meaning to the term *blasphemy*, I would call such moralizing the most outrageous blasphemy ever perpetrated against reason and humanity. You "blind leader of the blind!" instead of pointing out the causes of the disaster, and the heavy responsibility of those who had the supervision of the building for the purpose of avoiding similar occurrences in future, and appealing to the parents and teachers to cultivate in children reason and reflection, the only antidotes to fear, and a proper confidence and reliance in themselves so as to enable them to preserve presence of mind in emergencies, you merely preach blind faith in a Providence, who, if he exists, must be either devoid of goodness or power; for among the tens of thousands of lives daily lost by accidents, we see no evidence of his benign power to prevent them, no angels' wings are spread to prevent the fallen from being crushed, no tempests are hushed in the midst of their violence to save the mariner from shipwreck, no rivers have ever been dried up to prevent man from drowning. Where is his saving arm then? Oh! "but he permits all that for his own lofty purposes," and only helps those that help themselves! But enough for the present, lest this article grow to an unreasonable length.

Yours, for the cause of Truth,
Ernestine L. Rose
New York, Nov. 29th, 1851

# REVIEWS OF HORACE MANN'S
# TWO LECTURES
February–March 1852
New York, New York

Horace Mann was known for his innovations in education and for his expansion of public education in Massachusetts. In 1852, he was serving out the term of the deceased John Quincy Adams as a member of Congress. Eager to hear the views of an enlightened reformer, Rose attended Mann's lectures in New York City, delivered on February 17 and 29, 1852, on "Hints to a Young Woman." Listening to his lectures, Rose was dismayed by Mann's argument that men and women were essentially different in nature and merited different rights and responsibilities. She was particularly offended by Mann's "pandering to public opinion," by which she meant his reliance on biblical authority to support his views. Unintimidated by Mann's credentials, Rose answered his statements in writing, point by point and in a mocking sarcastic tone, taking him to task for his timid conventional views. As an internationalist, Rose knows of the Belgian Helen Maria Weber by reputation and begins by confronting Mann's characterization of the famed agriculturalist and women's rights advocate.

The *Boston Investigator* published Rose's reviews of Mann's two lectures in its issues of April 21 and 28, 1852. In the April 21, 1852 issue her review was accompanied by a letter to the editor and a "Letter to Mr. Mann." The date on the letter to Mann is February 18, 1852, indicating that Rose wrote it, and probably her first review, on the day following the first lecture. The review of the second lecture is not dated, but was likely written on March 1, 1852, or soon after. Published here are Rose's letter to the editor and her reviews of the two lectures. The parenthetical insertions are Rose's own and appeared in the original documents.

Gerda Lerner, preeminent scholar of the Grimké sisters, reported that Sarah Grimké also wrote a feminist response to Mann's lectures which she has reprinted with commentary in a collection of Sarah Grimké's writing (Lerner 1998, 65–68). In her letter to the *New York Tribune*, Grimké focused solely on Mann's point that woman's role has been chiefly as "mother of the race." Grimké argued that women could contribute more to society if men would participate more actively as parents. However, as Lerner observed, she wrote in such a mild and flowery manner that her radical point may have been missed by most readers.

❧

## LETTER TO THE EDITOR
Mr Editor:—It may perhaps appear to some of your readers like treading on forbidden ground, to attempt to criticize one who is to some extent considered a Reformer, a friend to Education, and consequently to

Progression. But, as my motto is, that there is no ground too sacred for man to tread, no subject too holy for him to investigate, and no one, not even a Member of Congress, so far above ordinary mortals as to forbid the idea of scrutinizing his public opinion and acts, I will comment on some of the views advanced by the Hon. Horace Mann in his two Lectures delivered in the city of New York on the 17th and 29th of February, on the subject entitled "Hints to a Young Woman," and endeavor to see how much truth, justice, and common sense we can draw from them for her benefit. And if you think my review of them, together with a letter I addressed to him after his first Lecture, worthy of a place in the *Investigator*, you will oblige your friend by giving them publicity.

Yours, for Human Rights,
Ernestine L. Rose

## LETTER TO MR. MANN

Hon. Horace Mann:—

Dear Sir,—Pardon the liberty of a woman, from a foreign land, in troubling you with a few lines, which, if they have not the merit of poetry, possess, I trust, sufficient truth to secure for them a candid and serious perusal. I listened attentively to your discourse, entitled "Hints to a Young Woman." The importance of the subject, the name and reputation of the gentleman who was to enlighten and instruct us, made me hope and expect—not that you would agree with me, or any of those who claim the rights of humanity in the rights of woman—but that whatever your opinions on the subject might be, you would treat it with earnest truthfulness which this all-important question demands, and your age and station warranted. I, for one, fear no opposition to the rights of woman, feeling assured that all the reasons and arguments that can be brought against that just cause will only benefit it: for, as gold comes out finer and purer from the fiery furnace, so does truth shine brighter and more beautiful after the fiery ordeal of reason and justice. Let the claims of woman to her just and inalienable rights be analyzed and tested by reason and justice, but let it be done in the earnest spirit of enquiry for the instruction of the thoughtful, and not in the way of burlesque, to amuse the thoughtless. And though we cannot expect this fair dealing from the ignorant, uncivil mass, we may, I think, justly expect it from a National Legislator, a Reformer, a well known friend of Education, and necessarily of human happiness and improvement.

But, while listening to your Lecture, I was almost forced to exclaim with one of old, "Can *any* good come out of Nazareth?"—can a politician be true to any subject that is not popular, when the Honorable gentleman before me can so easily stoop to pamper the vitiated taste of an already prejudiced public opinion, by giving the unthinking multitude the slang and ridicule they admire, instead of the arguments, truth, and common sense they so much need! Should, however, the mere fact of the slight difference in the organic structure of the sexes militate, in your estimation, against the rights of woman, you will please to remember that human rights and justice do not depend on the size or structure of the limbs, but on the simple yet all-sufficient authority of a human being, male or female; and while woman has no desire whatever to claim the size, weight, or dimensions of the other sex, she feels herself entitled to the same rights, privileges, and opportunities, not only to cultivate, but to use all the powers Nature has given her for the benefit of herself and the race. And I have yet to learn that the promulgation of truth, or the performance of a duty, even in the forum, "unsexes woman" any more than man, as stooping to falsehood only can dehumanize man or woman. Nor do I think that even "Miss Weber, Esq.," though her taste and vocation induced her to adopt the male attire, has lost any of the real refinement and grace of woman, which consists, not in the flimsy attributes given to her by superstitious folly and flattery, but in a well-cultivated mind and feelings that appreciate truth, justice, and her own dignity too well to deviate from what appears to her to be right, even for the sake of popularity—a refinement that "shiny buttons" cannot outshine.

Hoping you will not attribute the sins of commission or of omission in this letter to my sex, but to me, who feel keenly woman's wrongs, and earnestly wish for her rights, not for her benefit only, but for the benefit of all. I subscribe myself, very respectfully,

Ernestine L. Rose

## COMMENTS ON MR. MANN'S FIRST LECTURE

After some preliminary remarks, Mr. Mann said that he would at once call woman to her duties and responsibilities. "There is (said he) a new theory of the equality of the sexes, or woman's rights, spread abroad. The leader of this sect is Helen Maria Weber, of Belgium, who has adopted man's attire and behaves like a man. She wears the biped continuations, and a coat with shiny buttons. This Miss Weber, Esq., claims equality with man." Now the injustice, incivility, and unmanliness of thus introducing the name of a woman who is in a far distant land, and who was not known, probably, to ten persons in the whole audience, must be evident to every one of the least courtesy. Did Mr. M. know Miss Weber? did he know that she is a woman of high character and superior abilities?

a practical, scientific agriculturalist, who although yet young, has for years managed a large estate in a successful and excellent manner? If he knew this, why did he not inform the audience of these important facts, and candidly acknowledge that a woman can manage a business, that has been considered to belong exclusively to man? Did he not know her? Then how did he know that she behaved like a man? Did he presume it, from the fact of her wearing male attire? Is the influence of "biped continuations" so powerful as to change her acts? Then it would be very desirable to send a few dozen of honest intelligent men's coats and hats to Washington, for the use of Congress and the benefit of the people.

But what means it to act like man? Does it mean reflecting deeper, reasoning clearer, judging better, acting wiser? Then I hope we may all, the Hon. Lecturer included, soon act like man But "Miss Weber, Esq.," committed the unpardonable sin of claiming equality with man—and why not? But here comes the reason:—"The design and works of God have forbidden this commingling; to efface or modify the great distinguishing features which separate the sexes, would be to defy the Maker himself." Very logical, truly! To give woman the right to live, labor, and enjoy, and use her faculties to the best advantage in accordance with her taste and powers, would be to efface the distinguishing feature of the sexes, and consequently to defy the Maker!—The assumption of his premises and the perfect absurdity of the inference are too palpable to require any refutation. They have no substance to take hold of—they are mere phantoms that disappear with the least glimmer even of the rush-light of reason. But here comes the big gun:—"The human soul and feelings were created male and female as much as their bodies." Indeed!

As the Hon. Speaker made free use of the terms gospel, salvation, heaven, and all such expressions belonging to the unknown tongue, which he no doubt understands, he of course believes Revelation necessary to save the soul; but as one Revelation only was given, and that to man, to save man's soul, it follows that there is no Revelation to save the female soul at all! What is he going to do with the female soul? for, if the Creator is defied by woman's claiming social equality *here*, how can she intrude herself into *heaven*, and claim equality with man there? and she certainly could not be saved by male Revelation, seeing that "all things are male and female." I fear we shall have to leave this important decision for some farther "hints to a young woman." and so we will endeavor to face a still more formidable argument against woman's rights. "The structure is entirely different in the sexes, there is not one single organ in structure, position, and function alike in man and woman, and therefore, there can be no equality between the sexes."

I ask the Hon. Teacher's pardon, but the school-master must have been *"abroad"* when he took his lessons in physiology, or, as habit is powerful, he may have thought he was still teaching "the young idea how to shoot," when he made so gross, so absurd an assertion, which any boy or girl of fifteen would be ashamed to make. It needs no argument to confute it as it does that itself; but, for argument's sake, I will meet him on his own ground. Suppose, then, that the structure of the sexes is different—that the heart, lungs, liver, stomach, or any other of the organs requisite in the human economy are larger, smaller, situated a sixteenth of an inch higher, or lower, more to the right or the left, in man or woman what then? Does it follow that woman cannot, or must not be socially, civilly, and politically his equal? Does the female organization, such as it is, require food, raiment, and shelter to sustain life? Does her mind, her faculties, and powers, require cultivation and development to promote health and happiness? If so, and I don't think the Hon. Lecturer would deny it, is she not entitled to all the rights and privileges society can bestow, to enable her to promote her interest, health, and happiness in accordance with her powers, tastes and feelings irrespective of sex, the same as man?

But to make his argument more conclusive, or rather more ridiculous, he exclaimed, "As well might knives and forks, hooks, and eyes, buttons and button-holes claim equality, as man and woman." I will not presume to comment on this philosophical simile, it being the product of the "higher intellect of the sterner sex," but proceed. "It is true (said he) woman has been oppressed and degraded by man, and it is not to be wondered at: when we see her run to the extravagance of calling Conventions, and under the banner of Woman's Rights appear on the forum and make speeches, she unsexes herself, and loses the grace and delicacy of her sex, and gains none of the superior powers of the other." That is as modest as it is consistent. He admits woman is oppressed and degraded by man, but to claim and vindicate her right to call conventions and appear on the forum where she would have a chance to be heard, then "she unsexes herself," etc. Probably she might do better to leave the pleading of her cause to the Hon. Lecturer, who would deal with it very honorably, no doubt, but in the "division of labor" that trifling occupation was not assigned to the male sex, so *she* has to do it, and abide the sad consequences of "unsexing herself." But what does the Hon. Lawgiver really mean by that term? I fear we will have to send it to Washington for Congressional deliberation.

To carry out still farther the distinctive difference between the sexes, he instanced a comparison between Henry VIII and his daughter Elizabeth, Queen of England. "Henry VIII was made of ten thousand bears, but Elizabeth was made of ten thousand cats; do all these facts not prove that there is no equality between the sexes?" Very conclusively, so I will leave it for his benefit, and hear what he has to say on the perfect nothingness of woman. "What have been the rank and influence of woman for 6000 years? Man has immensely degraded her; she has been little more than the mother of a race—such a race! that it might be doubted if its increase would be a benefit to the world." What else, Mr. Lecturer, *could* have been the rank and influence of woman, than to be the mother of just *such* a race, bad as that may be, judging from some specimens, when she has been "immensely oppressed and degraded by man?" And did you, as one of that very race, not do your best to degrade her, when you endeavored to prove by false and absurd assertions regarding her nature and destiny, and still more false and ridiculous about the design of the Creator, that she was unfit to be considered the equal of man, and therefore undeserving of the same rights as he enjoys? And that for her to break down these unjust barriers that have kept her in an inferior state, and set her free to cultivate and carry out the powers and bent of her mind in accordance with the laws (design if you will) of her nature, "was to defy the Creator himself?" And will she not always remain in this degraded state as long as man arrogates to himself the right to command and force her to obey?—make laws and compel her to observe them? And if she revolts against that tyranny and degradation, and claims her rights as a human being, who, whatever the difference in her organic structure, has the same aims and objects in life a man has, does she not "unsex herself?" Think of these questions and answer them, not according to the popular notions on the subject, but according to reason and truth before you give the next "hints" to man or woman.

But after telling us that the race was so corrupt that (the deluge?) "Hydropathy would be the only cure for such a planet," he said, "For four thousand years the Jewish women did nothing but give birth to a race of unmerciful, stiff-necked men." The Hon. Lecturer was evidently partial to the Jews for excluding them from the corrupt race who ought to have a ducking for the benefit of the world. Well, perhaps that partiality arises from the fact that unmerciful and stiff-necked as the Jews are they still are the authors and originators of his religion, and a Jewish woman was the mother of his Redeemer. Well, gratitude is a virtue; and seeing how corrupt the race is, it is quite refreshing to find one mother's son possessing the amiable virtue of gratitude to God's (his God's) chosen people. But, said he, Protestantism and civil liberty rose in their strength, and man and woman, assumed a better and more appropriate station. Did they? Were their stations before that time different? Oh! yes! Protestantism, or Christianity, under any of its isms, has done much for woman, when we see a Protestant, Republican Legislator, Teacher, and Reformer turn a subject of such vital importance into a burlesque, and use every slur and slang phrase that the category of vulgar language can furnish him, to pamper an already vitiated taste!

But he made it all up, by flattering her about the "superior faith, grace beauty, and above all, her religious sentiments. The breath of life God gave woman was superior and nobler than the one he gave man"—so God must have had a male and female breath. "Woman was created a religious being, destined to lead man to Heaven; man was made of sterner muscles fit to be abroad and command, while woman's place is at home to educate her children." The great besetting sin of woman, or rather her principal weakness, namely, *credulity*, of which the priest ever knows how to take advantage, and fill her mind with superstition which gives him entire control over her, and is a main cause that keeps her in an inferior condition, is the only laudable trait of character Mr. Mann sees in woman, except to cook a good *dinner*, sew on buttons, etc.

But I would like to ask him, if "the souls are created male and female," how woman can educate the children? Not all the children, surely, for how can a "female mind or soul" take care of a "male mind or soul?" You might as well set a "cat" to educate a "bear." Perhaps he thought a soul or mind was not required for the occupation, as he probably only meant the feeding, washing, and dressing process, which, out of gallantry, he styled education Perhaps in his next "hints" he will teach us the *modus operandi*. But here again, how can he, created with a male soul or mind and feelings, teach us female souls, minds, and feelings? Oh! that accounts for the little use, I fear, we shall be able to make of the "hints to a young woman."

The Lecturer acknowledged that "Joan of Arc commanded an army, but she brought her sword back pure without a blood-stain—still the best place for woman is at home with her family; for a man to take care of children would be like an elephant hatching chickens." Perhaps, if woman had more the command, fewer swords would be stained with human blood, until they finally might be made into plough-shares. Mr. Mann wondered "how few great women there were. It is true, there is Mrs. Somerville, Miss Dix, and Mrs. Putnam. The women of Europe were nothing; there were more intelligent women in New-England, than in the whole continent of Europe. There is a lady in New-England who is so talented that students go to her for instruction; and while she is kneading her bread, she expounds to them the sciences, and gives quotations from the Greek." Well, small favors are thankfully received. I am quite glad there are *some* intelligent women, no matter where; but I fear his knowledge of the women of Europe is confined in rather less space than a nut-shell, or he would know a *little* more about them.

But fearing, lest the above-mentioned fact, that a woman may be so learned as to instruct students, male students, at the same time she kneads her bread, might upset his whole theory of the "division of labor" and have a bad influence on "a young woman," he added, "still in vigor of mind, sounder sense, reason, and power to command, man is superior; but in the feminine (soft?) qualities, in educating the children, (at the cradle) she is the most lovely." Mr. Mann acknowledged that "all the colleges except one, Oberlin, were closed against woman;" but still he wondered that "she has not done some more wonderful things; that she has not performed some acts of greatness." And thus by speaking partially for her education, and entirely against her equal rights with man, by alternately flattering and insulting her, denying her almost common sense, particularly causality, as "that was a masculine quality," and telling her what a delightful religious little creature she was, a perfect angel all but the wings, ended the first "Hints to a Young Woman."


## [COMMENTS ON MR. MANN'S] SECOND LECTURE

Mr. Mann commenced by saying, "I have endeavored to establish the fact that God created the two sexes on the division of labor. As mortals are created male and female, so labor and pursuits are of a similar character. Let woman have control of ornamental design, of copying, penmanship, proof-reading, and all such sort of labor, but the greatest pride of woman should be as a good house-keeper, as a scientific cook, to enable her to cook a good breakfast, and keep it nice and hot till her husband is ready for it, to take care of the wardrobe, and keep the buttons where they belong; but her greatest duty is at the cradle, to take care of and educate the children."

If we are to believe the literal Bible story, which the Lecturer seems to believe in, then it would appear that God did not intend man to labor at all, much less could he have created the sexes "on the principle of the division of labor;" for had not mother Eve, contrary to the command of God, eaten and induced the stack of ribs from which she was manufactured, to partake of the glorious little apple which transformed them into rational beings, and as such made it necessary for them to labor, they would have had no labor at all—no! not even a seat in Congress, a cradle to attend to, nor a button to sew on. But the Hon. Lecturer thought, perhaps, as woman commenced her career on this mundane sphere in the eating line, she had better stick to her trade; only he wishes her to improve on it. and become a "scientific cook!" Well, I wish so, too; but the great difficulty is, that as a certain taste and adaptation or peculiar faculties are required for proficiency in any art or science; and as, according to the Lecturer, (and I perfectly agree with him.) "the cuisine is a perfect laboratory worthy of a chemist's improvement," then it would be just as reasonable to expect all men to be painters, sculptors, or chemists, as to ask all women to be scientific cooks. If men and woman were educated in accordance with their predilections and tastes, it might so happen that some men might have the best capacity for the science of cooking, and some women for the science of government; and as for the "buttons," every girl ought to know how to sew on buttons and I am quite willing to give the same privilege to men particularly to the bachelors; but the Lecturer can certainly not insist that in the "division of labor," the Creator assigned the wardrobe to woman, for according to the Bible. "Did the Lord God make coats of skins [buttons and all] and clothed them."—[Genesis, iii.21.]

Mr. Mann having disposed of woman's destiny and calling proceeded to tell us what she was not fit for—namely, war; and after a long dissertation against war, he said, "It may be said that if women were legislators, war would die out, but I think not; the opportunity to gratify a passion would fire that very spirit into action." Here, again, I lack information. At the parceling out of labor between the sexes, on which side did the Creator place war? As fighting I should think must be laborious, judging from the fact that men have always been at war with each other, and that according to Scripture, by the direct command of God, it must follow that he placed war on the side of man, as a manly recreation If so, how could the Lecturer accuse his Creator of the injustice and barbarity of giving woman a passion for an employment which he did not design her to follow? But, as if to correct that unfortunate mistake, the Lecturer kindly wished to obviate the difficulty by keeping her from the opportunity of exercising it. I perfectly agree with this laudable desire, but I would humbly ask, does not the opportunity call that very passion out in man too? If so, would it not be better for all parties to prevent men too from being legislators? If, however, he was predestined a "fighting animal," then he might as well fight in the Senate as elsewhere. But here comes another inscrutability:—

"The law is not at all suited for woman. She lacks that hard, dry, calculating, passionless spirit, which was primarily [not now?] necessary; she lacks the unflinching nerve demanded in a judge, the endurance required in a juror." That the law is a dry subject, I doubt not; but seeing how soft most lawyers are, it does not appear to require a very hard head to master it, though it may require a very hard heart to carry it out. But as for the unflinching, passionless nerve and endurance of judge and juror, it strikes me, if the Lecturer were better acquainted with the vocation he thought particularly adapted to woman, he would know that the most unflinching nerve, the most passionless, patient endurance is required at the cradle, in the nursery, at the bed of sickness and of death. Does he doubt it? Let him—let the most unflinching nerve in the judge's chair, the most patient endurance of the jury-box try it. There is not a woman but would be perfectly willing to give them a fair trial. Is she not entitled to as fair a trial to the trying position of the lawyer, judge and juror before a verdict is pronounced against her admissibility at the bar except as a culprit? Has the Lecturer ever found a woman flinch from a trying position? Let him point her out, and she will be as great a curiosity as his arguments. But Mr. Mann seemed to doubt the validity of the above reasons himself, for he kept the biggest gun in reserve for the last shot:—

"Fancy to yourself, one husband's wife locked up in the jury-room with another wife's husband, and see them marching two and two after the court martial to and from the jury-room." Let him remember—*"Honi soit qui mal y pense!"* [Shame upon him who thinks evil of it!] The Lecturer, I ask pardon, was not as wise as a certain mayor of a country town, who, on apologizing to a prince who visited the town, for not firing cannons, gave eighteen reasons; the first was, the town had no cannons, with which reason the prince was so well satisfied that he dispensed with the other seventeen. Had we had the last of the above series of reasons first, we might with royal magnanimity have saved the Lecturer the trouble of giving, and us of hearing the other seventeen.

Thus leaving this hard subject, we come to rather a soft one:— "I see but one reason why woman should not preach the Gospel, and that is, she looks vastly better in acting and living the Gospel, than in preaching it in public." Here, at least, is a subject soft enough for woman. Legislating is apt to call out the fighting passions; the bar, the bench, and the jury-box require spirit, though a hard and dry one, patient endurance, and the "superior sense of man." But the Gospel, requiring no such encumbrances, is quite soft enough for woman, and woman for it; so that the only objection why she should not preach in public is that she does not look quite so well preaching as practicing, etc. I fear that, in the Lecturer's estimation, preaching the Gospel must have a tendency to distort the countenance; hence, in his tender solicitude for woman's beauty, he objects to her preaching in public. In private, in the kitchen, or at the cradle, it matters not *how* she looks—there she may preach to her heart's content. But what means this acting and living the Gospel? In the old romances called by that name, there are so many silly and contradictory stories, and most of them so chimerical and impractical that I am perfectly at a loss to know what *living* the Gospel means. The Arabian Nights might with far more benefit be lived and acted than the Gospel. Surely, the Hon. Lecturer would not advise woman to carry out the Gospel injunction to "hate father, mother, brother, sister, friends, children, and even their own life," to find grace in the Gospel-makers' eyes? But whatever it might mean, and however much it might improve the looks of woman, there is this objection to it, that it does not pay quite as well as preaching for half an hour every week in public at the rate of one, two, or three thousand dollars a year; and as the minister always has the pay without the practice, it certainly is nothing but fair to set him to work, if it is only for a little wholesome exercise, and let woman have the preaching and the pay. For my part, I would prefer to see woman more usefully and rationally employed, even if it did not pay quite so well; but if there are any of our sex who have a taste for such a lazy life, or are good for nothing else, then they have a perfect right to follow it.

Having disposed of law and gospel, we proceed to medicine. The Lecturer warmly and ably advocated woman's studying the medical profession. "I deem it in an especial degree adapted to woman, so as to enable her to attend to her own sex, and to her children. The term nurse is so identified with woman, that it entirely excludes the other sex." Mr. Mann spoke warmly of the influence the medical practitioner has on women, and the benefit it would be to have female physicians. It is needless to say that I fully and emphatically agreed with that part of the discourse, and it gives me pleasure to say that it was ably enforced, and I have no doubt did some good. But what exceedingly surprised me was, that he deemed woman possessed of sufficient unflinching nerve requisite to dissect the human body, to perform the most difficult and delicate operations, where the life of the patient often depends entirely on the steady nerve, cool, patient endurance of the practitioner, when he deemed her so entirely deficient in these very qualities as to be incompetent to dissect the law, sit in the jury-box, or pronounce a verdict ninety-nine times out of every hundred concerning some dollars and cents! He also recommended her to study botany, as it would be useful to her as a nurse; but said he—"Politics! politics! that any person could ever wish to see woman embarked upon this Stygian lake, is incomprehensible!" Here Mr. Mann drew a life-like picture of government, which he styled "the political and legislative bear-garden," assuring us that it is "the deepest, darkest sink of corruption, and hence woman ought not to have any thing to do with government." Oh! no, always excepting paying taxes, and being hung: and as she has no opportunity to gratify her own passion for war, she may furnish living targets for the use of government!

I have not the least idea of disputing the Lecturer's opinion on gov-

ernment, particularly as he can speak from personal experience. But that
such a description would have the effect to reassure and satisfy woman
that she is quite safe in leaving her best and dearest interests in the hands
of such a "set of animals" is rather doubtful, particularly as it might suggest itself to her mind that as the government is in such a lamentable,
disgraceful condition would it not be well, even as a mere experiment, to
send these legislative gentlemen home to be tamed, and let women take
their places as, according to the Lecturer's opinion, (and I fully believe
him) it could not possibly be worse, and there might be some chance for
the better.

But, "Peace!" cried the speaker, "Peace! Fancy to yourself the husband
and wife disputing on politics, the wife being nominated for office, and
the husband voting against her, and *vice versa*—one vote the Whig, the
other the Democratic ticket! What a horrible thing that would be! No!
no! that would never do." All this may be very convincing to some, but I
would humbly suggest, that before the Hon. Lecturer gives any more—
"hints to a young woman," old woman, or any woman, he study once more
ancient and modem history, and examine facts around us, and he will find,
that of all the causes of difference of opinion and dissension between man
and man, there is none so prolific of evil, so productive of rancor malice, deep-seated hatred, as religion. All other differences may be brought
to an end. In the arts and sciences, as soon as the facts connected with
them are ascertained, the dispute can terminate. Political dissensions, bad
as they are, only last about nine days before an election; that over, the
parties become sober again and laugh at their own and each other's folly
and are friends once more But the ill feelings produced by religious dissensions never end for the simple reason that there are no facts connected
with them to appeal to. The disputants know not what they differ about
it being a mere phantom, which each claims to see and understand, yet
none can grasp. Hence the unyielding, the unmerciful spirit of fanaticism.
Its cruelty does not end even with life; it extends as far at least as the
wishes of the fanatic goes, beyond the grave, and its fiend-like characteristic is, that the more honest and conscientious the believer, the more
mercilessly cruel the fanatic—for what is a fanatic but an honest believer?
"He that believeth not shall be damned," is the language of the Gospel,
and as every honest believer no doubt wishes to please his God, he naturally must wish to carry out this heavenly sentence on earth, hoping the
Lord will do the rest hereafter. How strange, then, it is, that in the face of
these facts, of which Mr. Mann can certainly not be ignorant, he should
recommend to woman religion, the Gospel, without any reference to the
evil consequences arising from a difference of opinion between husband

and wife, while he is so anxious lest woman's political opinions might be a source of trouble in the family, particularly as there is a remedy at hand, namely, if husband and wife could not agree to differ on politics, why then just let man cease to meddle with them altogether. He has had it long enough all his own way; let her have a chance to try her hand at it, and who knows but the time may come when man and woman will be so far civilized as to agree to differ in an amicable and friendly way whenever they should not be able to agree? and then man might be reinstated in all the glories of politics.

In describing the degrading influence of riches and luxury on woman, the Lecturer said, "So degrading were what we call women now, that a man might marry at least a dozen before incurring the charge of bigamy." I know not whether the influence of riches and luxury is less degrading to man than to woman, or that the influence of riches is any more degrading to woman than that of poverty, though it may produce a different result, and more in accordance with the taste of some. Again,—"The theory I have advanced assigns to woman the empire of home"—which means the cradle, the range, and the buttons; "but for the great prodigies the Admirable Crichtons of the female sex, to such I would say there is a realm of glory where each of them may be crowned." Here he very kindly advised woman to go into the highways and convert the outcast and vicious to virtue, and lead them to Heaven. "The sphere is wide and noble enough for God, and is it not for his last and best work, woman? Wide as the field now open to woman is, it must begin at home, and when she has done that, let extend it to other homes." After she has cooked her own breakfast let her cook her neighbor's. "Why should cities be great centers of suffering? Does woman pant for glory? Point her here; there is more glory in conquering a street than in all the Thermopylaes and Waterloos. Are there any here who have ambition to gratify? Let them lay it aside and practice religion, benevolence, and charity and the angels will call them sisters. They shall be mine, saith the Lord of Hosts, in that day when I make up my jewels."

Apart from the last bit of fancy work, the advice given is most excellent not only to women, but to the gods, and most earnestly do I wish that all the poverty, sin, and suffering could not only be alleviated, but the causes that produce them, of which the present inequality and condition of woman is one, removed forever But facts stare me in the face, and ask in the stern voice of justice who is to perform this living miracle? Woman! poor, degraded inexperienced, and helpless inferior woman! Does it require less unflinching nerve, less patient, passionless endurance to enter upon a warfare with vice and corruption, to remove the mountains and fill up the stream of pollution, the very contact of which contaminates, than preside at the bar and on the bench? And if here were any such "prodigies," any such "Admirable Crichtons of the female sex," who felt strong enough to defy alike the contamination of vice and the serpent tongue of slander and malice, what means have they at their disposal to quench that volcano of vice that threatens far surer destruction to the race than all the hells superstition ever invented? What they earn as scientific cooks, at the cradle, for sewing on buttons, or the pin-money their husbands kindly give them!!

Oh! of how little use are words, however beautiful in themselves, however well chosen and arranged, if they do not present reason and truth, and are not based upon facts? They are at best but like a basket of artificial flowers, showy and handsome from a distance, but valueless on nearer approach, for they greet with no perfume to vivify and gladden the spirit, and purify the miasmas of the physical and moral wilderness. How much better would it have been if the Lecturer, (pardon me, for suffering humanity requires plain speech) had given the proceeds of the two Lectures as an earnest of his admiration for the god-like (if that means good) qualities of charity he so warmly and justly recommended to woman; for not many yards from the very place where he exhorted woman to deeds of charity, could be heard the cry of anguish wrung from the pangs of hunger, sickness, and suffering! But alas! charity, like the Gospel, is not practiced by those that preach it, and like the minister, the Lecturer may have found out that it is far easier, costs much less, and brings much more to recommend all these sublime virtues which "God and his angels so much admire," but either cannot, or will not perform, than it is to practice them!

But enough of this. I am weary in head and heart, and will but say that if any of you, my sisters, who may read these lines, feel swelling up within you not only pity and sympathy for suffering humanity, but a rightful ambition to be great—"lay it [not] aside" like a garment which does not belong to you, but cherish it for the "good time coming," when woman will be recognized as the co-equal with man; like him, and with him, to be educated as a rational, intellectual, independent being; unflinchingly, unhesitatingly to use her powers when and wherever they shall best promote her interest, and the interest of the race; for then, and not until then, will this gigantic mountain of sin and misery that so weighs on society be removed, and virtue and happiness be enjoyed irrespective of sex.

Ernestine L. Rose

# SPEECH AT THE THIRD NATIONAL WOMAN'S RIGHTS CONVENTION: "A CHILD OF ISRAEL"
### September 8, 1852
### Syracuse, New York

Ernestine L. Rose was presented to this convention as "a Polish lady of the Jewish faith," although she had been an activist and public speaker in the United States for more than a dozen years. Rose's Jewish origins surfaced here perhaps because of the rise of the anti-immigrant Know-Nothing movement, which drew heightened attention to national origins and religious differences.

With the opening sentences of her first, brief speech at the convention, Rose reclaims control over her public identity, reintroducing herself on her own terms as "a daughter of poor, crushed Poland" and "a child of Israel." Rose uses her difference from the others as proof that women's demands for rights transcend national, ethnic, religious, and cultural differences, presenting herself as "an example of the universality of our claims." She goes on to counter the argument that women are not asking for their rights. Instead, she compares the apathy of many women to "poor inebriate[s]," grown so accustomed to their addiction that they are unaware they have a problem. Rose, as an Owenite, takes a modern view of addiction, viewing it as a disease to be remedied rather than as sinful behavior to be condemned. Her political strategy is based on the same philosophy: Do not attack your opponents as evil or ill-intentioned; instead, educate them.

~&~

It is of very little importance in what geographical position a person is born, but it is important whether his ideas are based upon facts that can stand the test of reason, and his acts are conducive to the happiness of society. Yet, being a foreigner, I hope you will have some charity on account of speaking in a foreign language. Yes, I am an example of the universality of our claims; for not American women only, but a daughter of poor, crushed Poland, and the down-trodden and persecuted people called the Jews, "a child of Israel," pleads for the equal rights of her sex. I perfectly agree with the resolution, that if woman is insensible to her wrongs, it proves the depth of her degradation. It is a melancholy fact, that woman has worn her chains so long that they have almost become necessary to her nature—like the poor inebriate, whose system is so diseased that he cannot do without the intoxicating draft, or those who are guilty of the pernicious and ungentlemanly practice of using tobacco until they cannot dispense with the injurious stimulant. Woman is in a torpid condition, whose nerves have become so paralyzed that she knows not she is sick, she feels no pain, and if this proves the depth of her degradation, it also proves the great wrong and violence done to her nature. * * *

Woman is a slave, from the cradle to the grave. Father, guardian, husband—master still. One conveys her, like a piece of property, over to the other. She is said to have been created only for man's benefit, not for her own. This falsehood is the main cause of her inferior education and position. Man has arrogated to himself the right to her person, her property, and her children; and so vitiated is public opinion, that if a husband is rational and just enough to acknowledge the influence of his wife, he is called "hen-pecked." The term is not very elegant, but it is not of my coining; it is yours, and I suppose you know what it means; I don't. But it is high time these irrationalities are done away, for the whole race suffers by it. In claiming our rights, we claim the rights of humanity; it is not for the interest of woman only, but for the interest of all. The interest of the sexes cannot be separated—together they must enjoy or suffer—both are one in the race.

# DEBATE AT THE THIRD NATIONAL WOMAN'S RIGHTS CONVENTION ON BIBLICAL AUTHORITY FOR WOMEN'S RIGHTS

*By Ernestine L. Rose and Antoinette L. Brown*

September 9, 1852

Syracuse, New York

In her second public appearance at the convention, Rose engages in debate with Antoinette Brown (later Antoinette Brown Blackwell), the first woman ordained as a minister in the United States, about the place of the Bible in women's rights reform. Their debate, with competing resolutions proposed by each of them, was a significant focus of discussion at the convention. Rose's resolution was passed following the debate. On the third and final day of the convention, in both the morning and afternoon sessions, Brown again raised the topic of biblical authority and this time the resolution was tabled. This debate would recur over many subsequent women's rights conventions, culminating in the great divorce debate at the 1860 national convention (See *11 May 1860*).

Rose and Brown were colleagues and friends who traveled the same lecture circuit, and would continue to do so. Though Rose engaged in sharp debate with Brown, she was always courteous, acknowledging that Brown had the same right to be a minister and interpret the Bible as a man did. Indeed, Rose hoped that Brown, with the same credentials and expertise, would best the male ministers at their own game, but preferably not at women's rights conventions. In January 1855, joined by Susan B. Anthony, Rose and Brown would make a comprehensive tour of central New York State, collecting signatures for a petition to the state legislature on women's rights (Kolmerten 1999, 164). Brown, as a minister, could more easily persuade those who sought religious justification for women's rights; while Rose was more persuasive with those who preferred rationalist secular political arguments. In any case, their debates brought drama to the lecture series.

The following speeches and resolutions are excerpted from *Proceedings of the Woman's Rights Convention, held at Syracuse, September 8th, 9th & 10th, 1852*, which were published the same year. Most of Rose's speech concluding the first day of Bible debate was also published as one of a series of Woman's Rights Tracts (No. 9) that were widely circulated at the time.

~&~

## ANTOINETTE L. BROWN

*Resolved*, That the Bible recognizes the rights, duties and privileges of Woman as a public teacher, as every way equal with those of man; that it enjoins upon her no subjection that is not enjoined upon him; and that it truly and practically recognizes neither male nor female in Christ Jesus.

God created the first human pair equals in rights. possessions and authority. He bequeathed the earth to them as a joint inheritance; gave them joint dominion over the irrational creation; but none over each other.—(Gen., 1, 28.) They sinned. God announced to them the results of sin. One of these results was the rule which man would exercise over woman—(Gen., 3, 16.) This *rule* was no more approved, endorsed, or sanctioned by God, than was the twin-born prophecy, "thou (Satan) shalt bruise his (Christ's) heel." God could not, from His nature, command Satan to injure Christ, or any other of the seed of the woman. What particle of evidence is there then for supposing that in the parallel announcement he commanded man to rule over woman. Both passages should have been translated *will*, instead of *shall*. Either auxiliary is used indifferently according to the sense, in rendering that form of the Hebrew verb into English.

Because thou hast done this, is God's preface to the announcement. The results are the effects of sin. Can woman then receive evil from this rule, and man receive good? Man should be blessed in exercising this power, if he is divinely appointed to do so; but the two who are one flesh have an identity of interests, therefore if it is a curse or evil to woman, it must be so to man also. We mock God, when we make Him approve of man's thus cursing himself and woman.

The submission enjoined upon the wife, in the New Testament, is not the unrighteous rule predicted in the Old. It is a Christian submission due from man towards man, and from man towards woman: "Yea, all of you be subject one to another"—(1 Pet., 5, 5. Eph., 5, 21; Rom., 12, 10, &c.) In 1 Cor. 16, 16, the disciples are besought to submit themselves "to every one that helpeth with us and laboreth." The same Apostle says, "help those women which labored with me in the Gospel, with Clement also, and with other my fellow laborers."

*Man is the head of the woman.* True, but only in the sense in which Christ is represented as head of His body, the Church. In a different sense He is head of all things—of wicked men and devils. If man is woman's head in this sense, be may exercise over her all the prerogatives of God himself. This would be blasphemous. The *mystical* Head and Body, or Christ and His Church, symbolize oneness, union. Christ so loved the Church he gave himself for it, made it his own body, part and parcel of himself. So ought men to love their wives. Then the rule which grew out of sin, will cease with the sin.

It is said woman is commanded not to teach in the Church. There is no such command in the Bible. It is said, (1 Cor. 14, 34), "Let your women keep *silence* in the churches; for it is not permitted unto them to *speak*." This injunction, taken out of its connection, forbids *singing* also; interpreted by its context, woman is merely told not to *talk* unless she does *teach*. On the same principle, one who has the gift of tongues is told not to use it in the Church, unless there is an interpreter. The rule enforced from the beginning to the end of the chapter is, "Let all things be done unto edifying." Their women, who had not been previously instructed like the men, were very naturally guilty of asking questions which did not edify the assembly. It was better that they should wait till they got home, for the desired information, rather than put an individual good before the good of the Church. Nothing else is forbidden. There is not a word here against woman's teaching. The Apostle says to the whole Church, woman included, "ye may all prophesy, one by one."

In 1 Tim. 2, 12, the writer forbids woman's teaching over man, or usurping authority over him; that is, he prohibits dogmatizing, tutoring, teaching in a dictatorial spirit. This is prohibited both in public and private; but a proper kind of teaching is not prohibited. Verse 14—a reference to Eve, who, though created last, sinned first, is merely such a suggestion as we would make to a daughter whose mother had been in fault. The daughters are not blamed for the mother's sin, merely warned by it; and cautioned against self-confidence, which could make them presume to *teach over man*. The Bible tells us of many prophetesses approved of God. The Bible is truly democratic. Do as you would be done by, is its golden commandment, recognizing neither male nor female in Christ Jesus.

## ERNESTINE L. ROSE

If the able Theologian who has just spoken had been in Indiana when the [Indiana State] Constitution was revised, she might have had a chance to give her definitions on the Bible argument, to some effect. At that Convention, Robert Dale Owen introduced a clause to give to a married woman the right to her property. The clause had passed, but by the influence of a minister was recalled; and by his appealing to the superstition of the members, and bringing the whole force of Bible argument to bear against the right of woman to her property, it was lost. Had Miss Brown been there, she might have beaten him with his own weapons. For my part, I see no need to appeal to any written authority, particularly when it is so obscure and indefinite as to admit of different interpretations. When the inhabitants of Boston converted their harbor into a tea-pot, rather than submit to unjust taxes, they did not go to the Bible for their authority; for if they had, they would have been told from the same authority, to "give unto Cesar what belonged to Cesar." Had the people, when they rose in the might of their right to throw off the British yoke, appealed to the Bible for authority, it would have answered them, "submit to the powers that be, for they are from God." No! on Human Rights and Freedom—on a subject that is as self-evident as that two and two make four, there is no need of any written authority. But this is not what I intended to speak upon. I wish to introduce a resolution, and leave it to the action of the Convention:

> *Resolved,* That we ask not for our rights as a gift of charity, but as an act of justice. For it is in accordance with the principles of republicanism that, as woman has to pay taxes to maintain government, she has a right to participate in the formation and administration of it. That as she is amenable to the laws of her country, she is entitled to a voice in their enactment, and to all the protective advantages they can bestow; and as she is as liable as man to all the vicissitudes of life, she ought to enjoy the same social rights and privileges. And any difference, therefore, in political, civil and social rights, on account of sex, is in direct violation of the principles of justice and; humanity, and as such ought to be held up to the contempt and derision of every lover of human freedom.

But we call upon the law-makers and law-breakers of the nation, to defend themselves for violating the fundamental principles of the Republic, or disprove their validity. Yes! They stand arrayed before the bar, not only of injured womanhood, but before the bar of moral consistency; for this question is awakening an interest abroad, as well as at home. Wherever human rights are claimed for man, moral consistency points to the equal rights of woman; but statesmen dare not openly face the subject, knowing well they cannot confute it, and they have not moral courage enough to admit it; and hence, all they can do is to shelter themselves under a subterfuge which, though solidified by age, ignorance and prejudice, is transparent enough for the most benighted vision to penetrate. A strong evidence of this, is given in a reply of Mr. Roebuck, member of Parliament, at a meeting of electors, in Sheffield, England. Mr. R., who advocated the extension of the franchise to the occupants of five pound tenements, was asked whether he would favor the extension of the same to women who pay an equal amount of rent? That was a simple, straight-forward question of justice; one worthy to be asked even in our Republican Legislative Halls. But what was the honorable gentleman's reply? Did he meet it openly and fairly? Oh, no! but hear him, and I hope the ladies will pay particular attention; for the greater part of the reply contains the draught, poor, deluded woman has been accustomed to swallow—Flattery:

> There is no man who owes more than I do to woman. My education was formed by one whose very recollections at this moment make me tremble. There is nothing which, for the honor of the sex, I would not do—the happiness of my life is bound up with it—Mother, Wife, Daughter, Woman, to me have been the Oasis of the desert of life, and, I have to ask myself, would it conduce to the happiness of society to bring woman more distinctly than she now is brought, into the arena of politics? Honestly I confess to you I believe not. I will tell you why. All their influences, if I may so term it, are gentle influences. In the rude battle and business of life, we come home to find a nook and shelter of quiet comfort, after the hard and severe, and I may say, the sharp ire and the disputes of the House of Commons. I hie me home, knowing that I shall there find personal solicitude and anxiety. My head rests upon a bosom throbbing with emotion for me and our child; and I feel a more hearty man in the cause of my country, the next day, because of the perfect, soothing, gentle peace which a mind sullied by politics is unable to feel. Oh ! I cannot rob myself of that inexpressible benefit, and therefore I say, NO.

Well, this is certainly a nice, little, romantic bit of Parliamentary declamation. What a pity that he should give up all these enjoyments, to give woman a vote. Poor man! his happiness must be balanced on the very verge of a precipice, when the simple act of depositing a vote by the hand of woman, would overthrow and destroy it forever. I don't doubt the Honorable gentleman meant what he said, particularly the last part of it, for such are the views of the unthinking, unreflecting mass of the public, here as well as there. But like a true politician, he commenced very patriotically, for the happiness of society, and finished by describing his own individual interests. His reply is a curious mixture of truth, political sophistry, false assumption and blind selfishness. But he was placed in a dilemma, and got himself out as he could. In advocating the franchise to five pound tenement-holders, it did not occur to him that woman may possess the same qualification that man has, and in justice, therefore, ought to have the same rights; and when the simple question was put to him, (simple questions are very troublesome to statesmen,) having too much sense not to see the justness of it, and too little moral courage to admit it, he entered into quite an interesting account of what a delightful little creature woman is, provided only she is kept quietly, at home, waiting for the arrival of her lord and master—ready to administer a dose of purification, "which his politically sullied mind is unable to feel."

Well! I have no desire to dispute the necessity of it, nor that he owes to woman all that makes life desirable—comforts, happiness, aye, and common sense too, for it is a well-known fact, that smart mothers always have smart sons, unless they take after their father. But what of that? Are the benefits woman is capable of bestowing on man, reasons why she must pay the same amount of rent and taxes, without enjoying the same rights that man does. But the justice of the case was not considered. The Honorable gentleman was only concerned about the "happiness of society."

Society? what does the term mean? As a foreigner, I understand by it a collection, or union of human beings: men, women, and children, under one general government, and for mutual interest. But Mr. Roebuck, being a native Briton and a member of Parliament, gave us a Parliamentary definition, namely: society means the male sex only; for in his solicitude to consult "the happiness of society," he enumerated the benefits man enjoys from keeping woman from her rights, without even dreaming that woman was at all considered in it; and this is the true Parliamentary definition, for statesmen never include woman in their solicitude for the happiness of society. Oh, no! she is not yet recognized as belonging to the honorable body, unless taxes are required for its benefit, or the penalties of the law have to be enforced for its security. Thus, being either unwilling or afraid to do woman justice, he first flattered her, then, in his ignorance of the true nature of woman, he assumed, that if she has her rights equal with man, she would cease to be woman—forsake the partner of her existence, the child of her bosom, dry up her sympathies, stifle her affections, turn recreant to her own nature. Then his blind selfishness took the alarm, lest, if woman were more independent, she might not be willing to be the obedient, servile tool, implicitly to obey and minister to the passions and follies of man; "and as he could not rob himself of these inexpressible benefits, therefore he said, No."

Such are the lofty views of statesmen on woman, that equality of rights, the only and sure means to enlighten and elevate man, would degrade and corrupt woman. The genial rays of the sun of freedom, that vivify, cheer and ennoble him, would chill the heart and destroy the affections in her, and therefore it is inexpedient to give her her rights, "to bring her more distinctly into the political arena." Oh, yes! the Turk deems it inexpedient (for the happiness of society,) to give woman any personal

freedom, therefore he encloses her in a harem. It is a well-known characteristic of tyrants and cowards, when they dare not face a question of right,
to shelter themselves under expediency. It was inexpedient for Nicholas of
Russia to allow Hungary to free herself from Austrian oppression, therefore he sent his infernal machines to prevent it. It was expedient for Louis
Napoleon to destroy the Roman Republic, and inexpedient to await the
issue of another election, and therefore he violated his oath, and, with
bayonet in one hand and musket in, the other, compelled his re-election.
The bright and noble spirits of France were inexpedient to his treach-
ery, so he incarcerated them, or banished them from the country—all
these are measures of expediency. Thus in the more despotic countries of
Europe, it is expedient for the rulers to deprive the people of every vestige
of freedom. In constitutional England, it is already expedient to advocate
(and I hope they soon will obtain it) the extension of the elective franchise to every man who pays five pounds rent, but it is yet inexpedient to
give woman the same privilege.

And here, in this glorious land of freedom, a Republic that has proclaimed equality of rights—that has written on its banners universal
suffrage—even here it is yet deemed by the wiseacres of the nation, expedient to exclude half of its population from that universality. And do you
know, my friends, the reasons given for all these measures of tyranny and
oppression? Why, the happiness of society. But the question we ask, is
not whether woman shall forsake her household, like man, to intrigue in
politics, fight at elections, marshal armies, or direct navies. The question
at issue is whether woman, as a being amenable to the laws under which
she lives, shall have a voice in their enactment—as a member of the
social compact, shall participate and control those institutions to which
she is made subject! Or shall man, in his assumption of power, continue
to deprive her of her natural and inalienable rights, prescribe her sphere
of action within the least possible limits, restrict her education, and the
development of her powers to the lowest degree, cripple her physical,
mental and moral energies, that he may have a docile, obedient slave to
do his bidding?

These are questions not of expediency, but of right; not of charity, but
of justice. And yet, though we might well leave the issue of our cause on
its own merits, I would be perfectly willing to meet the opposers of our
claims on their own grounds, and convince them that even on the question of expediency they have not an atom of ground to stand upon. The
greatest objection I have yet heard, in public or private, against woman's
political rights, is the corruption of the present state of party politics. It
is represented to be in so low and degraded a condition, that no one can

enter the political arena without contamination, and therefore woman must be kept from its very atmosphere. Now, without disputing the validity of the testimony, as humiliating confessions come mostly from gentlemen belonging to these honorable bodies, I would ask, what is to be done? Leave forever our Legislative Halls, the Stygian pools, as the honorable Horace Mann calls them, that they now are? For what rational hope have we that they will ever become purified unless woman takes them in hand, seeing that man has had the exclusive possession of them so long, and they only seem to grow worse. No! no! something must be done. Expediency, "the benefit of society," calls for woman's "purifying influence," for "the perfect, soothing, gentle peace which the politically sullied minds" of our legislators, seeing how they fight in Congress, "are unable to feel." Let woman then, be with him wherever duty calls her, and she will soon cleanse the Legislative Halls, as she has cleansed and purified the festive board of the excess that existed there.

"'Tis not well for man to be alone"—Mother, Sister, Wife, Daughter, woman must be with him, to keep him in his proper sphere. Do you doubt it? Then look at exclusive assemblies of men, and even among the best you will perceive the rude, uncultivated nature of Adam, before mother Eve civilized him, by making him partake of the Tree of Knowledge. Expediency, therefore, as well as justice, demands that woman should have her political, civil and social rights, that she may be better able to "soothe, quiet," and aid man, abroad as well as at home. And the beneficial effects to society will soon be apparent; for as she will be better educated, have all her powers developed, her judgment expanded, she will be more competent to fulfill the various duties devolving upon her—as mother, to train her sons (aye, and her daughters, too,) in the way they should go, from which, when they grow old, they will not depart; as wife, more truly affectionate, so that when the husband's head will rest on her throbbing bosom, she would be able to give him counsel and courage, as well as rest; and though at the marriage ceremony she might not be willing to say "Obey," she will substitute the far better word, Assist. As a companion, she would be more interesting and instructive, and as a member of society, more useful, honorable and happy.

# SPEECH AT ROBERT OWEN'S BIRTHDAY CELEBRATION
May 13, 1853
New York, New York

This event, on Robert Owen's eighty-third birthday, was the second freethought community celebration where Rose presided that year, the first being the annual Thomas Paine celebration in January. In her speech Rose sketches, with respect and admiration, the life of Robert Owen. She honors the qualities of character that led Owen, the successful industrialist, to devote much of his life and fortune to shaping a better world. As a marketer of colognes and the wife of a skilled craftsman and shop-keeper, Rose understood and respected the qualities that made for Owen's success in business. Her speech was printed by the *Boston Investigator* on June 1, 1853, as part of its report called "Anniversary of Robert Owen's Birth-Day Celebrated in New York." Lucy Stone's attendance at the event was mentioned in the report, perhaps signaling growing recognition of Women's Rights advocates by the freethought press.

⤙⤙

*My Friends:*—With unspeakable pleasure do I rise to welcome the natal day of the world's greatest and purest philanthropist, Robert Owen. It is ever a pleasing duty to honor the day that gave birth to a great and noble being, for every good man is a blessing to society. But the grati-fication this evening must be greatly enhanced to us all by the pleasing consciousness that our venerable and beloved friend, whose eighty-third birth-day we meet to celebrate, is yet among us; and though the wide ocean separates him from our midst, yet his benign influence, his gentle and benevolent spirit, will, I am sure, be felt among us on this interesting occasion. On the 13th of May, 1770, a bright and glorious star appeared in our social and moral horizon, whose effulgent rays penetrated into the deep and dark recesses of our social existence, and disclosed to our mental vision the cliffs and shoals, and quicksands of ignorance, selfishness and vice, against which the dearest hopes and the best interests of mankind have been wrecked; and unless they were uprooted from their very foun-dation, and the streams of life cleansed and purified, would ever impede the progress of man to knowledge, virtue and happiness.

. . . . . .

His life was the most useful and interesting that ever fell to the lot of man. At a very early age he struck out for himself a course of life, which he pursued with an energy, consistency and perseverance, unequalled in the history of man. At the age of ten he left his native place in Wales for the great commercial emporium, London, with less than ten dollars in his pocket to commence the world with. While yet a mere boy he entered the arena of commerce, and contended most successfully for the prize of genius, persevering industry and application. One or two points of his early life will give you some idea of his youthful character. At eighteen he commence[d], with a partner, a machine-making establishment, employing forty men. Soon after, he added the commencement of cotton spinning by the newly invented machinery. At twenty, hearing a Mr. Drinkwater, proprietor of the first fine cotton factory, in Manchester, employing five hundred hands, advertise for a manager, Mr. Owen presented himself. "You are a boy," said Mr. Drinkwater. "That would have been an objection to me four or five years ago," was his reply; "I am a man now, and have some experience in this business." "What experience?" "I work three mules, and am making three hundred pounds a year." "How many times a week do you get drunk?" This was too much for the young philosopher, he colored up to his very temples, and replied very indignantly, "I never was drunk in my life!" "What salary do you ask?" "Three hundred pounds." "Three hundred?" said Mr. D., with astonishment; "why, there have been dozen here this morning, some of them double your age and they don't ask half that sum." "Very well," said Mr. Owen, "I am making three hundred a year in my own business, and I cannot come for less." "Let me see your establishment." They went, Mr. Drinkwater examined it in silence. "Well," said he, "come to me tomorrow, you shall have what you ask." Six months after, Mr. D. sent one morning for his manager. "Stay with me three years," said he, "I will give you four hundred next year, five hundred the year after, and then you can be a partner with me if it suit you." At the end of four years Mr. Owen entered into a more extensive partnership, and built the original Charlton mills in Manchester, over which he had almost entire control. Thus, commencing life with such genius, foresight, self-reliance, industry and perseverance, as his stock in trade, is it surprising that he was so eminently successful in life? He amassed a princely fortune, and offered it at the shrine of humanity.

His great object in life has been to benefit mankind—in his own words, to "peaceably revolutionize the mind and practice of the race." For this purpose, he set to work, by precept and example, to diffuse knowledge, based on the inscrutable laws of human nature; to infuse the benign spirit of charity and kindness into every heart; to teach mankind that the law of kindness is the most effective law in the well training of man; that if we want to have man rational, consistent, virtuous, and happy, we must remove the causes that have a tendency to make him irrational, inconsistent, vicious, and consequently miserable; for it is an eternal truth, that as long as the causes are allowed to remain, the effects must remain also. His whole life demonstrates that he had no private end to gain, no private ambition to gratify; were that his object, he had it at his command. In 1828, the Mexican government offered Robert Owen a district one hundred and fifty miles broad, extending from the Gulf of Mexico to the Pacific Ocean, along the line that separates Mexico from North America, including what is now called the golden regions of California, to be under his entire jurisdiction. The governments of England and the United States of America greatly favored the project. Mr. Owen accepted the offer, under the condition that the government should grant perfect religious freedom to every sect and every individual. This was generously acceded to by the government and the people; but the monks, the ever active and sworn enemies of religious liberty, so strenuously opposed the measure that it was finally defeated; and Robert Owen, ever true to himself and to the cause of freedom, declined the offer.

Nor has his life-long labor of love been in vain—for though the full carrying out of his principles and plans for the emancipation of the race from disunion, sin and suffering is yet among the things to come, yet no reformer probably ever lived who has seen so much of his principles and views adopted as Robert Owen. The great truth that the combined powers of organization, and the influences of education and position operating upon the organization from birth through life, form the character of man just what it is at any given period of his existence, has had its salutary effects upon society. All the moral reforms are based on this truth. The old erroneous idea of the depravity of human nature is daily giving way to philosophical inquiries into the nature of the causes and influences that produce depravity, vice and misery; and just in proportion as this truth is perceived, and the corresponding remedies applied, so is moral reform successful. His lofty conceptions, expanded mind, and great heart, embraced all reform—his platform was broad enough for the whole human family. On the fifth of May, 1834, he formed a society (to which I had the pleasure to belong) called the "Association of all Classes of all Nations, without distinction of sect, party, sex, country, or color." His wealth, energy and life had been devoted to the service of humanity, and he has reaped the rich reward of his holy devotion; for as every good act brings its own reward, so has he lived a life of serene happiness, of perpetual sunshine, that has shed a bright luster on his old age, and makes his declining days go down like that bright luminary in his full glory after a cloudless summer's day. And if the promulgation of "truth without mystery, mixture of error, or the fear of man"—if the diffusion of correct knowledge, based on the inevitable laws of man[']s nature—if peace, mercy, charity and kindness, can ever benefit mankind, then, indeed, may Robert Owen be justly considered a benefactor of the race.

# SPEECH AT THE HARTFORD BIBLE CONVENTION: "TRAMPLE THE BIBLE, THE CHURCH, AND THE PRIESTS"

June 4, 1853
Hartford, Connecticut

The Hartford Convention was part of a history dating back to the 1820s of debates on the Bible between the Infidels and the Bibles as the defenders of divine authorship were called. Freethinkers organized the Hartford Bible Convention as a forum for a whole range of reformers, such as William Lloyd Garrison of the abolitionist movement and Ernestine L. Rose representing women's rights, to address the question: Was the Bible an inspiration of God? Joseph Barker from England, a former Methodist minister turned freethinker, chaired the convention, which ran from June 1–5, 1853. The convention grew rowdy as theology students from nearby Trinity College repeatedly disrupted Infidel speeches with catcalls and hisses, and finally by turning off the lights. Garrison's presence at this Convention is noteworthy, as he did not often attend freethinker gatherings, and the antislavery movement was deeply influenced by Christian religious thought. Many radical abolitionists, especially Garrisonian abolitionists, were deeply disillusioned with the failure of the churches to speak out against slavery, the central moral issue of the time. This disappointment fed the "come-outer" movement that called upon abolitionists to come out of the churches until the clergy remedied their failure to condemn slavery fully and forthrightly as inconsistent with Christianity.

Rose's first speech at the convention, delivered the evening of June 4 was frequently interrupted by noisy responses, both positive and negative. At the conclusion of the speech, Rose asserted that the Bible, like all religious texts, exists to subjugate women, and exhorted the women present: "[D]o you wish to be free? Then you must trample the Bible, the church, and the priests under your feet." Coming from a woman, this declaration immediately created an uproar. One might even question whether Rose intended to end on such an incendiary note, or had to cut her speech short because of the response. In her second address to the convention, the following day, she began by recapping some of what she had said in her first speech, mentioning that it might not have been heard "owing to the confusion last evening." Her exhortation was also extensively reported in the press. The notoriety it created followed Rose onto many other platforms, where she was attacked as an atheist and sometimes refused the use of meeting halls to lecture on women's rights and abolition.

In fact, Rose's words simply express—albeit in vividly dramatic language—the belief of radical freethought that religion indoctrinated its followers to distrust their own rational understanding of the world and led them to submit to the domination of both religious and secular leaders. Since Rose believed that all human progress depended upon rational understanding and rational choices, it followed naturally that the Bible, which represented a nonrational authority, therefore needed to be cast aside in order for freedom and liberation to occur. Words in parentheses and brackets come directly from the Proceedings.

Shortly after the convention, on June 14, 1853, Rose wrote a letter to the *Boston Investigator*, offering her own account as a participant-observer at the convention. It was published in the paper's edition of June 29, 1953.

~&

My friends,—I rise under peculiar disadvantages: one is, that it is so late, and another that the ground has been most ably, eloquently, and masterly occupied by the various speakers who preceded me. Under these circumstances I would prefer not to speak at all, were it not for the fact that this movement seems to be one of the highest and greatest importance that has taken place in our age—(Applause)—of more importance even than the one that has so long lain at my heart, the rights of woman—(Applause)—for it is closely connected with it; and as woman has not been represented here, I feel it my duty to raise my voice and protest against the Bible, or, as it is called, the Word of God; for if a line of demarcation could be drawn of the injurious effects produced by the errors of that book on man or woman, I would say most emphatically, that on account of the inferior education and experience of woman, the errors of the Bible which have been palmed off upon society as emanations from some superior wisdom and power, have had a far more pernicious effect on the mind of woman than of man, for knowledge and experience are the only safeguards against superstition; and as woman has received less of the light of knowledge, superstition has had a stronger hold on her mind, and has enslaved her far more than man. (Applause, hisses, and cries of "Shame, shame.")

Mrs. Rose, on looking around at the confusion, said—My conviction is, that man always acts as well as he can; and if I see my poor unfortunate fellow being act as it appears to me inconsistent and irrational, I can but pity him for it. (Applause.)

The question under consideration, I believe, is the origin, influence, and authority of the Bible, or, Is the Bible an emanation from, or inspiration of, God? It seems to me that it would have been more in order had we commenced by inquiring what is meant by the term God, or Divine; but here again a difficulty presents itself, Where shall we commence to make the inquiry? If we go back to past ages, to the very infancy of the race, and from thence come up to the present time and hour, and ask the definition of God, the answer would be that, just what any age or people considered their *beau-ideal* of greatness, of wisdom, of virtue, and of perfection, they embodied in one grand idea, and called it God. (Renewed and long-continued disturbance in the gallery.) I will wait till I can be heard. (Renewed confusion.) This confusion is an evidence of the influence of the Bible. (Hissing.)

The Bible tells them that woman "should not speak in public." Oh, no, she must not raise her voice in behalf of truth and humanity, and if she does, she is met with confusion and riot by the believers in that doctrine; but after all, that is the best argument that can be brought in support of the Bible. With the sword it has been promulgated, with riot and confusion it must be supported. (Applause and hisses.) Yes! if we go back to the past, we find that men in all ages, all countries, conditions, and states, have always embodied what to them appeared the acme of perfection, and worshiped it. In those ages wherein the warrior, the conqueror, the hunter has been considered the most perfect and noble beings in the conception of men, they have cut out images of stone, wood, silver, and gold, to embody the various attributes, and knelt down and worshiped them; and as we came up from the long past, through all ages, without mentioning the various gradations, for time is short, to the present time, we still behold the same. The opinions only as to what constitutes greatness, goodness, and perfection, have changed; the tastes have become more refined, the feelings more humanized, the minds more enlightened and consistent. Man, in fact, has become more civilized; therefore the *beau-ideal* of his conception, or the idol of his imagination, is so too. Thus, instead of cutting out an image of the grosser materials, or painting it on the canvas, and then kneeling down to worship it, he shuts his eyes and beholds the embodiment of what appears to him to be the greatest, best, and noblest of human attributes, on the retina of his imagination, and bows down his head and pays homage to it; but however gross or refined, it is ever a likeness of himself, or what he would wish to be.

It has been a great mistake to say that God has made man in his image, for man in all ages and times has made his God in his image, and hence we have as great a variety of religions and gods as we have stages and gradations of man's perception of the true, the beautiful, and the noble, from the darkest ignorance and harbored to the present comparative state of knowledge and civilization. (Prolonged applause, hissing, and hooting.) Hiss on, if it does you any good. I give utterance to these convictions to aid in man's emancipation from the superstition and ignorance from which he has so long suffered. I know but too well what it is to go against the long-cherished and time-honored prejudices and superstitions. It is no pleasant task to go against the current, but there is a sense of duty that balances all unpleasantness, even hissing and hooting, and all, that is more potent than all persecutions, that brings a peace of mind, content, and happiness that none can feel but the mentally free. (Applause.) But to the subject. The Rev. Mr. Turner denied the objections brought against the Bible, saying that objections were not arguments; but I would respectfully remind him, that denials are not arguments, and it would have been better to confute the arguments that were brought against the Bible, than to do nothing but constantly deny them. (Applause.)

To judge of the inspiration of the Bible we must examine the Bible itself, and as its contents will appear consistent or inconsistent, so we must pronounce it based upon truth or error, for truth is always consistent with itself, and with every other truth, while error is always inconsistent. Now, when we examine the Bible in its commencement, we find its account of creation is perfectly inconsistent with, and contrary to, the sciences of geology, astronomy, physiology, and all well-ascertained facts based upon science and truth; and therefore we are justified in saying that whosoever wrote or inspired that part of the book must have been utterly ignorant of all these sciences; and as we proceed, we find so many inconsistencies, vices, and cruelties, that it is impossible to ascribe them to a wise or kind and benevolent power or being. (Hissing, stamping of feet, and whistling in the gallery, and cries of "Go on, go on.") My friends, there was once a time when I had a voice strong enough to speak against all opposition, and be heard, but that time is past. My constitution has been somewhat broken, and mainly broken in the great conflict against error. I had hoped that whatever our opponents might think of my opinions, they would behave like gentlemen, though believers and defenders of the Bible. (Cries of "Hear, hear.") [A lady said—"If you have a heart to speak on, speak on."] (Great applause.) I thank my sister for saying so. I have a heart to speak, and I will speak. (Tremendous applause.) My friends, you who do not know how long and how ardently I have wished for such a movement, can have no idea how I rejoice in this Convention, even hissing and all. (Applause.) The time was, some twenty-five years ago, when I stood alone on a platform—(Voice, "Where?")—for precisely the same noble cause, to defend the rights of humanity against the assumptions, superstitions, and errors of the Bible, without knowing that there was another human being in the wide world who thought as I did, and there and then I bore testimony against the same errors that I do now. (Applause and hissing.)

[The Rev. Mr. Turner expressed his hopes that Mrs. Rose would not be interrupted.]

As we proceed in our investigation of the Bible we find it inculcates war, slavery, incest, rapine, murder, and all the vices and crimes that blind selfishness and corruption could suggest; many have been enumerated here to-day, but it is utterly impossible to enumerate all. That book has been a two-edged sword to men; it has united them in nothing but persecution; to woman it has been like a millstone tied to her neck to keep her down; it has subjected her to the entire control and arbitrary will of man. It has libeled human nature, and libeled the very God of whom it speaks—it represents him as having created man in utter ignorance of consequences, as having created one sex, and pronounced it all to be very good, but found out that "it was not good for man to be alone," therefore he created woman—not for the same aims and objects of life that he created man—oh! no; but because he found, contrary to his expectation, that it was not well for him to be alone. So, after he had finished his work, and rested, he had to go to work again and make woman. This might be sublime if it were not ridiculous. And yet, do you know, my sisters, that most of the subjugation of woman, the tyranny and insult heaped upon her, sprung directly or indirectly from that absurd and false assumption. It is an insult to the supposed Creator to say he created one-half of the race for the mere purpose of subjecting it to the other, as well as a libel on the nature and powers of woman, to say that there is no other aim nor destiny in her existence except to be a mere plaything or a drudge to man, as the circumstances may require. The writers of all such parts of the Bible, where it libels her nature and powers, and therefore restricts her rights more than man's, were alike devoid of a knowledge of her nature and destiny, and of wisdom, justice, and humanity.

Yes, in reading that book understandingly, and judging it by its own contents, it tells us in language not to be misunderstood, that instead of being an emanation for some exalted wisdom and goodness, it is simply the work of different minds, existing in different ages, possessing different degrees of knowledge and principle; and in accordance with their state of progress, their knowledge, and feelings, so did they write—they could do no better. I have charity and forbearance for the writers of the Bible. Had they had loftier conceptions, juster ideas, kinder feelings, and a more accurate knowledge of Nature in general, and human nature in particular, they would have written quite a different Bible. As it is, it seems to me to be a concoction of incongruities, absurdities, and falsehoods almost impossible to conceive. It is true we find some excellent sentiments in it, such as "love thy neighbor as thyself," "do unto others as you would others should do unto you," and some others equally good; and though they are not original with the Bible, they are still beautiful sentiments; but as arbitrary commands they never can be carried out, for man is a being that requires a reason and a motive for his actions. Give him the reason and motive to love his neighbor as himself, in the knowledge of human nature and the relation he sustains to his fellow-man; convince him that he can find happiness only in proportion as he endeavors to promote the happiness of others—not only of those immediately connected with him, but of the race, for the race is but the great family of man, of which every individual is a member; and depend upon it, there will be no necessity for arbitrary commands with promised bribes and artificial rewards for the observance, and threats of penalties and artificial punishments for the non-observance of the great moral law nature has implanted in man for his rule of action, but which ignorance and error, called religion, has stifled by making mere belief of more consequence than works. A blind faith in things unseen and unknown is upheld as the greatest virtue in man.

The idea that "he that believeth shall be saved, and he that believeth not shall be damned," has caused more mischief to man than all the rest of the Bible could ever have benefited him, for it has produced all the persecution and ill-will on account of belief; and it is evident to my mind that the writer of this passage was utterly ignorant of the nature and formation of belief, or he would have known that there can be no merit in belief, nor demerit in disbelief, for it is not in our power to believe or disbelieve by a mere effort of the will. In childhood, belief is given to us the same as our food; we can make a child believe that what we call black is white; and if we tell it that it is of the highest importance, that its happiness here and hereafter depends upon its being called white instead of black, and any one who dares to call it by any other name is a bad man, an enemy to the power who wished it to be called white, and an enemy to man, whose safety here and hereafter depends upon its being called white, that child, if grown up, and possessed of an ardent, sincere, and conscientious temperament, would lay down his life, or sacrifice the lives of others, in support of black being white; and yet it would be black for all that. Thus we can make a child believe error to be truth, and it may die or sacrifice the lives of others in maintenance of it, and yet the error is not truth but error.

[Here Mrs. Rose was interrupted by hissing, hooting, and stamping. Some gentleman asked if such disturbances were the kind of arguments by which they expected to sustain the Bible? He hoped not. Mr. Barker said, "As we can not do the Bible justice without their assistance, they, the disturbers, are willing to assist us." At this point, some one having gained access to the gas-meter, turned off the gas, and for some minutes a continual hissing, shrieking, stamping, drumming of canes, and whistling was kept up by the rioters, mainly occupying the gallery, the body of the church having been occupied almost entirely during the Convention by peaceable and well-disposed auditors, who during the enactment of this scene mostly sat in silence. The utter confusion made it impossible to hear any voice that might have appealed to any sense of decency and propriety perhaps yet existing in the minds of rioters. The lights being restored, Mrs. Rose proceeded with her remarks, and said:]

When the lights were extinguished, it reminded me of one of the true things we find in the Bible, that some there are "who love darkness better than light." (Laughter and applause.) Just before that demonstration I endeavored to impress upon your minds how easily a child may be made to believe a falsehood and die in support of it, and therefore there can be no merit in a belief. We find in the various sects in Christendom, among the Jews, Mohammedans, Hindoos, in fact, throughout the entire world, that children are made to believe in the creed in which they are brought up. The children of the sect called Thugs[1] are made to believe in their creed, their Bible—for they, too, have a Bible, and priests to interpret it, and Bibles are always written so obscure as to require priestly interpreters—which tells them they are governed by a goddess; they seem to favor the rights of woman. (Applause.) Their means of salvation is to strangle every one they come in contact with who does not believe as they do; and the more Infidels and heretics they strangle the surer their reward in heaven, and the most pious and conscientious among them try to bring the most human sacrifices; and as humanity is not quite dead even among them, so they have quite a refined way to dispatch their victims; they have a silken cord made into a lasso, and when they come in contact with an unbeliever, they throw it adroitly over his head, and by a quick pull strangle him without the shedding of blood, and almost without a struggle. So strongly is humanity engrafted in man, that in spite of all the errors and superstitions called religion, it has not entirely been destroyed. (Applause.)

(Referring to some loafer in the gallery, with his boots hanging over the railing) I do not know but exhibiting the boots over the railing may be a part of the defense of the Bible, but whether it is so or not, we live in an enlightened age, in the free United Sates of America, where every one may do as he pleases, so long as he does not interfere with the rights of other, even to exhibit his boots or discourse in favor of the Bible. (Applause and hissing.)

Thus we see that children acquire their belief as they acquire any other habit. In after life [meaning adult], when we are more capable of reasoning, comparing, and reflecting, belief depends on the amount of evidence. If the evidence is strong enough to convince the mind, an assent is elicited; if the evidence is not strong enough to convince the mind, we can not believe; and the amount of evidence sufficient to convince one mind may not be enough to convince another; but whether the evidence is convincing or not, there can be no particle of merit in belief, or demerit in disbelief. No one within the reach of my voice can persuade himself that he hears me not, nor can any one out of it that he hears me, any more than he can believe that two and two make five, after he has been made to know that they make four. Yet in spite of this truth in connection with the formation of belief, all religions have been based on the false supposition that we can believe as we please, or as the priest wishes us to, and therefore we were promised rewards for believing, and punishment for disbelieving, the fashionable superstitions called religion.

Christianity is based on this error, my friends. I say it not in anger, but in sadness of heart, that all cruelties, persecutions, and uncharitableness, from the time of the Inquisition to the present hissing, have been in consequence of that irrational and pernicious sentence, "He that believeth shall be saved, and he that believeth not shall be damned." (Hissing.) That is perfectly consistent with your belief. But convinced as I am of the truth of the formation of human character, and of the inconsistencies, errors, and falsehoods of the Bible, in teaching a doctrine contrary to truth and to nature, I must come to the conclusion, that no very good, wise, exalted power or being could have been the author of it.

Now a few words as to its influence. As the Bible is based on error, what can its influence be but pernicious? For as truth is always beneficial, so is error always injurious. If we examine the history of Christianity, we will find that every step of its progress has been made in blood, and every atrocity committed has found authority in the Bible. When the tyrant of Russia and his despotic coadjutor of Austria subjugated poor, bleeding Hungary, they brought authority from the Bible. They told them that all power was of God—kings, priests, and emperors reign by the grace of God. "Oppose not those in authority; submit to the powers that be, for they are of God," has been the motto of every tyrant and every usurper; and when the burden has become too heavy to bear, the yoke too severe, and man could bear the oppression no longer, and tried to cast it off, he has ever been met with the cry of Babel to God's authority, which must be enforced with the point of the bayonet. The Pope has oppressed and all but destroyed poor Italy with the authority of the Bible. When the tyrant of Russia held his iron heel on the neck of my own poor, prostrate native land, Poland, he brought the same authority. When with the iron rod, that terrible thing called a scepter, said to have been given from heaven, the usurper sways the liberties and lives of millions, he brings good authority from the Bible. (Loud hissing.) Do you hiss the Bible,

or Russia? (Applause.) My friends, a most terrible outrage has been perpetrated on a poor humanity; there never has been a heart broken, a tear
drawn from the eye, a drop of blood from the human heart, nor a sigh
of agony from the expiring victim, but the perpetrators of these horrid
inhumanities have found authorities for it in the Bible. It is a sad reflection on man, that he could be so enslaved by the authority of a book. No
one knows its origin, in itself the most unintelligible, unreasonable, and
inconsistent that could ever have been concocted by the mind of man.
(Disturbance.)

It is to be regretted that disorder takes the place of order; but this
confusion of acts proceeds from the confusion of mind, in consequence
of the confusion of ideas taught by the Bible; here is its source and its
influence. The disorder of this book has filled man's mind with disorder,
and when the mind is a chaos, how can his actions be order? What do we
claim in this Protestant republic? Why only what it professes to guarantee
to every one, namely, freedom of speech; and look at the conduct of the
believers and defenders of the Bible; but their disorder and riot is the best
argument they can bring in support of it. Martin Luther once received the
same argument from the Church of Rome. (Hisses.) Do you hiss Luther,
or the Pope? (Applause.) Luther protested against the Church of Rome
and her Bible; he called her a harlot, a falsehood, a libel upon human
nature, religion, and God; he claimed the right of conscience and of private judgment; we, too, claim it here. Since his time, Protestantism has
gone on constantly protesting; we, too, protest against the right to shackle
the mind and prevent private judgment and freedom of speech; our protest here is in consequence of the protest of Luther; do you dislike it?
Throw your minds back to that time and hiss him to your heart's content.
(Applause and hissing, and drumming of feet and canes.)

According to the Bible in the hands of the Pope, there is no freedom
of opinion, no variety of sects, no private judgment; his Bible tells him
only to subject human rights, reason, and judgment to his despotic rule.
(Applause and hisses.) Protestantism professes to give freedom of conscience and of speech. Make your choice between the Church of Rome
and Protestantism, and abide by it. (Tremendous applause and hissing.)
And yet the Bible, as a history of the past—as reminiscences of other
times and people—would be interesting enough, provided it was not
palmed upon us as a guide for our age and time; as well might you force a
man, at forty, to wear his swaddling clothes, because they were once fit for
him. The time I trust will come—is already at hand—when the Bible, like
any other book, will be subjected to the test of reason, the light of knowledge and of truth, and by that test either stand or fall, and every man

will adopt what appears to him good, and reject what appears to him bad and inconsistent. But on account of its having been forced on man as an infallible rule of life, it has been more instrumental to keep him in ignorance, degradation, and vice, to prevent his elevation and development, to produce war, slavery, intemperance, and all the evils that afflict the race, than any and all the books that have ever been concocted by man. (Renewed hissing, indecent expressions, and disturbance.) All this does not disturb me nor ruffle my temper; it is only an additional evidence to me of the pernicious influence of the Bible. This is a practical illustration of it. I have stood more than this in opposing error, and I can stand this. It inspires me with no other feeling than pity and commiseration for such irrationality; but it is late, and I had better save my voice; it may be wanted to be raised in the same holy cause at some other time. (Applause and hissing in the gallery.) To you, my sisters, I would but say, that the defenders of the Bible have given you a most practical evidence of the rights and liberties Christianity has conferred upon you. The Bible has enslaved you, the churches have been built upon your subjugated necks; do you wish to be free? Then you must trample the Bible, the church, and the priests under your feet.

Mrs. Rose took her place amidst deafening applause, hisses and confusion. . . .

**NOTE**

1. Elinor Gadon, Women's Studies Research Center Scholar at Brandeis University, and expert on Indian goddess religions, commented as follows on Rose's characterization of the thugees: "Alas, Ernestine was taken in by some British propaganda that does have some small reality. In the nineteenth century there were groups of thugees (origin of the word "thug") who worshipped Kali [Goddess of death and destruction] and practiced banditry and murder" (Gadon 2006). Though Rose comments, probably as a joke, that the thugees worship of a goddess suggests they favored women's rights, Gadon does not agree that the thugees believed in the rights of human women, only in the power of their goddess.

# LETTER TO THE EDITOR: DESCRIBING
# THE HARTFORD BIBLE CONVENTION
June 14, 1853
Hartford, Connecticut

Shortly after the convention, on June 14, 1853, Rose wrote a letter to the *Boston Investigator*, offering her own account as a participant-observer at the convention. It was published in the paper's edition of June 29, 1853.

⌐&

Mr. Editor: . . . To any one capable of realizing the spurious and superstitious origin given to that book [the Bible], its falsely assumed authority, and, above all, its pernicious influence, the immense importance of such a Convention must be plainly apparent. It would be impossible for me to give anything like an adequate idea of the amount of heartfelt interest it created. A few allusions to the proceedings upon the occasion, are all I shall attempt to offer.

. . . . . . . .

The Hall, in which the Bible Convention was held, will accommodate, it is said, about 1600, and it was well filled at every session. In the evenings, especially, it was crowded, every standing-place being occupied even to the outside of the doors. As for the debates, I need hardly tell you that on one side there were plenty of speakers who clearly and forcibly demonstrated the falsity, inconsistency, and corruption of the Bible, as a whole; and many more would willingly and ably have lifted their voices on the same side, but for want of time had no opportunity. The speeches made by the President, William Lloyd Garrison, Henry C. Wright, Andrew Jackson Davis, and others, were unanswerable and unanswered. Not a solitary argument was disposed of by the defenders of the Bible. They had just wisdom enough to know they could not do it.

However, on Saturday evening, last but one of the Convention, they seemed to concentrate their forces and to use the best and only argument at their command in favor of their Bible—namely, disturbance, confusion, and riot! I was speaking at the time, and it appeared to be taken advantage of as the signal for the tumult that followed. That they should have been rather more afraid of the voice of a woman raised against their idol than the voice of a man, is perfectly natural; for they knew too well that so long as they can keep woman in ignorance and subjection, they are safe in their irrational and nefarious practices, for the churches rest upon her subjugated humanity, and that if she once breathes the vivifying breath of knowledge and of truth, when the extension of human rights and freedom shall enable her to do her own thinking and acting, when the light of Reason based on human rights shall lift her out of her present prostrate and enslaved condition and enable her to stand erect in the full dignity of her humanity, the churches will fall, and the priest's, like Othello's occupation, will be gone! And knowing well that knowledge disperses darkness, they showed their ignorance by thinking that by letting off the gas, the light of knowledge could be prevented from shining. But whoever were the instigators and managers of the pious mob, they used the best arguments they had, and I am sure I had perfect charity for them for doing the best they could in their position. I spoke full an hour on Saturday evening, and more than an hour and a half on Sunday afternoon—on the latter occasion without the Hall being darkened, for the priests could not turn off from us the light of the sun, or depend upon it, they would!

. . . . . . . .

In conclusion, allow me to say, that the signs of the times are encouraging. Freedom's car is on progression's track, and no obstacle of priest or superstition can throw it off. Humanity's motto is, Onward and upward! "Silence will not retard our progress, and opposition will give increased celerity to our movements."

Yours, in the cause of Truth and Right,
Ernestine L. Rose
New York, June 14, 1853

# SPEECH AT THE ANNIVERSARY
# OF WEST INDIAN EMANCIPATION
August 4, 1853
Flushing, New York

This speech was made at an outdoor celebration in Flushing, today's borough of Queens in New York City. The event was the antislavery movement's version of an Independence Day picnic, and indeed, the setting brought forth in all of the orators a style of Fourth of July oratory popular during that period. The celebration of "West Indian Emancipation," commemorated the nineteenth anniversary of the British emancipation, in 1834, of enslaved people in Caribbean colonies, then called the West Indies. This was, of course, decades before the Civil War and the emancipation of slaves in the United States. Abolitionists loved playing on the irony of "the cradle of liberty" being outdone in progress for human liberation by its colonial "mother country."

The *National Anti-Slavery Standard*, news organ of the American Anti-Slavery Society, reported that participants came by steamer boat from Fulton Street in Manhattan. Heavy rain the day before had discouraged some from attending, but those who braved the weather saw the sun come out at 10:15 a.m. "over a fine view of the grove . . . on a bluff-like elevation." The chair, New York Anti-Slavery Society President Lauren Wetmore, opened the event, declaring that the participants were gathered to celebrate "the greatest event of modern times, 800,000 persons transformed from chattel[s] to free men." Robert Hamilton and Ezekial Dias, described by the *Standard* as "two colored men," sang a hymn to the tune of a Scottish melody. William Lloyd Garrison, detained by a railroad accident, arrived late and was greeted with great applause. After a recess for picnicking, Garrison spoke at some length "to hearty applause," followed by Ernestine L. Rose and other speakers.

While this is Rose's first extant speech on the abolition of slavery, it was almost certainly not her first speech on the subject, judging by her account, contained within this document, of her visit in 1847 to South Carolina, as well as by other reports. The text of Rose's speech (as part of a report of the entire event) was reproduced in both the August 13, 1853, edition of *The National Anti-Slavery Standard* and the August 19, 1853, edition of the *Liberator*, William Lloyd Garrison's paper. The fact that the speech has survived and is known to modern readers is due in no small measure to its rediscovery by Morris U. Schappes, a historian of secular Jewish life in the United States, and subsequent publication, with commentary by Schappes, in the *Journal of Negro History* (1949, 344–55).

❧

Friends—I can hardly leave this place without raising my voice in unison with those who have spoken here. Indeed, the exercises of this celebration would not appear to me complete, without having [a] woman raise her voice in this great and noble cause (applause); for when has any good cause been effected without her co-operation? We have been told, to-day, that it was a woman that agitated Great Britain to its very centre, before emancipation could be effected in her colonies. [For more on the role of women in abolishing slavery in Great Britain, see Clare Midgley, *Women against Slavery: the British Campaigns, 1780–1830.* London: Routledge, 1992.] Woman must go hand in hand with man in every great and noble cause, if success would be insured.

I love to attend such anniversaries; I think the effect is very beneficial. Many such are celebrated in this country. New England celebrates the anniversary of the landing of the Pilgrim Fathers, and well she may; for when those Pilgrim Fathers left their native shores, it was to obtain that civil and religious freedom which was denied them in the mother country; and in so far as the same freedom is desirable for all, it is perfectly right and proper that their descendants should keep the anniversaries of the landing of their ancestors. Thousands attend these anniversaries, I doubt not, with joyful hearts and grateful memories; and though I am not myself an American by birth, and have never had the pleasure of attending such an anniversary, yet my heart is always with those who do, for they hail a day of freedom. But there are other anniversaries kept in this country, one of which I presume you all love to celebrate; and that is the anniversary of the Declaration of Independence. That great and glorious day did not create, but gave to the world a great truth—that all men are born free and equal, and are therefore entitled to life, liberty, and the pursuit of happiness. My heart always rejoices in that day, and I shall never forget the emotions I felt when I first witnessed its celebration in this country. It seemed to me as if the sun shone brighter, the birds sang sweeter, the grass grew greener. Everything in nature seemed transformed from deformity to beauty. Ah, were only that great, noble truth of the Declaration of Independence carried out, as it ought to be, there would be no need of our meeting here to-day. (Applause.) Then indeed might we all rejoice when the Fourth of July arrives. But whether it is carried out or not, the truth remains the same. Alas! that it should come up in judgment before this great nation! But though I rejoice when that great day comes round, I cannot help contrasting, as I sit here to-day, the event which that commemorates with the one which we are met to-day to commemorate.

All my feeling and principles are republican; I may say I am a republican by nature; but in comparison to the liberation of 800,000 slaves, the Declaration of Independence falls into utter insignificance. (Applause.) It falls short, just as theory falls short of practice. (Applause.) There is almost an immeasurable distance between the two. The one was the utterance of a great truth, that will last forever; the other was a practical application of it. How different the results! the Declaration of Independence—has it yet abolished Slavery? But the great act of emancipation of 800,000 human beings has shown to the world that the African race are not only capable of taking care of themselves, but are capable of enjoying peacefully as much liberty and as much freedom as the white men. Thus it has done far more towards the cause of freedom—towards emancipation from all kinds of slavery—than the Declaration of Independence did. (Applause.) For in spite of that Declaration—in sadness and sorrow do I say it—the United States of America are guilty of outrage and recreancy to their own principles in retaining slavery; while Great Britain, without that Declaration, having yet a great deal of oppression and tyranny in her midst, has shown a noble example to the world in emancipating all her chattel slaves.

It is utterly impossible for us, as finite beings, with the utmost stretch of the imagination, to conceive the depth and immensity of the horrors of slavery. I would that, instead of speaking and listening to-day, we could all sit down in perfect silence, and each and every one of us ask ourselves what is it to be a slave? What is it to emancipate eight hundred thousand slaves? We have the evil among us; we see it daily and hourly before us; we have become accustomed to it; we talk about it; but do we comprehend it—do we realize it—do we feel it? What is it to be a slave? Not to be your own, bodily, mentally, or morally—that is to be a slave. Ay, even if slaveholders treated their slaves with the utmost kindness and charity; if I were told they kept them sitting on a sofa all day, and fed them with the best of the land, it is none the less slavery (applause); for what does slavery mean? To work hard, to fare ill, to suffer hardship, that is not slavery; for many of us white men and women have to work hard, have to fare ill, have to suffer hardship, and yet we are not slaves. Slavery is, not to belong to yourself—to be robbed of yourself. There is nothing that I so much abhor as that single thing—to be robbed of one's self. We are our own legitimate masters. Nature has not created masters and slaves; nature has created man free as the air of heaven. The black man and the white man are equally the children of nature. The same mother earth has created us all; the same life pervades all; the same spirit ought to animate all. Slavery deprives us of ourselves. The slave has no power to say, "I will go here, or I will go yonder." The slave cannot say, "My wife, my husband, or my child." He does not belong to himself, and of course cannot claim anything whatever as his own. This is the great abomination of slavery, that it deprives a man of the common rights of humanity, stamped upon him by his Maker.

Not being a native of this country, I have probably had some different

ideas with regard to the working of slavery from what many abolitionists have. I do not belong to any abolition Society, as my friend by my
side said he was compelled to belong to the Garrisonian Society (laughter); but with my whole heart, mind and soul, I bless him for having been
the great and noble voice of humanity to this country for emancipation.
(Applause.) I go for emancipation of all kinds—white and black, man and
woman. Humanity's children are, in my estimation, all one and the same
family, inheriting the same earth; therefore there should be no slaves of
any kind among them. There are ties that bind man to man far stronger
than the ties of nation—than the political and commercial ties—ay, even
stronger than the ties of relationship; and these are the ties of humanity.
Humanity, the great mother of all, has thrown around us ties, sympathies
and feelings which are more endearing, more effectual, and more noble,
than any other that have ever bound man to man.

Our friend who has addressed you to-day has mentioned the fact that
the opposers of emancipation are fearful that the South will not trade with
the North. No greater folly was ever conceived. The South forsake the
North! What will they do? Six years ago, I was in Columbia, S. C. A senator, returning from Washington, made a speech there, in which he talked
a great deal about Abolitionists and Disunionists of the North. A young
lawyer, who boarded at the same hotel where I stopped, came home full
of these ideas, and commenced a conversation with me on the subject of
slavery; and he was so full, that he could scarcely find time to express his
indignation. "We don't want the North," said he, "we are independent of
the North, and we can afford to dissolve the Union to-day." I let him go
on for some time, for I knew he would run himself out. (Laughter.) After
he had done so, I told him I did not wish to have the Union dissolved; I
would like to stick to you, because you need us. (Laughter.) I then asked
him, "Wherein could you be independent of the North? Who are your
teachers and professors? Northern men. Who weaves your cloth and
bedecks you? Northern laborers. Who grows much of the food that nour-
ishes you? Northern men." (Indeed, so greatly impoverished is the land
in the South that it is a positive fact, that I once saw a cow held up while
she was fed.) (Great laughter.) "Just remember, my dear Sir," said I, "that
from your head to your feet, you were manufactured at the North; directly
or indirectly. (Laughter.) From him who first taught you your alphabet,
to the professor who gave the finish to your education, and taught you
to make black appear white, they were all Northern men. Nevertheless,
I don't want to see the Union dissolved; for as long as we are united, we
have an influence over you; indeed, you stand so greatly in need of us that
I should be very sorry to leave you." (Laughter.)

Mrs. R. here made an appeal in behalf of the principle of refusing to consume slave products, believing it would have a great tendency to abolish Slavery. Not being able to find a market for their products, the slaveholders would have either to go to work to feed their slaves or free them. And as for working, there was an entire inability on the part of the slaveholder. He was a poor, miserable, inactive, lazy, unfortunate creature, and with all heart and soul she pitied him. (Laughter.) When I first stepped on slave soil, said she, I read the curse of Slavery upon it. A gentleman once asked me in the South, what I thought, on the whole, of South Carolina. I told him: "I am sorry to say that you are a century, at least, behind in the means of civilization." (Laughter.) He wanted to know why I thought so. I said: 'The only civilization you have exists among your slaves: for if industry and the mechanical arts are the great criterion of civilization (and I believe they are), then certainly the slaves are the only civilized ones among you, because they do all the work." (Laughter.) (In Charleston and Columbia, S.C., the slaves are painters, glaziers, carpenters and masons; in fact, all the trades are filled with slaves. The owners cannot do any kind of manual labor, because it is disgraceful, so that everything is done by slaves.) He told me I had to thank my stars for being a woman. (Laughter.) I said I always thanked my stars for being a woman (renewed laughter), but I wanted to know wherein I had to thank my stars in that particular instance. Said he, "Our State has made provision for many cases, but not for all. For instance—when we catch a good Abolitionist, we give him a coat of tar and feathers." (Laughter.) I then told him that, as for me, I was an Abolitionist in the fullest sense of the word (applause), and be I a woman or not, said I, you are so exceedingly lazy and inactive here that it would be an act of charity to give you something to do, were it even to give me a coat of tar and feathers. (Great laughter and applause.) To say that he was enraged would express no idea whatever. (Laughter.) Then I said to him, "My dear sir, you have to thank yourself for this altercation; I did not begin it; I knew your weak spot, and did not wish to touch it. (Laughter.) You thought that I would be a coward and recreant to my sentiments. I tell you, sir, that if I had never been an Abolitionist before, I would have become one here, and you would have helped to make me one." (Applause.) Let a Northern man or woman go to the South, and the moment they touch the slave soil, they are looked upon as if they had come prepared to steal Negroes, and they never will let you alone, no matter how silent you may be; they will commence to draw you out and discover what your principles are. And it is a shame to acknowledge it, they find too many cowards from the North, who are recreant to their own principles; and having succeeded so many times with persons of this character, they think they can always succeed. They think that, for the sake of getting into society and being patronised by the higher classes, you will say, "O yes, your institutions are the best that can possibly be for your portion of the Union."

It has always appeared to me to be the greatest error and absurdity to suppose that the South is ever going to forsake the North. Where are they to go? It was a sheer political trick, raised for the purpose of making political capital, when our politicians in 1850 raised the cry—which (looking at the reporters present) of course the newspapers had to echo (laughter) that the Union was in danger. There was not a man of sound sense in the South, I venture to say—and there are many such—that believed it for a moment. It was got up by political gamblers of both sections, for the purpose of making capital. If you could only estimate the immense injury that Slavery does, not only to the South, but to the North—in fact, the whole world—you would say, "Leave us, if you will; we will willingly give you a passport, if you will rid us of this encumbrance."

Our friend Garrison has repeated to us the many blessings resulting from upright actions. Yes, every act brings its own reward or its own punishment. Every good act produces its own corresponding reward, and every bad act its corresponding punishment. How, then, must not only the South but the North be punished in consequence of that great, immeasurable wrong of Slavery? Oh, the shame and outrage that, for one single moment, that great blot should be suffered to remain on the otherwise beautiful escutcheon of this republic!

But permit me to say that the slaves of the South are not the only people that are in bondage. All women are excluded from the enjoyment of that liberty which your Declaration of Independence asserts to be the inalienable right of all. The same right to life, liberty, and the pursuit of happiness, that pertains to man, pertains to woman also. For what is life without liberty? Which of you here before me would not willingly risk his or her life, if in danger of being made a slave? Emancipation from every kind of bondage is my principle. I go for the recognition of human rights, without distinction of sect, party, sex, or color. (Applause.)

## SPEECHES AT THE NEW YORK STATE
## WOMAN'S RIGHTS CONVENTION
## ("THE MOB CONVENTION")

*By Ernestine L. Rose, Mathilde Franzisca Anneke, and Others*
September 9, 1853
New York, New York

In the fall of 1853, New York City was crowded with visitors to the first "World's Fair" to be held in the United States, at a newly constructed Crystal Palace inspired by the famous structure in London. In September of that year, three reform conventions were held in close proximity to one another: the World's Temperance Convention organized by Susan B. Anthony, an abolitionist convention, and the New York Woman's Rights Convention. Although women were an important constituency of the temperance movement, they were not allowed to speak at this World's Temperance Convention. This fact may have represented a turning point for Susan B. Anthony, helping convince her to fully commit her energies thereafter to the women's rights movement. Because these reform movements had overlapping constituencies, the conventions were positioned so that reformers could attend all three. Organizers may also have hoped to attract new people by holding their conventions during this period of expanded tourism. The conventions were overrun with attendees ranging from curiosity seekers to violent opponents of rights for women and African Americans. At the Woman's Right Convention, held at the Broadway Tabernacle in Manhattan on September 8 and 9, the audience caused so much disruption that it was dubbed "the Mob Convention." In her Farewell Letter of May 1856, Rose remembered this convention as one of the most violent and threatening meetings she had ever attended.

Ernestine Rose made the Married Women's Property laws in New York State the focus of her prepared speech on September 9, since the convention provided a prime opportunity to reach state legislators by means of energizing New York residents. In her speech, Rose satirized the existing laws governing married women's property and widow's inheritance, to the great amusement of some in the crowd, and the consternation of others.

That evening, at the convention's final session, its president, Lucretia Mott, turned the chair over to Ernestine L. Rose. Were police intervention required to maintain control, Mott, as a pacifist Quaker could not, in conscience, call for forcible action, while Rose, as a person who believed in laws to remedy social problems, was willing to do so to protect public safety. It is not clear from the printed proceedings of the convention whether any police actually arrived, although the document does note: "Owing to the tumult and noise which prevailed during the greater part of the proceedings, it is quite possible that some portion of the speakers' words were lost, and other portions incorrectly heard. The Report will be found as accurate as the circumstances permitted."

During this final session, Rose extemporaneously translated the speech of

Madame Mathilde Franzisca Anneke, who had immigrated to the United States following the failed uprisings of 1848 in Germany. In the United States, she was editor of a German-language newspaper for women called the *Frauen-Zeitung*, published in Newark, New Jersey, and later in Milwaukee, Wisconsin. Rose has been called the translator of the women's rights movement because of her knowledge of French, German, and Polish (Anderson 2000, 20–21).

⁓

## SPEECH ON MARRIED WOMEN'S PROPERTY LAWS

As to the personal property, after all debts and liabilities are discharged, the widow receives one-half of it; and, in addition, the law kindly allows her her own wearing apparel, her own ornaments, proper to her station, one bed, with appurtenances for the same; a stove, the Bible, family pictures, and all the school-books; also, all spinning-wheels and weaving-looms, one table, six chairs, tea cups and saucers, one tea-pot, one sugar dish, and six spoons. (Much laughter.) But the law does not inform us whether they are to be tea or table spoons; nor does the law make any provision for kettles, sauce-pans, and all such necessary things. But the presumption seems to be that the spoons meant are teaspoons; for, as ladies are generally considered very delicate, the law presumed that a widow might live on tea only; but spinning-wheels and weaving-looms are very necessary articles for ladies nowadays. (Hissing and great confusion.)

Why, you need not hiss, for I am expounding the law. These wise law-makers, who seem to have lived somewhere about the time of the flood, did not dream of spinning and weaving by steam-power. When our great-great-grandmothers had to weave every article of apparel worn by the family, it was, no doubt, considered a very good law to allow the widow the possession of the spinning-wheels and the weaving-looms. But, unfortunately for some laws, man is a progressive being; his belief, opinions, habits, manners, and customs change, and so do spinning-wheels and weaving-looms; and, with men and things, law must change too, for what is the value of a law when man has outgrown it? As well might you bring him to the use of his baby clothes, because they once fitted him, as to keep him to such a law. No. Laws, when man has outgrown them, are fit only to be cast aside among the things that were.

But I must not forget, the law allows the widow something more. She is allowed one cow, all sheep to the number of ten, with the fleeces and the cloth from the same, two swine, and the pork therefrom. (Great laughter.) My friends, do not say that I stand here to make these laws ridiculous. No; if you laugh, it is at their own inherent ludicrousness; for I state them simply and truly as they are; for they are so ridiculous in themselves, that it is impossible to make them more so. . . .

[Rose spoke further on issues of inheritance later in the day.]

In allusion to the law respecting wills, I wish to say that, according to the Revised Statutes of our State [New York], a married woman has not a right to make a will. The law says that wills may be made by all persons, except idiots, persons of unsound mind, married women, and infants. Mark well, all but idiots, lunatics, married women, and infants. Male infants ought to consider it quite an insult to be placed in the same category with married women. No, a married woman has no right to bequeath a dollar of the property, no matter how much she may have brought into the marriage, or accumulated in it. Not a dollar to a friend, a relative, or even to her own child, to keep him from starving. And this is the law in the nineteenth century, in the enlightened United States, under a Republic that declares all men to be free and equal.

## ERNESTINE ROSE'S TRANSLATION OF STATEMENT BY MATHILDA FRANZISCA ANNEKE

I wish to say only a few words. On the other side of the Atlantic there is no freedom of any kind and we have not even the right to claim freedom of speech. But can it be that here, too, there are tyrants who violate individual right to express our opinions on any subject. And do you call yourselves republicans? No; there is no republic without freedom of speech.

[Ed. Note: As the uproar continued, Wendell Phillips, the renowned Boston Brahmin orator, appealed to the rioters' self-respect, addressing them as fellow citizens of a great country. He reminded them that New Yorkers had welcomed other freedom fighters and refugees from the liberation struggles of Europe, and urged them to give Madame Anneke, who had "faced the cannon of Francis Joseph of Austria," the same respect. Then Madame Anneke continued:]

I saw this morning, in a paper, that the women of America have met in convention, to claim their rights. I rejoiced when I saw that they recognized their equality; and I rejoiced when I saw that they have not forgotten their sisters in Germany.

. . . . . . . .

Before I came here, I knew the tyranny and oppression of kings; I felt it in my own person, and friends, and country; and when I came here, I expected to find that freedom which is denied us at home. Our sisters in Germany have long desired freedom, but there, the desire is repressed as well in man as in woman. There is no freedom there, even to claim human rights. Here they expect to find freedom of speech—here, for if we cannot claim it here, where should we go for it? Here, at least, we ought to be able to express our opinions on all subjects; and yet, it would appear, there is no freedom, even here, to claim human rights, although the only hope in our country for freedom of speech and action is directed to this country for illustration and example. That freedom I claim. The women of my country look to this country for encouragement and sympathy; and they, also, sympathize with this cause. We hope it will go on and prosper: and many hearts among the ocean of Germany are beating in unison with those here.

[Madame Anneke was once again interrupted, Phillips again attempted to quell the uproar, but was not able to do so. At that point, Ernestine Rose mounted the podium and spoke:]

"As presiding officer for this evening, I call upon the police. The Mayor, too, promised to see that our meetings should not be disturbed, and I now call upon him to preserve order. As citizens of New York, we have a right to this protection, for we pay our money for it. My friends, keep order, and then we shall know who the disturbers are.

[Phillips yet again tried to speak.]

Mrs. Rose: I regret that I have again to call upon the police to keep order; and if they are not able to do it, I call upon the meeting to help them.

# SPEECH AT THE FOURTH NATIONAL WOMAN'S RIGHTS CONVENTION: "THE DOUBLE STANDARD OF SEXUAL MORALITY"

October 7, 1853
Cleveland, Ohio

At this convention Rose spoke several times, but her most eloquent and distinctive speech addressed the double standard of sexual morality for women and men. She spoke of the women who were ostracized and condemned by society for violating strict codes of sexual conduct, often as a result of being victimized by unscrupulous men, who themselves suffered no approbation of any kind. For Rose, such warped and hypocritical social conventions were symptoms of the general condition of inequality between men and women, which in turn was created by laws that were "framed in ignorance . . . sanctioned by superstition and enforced by power." As the debate continued, she added "pulpit-preachers" to the list of those responsible.

In her speech, Rose refers to a "declaration of independence" for women; this is the Declaration of Sentiments from the 1848 Seneca Falls convention, closely modeled on the U.S. Declaration of Independence. It had been read aloud earlier that day. Also mentioned is another declaration of women's rights, which was included in a letter from reformer William H. Channing, also read aloud; it had been agreed that both documents would be drawn upon in creating a declaration for the present convention. Rose, in a sense, modeled woman's resistance to the influence of men in her introductory remarks on the first day of the convention, urging women not to abandon their planned women's rights meeting to respond to a last-minute invitation to an antislavery meeting. "We might congratulate ourselves that man has advanced so far as to invite a Woman's Convention to attend his Convention; but surely it will not advance our cause to adjourn sooner, in order to meet his advances," she declared.

⤙

[S]omething was said by one of my sisters, with regard to the statement [the Seneca Falls "Declaration of Sentiments"], that man purposely played the tyrant over woman. I trust that it is well understood—if not, I will repeat it as one of my views and principles, and I presume it will not be too presumptuous, to say, it is the principle of all the friends who advocate this cause; we do not fight with man himself, but only with bad principles. Man is inconsistent, and he has been made, through that inconsistency, tyrannical. Man has been unjust, because bad laws always will make bad men. We have had bad laws, hence man has been bad; but so thoroughly good is human nature, that in spite of bad laws, man is not as bad as he might be, under them. We make no complaint against individual man, for he is under the laws of the past; and humanity does not allow him to carry out, to the full extent, the bad provisions of the laws under which he lives. You will say, these laws were made by man. True! but they were framed in ignorance, ignorance of the ultimate end or aim of the human being, man or woman, and ignorance of the relations of the sexes. They were sanctioned by superstition and enforced by power. This is an additional reason why we wish all these laws altered, for it can be no otherwise than inconsistent, when one half of the race frame laws for the other half. Man is not now, in the full sense, man; any more than woman is, in the full sense, woman. It requires both to enact rational and proper laws for the rational government of both; and this is the reason why we claim our rights fully, fearlessly and entirely.

I blame no one. My creed is, that man is precisely as good as all the laws, institutions and influences, [in] operation upon his peculiar organization, allow him to be; and therefore I see an additional reason and feel an additional motive, to point out our present laws and institutions. For so long as they are wrong, man will act unjustly; therefore we must have them altered. Remove the causes that produce transient effects, and the effects will not exist. But I heartily endorse the proposition offered here, to come forth with a declaration of sentiments. I second it as no less great, noble, and important, than the first honorable declaration of Independence; those great immutable truths which have gone forth all over the world, and have given to man hope, and life, and light. Yes, this declaration of woman's independence is even more far-sighted and sublime. For although truly a result of that declaration itself, it was never before dreamed that woman would be included in it. Is it not obedience to old laws, received from old and barbarous ages, and tyrannical lands, which has prevented, hitherto, the application of that declaration, to woman? And while they continue to sustain and execute the laws which oppress half the race, this new declaration, based upon the self-evident truths of the old declaration, is of paramount importance.

I also approve of the letter of Mr. Channing. I revere Mr. Channing, although I do not name him, Reverend. I thought that in a republican country, titles would not exist. A title never can honor a man, but a man may honor the station which a title attempts to indicate. I agree almost entirely with that letter—nay, entirely. I only differ from the remark afterward made by my friend, Antoinette L. Brown, with regard to altering that part which says, that habitual drunkenness should be a reason for divorce. She thought it should be only a cause for legal separation. I would ask her if such legal separation should have the same force as a divorce?

Miss Brown:—It should not allow the parties to marry again.

Mrs. Rose. What constitutes marriage? The violation of that, whatever it is, is a sufficient ground for a legal, social, and entire separation between them; and that is divorce. But, I will not enter upon the discussion of that subject, at present. I trust it will come up during this Convention, or, if not here, during some other of our Conventions; for it is of vital importance. We must come to it, we must face it. I know well and have known it for years, that this subject will encounter more prejudice and in consequence more difficulties than any subject hitherto brought before the public; and hence it is all the more necessary to meet, and discuss it. It lies at the foundation of things, and whenever it is brought up and I have an opportunity, I will speak more on the subject; but here I must leave it.

I wish to read a passage which has been already read in this Declaration of Independence. To me, it is beautiful, because it is true. It is of the utmost importance and should be dwelt upon. "He has created a false public sentiment by giving to the world a different code of morals for man and for woman, &c." My Friends, I have read it imperfectly, for English is still difficult to me—have you heard it, have you understood it? I acknowledge no different standard of morals for the sexes; there is none in nature, in truth, and should be none in practice. But a different code is recognized in practice in all our Society, in all our Law, in all our public opinion, that greatest of all tyrants. All those have established a different code of morals for the sexes, and hence comes so much of immorality, so much of crime, so much of suffering.

It is time to consider, whether, what is wrong in one sex, can be right in the other? It is time to consider, whether, if woman commits a fault,— but too often from ignorance, from inexperience, or from poverty, (the consequence of her degradation and oppression)—whether when such a being, in her helplessness, in her ignorance, in her inexperience and dependence, not having had her mind developed, nor her higher faculties exercised, not having been allowed to mingle in honorable society, and gain needful experience, and therefore unacquainted with human nature, or rather, perverted nature, as it too often is,—whether, when such a being is drawn into sin, often through appeals to her tenderest and best feelings, and in consequence also, of being accustomed to look up to man as her superior, her guide, and master—when a being, thus brought up, and thus situated, is drawn down to sin, and has broken the law of society, whether such a being should be cast out of the pale of humanity—while he who led her into it, (if not the main, the great secondary cause of it) he who is endowed with the superior advantages of education and experience, he who has taken advantage of that weakness, and that confiding spirit, which the young, particular, always have,—I ask, if she, the victim, is cast out of the pale of humanity, shall the despoiler go free? (Cries of no! no! no!) And yet, he goes free!

My friends, I speak warmly, because I feel deeply for the degradation of woman. Look into your societies; look into your newspapers; look everywhere, anywhere; look at the helpless beings who crowd our cities! Have these poor creatures been born with the mark of Cain upon their foreheads? Nature cries, no! To what then is it owing, but to the wrongs of which they have been victims! but to the fact, that woman is made to believe that she is created to be only the tool or plaything of man; to be dependent upon him, instead of dependent upon her own rectitude, dependent upon her own faculties. In that doctrine of dependence upon man, lies one of the great causes at least, of the evils which lead so many young and lovely creatures to a premature and dishonored grave. And ye men before me, when you read in the newspapers the terrible account of some woman who has been brought to so low and terrible a condition, as to violate the strongest law of her nature, the moral law of her being; do you not know that it is the result of ignorance and dependence?

I pity man, but I blame him not. It is owing to unjust, perhaps unwritten laws, and our supposed duty to recognize them as laws. Ah! if there should be one before me, who has been brought to that unhappy condition to which I have alluded, and has been forced to degrade herself in her own estimation, to prostitute her mind and body to lust! how deep lies the guilt at the door of society, not only at her own. They have driven her to it,—and yet man, the author of it, in as far as he was the law-maker, and in as much as he is the stronger,—in ninety-nine cases in a hundred, particularly if he can keep up his position in the Church and give money to Bible and Tract Societies,—is honorable in society. I do not state this to cast odium upon these religious societies, or upon the churches. I say it because I know it to be a fact. Such men are to be found in the best society: among our aldermen, our church-officers, in the Legislative halls, in Congress at Washington, and who knows but in the Presidential chair itself. Read your papers, and see how often ministers are brought up for taking advantage of some weak member of their congregations,—or rather, how seldom they are brought up for it, while their poor victims are thrust out from the pale of humanity. And though she has violated only one single law, (and I say it with anxious sorrow) woman is the first to thrust her out from her own companionship, while she, who thrusts her out, is often quite flattered with the attentions of the gentleman who made her his victim. Yet I blame her not any more than man. The same ignorance, the same falsity has made her as inconsistent as it has made him. The same laws removed, only can remove these evils.

Yes, my friends, I am willing to acknowledge, that at present, woman,—the majority of women,—are as much opposed to their nearest and dearest interests, as man is. The reason is obvious. She has been made to believe in, and to depend only, upon the opinions of man. She thinks man is opposed. She lives entirely upon the flattery and adulation of man. She has no object sufficient in life, no confidence in her own principles, nor in her own powers; and therefore, so long as she thinks it unfashionable among men, so long will she go against it. Hence the great necessity to make our truths, legal truths,—for when once they are legal, they will become fashionable, and fashionable ladies will go for them.

I have been told, time after time, by ladies—"We claim our rights! why we have rights enough. We don't want any more rights." An allusion was made here yesterday to tyranny; the question was asked, whether woman would be a tyrant, if she obtained her rights?—My friends, analyze that phrase: "We have rights enough!" that sentiment, "And we don't want any more rights!"—It is equivalent to saying, "I have rights enough, therefore you are not entitled to yours." There is tyranny in such experience, and such women are tyrants. For it is a law of nature, that he who can submit to be a slave, only wants the opportunity, to become a tyrant. He who will place your yoke on his own neck, just give him the opportunity, and he will reverse it, and place the yoke on your neck.

Yes, woman can be a tyrant as great as man, and the more ignorant, and submissive she is now, the greater tyrant she may be for it. [B]ut he who can appreciate human rights, he who values the noble spirit of humanity, he who truly recognizes the entire equality of human beings, will never desire to infringe upon the rights of a single member of humanity. Just in proportion as man can be a slave, can he become a tyrant.

But I did not intend to make a speech, I rose to move, and will now move that a committee be appointed to take this declaration of Independence, and the Declaration of Mr. Channing, and either combine the two, or frame a new one.

[The convention's president, Asa Mahan, objected to the idea that the "male sex" alone had created the double standard Rose described, arguing that women were equally, if not more, to blame for this kind of "public sentiment."]

Mrs. Rose:—I heartily agree that we are both in fault; and yet we are none in fault. I also said, that woman, on account of the position in which she has been placed, by being dependent upon man, by being made to look up to man, is the first to cast out her sister. I know it and deplore it; hence I wish to give her her rights, to secure her dependence upon herself.

In regard to that sentiment in the declaration, our friend said that woman created it. Is woman really the creator of the sentiment? The laws of a country create sentiments. Who makes the laws? Does woman? Our law-makers give her ideas of morality.

Mr. [Joseph] Barker:—And the pulpit.

Mrs. Rose—I ought to have thought of it, not only do the law-makers give woman her ideas of morality, but our pulpit-preachers. I beg pardon—no I do not either—for Antoinette L. Brown is not a priest. Our priest[s] have always made or recognized in daily life, distinctions between man and woman. Man, from the time of Adam to the present time, has had utmost license, while woman must not commit the slightest degree of "impropriety," as it is termed. Why, even to cut her skirts shorter than the fashion, is considered a moral delinquency, and stigmatized as such by more than one pulpit, directly or indirectly.

You ask me who made this sentiment; and my friend yonder says, woman. She is but the echo of man. Man utters the sentiment, and woman echoes it. As I said before—for I have seen and felt it deeply—she even appears to be quite flattered with the destroyer of woman's character—aye, worse than that, the destroyer of woman's self-respect and peace of mind—and when she meets him, she is flattered with his attentions. Why should she not be? He is admitted into Legislative halls, and to all places where men "most do congregate;" why, then, should she not admit him to her parlor? The woman is admitted into no such places; the Church casts her out; and a stigma is cast upon her, for what is called the slightest "impropriety." Proscribed by no true moral law, but by superstition and prejudice, she is cast out not only from public places, but from private homes. And if any woman would take her sister to her heart, and warm her there again by sympathy and kindness, if she would endeavor once more to infuse into her the spark of life and virtue, or morality and peace, she often dare not so far encounter public prejudice as to do it. It requires a courage beyond what woman can now possess, to take the part of the woman against the villain. There are few such among us, and though few, they have stood forward nobly and gloriously. I will not mention names, though it is often a practice to do so; I must, however, mention our sister, Lucretia Mott, who has stood up and taken her fallen sister by the hand, and warmed her at her own heart. But we can not expect every woman to possess that degree of courage.

# TESTIMONY BEFORE SELECT COMMITTEE
# OF THE NEW YORK STATE ASSEMBLY
March 3, 1854
Albany, New York

Following the New York Woman's Rights Convention of February 14–15, 1854, the first to be held at the state capital, reformers who were able to stay on in Albany presented their petitions to committees of the New York State Assembly. According to a report in the *Albany Transcript*, "Rose's speeches . . . were the most applauded during the Convention by the New York Legislature." Rose addressed the issues "in an ingenious and plausible manner. Her remarks were listened to with the most profound attention, and she was encouraged by frequent and prolonged applause. . . . [A]s a whole her speech which was of great length and ability, appeared to be favorably received."

Rose's subsequent testimony before the legislative committees may not have been so well received, especially by opponents of women's rights. When Rose and William Channing spoke to a Senate select committee on March 1, the *Albany Register* reported, "The Honorable senators quailed beneath the trial." On March 3, Rose joined Susan B. Anthony in addressing a select committee of the Assembly. The *Evening Journal* described their appearance "before the Senate Committee of Bachelors": "The only effect produced was a determination more fixed than ever, in the minds of the Committee to *remain* Bachelors in the event of the success of the movement. . . ." (Gordon 1997, 263n)

Her colleagues were even more pleased with Rose's presentation than the *Albany Transcript*. Susan B. Anthony reported in a letter to Lucy Stone:

> . . . We have had a most glorious hearing before our Assembly Committee, the one to whom was referred our Petition for the Just and Equal Rights of Women. All the members, save one, are quite liberally disposed. Mr. Channing and Mrs. Rose were the only members of our committee who could be present at the hearing. . . .
>
> After the presentations of the statement to the Senate by Channing, Mrs. Rose and Mr. C. made good arguments—as good as they could under the circumstances. The Senate Committee were very frivolous and wanting in common politeness. I read the document presented to the Assembly Committee. Mrs. Rose followed with an hour's close argument. We expected Mr. C. to follow her, but he thought best that the impression made by Mrs. R. should not be marred. [N.B. is the end of quote] (Gordon 1997, 262)

What follows is an excerpt of Rose's testimony, published in the March 4, 1854 edition of the *Albany Argus*. Though brief and incomplete, this document is an important example of Rose's frequent, but rarely recorded, advocacy before a legislature. Rose spoke before legislative committees in Massachusetts, Michigan, and many times before the State Legislature in New York, but there is little documentation of her words on those occasions, perhaps at least in part because of a fire in the New York State archives in a subsequent period.

჻

The right of petition is of no avail unless the reform demanded be candidly considered by the legislators. We judge of the intellectual inferiority of our fellow-men by the amount of resistance they oppose to oppression, and to some extent we judge correctly by this test. The same rule holds good for women; while they tamely submit to the many inequalities under which they labor, they scarcely deserve to be freed from them. . . . These are not the demands of the moment or the few, they are the demands of the age; of the second half of the nineteenth century. The world will endure after us, and future generations may look back to this meeting to acknowledge that a great onward step was here taken in the cause of human progress.

[Mrs. Rose took her seat amidst great applause from the galleries and lobbies. The Committee adjourned.]

# ATTACK IN THE *ALBANY REGISTER* AND ERNESTINE L. ROSE'S RESPONSE

By Editors of the Albany Register *and Ernestine L. Rose*
March 6 and 7, 1854
Albany and New York, New York

After Rose had addressed committees of the New York State Legislature in public hearings, she was viciously attacked in the March 6, 1854, edition of the *Albany Register*. While ridiculing all women's rights reformers, the paper saved its most hate-mongering invective for Rose. Its diatribe rested entirely on sexist, racist, and anti-immigrant rhetoric, and warned against the infidel Rose's "efforts to obliterate from the world the religion of the Cross"—whether because she was a Jew or an atheist, or both, is not clear. Rose ably and immediately defended herself, and the work of all reformers and freedom fighters. In a letter to the editor that is a model of eloquent restraint, considering the article that inspired it, she used language that she frequently employed to praise the values of her adopted country, while urging greater efforts to live up to those values. Rose's letter is dated March 7; the date of its publication has not been verified.

❧

## "WOMAN'S RIGHTS IN THE LEGISLATURE," *ALBANY REGISTER*

While the feminine propagandists of women's rights confined themselves to the exhibition of short petticoats and long-legged boots, and to the holding of Conventions, and speech-making in concert-rooms, the people were disposed to be amused by them, as they are by the wit of the clown in the circus, or the performances of Punch and Judy on fair days, or the minstrelsy of gentlemen with blackened faces, on banjos, the tambourine, and bones. But the joke is becoming stale. People are getting cloyed with these performances, and are looking for some healthier and more intellectual amusement. The ludicrous is wearing away, and disgust is taking the place of pleasurable sensations, arising from the novelty of this new phase of hypocrisy and infidel fanaticism. People are beginning to inquire how far public sentiment should sanction or tolerate these unsexed women, who make a scoff of religion, who repudiate the Bible and blaspheme God; who would step out from the true sphere of the mother, the wife, and the daughter, and taking upon themselves the duties and the business of men, stalk into the public gaze, and by engaging in the politics, the

rough controversies, and trafficking of the world, upheave existing institutions, and overturn all the social relations of life.

It is a melancholy reflection, that among our American women who
have been educated to better things, there should be found any who are
willing to follow the lead of such foreign propagandists as the ringleted,
glove-handed exotic, Ernestine L. Rose. We can understand how such
men as the Rev. Mr. May, or the sleek-headed Dr. Channing may be
deluded by her to becoming her disciples. They are not the first instances
of infatuation that may overtake weak-minded men, if they are honest
in their devotion to her and her doctrines. Nor would they be the first
examples of a low ambition that seeks notoriety as a substitute for true
fame, if they are dishonest. Such men there are always, and honest or dishonest, their true position is that of being tied to the apron-strings of
some "strong-minded woman," and to be exhibited as rare specimens of
human wickedness, or human weakness and folly. But, that one educated
American woman should become her disciple and follow her infidel and
insane teachings, is a marvel.

Ernestine L. Rose came to this country, as she says; from Poland,
whence she was compelled to fly in pursuit of freedom. Seeing her course
here, we can well imagine this to be true. In no other country in the world,
save possibly one, would her infidel propagandism and preachings in regard
to the social relations of life be tolerated. She would be prohibited by the
powers of government from her efforts to obliterate from the world the
religion of the Cross—to banish the Bible as a text-book of faith, and to
overturn social institutions that have existed through all political and gov-
ernmental revolutions from the remotest time. The strong hand of the law
would be laid upon her, and she would be compelled back to her woman's
sphere. But in this country, such is the freedom of our institutions, and we
rejoice that it should be so, that she, and such as she, can give their genius
for intrigue full sway. They can exhibit their flowing ringlets and beautiful
hands, their winning smiles and charming stage attitudes to admiring audiences, who, while they are willing to be amused, are in the main safe from
their corrupting theories and demoralizing propagandism.

The laws and the theory of our government suppose that the people
are capable of taking care of themselves, and hence need no protection
against the wiles of domestic or foreign mountebanks, whether in petticoats or in breeches and boots. But it never was contemplated that these
exotic agitators would come up to our legislators and ask for the passage
of laws upholding and sanctioning their wild and foolish doctrines. That
was a stretch of folly, a flight of impudence which was hardly regarded as
possible. It was to be imagined, of course, that they would enlist as their

followers, here and there one among the restless old maids and visionary wives who chanced to be unevenly tempered, as well as unevenly yoked. It was also to be assumed, as within the range of possibility, that they might bring within the sphere of their attractions, weak-minded, restless men, who think in their vanity that they have been marked out for great things, and failed to be appreciated by the world, men who comb their hair smoothly back, and with fingers locked across their stomachs, speak in a soft voice, and with upturned eyes. But no man supposed they would abandon their "private theatricals" and walk up to the Capitol, and insist that the performances shall be held in legislative halls. And yet so it is.

This Mrs. Ernestine L. Rose, with a train of followers, like a great kite with a very long tail, has, for a week, been amusing Senatorial and Assembly Committees, with her woman's rights performances, free of charge, unless the waste of time that might be better employed in the necessary and legitimate business of legislation, may be regarded as a charge. Those committees have sat for hours, grave and solemn as owls, listening to the outpourings of fanaticism and folly of this Polish propagandist, Mrs. Ernestine L. Rose, and her followers in pantalets and short gowns. The people outside, and especially those interested in the progress of legislation, are beginning to ask one another how long this farce is to continue. How long this most egregious and ridiculous humbug is to be permitted to obstruct the progress of business before the Committees and the Houses, and whether Mrs. Ernestine L. Rose and her followers ought not to be satisfied with the notoriety they have already attained. The great body of the people regard Mrs. Rose and her followers as making themselves simply ridiculous, and there is some danger that these legislative committees will make themselves so too.

## RESPONSE BY ERNESTINE L. ROSE

Mr. Editor: In your paper of Monday the 6th inst., I perceive you pass judgment upon the woman's rights cause, upon those engaged in it, and particularly upon myself—how justly, I leave to your conscience to decide.

Every one who ever advanced a new idea, no matter how great and noble, has been subjected to criticism, and therefore we too must expect it. And, in accordance with the spirit of the critic, will be the criticism. Whether dictated by the spirit of justice, kindness, gentleness, and charity, or by injustice, malice, rudeness, and intolerance, it is still an index of the man. But it is quite certain that no true soul will ever be deterred from the performance of a duty by any criticism.

But there is one thing which I think even editors have no right to do, namely: to state a positive falsehood, or even to imply one, for the purpose of injuring another. And, as the spirit of charity induces me to believe that in your case it was done more from a misunderstanding than positive malice, therefore I claim at your hands the justice to give this letter a place in your paper.

In the article alluded to, you say: "Ernestine L. Rose came to this country, as she says, from Poland, whence she was compelled to fly in pursuit of freedom." It is true that I came from Poland; but it is false that I was compelled to fly from my country, except by the compulsion, or dictates of the same spirit of "propagandism," that induced so many of my noble countrymen to shed their blood in the defence of the rights of this country, and the rights of man, wherever he struggles for freedom. But I have no desire to claim martyrdom which does not belong to me. I left my country, not flying, but deliberately. I chose to make this country my home, in preference to any other, because if you carried out the theories you profess, it would indeed be the noblest country on earth. And as my countrymen so nobly aided in the physical struggle for Freedom and Independence, I felt, and still feel it equally my duty to use my humble abilities to the uttermost in my power, to aid in the great moral struggle for human rights and human freedom.

Hoping that you will accede to my (I think) just claim to give this a place in your paper.

I am, very respectfully,
Ernestine L. Rose
New York, Mar. 7, 1854

# DIARY OF LECTURE TOUR TO THE BORDER SOUTH WITH ERNESTINE L. ROSE

*By Susan B. Anthony*

March 24–April 14, 1854

Washington, D.C.; Northern Virginia; Baltimore,
Maryland; and Philadelphia, Pennsylvania

Almost immediately after the legislative hearings in Albany, Rose and Anthony set out on a lecture tour to the nation's capital and surrounding states in the Border South region, with the goal of "bringing women's rights to the South." By then, Rose was already an experienced and renowned orator. Anthony, who was just beginning to be active in the women's rights movement, used her considerable skills for organizing and planning to manage the tour.

Excerpts from the diary of Susan B. Anthony are included in this volume on Rose because Anthony's observations, as a colleague and friend, writing in her private journal, provide an important perspective on Rose from a contemporary who was her colleague in reform and who traveled with her; their challenging mission to spread the ideas of women's rights in the nation's capital and the Border South.

Rose had been pressing for the next national women's rights convention to be held in Washington, D.C., later that year, hoping to use the opportunity to influence Congress (Kolmerten 1999, 140–41), but instead Philadelphia had been chosen as the convention site. Rose was determined to be heard by lawmakers nevertheless. The women's request for use of a hall at the Capitol building was refused by the chaplain, on the grounds that Rose "failed to recognize the Divine." DuBois (2001, 13) has written with great empathy on the irony of Anthony's later attempting to comfort Rose with the gift of a church program when she had been excluded from the nation's capital as a Jew and an atheist. Then, Anthony rented a room at Carusi's Saloon, an elegant public assembly hall near the National Mall. Rose spoke the first night to 100 people, but by the third night to an audience of 500, including many members of Congress. Nonetheless, the tour lost money (Kolmerten 1999, 142–46). After Washington, D.C., the women traveled to northern Virginia and Baltimore, where they witnessed slavery firsthand. On their way back to New York they stopped in Philadelphia, where they met with prominent reformers. Their experiences and conversations were faithfully recorded by Anthony, an inveterate diarist, letter-writer, and scrapbook-keeper, whose personal papers have become a primary source of information about the early fight for women's rights, and the women who waged it.

It was while on this tour together that Rose felt comfortable enough to tell Anthony of her feelings upon hearing at the convention at Syracuse in 1852 that Lucy Stone and Wendell Phillips were opposed to allowing foreigners to vote.

**March 24**

Directed tickets to Mrs. Rose Meeting on Political and Legal Rights of Woman this evening at Carusi's Saloon, to both Representatives and Senators, in all about 300 in number. Asked the Speaker of the House for the use of the Capitol on Sunday A.M. He referred me to Mr. Milburn the Chaplain. Called on him. He could not allow her to speak there because she was not a member of some religious society. I remarked to him that ours was a country professing Religious as well as Civil Liberty and not to allow any and every faith to be declared in the Capitol of the nation, made the profession to religious freedom a perfect mockery. Though acknowledging the truthfulness of my position, he could not allow a person, who failed to recognize the Divine, to speak in his place. . . .

**March 26**

Went to the Capitol and listened to Mr. Milburn on Home Life. He said many good things and many things that indicated gross ignorance, misrepresentation. Said "It is here in the home that most men and all women's chiefest duties lie." . . .

Called also at Gerrit Smith's . . . [a well-known abolitionist, philanthropist, member of Congress, and cousin to Elizabeth Cady Stanton].

Mr. Smith said he wished to share with us in the pecuniary loss of one meeting and insisted on my accepting a Bill which I afterward learned to be a $20 bank note. Expressed himself very glad that Mrs. R. had come to Washington. . . .

**March 29**

Left Washington at 1/4 to 9 o'clock for Mt. Vernon, where we arrived about 1 o'clock. The weather cold and windy, but more mild than the day before. The location of Washington's home is most beautiful and commanding, but, oh, the air of dilapidation and decay that everywhere meets the eye, the tottering out-buildings, the mark of slavery o'ershadow[ing] the whole. Oh, the thought that it was here, that he whose name is the pride of this nation was the *Slave Master*. The humorous, little buildings surrounding, or rather in [the] rear of the great house plainly tell the tale—a Slave, Woman, the cook of the present owner, Grand Nephew of Gen. Washington, told me these buildings were the Servants' Quarters.

The tomb is humble indeed. It would seem that, if the profession of reverence for the "Father of his Country" were *real*, that this home of Washington would be rescued from the curse of slave labor, and made to blossom in the sunshine of free labor. . . .

(P.M.) This noon, I ate my dinner without once asking myself, are these human beings who minister to my wants *Slaves* to be bought and sold and hired out at the will of a master? And when the thought first entered my mind, I said, even I am getting *accustomed* to *Slavery*, so much so that I ceased continually to be made to feel its blighting, cursing influence, so much so that I can sit down and eat from the hand of the bondsman, without being once mindful of the fact that he is such.

Oh Slavery, hateful thing that thou art, thus to blunt the keen edge of men's conscience, even while they strive to shun thy poisonous touch.

I learn to-day that the present owner of Mt. Vernon is an *intemperate* man. This fact added to slave holding accounts for the ruinous state of the Plantation.

A white woman here, a slave holder, says she frequently gets perfectly disgusted with Slavery, the *Licentiousness* between the White men and the Slave women is so universal and so revolting, *free* colored women will boast of rooming with a white man for a whole week. The Proprietor of this City Hotel hires slaves of their masters. . . .

**March 30**
Baltimore . . . There is no promptness, no order, no anything about these Southerners. I have had Pro Slavery People tell me just go South once, and see Slavery as it is, and then you will talk very differently. I can assure all such, that contact with Slavery has not a tendency to make me hate it less. No, the ruinous effect of the institution upon the white man alone causes me to hate it. . . .

. . . finally decided to take rooms at Mrs. Waters, 49 Hanover.

Every thing is plain but so far seems cleanly. Learned from the chambermaid Sarah that she and others of the Servants were Slaves. It is perfectly astonishing to see what an array of Servants there is about every establishment. Three Northern girls, with the engineering of a Northern boarding house keeper would do all the work of one dozen of these men, women and children, whether slaves or free. Such is the baneful effect of slavery upon labor.

The free blacks who receive wages, expect to do no more work than do the *slaves*. Slave labor is the standard and it needs but a glance at Southern life to enable an Abolitionist to understand why it is that the Northern man is a more exacting slave master than is a Southern one. He requires of the slave an amount of labor equal to that he has been accustomed to get from the well paid Northern free laborer. . . .

**April 2**
A little colored boy came into our room with Sarah, the Chambermaid.

Said Mrs. R., whose boy is that, Sarah? He belongs to Mrs. Waters, Miss. Where is his mother? She is Cook in the kitchen, Miss. Where is his Father? On the Eastern Shore, Miss. Is he a Slave? Yes, Miss. Does he come to see his wife? No, Miss, not since my mistress moved to the City. Has the Cook any more children? Yes, Miss, two more little boys younger than this. Oh, how did my blood run chill.

Before this I said to Sarah, are you *free*, Sarah? No, Miss! Do you belong to Mrs. Waters? No, Miss, she hires me of my Master for $8 per month. And don't you get any portion of it? No, Miss, only my Master gives me my clothes. Does he keep you well clothed? Sometimes, Miss, and sometimes I gets short. And don't you have any pocket money of your own? Yes, Miss, what the ladies gives me. Sarah is a bright girl, fine expression of face. Oh how I long to probe her soul in search of that Divine spark that scorns to be a slave. But then would it be right for me by so doing to add to the burden of her wretched life?

## April 4

Mrs. Rose meeting small. Sold only about 54 tickets. Some 60 free tickets present. The people are so *afraid* that some thing will be said on Slavery that they will not countenance the meeting, and more than that there is at the bottom a sad want of intelligence. Science and literature have no charms for them any more than the Reforms. . . .

## April 6

I lectured this evening by invitation from the Marion Temperance Society of Baltimore. Had a full house. The meeting was called to order by the President of the Society and opened by prayer by an old man who made the stereotype prayer of Stephen S. Foster's Slave holder—"O Lord, we thanks thee, that our lives have been cast in places and that we live in a land where every man can sit under his own vine and fig tree, and none dare to molest or make him afraid." Oh, how did my blood boil within me and then to go on with my lecture and not protest against a man's telling the Lord such terrible falsehoods. . . .

## April 8

. . . Went out to the Post Office, found no letter, feel very much disappointed at not hearing from home while here this week. Got the Morning Papers, and gave most of the Editors a copy of Mrs. Stanton's Address [to the New York Assembly]. . . .

Mrs. R. and myself were talking of the *know nothing* organizations [the anti-immigrant American Party], when she criticized Lucy Stone and Wendell Philips with regard to their feelings toward foreigners. Said she had heard them both express themselves in terms of prejudice against granting to foreigners the rights of Citizenship.

I expressed disbelief as to either of them having that narrow, mean prejudice in their souls. She then said I was blinded and could see nor hear nothing wrong in that clique of Abolitionists. She thought she, being connected with no Society or association, either in religion or reforms, could judge all impartially. I then ventured to say that Kossuth's non committal course while in this country, it seemed to me, she did not criticize as she would an American. She thought she did, and could see reasons why he pursued the course he did. [Kossuth was a Hungarian freedom fighter who came to the United States to gain support for the struggle in Hungary, but avoided criticism of slavery in order not to alienate potential supporters in the south.] Yes, said I, you excuse him, because you can see the causes why he acted and spoke thus, while you will not allow me to bring forward the probable cause of Lucy's seeming fault. It seemed to *me* that *she* could not ascribe *pure motives* to any of our Reformers, and while to her it seemed that I was blindly bound to see no fault, however glaring. At length in the anguish of my soul, I said, Mrs. Rose, there is not *one* in the Reform ranks, whom you think true, not one but whom panders to the popular feeling. She answered, I can't help it. I take them by the words of their own mouths. I trust all until their words or acts declare them false to truth and right and, continued she, no one can tell the hours of anguish I have suffered, as one after another I have seen, those whom I had trusted, betray falsity of motive as I have been compelled to place one after another on the list of panderers to public favor. Said I, do you know Mrs. Rose, that I can but feel that you place me too on that list. Said she, I will tell you when I see you untrue. A silence ensued. While I copied the verse from the hymn sung in Church this A.M., and subscribed it Susan B. Anthony, for her dear friend Ernestine L. Rose, as I handed it to her, I observed tears in her eyes. Said I, Mrs. Rose, have I been wicked and hurt your feelings? She answered, no, but I expect never to be understood while I live. Her anguish was extreme. I too wept, for it filled my soul with anguish to see one so noble, so true (even though I felt I could not comprehend her) so bowed down, so overcome with deep swelling emotions. At length she said, no one knows how I have suffered from not being understood. [I said] I know you must suffer and heaven forbid that I should add a feather's weight to your burdens.

Mrs. Rose is not appreciated, nor cannot be by this age. She is too much in advance of the extreme ultraists even, to be understood by them. Almost every reformer feels that the odium of his own ultraisms is as much as he is able to bear and therefore shrinks from being identified with one in whose view their ultraism is sheer conservatism. This fact has been most plainly brought home to me. Every[one] says, "I am *ultra enough*, the mercy knows; I don't want to seem any more so by identifying myself with one whose every sentiment is so shocking to the public mind." . . .

## April 11
Philadelphia . . . Contrary to Mrs. R['s] expectation, Mrs. Mott expressed herself in favor of having a meeting, and Mr. Mott sallied out forthwith to secure a Hall, Spring Garden Institute for Thursday and Samson St. Hall for Friday evening. It seems quite good to me to have some one take the burden off my shoulders. . . .

## April 13
I went to the Female Anti Slavery Society. In attendance was a young lady, Virginia ————, of Maryland. She and her sister had left them by their Father, *three* slaves worth $1000, each of whom they set at liberty. Beside these three, their Father left 13 slaves, all of whom save one they have been instrumental in freeing. This one is a Cooper, and belongs to their only brother, who is ill and not expected to live long. He has an offer of $800 for the slave but tells the girls, if they can give him $400 he will take it and thus set the last of the 16 at liberty. Virginia has raised over $200 and I hope she may succeed in getting the remaining $200. In consequence of their Slaves, she and her sister have been compelled to resort to day labor. She has a fine expressive face. It is indeed noble to see two such young girls make such a sacrifice of their all. . . .

## April 14
Dined at James Motts. Abby Gibbons, Sarah Grimpke [Grimké], Thomas Curtis, [and other] invited guests. . . . We had a . . . chat, spiritualism as usual being the principle topic. Mrs. Rose and Mr. Curtis believing the spirit inseparable from the body, of course, were on the unbelieving side while Sarah Grimpke was all enthusiasm in the faith. . . . The rest of the company, with myself, seemed not to know whether or not there is any truth in these modern manifestations.

Mrs. R returned . . . immediately after dinner to rest for the meeting to be held at Samson's Street Hall. I remained and with Lucretia [Mott] and Sarah Grimpke and myself on one side and Thomas Curtis on the other had an argument as to the probable future existence of the mind or soul or spirit of man. Not an argument could one of us bring other than an intuitive feeling that we were not to cease to exist when the body dies. While Mr. Curtis reasoned (as has Mrs. Rose often done with me) that all things in Nature die, or rather that the elements of all things are separated and assume new forms, then if the soul, the vital spark of man lives eternally so must the essence of the tree, the animal, the fern and the flower. There certainly is no argument to be brought against such reasonings. But if it be true that we die like the flower, leaving behind, only the fragrance . . . while the elements that compose us go to form new bodies, what a delusion has the race ever been in, What a dream is the life of Man. . . .

# LETTER TO THE EDITOR:
## "SLAVERY AND REFORM"

By Susan B. Anthony
April 14, 1854
Baltimore, Maryland

In April 1854, Susan B. Anthony wrote a letter to the *Liberator*, William Lloyd Garrison's abolitionist newspaper, reporting on her women's rights tour with Rose through the Border South states. The trip demanded great courage from both women, not only because women's rights reformers had not traveled south before, but also because Rose was not willing to side-step the issue of slavery when it was raised, as was expected in the slave states in deference to their "pet institution." In her letter, Anthony describes Rose as "an out and out abolitionist."

Anthony describes one lecture in which Rose built an argument for "disunion." Radical abolitionists were actually the first secessionists, believing that separating North and South was preferable to accepting the demands and manipulations of the slave-owning states in the interests of preserving the union. A particularly egregious example was the compromise reached on the "Nebraska Question." The Kansas-Nebraska Bill was introduced by Stephen Douglas, the Democratic senator from Illinois (and future rival of Abraham Lincoln—who himself rose to national prominence by opposing the bill). The bill sought to curry favor with the South and encourage settlement in the territories by permitting each new state to vote slavery up or down. Its passage, later in 1854, superseded the Missouri Compromise of 1820, which had held the spread of slavery in check. At the New England Anti-Slavery Convention in Boston the following year, Rose would describe this event in Washington as a turning point in her thinking on disunion: "[W]hen I went home from that lecture, I said to a friend of mine, 'If I have not succeeded in convincing anyone else, I have succeeded,—and I am very happy to know it,—in convincing myself.'"

Anthony kept close track of how their tour was received in the local press. At one point, she takes issue with a Washington newspaper for misunderstanding and misstating Rose's views; she also accuses some of the antislavery press in the area of not covering Rose's speeches because she was a woman and a non-Christian. Anthony's report to the *Liberator*, written in the form of a letter to its editor, Garrison, appeared under the heading "Slavery and Reform" in the issue of April 14, 1854.

❧

Baltimore, April 1854

Dear Mr. Garrison:

From the land of slavery I write. There is no mistaking the fact. The saddening, hateful evidences are on every side. Pro-slavery people, both of the North and the South, have often said to me, "Just go South, and see slavery as it really is, and you will cease to speak of it as you now do." How strangely blind must that person be, who hates slavery less, by coming in closer contact with its degrading influences! How wanting in true nobility of soul must he be, who can hear a human being speak of himself as being the property of another, without evincing the least discontent! How unworthy the boon of freedom is the man who sees himself surrounded, for the first time, with beings wearing the human form, from whose faces slavery has blotted out almost every token of that Divine spark within, that aspires to a higher, a nobler life, that scorns to be a thing,—and, from the very depths of his soul, hates not slavery more than it were possible for him ever to have done before! I hate slavery less? Heaven forbid!

I have been traveling in company with Ernestine L. Rose the past three weeks, during which time Mrs. Rose has lectured on Woman's Rights in Washington, Alexandria and Baltimore. Her meetings have all been but thinly attended, compared with our Northern meetings. Still, the people here call the audiences large, and quite equal to the number who usually attend literary or scientific lectures. But few people here seem to be in the least interested in any subject of reform. The only thing that in any way alarms them is the fear that some word shall be uttered which shall endanger their "pet institution." In making application for a hall in this city, the proprietor said to me, "You know we are a sensitive people, and don't like to allow persons to speak in our halls, who will introduce topics foreign to those they announce." I said, "I suppose you refer to the subject of slavery?" He answered, "Yes." "Well, sir, I wish you to understand that Mrs. Rose is an out and out abolitionist. She is here now to speak on Woman's Rights, and wishes the hall for that purpose; but if she should feel disposed, as I hope she will, to give an anti-slavery lecture, she will duly inform all parties concerned of her intentions." Thus is it with the editors, and thus is it with the people. All are afraid of us; if we don't say any thing, our very presence seems to arouse their suspicions. Still, notwithstanding this ever-present apprehension lest a word shall be dropped touching the *tender* subject, all the editors, in the different cities we have visited, have been very respectful in their notices of Mrs. Rose, both before and after her meetings.

Mrs. Rose's third lecture in Washington was on the "Nebraska Question, as deduced from Human Rights." The only paper that reported any thing of her speech was the *Washington Globe*, which, though it spoke most highly of her as a lecturer, misrepresented her, by ascribing to *her* the arguments of the South. She did not say that "she was aware that it was almost an utter impossibility, in the present state of society, to bring about the abolition of slavery." Nor did she say that "the slaveholder could no more be expected to relinquish his hold on his slaves, than the Northern capitalist to relinquish is grasp upon his bag of hard-earned dollars"; but that she knew such were the arguments of the South. Mrs. Rose's whole speech was marked with bold denunciation of the institution that robs man of his first inalienable right—the right to himself. She said that there was no possible argument that could have a feather's weight in the balance against human freedom, and that, though no advocate of disunion, still, if she were convinced that slavery could be abolished by a dissolution of the Union, she would rather see, not only the North separate from the South, but State from State, and city from city, than that the curse of slavery should longer continue.

While Mrs. R. could see some reasons why the South should desire an acquisition of slave territory, in the well-known fact that their lands are impoverished by slave labor, there was no excuse for the North. She could feel pity and commiseration for some men of the South, while for Northern recreants she felt the most utter contempt. She said the introduction of the Nebraska bill, and its consequent agitation throughout the Union, would be productive of great good to the cause of freedom, it mattered not whether it was passed or not. She commented severely on Douglas and consigned him on the fate of John Mitchel [an Irish nationalist who escaped to the United States where he edited a pro-slavery journal], and all others before him, who have attempted to get themselves place or power, by pandering to the prejudices of the South.

Strange is it may seem, the *National Era*, the only paper in Washington that makes any professions of being on the side of human freedom, took no notice of the fact of Mrs. Rose having spoken in that city on the subject of slavery. Can it be possible that its editor's love for the poor down-trodden slave is so weak as to allow the prejudices of sect or sex to hold it in abeyance? Can it be that he panders to the narrow, mean, bigoted sectarianism that recognizes no anti-slavery, save that bounded by 'time-worn creeds,' no divine right of utterance, save that of *man* alone?

I speak this evening on the subject of Temperance by invitation from the "Marion Temperance Society," of this city, of which Dr. J. E. Snodgrass is a member, and the Society which fully sustained him in contending for the right of woman in the "*Half-*World's Temperance Convention" last September.

Mrs. Rose gives her last lecture in Baltimore to-morrow evening, after which we return to New York, stopping only at Philadelphia.

May the day soon come when justice and equality shall be fully established between all mankind without distinction of sex or color!

Susan B. Anthony

# SPEECH AT THE FIFTH NATIONAL WOMAN'S RIGHTS CONVENTION: "A GREAT AND IMMUTABLE TRUTH"
### October 18, 1854
### Philadelphia, Pennsylvania

Rose was president at the 1854 National Woman's Rights Convention, held in Philadelphia. Presiding in the city where the founding documents of the nation were signed provided a perfect opportunity for Rose to link women's struggle for their rights to the American Revolution and to the founding "principles of the nation." In this speech, she argues that both the Declaration of Independence and its "great and immutable truth" of inalienable rights, as well as the treasured national creed of "no taxation without representation" demand that women be given equal rights with men. Rose had been making these arguments based on the foundational principles of the republic since 1836 in her speeches called the "Science of Government": these were credited by the next generation of suffragists as fundamental to the women's rights movement (National American Woman Suffrage Association 1940, Appendix 3, 159).

The *New York Tribune*, reporting on the 1854 convention, praised Rose's eloquence and ability as chair of a public meeting: "Mrs. Rose, the President, did her duties with great dignity, and her occasional short addresses showed wide experience, and a more highly cultivated mind, perhaps, than any of the other ladies possessed."

⤙⤚

There is one argument which in my estimation is the argument of arguments, why woman should have her rights; not on account of expediency, not on account of policy, though these too show the reasons why she should have her rights; but we claim—I for one claim, and I presume all our friends claim—our rights on the broad ground of human rights; and I for one again will say, I promise not how we shall use them. I will no more promise how we shall use our rights than man has promised before he obtained them, how he would use them. We all know that rights are often abused; and above all things have human rights in this country been abused, from the very fact that they have been withheld from half of the community.

By human rights we mean natural rights, and upon that ground we claim our rights, and upon that ground they have already been conceded by the Declaration of Independence, in that first great and immutable truth which is proclaimed in that instrument, "that all men are created equal," and that therefore all are entitled to "certain inalienable rights, among which are life, liberty, and the pursuit of happiness." Our claims are based upon that great and immutable truth, the rights of all humanity. For is woman not included in that phrase, "all men are created free and equal"? Is she not included in that expression? Tell us, ye men of the nation, ay, ye wise law-makers and law-breakers of the nation, whether woman is not included in that great Declaration of Independence? And if she is, what right has man to deprive her of her natural and inalienable rights? It is natural, it is inherent, it is inborn, it is a thing of which no one can justly deprive her. Upon that just and eternal basis do we found our claims for our rights; political, civil, legal, social, religious, and every other.

But, at the outset, we claim our equal political rights with man, not only from that portion of the Declaration of Independence, but from another, equally well-established principle in this country, that "taxation and representation are inseparable." Woman, everybody knows, is taxed; and if she is taxed, she ought to be represented.

I will simply here throw out a statement of these principles upon which our claims are based; and I trust each separate resolution will be taken up by this Convention, fully canvassed and commented upon, so as to show it not only an abstract right, but a right which can be wisely made practical.

Again, it is acknowledged in this country, and it is eternally true, that "all the just powers of government are derived from the consent of the governed." If so, then, as woman is a subject of government, she ought to have a voice in enacting the laws. If her property is taxed to maintain government, she ought to have a voice in forming that government. If she has to pay taxes to maintain government, she ought to have a voice in saying how those taxes shall be applied.

On these grounds we make our claims, on natural, humane, eternal, and well-recognized laws and principles of this republic. On these grounds we ask man to meet us, and meet us in the spirit of inquiry, in the spirit of candor and honesty, as rational human beings ought to meet each other, face to face, and adduce arguments, if they can, to convince us that we are not included in that great Declaration of Independence; that although it is a right principle that taxation and representation are inseparable, yet woman ought to be taxed, and ought not to be represented; and that although it is an acknowledged principle that all just power of government is derived from the consent of the governed, yet woman should be governed without her consent. Let them meet us fairly and openly, let them meet us like rational men, men who appreciate their own freedom, and we will hear them. If they can convince us that we are wrong, we will give up our claims; but if we can convince them that we are right in claiming our rights, as they are in claiming theirs, then we expect them in a spirit of candor and honesty to acknowledge it.

# SPEECH AT THE THOMAS PAINE
# CELEBRATION: "THE RIGHTS OF WOMAN"
January 29, 1855
New York, New York

Early in what was to become her most prolific year, Rose attended the annual Thomas Paine Celebration, where she responded to a toast to "The Ladies—May they have the courage to express their opinions, and talent to command attention." Rose offered a witty dinner speech that nonetheless had serious intent. Lacking neither courage, opinions, nor talent, Rose demonstrated that the "Rights of Man," as outlined in Paine's famous work, had always included the rights of woman. She asked those present to sign two petitions that she had brought with her from her recent lecture tour of New York State.

Later in the evening, Rose would make a second, brief toast: "Robert Owen—Though a convert to Spiritualism, may he long deprive the spirits of any other world of his valuable and interesting company, for the benefit of the spirits of this world." Word of Owen's adoption of spiritualist beliefs must have recently reached Rose in New York. A year and a half later in London, she was able to discuss this emerging difference between them in person and then wrote about it for the *Boston Investigator* (see *1856 July 6*, Travel Letter No. 2). A few years later, at a "Free Convention" of radicals and reformers in Rutland, Vermont, Rose was asked whether she had been swayed from her materialist views by Owen's embrace of spiritualism. Rose responded that, if Owen himself had told her he had seen a three-decker building pulled through the streets of New York by a mouse, she would say to him: " I believe that you believe you have seen it, but that can be no authority for me [Hear! Hear!]" (Kolmerten 1999, 205).

An account of the evening, including transcripts of the toast and speeches, appeared in the *Boston Investigator* on February 14, 1855.

⁓

My friends—I am happy to have met with you once more on this interesting occasion; it is indeed delightful to meet where the old and the young can unite in social and intellectual enjoyment. What a pity the world had only one Thomas Paine! . . . I cannot help regretting that there were not at least fifty-two so as to celebrate one birth-day every week. I would not object to call them Sabbath or rest, not exactly such as instituted by the church, who, while it compels us to refrain from labor, provides us with no other recreation than to doze or yawn in a richly cushioned pew, or fare worse, and receive a copious dose of brimstone from some good old Orthodox, brimstone-loving minister. But I mean one evening in the week, to cast off the burden of business, leave the god of Mammon to take care of himself, and the golden calf, at whose shrine every one bends not only the knee, but alas! the head and heart too, and meet in intellectual and social union, to unbend the head and open the heart for the reception of enjoyment and to impart it to others as the only basis of our own. . . .

I have just returned from a lecturing tour in ten counties of this State, and I feel that the mind wants rest as well as the body. I have interrupted my journey for the pleasure of being with you this evening; for when the heart and head are severely taxed, they require social recreation to restore a healthy equilibrium to the system. The object of my mission was to rouse the people to the presumptive evidence that the immutable truth upon which the Declaration of Independence is based, and which immortalizes the name of Thomas Jefferson, namely, that "all men are created equal, and endowed with inalienable rights to life, liberty, and the pursuit of happiness," includes woman too. Self evident as this truth is, yet it is no easy task to enforce it upon minds who never had a correct conception of the true principles upon which alone a republic can securely stand, who are so thoroughly Know-Nothing as to be ignorant that human rights recognize no sex, country, or color.—It is easier to win a battle than to conquer minds filled with Know-Nothingism. [The American Party popularly known as the Know-Nothing movement was a powerful but short-lived U.S. political force that was nativist, anti-immigrant, and especially anti-Catholic. It was at its height in 1855.] It requires far more true courage and persevering heroism to carry on a moral war than a physical one. It is much easier to take a fortress, composed even of granite, than to storm a citadel of prejudice sanctified by superstition, engrafted by age, and strengthened by habit; and well might those who are engaged in this moral war exclaim: "These are the times that try women's souls." [The famous phrase "These are the times that try men's souls" was the opening line from the first of a series of pamphlets, titled *The American Crisis*, that Thomas Paine began writing in 1776, after the start of the American Revolution.]

. . . . . .

But we have one great advantage over physical war, for while the breaks and inroads the Allied armies make on the walls of Sebastopol are constantly filled up and repaired by the enemy, the breaks and inroads we make on the stronghold of conservatism, ignorance, and error, can never again be repaired; a breach once made goes on widening of itself, every stone removed helps to undermine the foundation until the whole superstructure will crumble at our feet. [The Siege of Sebastopol was a turning point in the Crimean War (1853–1856), which pitted Imperial Russia against the Allied forces of Britain, France, and the Ottoman Empire.]

But I will draw my remarks to a practical conclusion. I am a great admirer of the wisdom of Solomon; and he said there is a time and a season for all things. Now it seems to me that a celebration to commemorate the birth day of the author of the "Rights of Man," is just the time to do something for the "rights of women," and I feel myself in the position of the Frenchman, who, on seeing a crowd gathered around a poor man, for whom they expressed much sympathy, took a dollar from his pocket, and said, "I pity him with one dollar; with how much do you pity him?" Friends, I honor the author of the Rights of Man, with the endeavor to promote the rights of woman, and I hope you will evince your devotion to him by giving us your signatures to two petitions to be sent to our Legislature—one for the just and equal rights to property, offspring, a trial by a jury of our peers, etc., and the other for the elective franchise; and if you don't wish to sign both, then give us your names to the elective franchise, for if we have that secured to us, we will take good care to secure to us all the rest.

Thus, my friends, as I fully appreciated the sentiment given to the ladies, I have taken courage to express my opinions, and being conscious of the kind attention you paid to me, you must pardon me if I take it for granted that it is owing entirely to my talent to command it. But gentlemen, we wish to convince you that, while we claim equal rights, we are willing to return equal compliments, for politeness recognizes no sex. So, allow me to offer you, in the name of the ladies, the following toast:

The Gentlemen—May they have the wisdom to appreciate our opinions and the justice to acknowledge them.

# TESTIMONY BEFORE SELECT COMMITTEE OF THE NEW YORK STATE ASSEMBLY

By Boston Investigator
February 18, 1855
Albany, New York

In an effort to keep the pressure on the New York State Legislature, begun at the prior year's hearings, women's rights advocates returned to Albany in 1855. Under the heading "Just and Equal Rights of Women," the *Boston Investigator*, on March 14, 1855, reprinted an account published earlier in the *Albany Register*, reporting: "The select Committee of the Assembly to which was referred the petition for Woman's Rights . . . granted a hearing to the petitioners, who were represented by the Rev. Antoinette L. Brown, Miss Sarah [*sic*] B. Anthony, and Mrs. Ernestine L. Rose, in the Assembly Chamber, Saturday evening," February 18. The account described the testimony of Brown and Rose, who argued for improved child custody rights and other marital and inheritance rights, as well as the enfranchisement of women.

∼❧

Mrs. Ernestine L. Rose followed [Rev. Antoinette L. Brown], alluding first to the fundamental principle of our Revolutionary fathers, that "all men are created equal," and said, that under that principle, all that women asked had been granted already. She only asked in fact what is granted in theory—the right of life, liberty, and the pursuit of happiness. Will any one say woman is not included in that glorious Declaration? That principle required no sex, for it was based upon humanity and mind, and they know no sex. Happiness and misery, life and death, recognize no sex. In all the essentials of human life, woman is like man. Where the dividing line begins or ends, we need not seek to know. Her claims are based above these, and she claims nothing she ought not to possess, and she ought to take no less, for principle knows no compromise.

She repeated the idea, that without the right to the elective franchise, woman was not secure in the possession of any of her rights; and replied to the objections urged to it. She thought it time that woman helped man in securing peace and quiet at the ballot-box.

It was urged that woman, with political rights, would neglect her family. She replied that she would know better her duties to her family, and would the better discharge them. It was asked why, when woman was represented by her father, brother, and son, she should seek to represent herself? The question was worthy of consideration, but she claimed that even if not wronged by their representation, self-representation would be her right. But facts were stubborn things, and she could cite facts to show her position.

The statute-books say "he" and "his," and in but few instances "she" and "hers."

It is said, "husband and wife are one;" aye, said she, but that *one* is the *husband*. She wished they were truly one; if so, there would be far less reason for the claims she urged. When woman marries, in almost every sense she dies legally. If she commits crime in the presence of her husband, *he* is held responsible.—The laws make no distinction between man and man, but between man and woman. She is in our statute-books classed with infants and idiots.

The distinction should be between good men and bad men, between right and wrong, not between the sexes.

Mrs. R. noticed, in detail, the laws of our land, dwelling upon the property-features of existing laws respecting women. She alluded to the legal right possessed by the husband to take the earnings of his wife, and spend for liquor. The husband has entire control over her, and all business must be transacted in his name, let his character be ever so bad. She desired that woman be allowed to control her own earnings when the husband did not provide. It was just at least, that the laws pertaining to co-partnership, be applied to husbands and wives. The right of the husband to bind out the children without the consent of the mother, was a base injustice to woman.

She claimed equal rights for the mother in this particular, and urged the passage of a law upon these subjects, now before the Legislature.

Woman was a piece of property, belonging to father, guardian, or husband, transferred from one to the other—her feelings lacerated, from the cradle to the grave. And oppressions inflicted upon woman must fall back upon man. Her place was to furnish the foundation for the after-character of her child, and upon that child would be visited the effects of a mother's position and treatment. Human rights, human freedom was necessary to the ennobling of any human being. The claim of woman is not for herself alone; it is for society at large.

Mrs. R. denied that to man alone belonged the head, and to woman the heart, claiming that both head and heart were necessary for a human being, and that a figure of speech ought not to be the basis of our laws.

Woman never had the chance to prove what she might be. Insult is added to oppression when man says her capacity is unequal to his. It is yet to be seen, under a more favorable state of things, what her capacity is.

When woman has her full rights in forming and executing laws, her rights to property and her offspring, then will there be a union of the intellect and the sentiment in man and woman, and her real capacity can be truly estimated.

She protested against the injustice of the laws that give the wife only the use of one-third of the property at the death of her husband, but upon her death gives him all. And also against the implication, from that law, that the mother had not a heart for her children's wants as a father had.

She did not desire much legislation; we had too much already; but only that laws be just and equal. Right always rewards itself, and wrong punishes itself.

After the close of her remarks, members of the committee and individuals in the audience sent up quite a number of questions respecting the effect of granting to woman the elective franchise, which Mrs. Rose answered, in a characteristic manner, and greatly to the entertainment of the audience.

# SPEECH AT THE NEW ENGLAND ANTI-SLAVERY CONVENTION: "ALL FREE OR ALL SLAVE"

*By Ernestine L. Rose, with Comment*
*by Wendell Phillips*
May 30, 1855
Boston, Massachusetts

Rose brought unique perspectives to this convention. As she often did, she called upon her experience as an immigrant, contrasting the bright promise the United States represented to the "dark and bitter" reality of slavery. Her European background and education and her reading in science also gave her confidence to critique the racialized "science" that was used to justify slavery. While some who opposed slavery nevertheless accepted the inferiority of African Americans, Rose always insisted upon exposing and condemning not only slavery but racism in all its forms. In this speech, Rose also continues and extends her argument for disunion, insisting that while slavery exists anywhere in the nation, there are no "free states"—the United States can only be "all free or all slave." Concluding with an Owenite flourish, Rose hails "human freedom, irrespective of sex, or sect, or color, or country."

Others mentioned in Rose's speech include Anthony Burns, who escaped to Boston with the help of abolitionists resisting the Fugitive Slave Law of 1850 and Rev. Thomas Wentworth Higginson, a Unitarian minister, who was also a radical Garrisonian abolitionist who led the raid to free Burns when he was captured and imprisoned. A group of abolitionists subsequently contributed to purchase Burns's freedom. Higginson would go on to lead a Black regiment during the Civil War, and then to write of his experience.

Rose was followed on the platform by one of the greatest orators of the abolitionist movement, Wendell Phillips, who praised not only Rose's words but "the life behind it," saluting her early efforts in reform. Phillips's good looks, height, and patrician bearing enhanced his charisma. He was able to face down mobs, and to move audiences with the unaffected simplicity of his language. Both Higginson and Phillips were stalwart supporters of women's rights as well as abolition and other reforms.

Rose spoke against slavery many times and in a variety of settings, yet this speech is the only one I found that was given at an antislavery convention. This speech took place on the second day of the convention, which ran from May 29–31; it was published in the *Liberator* on June 8, 1855.

❧

It gives me unspeakable pleasure to have the opportunity to make my voice heard here before you in behalf of human freedom. It gives me, indeed, great satisfaction to be able to enter my protest against that terrible scourge that afflicts, not only the colored slave, nor, indeed, the South, but which afflicts the whole United States of America. It gives me great gratification in being able to do my duty in entering my protest against that eternal crime against humanity—the holding of a man as a slave; and also against that great incomprehensible inconsistency, that slavery should exist in a country that calls itself a Republic.

Mr. Higginson well vindicated here the position of Russia. Truth is consistent; Error is always inconsistent. Truth is a unit, consistent with itself, and consistent with every other truth. And as Truth is, so also is Freedom. Human freedom, also, is a unit, and consistent with itself, and where freedom is, slavery cannot be. In comparing the two countries, Russia and America—alas! that we should be able to institute a comparison between such a dark and benighted land and one that calls itself a Republic—yet, sad as the fact is, it is nevertheless true that in instituting a comparison between the two countries, Russia dark and benighted as she is, much as she oppresses man, we at least must give her the credit of consistency, for she professes no freedom; while here, with all the glorious professions of republicanism and freedom, the whole land is cursed with the odious system of slavery. I remember I was but a little child, hardly able to understand the import of words, that I had already listened to them who pronounced it the Republic of the United States of America; and even then, though entirely unable to appreciate the import, the nobility of it, yet, somehow or other, it touched a vibrating chord in my heart, and I thought, if I live to grow up a woman, O how I should like to see *a Republic*! (Applause)

I did grow up, and attained that great hope; and, friends, I well remember—I doubt whether I should ever forget—the sensations and emotions I experienced when I first placed my foot on the soil of a Republic;—nay, more, the first Fourth of July that I spent here. Why, everything in nature appeared to change and become superior. The sun shone brighter; the trees looked more beautiful; the grass looked greener; the birds sang sweeter; all the beauties of nature became enhanced in my estimation, for I viewed them all through the beautiful rainbow colors of human freedom. (Loud cheers.) Alas! I little knew then what I should experience if I remained longer. Had I left this country on the fifth of that July, I should have gone away with the glorious emotion that there was one spot of earth on the whole globe where a man may stand, and call himself fully and entirely his own. But I remained here too long; and what a change has 'come over the spirit of my dreams'! All the enchantments have disappeared, one by one. Not, indeed, the enchantments of what a Republic ought to be, or the beauties that would result from a true

Republic, but the enchantments of the idea that there was such a Republic in this new world. Instead of the poor fugitive from the old world coming to this place of refuge and calling himself a freeman, we have to send the poor fugitive from the new world to the old, to an aristocratic monarchical government and there however oppressed he may be in many instances, at least, he may call himself, his wife and children—except, indeed, in Russia—his own.

It gives me no pleasure, I assure you, my friends, to dwell upon the dark side of humanity. I wish I could always dwell upon the bright and fair side; but facts and truth always demand plain utterance. This country has sent forth to the world a great and glorious truth—that eternal truth of the equality of men upon which the Declaration of Independence is based—that "all men are created equal; and endowed with an inalienable right to life, liberty, and the pursuit of happiness." That declaration, wafted like a bright vision of hope on the breezes of heaven to the remotest parts of the earth, to whisper freedom and equality to the downtrodden millions of men. And yet, while that declaration is thus wafted by the genius of freedom all over the earth, here, under its shadow, the children that had been born and brought up here are subjected to dark and bitter bondage. This country, therefore stands before the moral consistency of the world, to be judged thereby. From monarchical and despotic countries we do not expect much; but those countries have a right to hold you to your professions. The Quakers say, that according to the light you possess is the demand made upon you. It is a true and correct saying. According to your professions, we have a right to hold you responsible; and therefore, this country stands responsible for its false and hypocritical professions without carrying out the great, eternal truth of the equality of man. (Cheers.)

You all know about the evils of slavery. It would be presumption, as well as folly, in me, even to describe what slavery is. No man can place himself in the position of the slave as adequately to describe the horrors of that relation. He only who has experienced them, and who has felt, at the same time, the flame of freedom burning within him, can tell what slavery is. I have heard many eloquent speeches from this platform, and from other anti-slavery platforms, but I was never so affected as I was this morning by the few simple words that fell from the lips of Anthony Burns. (Applause.) He stood here as a living, breathing, moving witness of the great iniquity of slavery. Only one year ago, he was doomed to slavery once more; and were it not that a few benevolent men were untiring and persistent in their determination to rescue him, cost what it would, Anthony Burns would not have been here this morning to give his evidence, as he did, to the large audience that, slave as he was, crushed and oppressed as he was, chained, not only in body, but also in mind, nevertheless, he was a man; for there was the love of freedom and the determined purpose to achieve it whenever the opportunity was afforded. And when he told of the pleasure he felt in being able to stand here, I appreciated it, I felt it; it touched my heart as no other speech, no matter from whose eloquent lips it fell, had ever touched me, and confirmed me in my estimation of the depth of infamy involved in keeping human beings in the darkness of bondage.

Who can tell what Anthony Burns might have been, had he been deemed free from the moment he drew his first breath? How often do we hear the South say that slaves are not the same as white men—that they are not human beings! Why, it is only as if it were yesterday that any portion of the slaveholders,—and not only the slaveholders at the South, but the slaveholders at the North,—acknowledged that the colored man is a human being at all. And there are many now who take that position. Even scientific men have come down from the glorious heights of science low enough to be bought by Southern gold, and endeavor to prove that the colored man is a different being from the white man, and therefore it is right to hold him as a slave. I will not attempt to enter into any consideration of this subject, for there is no need of it. Like or unlike, he is a human being; and I will use the same argument with regard to him that I use when pleading—no, not when pleading—when *claiming* the rights of woman. Like or unlike, he is a human being, and entitled to all the rights that humanity can bestow and man can enjoy. (Applause.) It is worse than time lost to enter into any such consideration, because human beings do not depend on the shade of color; they do not even depend on a somewhat different construction, or somewhat different shape of body, or somewhat different shape of mind. I will say of the slave, as I often say when claming the rights of woman—humanity recognizes no color, mind recognizes no color; pleasure or pain, happiness or misery, life or death, recognizes no color. Like the white man, the colored man comes involuntarily into existence. Like him, he possesses physical, moral, and mental powers, upon the proper cultivation of which depends his highest happiness. Like him, he is subject to all the vicissitudes of life. Like him, when he breaks the laws of his being he has to pay the penalty. Like him, when he breaks the laws of the land, he has to endure the punishment. Like him, he ought to enjoy or suffer—but he only suffers—with the prosperity or adversity of his country; and therefore, like him, he ought to have all the rights and all the privileges that the country can bestow. (Loud applause.) Is that any more than any man ought to claim, and ought any man to be satisfied with less?

But if it be a fact that the color of a man, that his having been born in a certain geographical position, gives another man a right to enslave him, I would say, as I often say when advocating the equality of the sexes, why not reverse the order, and let the white man know what it is to be subject to eternal bondage? Let not this bondage remain only with the black man.

I have named here none of the evils of slavery. It were vain for me to attempt to do so. You can all understand it as well as I can, as I have never been in the position of a slave. It not only deprives a human being of his own identity, of his own person, but it subjects him eternally to the bitter degradation of bondage. I need not tell you of the pangs and misery caused by slavery, arising from the fact that the nearest and dearest bonds are severed and broken asunder. I need not depict before your eyes that parents and children are placed alternately on the auction-block, and they are bid off and knocked down like merchandise, and then separated, never again to behold each other. I will not repeat these things, for you know them too well.

As I said before, the curse of slavery is not confined to the poor black victim alone; but my friends the whole country is cursed by slavery. The Southern white population are cursed by it; and so much is my mind of a universal tendency, that while I deprecate slavery and slaveholding, while all my sympathies gush forth for the poor slave I cannot withhold some pity and commiseration for the slaveholder too; for it is an eternal principle of right, that the evil-doer shall be punished by the evil he inflicts upon others; and terribly cursed and punished is the South by the evil they inflict on the poor slave, by a violation of all human rights, by a violation of all the dearest principles of humanity.

I will not enter into an explanation here of the various ways in which the South is cursed through slavery. The very soil shows it; hence the necessity for a constant endeavor to obtain the accession of new soil; for without it they cannot live. Their industry shows it, for wherever slavery exists, industry is looked upon with contempt. Wherever slavery exists, labor is degraded. Wherever slavery exists, the mind, not only of the slave; but of the tyrant slaveholder is prostrated and degraded. And this influence affects not only the South, not only the slaveholder and the slave, but it extends to the North. The evil of slavery has shown itself of late yet more distinctly than ever before. I heard Mr. [Stephen] Foster say this morning, that he was glad when the Fugitive Slave Bill was passed and he seemed to rejoice that the influence of slavery was beginning to be better understood than formerly. I, too, rejoice in it. Whenever there is a disease in the system, it is always better to have it thrown to the surface than to have it confined internally, for two reasons;—one is, it shows the strength of nature to throw it off; and the other is, to give the skillful physician a better knowledge of how to attack the cause of the disease.

Slavery has shown itself distinctly within the last five years. Until that time, it was more confined to the South; at any rate, we did not so distinctly perceive it here at the North. At the time when the Fugitive Slave Bill was enacted it commenced showing itself out on the surface. I was one of those who, at that time, did not understand its bearings. I deeply deplored that the disease existed here at all. I deeply deplored the fact that slavery cursed the land, but I said at the time, I am glad that the disease is coming to the surface. I am glad that it is beginning to encroach more and more upon the North. It seems to be a fact that a man can never appreciate a thing so well until it is brought home to himself. That Fugitive Slave Bill brought the subject home to tens of thousands in the falsely so-called free States. I say *falsely so-called*, for if they were truly free, there would be no slavery in this country. If they were truly free, they could have no union or *com*munion with slavery, for freedom and slavery can no more exist together than truth and falsehood. It is all true or all false; all free or all slave, and as we are not all free, we are all slaves and we are all slaveholders to some extent; at any rate in aiding and abetting, unless we raise our voice against it and use the utmost efforts in our power to disunite, to break that unholy Union—for it is not a righteous Union—of wickedness, of crime, of sin, and of shame. A Union of freedom and slavery cannot exist any more than fire and water.

When the South took the second great step to encroach upon the North, I hailed it as the forerunner of freedom,—that was the Nebraska Bill. Whatever the Union might have been before that Bill was passed, the slender thread which held it together is now snapped asunder—and who has done it? Did the Abolitionists and Disunionists, snap that thread asunder? This slender link which once held the Union together is broken—who broke it? The South. The infamy,—if infamy there is to be attached to the dissolution of the Union,—will be attached to the South; for it was the South or Southern slavery, that snapped the link; and the snapping of that link is the surest forerunner of the dissolution of that false, corrupt Union, where there is no liberty and no humanity. (Applause.)

My friends, I was not always of this opinion. Not more than a year ago last March, I was in Washington and while there, I spoke on the Nebraska Bill. When I went to the lecture-room, I had no idea that I was a Disunionist; I never knew it; I never suspected it. But while there, in speaking of the Nebraska Bill, I endeavored to find some reasons to show why the Union need not be dissolved, and yet slavery be abolished—for I had been anti-slavery all my life-time. While I thus endeavored to find the reason and suggest the means for abolishing slavery, without dissolving the Union, I convinced myself of the impossibility of it, and I said so at the time; for, like a true Quaker, I always depend upon the 'moving of the Spirit' for the time being, and whatever comes into my mind I give utterance to it; and when I went home from that lecture, I said to a friend of mine, "If I have not succeeded in convincing anyone else, I have succeeded,—and I am very happy to know it,—in convincing myself." (Loud cheers.)

Yes, my friends, we often hear it said, by politicians, Free Soilers, and others, that there is no need to dissolve the Union, because the Constitution of the United States is not a pro-slavery, but an anti-slavery instrument. I will not enter into any discussion on this point. I will simply say, "Take your alternative, and abide by the consequences. If on the other side, the Constitution is a pro-slavery instrument then it is not fit for a Republic, and therefore must be annulled, and a free Constitution formed. But of course the South will not submit to this, and therefore there will be a dissolution of the Union." If, on the other side, the Constitution is an anti-slavery instrument, then, in the name of mercy, how dare the South call for the protection of the general government in the nefarious traffic in slaves? This would be the surest way to dissolve the Union; and, sir, I would say to those Free Soilers who insist that the Constitution is an anti-slavery instrument that I am glad to hear it. If it is an anti-slavery instrument, then rescue it from the hands of the slaveholders, and say to them—"You must abolish slavery, or you cannot come under the banner of this Republic, which is based on this instrument—the Constitution of the country." (Cheers.) So, in either case, whether it is a pro-slavery or an anti-slavery instrument, by that instrument itself, Disunion must come. There can be no Union between freedom and slavery, unless, indeed, we are prepared to unite more fully with the South, and go more deeply into slavery than we have ever gone before; and then, at any rate, we shall be more consistent than we have ever been before.

. . . . . . .

# LETTERS TO THE EDITOR:
## LECTURE TOUR OF "THE WEST"
## AND THE LEGACY OF FRANCES WRIGHT
By Ernestine L. Rose, with Joseph Barker
November 20, 1855
New York, New York

In this letter, Rose provides an overview of a lecturing tour of some two months' duration, covering Ohio, Michigan, and Indiana, which were then considered "the West." She traveled with Joseph Barker, a freethinking former minister from England who had shared the platform with her at the Hartford Bible Convention of 1853. Most of this tour centered on the freethought movement, but it included several lectures on women's rights. The letter is notable for its poignant description of Rose's feelings upon visiting the grave of Frances Wright, an earlier Owenite lecturer whom Rose considered the model of a courageous woman. Wright was buried in Cincinnati, where she had made her national reputation through a series of three lectures on freethought in 1828 (Post 1943, 141–44). Written on November 20, 1855, Rose's letter was published in the *Boston Investigator* on December 5.

∾

Mr. Editor:—Having just returned from a lecturing tour in the West, it may not be uninteresting to your readers to have a short sketch of it.

I left home on the 16th of September for Salem, Ohio, (the place of residence of Mr. Joseph Barker,) to attend a Convention of the "Progressive Friends." The meetings were well attended, and the various reforms brought up for discussion elicited much interest; but the most exciting subject was the influence of a belief in future reward and punishment on the life and actions of man in this world. Some thought that without such a belief, man could not be restrained from crime, and they adduced the organs of Veneration, Benevolence, Conscientiousness, and Hope, as a proof of a future existence. In reply, I endeavored to show that, so far from these organs proving a future, they had nothing whatever to do with it; they belonged entirely to our present existence, and that the belief in a future, so far from restraining man from crime, made man neglect this life, and kept him ignorant of a knowledge of his nature, the relation he sustains to his fellow man, and led him to the commission of crime, from which true knowledge only in opposition to all superstitions can ever free him.

On the last morning of the Convention, I proposed to change the name from "Progressive Friends" to that of "Friends of Human Progress," as being of a broader and more universal significance, and after some debate the new name was adopted. When the Convention adjourned, I lectured on the Education and Social Position of Woman.

From Salem I went to Adrian, Michigan, where I lectured twice on Woman's Rights and the Formation of Human Character. From thence I went to Battle Creek, and attended the Michigan Anti-Slavery Anniversary. . . . [Rose describes speaking in Battle Creek and twice in Ypsilanti.] Then I went to Ann Arbor; and from thence through Detroit I went to Cincinnati to attend our National Convention, which lasted two days only. The evening meetings were very well attended; but, take it altogether, it was not as well attended nor as interesting as our National Conventions in the East have been.

While in Cincinnati, I attended Dr. Buchanan's Anthropological class several times. I was exceedingly interested, and most truly regretted that I would not remain and attend the whole course. The subject is of vast importance, and he imparts his instructions with ability and seriousness, illustrating the various parts in a clear and happy manner, in the way of familiar conversation, which relieves the tediousness of investigating so complicated a science, and makes it very interesting, while it conveys to you all the knowledge requisite for your information. Dr. Buchanan is indefatigable in his efforts to propagate the "science of man." In addition to his daily labors as Professor in the College, he attends to his private class three times a day, two hours each time, and I must add with deep regret that such noble talents and devoted labors are spent to comparatively so small a class, while the same efforts could give instruction to at least one hundred or more. But so it is. I may be mistaken, but I think Dr. Buchanan would be far more appreciated and would have a wider field for labor in this city than he can ever have in his present location.

Before leaving Cincinnati, I visited, in company with Mr. Barker, the last resting-place of our noble friend, Frances Wright. The profile on her monument is tolerably good, but it does not give the soul that animated the original while alive. The place, the remembrance of the high-minded woman that rested there, her devotion to the race, her noble efforts to benefit society by the spread of useful knowledge, her love of human freedom and human rights, her opposition to superstition and intolerance, and the bitter persecutions she suffered in consequence, which have not ceased even though she is no more—were very suggestive to my mind and called up deep thoughts, earnest feelings, and a stronger devotion to the cause of freedom and of right for which she had to suffer so much. But more anon.

From Cincinnati I went to Indianapolis to attend a Woman's Rights Convention. It is the place where Robert Dale Owen worked so nobly to obtain the right of married woman to her property, and which, after it had been carried, was recalled again and lost through the influence of a minister by bringing the whole force of Bible arguments to bear against woman's right to property. So much for having priests in legislative halls! From Indianapolis I went to Winchester, and then to Mansfield, Ohio, where I spoke twice. In Dayton I spoke four times on the education and rights of woman, the formation of human character, and on the antagonisms of society. . . .

On my way home, I passed two days at Joseph Barker's. He was just preparing to go to Philadelphia to give a course of lectures. I expected to have spoken in Randolph, but I felt so over-fatigued from constant traveling and speaking, that I deemed it most prudent to proceed home, where, after two months' journey, I arrived safely.

The seeds of Social and Moral Reform have been sown in some of the Western States; but still it requires the labor, care, and culture of free and enlightened minds to make them spring up and bear the fruit of knowledge, freedom, and right, for as yet superstition has got a very strong hold on the minds of the people; and the clergy, the planters, cultivators, and guardians of error and superstition, do all they can to keep the minds of the people in ignorance and in darkness, well knowing that as darkness flies before light, so does superstition before knowledge; and the minds of the people once enlightened, *they* will lose their strong hold upon them.

Yours, for freedom,
Ernestine L. Rose

# LETTER TO THE EDITOR: "MRS. ROSE AND THE *BANGOR MERCURY*"

December 1855
New York, New York

Rose had been invited to address an antislavery society meeting in Bangor, Maine, but soon found herself caught up in controversy when a local minister hostile to the freethought movement attacked her in the local newspaper. Because the *New York Tribune* had referred to the *Bangor Mercury* article, Rose responded in a letter to the editor of the *Tribune*. In her letter, she included excerpts from the *Bangor Mercury* piece—in which she was attacked as a woman, a foreigner, and a Jew, as well as an "infidel"—and defended herself point by point. The *Mercury* articles did not dissuade local abolitionists, who refused to withdraw their invitation to Rose. The letter was printed in the *Boston Investigator* on December 26, 1855; there is no record of the date of its writing, or of its publication in the *New York Tribune*.

∾

To the Editor of the *New York Tribune:*

Sir:—On my return from a lecturing tour in the West, I saw a short paragraph in the *Tribune* of the 6th, with my name in it, occasioned by some remarks in the Bangor *Mercury*. Wishing to know what it all meant, I procured the *Mercury* of the 3d, 10th, and 17th of Nov., in which, in some articles in reference to a course of lectures to be given in Bangor, to which I have been invited as one of the speakers, I found a most brutal attack upon me.

From the tenor of those articles it is evident that the writer meant others who were invited to lecture in the course as well as me; but being too cowardly to attack any of them personally, he concentrated his whole malice upon me, feeling himself quite safe as I am only a woman, a foreigner, and (as the sectarian world calls me) an "Infidel" at that.

Well, he is safe, for, as far as my own feelings and dignity are concerned, I treat it with the silent contempt it deserves. I stand before the world as I am, unprotected and unsupported by sect or party. I have not the advantage of a *profession* of religion, which, like an impenetrable cloak, covers a multitude of sins. My opinions are publicly given, and I fear no investigation of them.

In principle I know no compromise, I expect no reward, I fear no opposition, and can therefore afford to pass by in silence the outpourings of a bitter spirit, and only pity him who possesses it.

But I think it my duty to point out at least some of the false statements to show the merits and reliability of the author by the truthfulness of his assertions, and not wishing to send it to the editor of the *Mercury*—for a man who evidently takes pleasure to calumniate and slander a person of whom he is utterly ignorant, cannot possess manliness, justice and honor enough for me to reply to him personally—I therefore ask it of you as a favor, as some remarks including my name in reply to some of his articles have appeared in the *Tribune*, to give this a place in your paper, and greatly oblige

Yours, very truly,<br>
Ernestine L. Rose

*Extracts from the Bangor Mercury:*

In an article in reference to some of the speakers invited to lecture in Bangor the editor says:

"We referred particularly to the engagement of Mrs. Ernestine L. Rose, the President of an Infidel club in New York, whose speeches at the annual Tom Paine festivals have, for half-a-dozen years, surpassed anything with which we are acquainted in ribald blasphemies against the Christian religion."

"On the anniversary of Tom Paine's birth-day every year this Association get up a supper, at which Jesus Christ is uniformly treated with the choicest blasphemies of which its members are capable. The presiding officer at these celebrations for at least half-a-dozen years past has been a *female* born of Jewish parents in Poland. Her Tom Paine festival speeches are as famous as infamous. Everybody accustomed to read a certain class of New York newspapers must have been time after time disgusted with the reports of her loathsome ribaldries against Christ and Christianity."

"For ourselves we do not hesitate to confess that we know of no object more deserving of contempt, loathing, and abhorrence than a *female* Atheist. We hold the vilest strumpet from the stews to be by comparison respectable."

But enough of this. Were it not that I had to give some extracts as specimens of the whole, I would not soil my fingers to copy language evidently dictated by the very spirit of malice, whose pen was dipped in the venom of bigotry and intolerance. I am no believer in "natural depravity," and therefore I must attribute it to *very inferior, vitiating* influences, to have had a tendency *so grossly* to deprave and vitiate his mind, and he deserves truly to be pitied; but not the less do I pity any cause or religion that has such an advocate to support it. *He* evinces the *same* spirit that crucified Christ for a difference in his belief, and that led the poor victim to the stake for disbelieving in the infallibility and power of the Pope.

The statements that:—

1. "I am the President of an Infidel Club."

2. That "at the celebration of Thomas Paine's birthday, Christ is uniformly treated with the choicest blasphemies."

3. "That I have been the presiding officer of these celebrations at least half-a-dozen years,"

I simply pronounce unqualified, unmitigated falsehoods, deserving of as little notice as their unfortunate author is of trust. As for the sentiments contained in my Paine Celebration speeches, I simply ask, Has he seen them? Then I pity the perversity of his mind so grossly to misrepresent them. Has he not see them? Then he deserves equal pity for his dishonesty. I pity him, for both these speeches are before the world and speak for themselves.

To the fact that I have attended the Paine Celebration, and once had the pleasure of presiding, I most cheerfully plead guilty; and though if Thomas Paine were alive, we would not agree on some subjects—as he believed in some things in which I cannot believe—yet it gives me great pleasure to pay him my tribute of profound respect for his devoted patriotism, his self-sacrificing spirit to the cause of freedom, his invaluable services to this country at the time of her need, his love to man, his unflinching adherence to truth, and his fearless opposition to tyranny and oppression—whether from the throne or the church; and I endeavor to carry out as far as it lies in my power his beautiful and noble motto:—

"The world is my country, and to do good my religion."

Yes! he who can appreciate Truth, love Virtue, and feel the ennobling sentiments of Justice and Gratitude, may find enough to honor in the author of "Common Sense," the "Rights of Man," and the "Age of Reason," although on some subjects he might differ from him.

In conclusion, I will say that, if the writer of these ignoble sentiments is not so *utterly* debased as to be entirely devoid of justice and honor, I call upon him to publish my Paine speeches; but if he is, alas! how deeply must he have sunk, and how greatly does he need our pity, charity and help!

Ernestine L. Rose

1856-1860

# SPEECH AT THE THOMAS PAINE CELEBRATION: DEFENDING HERSELF, THOMAS PAINE, AND FREETHINKERS

January 28, 1856
New York, New York

At the 1856 Paine celebration, a toast, the second of the evening, referred to the recent attacks against Rose in the *Bangor Mercury*. The toast was made to "Mrs. Ernestine L. Rose—Though a rose to her many admirers, yet she has proved a thorn to her slanderers in Bangor." According to the account in the February 13, 1856, edition of the *Boston Investigator*, "The toast was received with thunders of applause, in the midst of which Mrs. Rose ascended the platform, and when silence was obtained," gave the speech that follows. Rose used the recent attacks on herself as a starting point to defend her hero, Thomas Paine, and the ideals they shared and makes a strong case for the freethought movement's approach to life and death.

∽

Mr. President and Friends—I thank you for the kind sentiment expressed towards me, but you must pardon me if I remonstrate with you about it. To be subjected to the inquisitorial fire of priestly intolerance might, indeed, be expected, but I think it hardly fair in you to toast me alive, and that in my presence. Nevertheless, allow me to assure you that I am very happy to meet you once more on this interesting occasion, for there is a three-fold benefit in celebrating the natal day of the "author-hero of the Revolution," Thomas Paine.

1st. The gratification that springs from the performance of a duty prompted by justice and gratitude towards one who has proved himself, by a life-long devotion to the cause of freedom, truly to deserve the title of the "Friend of Man."

2d. In upholding his noble deeds, generous motives, self-sacrificing spirit, and great moral courage, in endeavoring to free the human mind not only from kingly but priestly despotism—for it is easier far to face the lion in his den than to attack superstition and priestcraft in their stronghold—we not only perform a duty to him, but give an incentive and encouragement to enable us fearlessly to perform our part in the great drama of life, for the "times that tried men's souls" are not yet over, and in the conflict for human rights the sterling worth of woman's soul is often tried too.

3d. To make Thomas Paine better known—for though he lives in his acts, in the signal services he rendered this country in the time of need, and is known by his "Common Sense," the "Rights of Man," and the "Age of Reason," yet the mass of the people are utterly ignorant about him, or what is worse still, know him only as his enemies painted him. Were it not for that, they could easily receive the simple statement of facts, and learn to know and appreciate him as he was, for truth is easy to learn when the mind is free from error; but their minds have been filled with falsehood, coined by his priestly enemies, and distributed from the pulpits and the press—hence truth cannot find access.

As you alluded to the attack made upon me, I presume I ought to say something on the subject—nor would it be out of place, for it was based upon the event which brought us together this evening. But the abuse is far too gross for me to speak about, or for you to hear; suffice it to say, that it seemed more like the outpourings of the concentrated essence of malice, prompted by the spirit of a fiend, than from a human being, simply on account of a difference of opinion. The charges upon which the attack was based were, that I presided at the anniversary of Paine's birth-day, where, they said, "Jesus Christ was uniformly treated with the choicest blasphemy of which its members are capable," and that I made speeches on such occasions which were as "famous as infamous," &c., &c. So you see you were implicated with me. Misery, they say, likes company. I think glory likes it as well; and as you were participators in the crime, I am perfectly willing you should partake of the glory also. Every one who attended the Paine celebration, and even some who probably never attended, but who were guilty of thinking for themselves and express-ing their thoughts freely, were included in the attack. Waldo Emerson, Wendell Phillips, Theodore Parker, and Harriet Martineau were freely mentioned, but not daring to attack them personally, I was honored with a place in the front rank, to receive the entire contents of the battery of priestly intolerance, meant for all. It is, indeed, an honor to suffer for such men, and such a cause—but it harmed me not—for the battery contained only smoke, which cleared off and left the atmosphere brighter and purer than before.

In justice to Bangor, I must say, that the author of these infamous attacks was not a citizen of that place; for though they appeared as edito-rials in the *Mercury*, yet it was well understood—as I was informed—that the poor, silly editor was only a tool of a notorious character who moved there from this city; one of whom the *Tribune*, in reference to some mis-representations in connection with the affair of the Book Publishing Society, said, "I mean no less a character than the Rev. Rufus Wilmot

Griswold, D.D., a person so notorious in this community, as to trace a calumny to him suffices effectually to dispose of it." But, being unable to effect the object, the Rev. Mr. Little, of Bangor, came to his aid, and, unitedly, they used their power and influence, by private letters and public appeals, to induce the committee to break their engagement with me, or to prevent the people from hearing me; and yet, although the Rev. Mr. Little, in a long, abusive article, said, "I will use all moral means (moral with a vengeance!) to thwart Mrs. Rose's influence, so help me God," the committee did not violate their word, and the people did come to hear. Most nobly did they, by their presence, exonerate themselves from any participation in these fiendish attacks, and vindicate and sustain the right to freedom of speech; and the result, I doubt not, will be good. Moral freedom has gained a victory; the people will, I hope, be aroused to the fact which history and every day's experience demonstrate, viz.: that the priesthood in all ages arrogate to themselves the right to dictate and control the actions of society. Clerical assumption, if unchecked, knows no bounds. But, thanks to the noble martyrs of freedom, the power has been wrested from their grasp; the poisonous fangs have been extracted; and though they still endeavor to bite, it is quite harmless now. But I am happy to say that there are noble exceptions, as evinced by the Rev. Mr. Battles, who most nobly fought the battle of freedom in Bangor. But, as a class, history bears me out that the assertion is true, they have ever proved themselves the greatest hindrance to progress, and the sworn enemies to reform and reformers, who, if they could not destroy, they slandered and vilified. This is evident in their treatment of Thomas Paine. Every member of this republic ought to feel it a duty to pay a tribute of respect to one who devoted his time, talents, energies, and means to the cause of human rights.

But so pernicious has been the effect of falsehood, that the sense of justice and gratitude has been stifled, and he is treated with abuse and opprobrium. The pretext for it is, that during the latter part of his life he was intemperate. Well, suppose it were true—which it is not; we have ample living testimony to disprove it—what then? Are the truths he uttered less true?—the services he rendered this country less valuable?— or his works less instructive and beautiful? Rightly cultivated minds and feelings unperverted by prejudice would, while contemplating his virtues, regret that one so intellectually great and nobly true should, in common with his kind, have been subject to the frailties of human nature, and have fallen a victim to a weakness that has hurried some of the wisest and best to an untimely grave, and while honoring all that was good in him, would throw the mantle of charity over his one failing. But while ministers of church and state who have filled a drunkard's grave are honored and eulogized, this presumed fault in Thomas Paine is so magnified as to overshadow his whole character. And not only in his life, but in his death, is he misrepresented; his death has been painted in the darkest colors, and held up to frighten children of a larger growth. The denial of this falsehood by his doctor, nurse, and a host of others, has no effect. It still is the theme of his enemies; but what, I ask, has his death to do with his life? The life of a man belongs to the world, for he is an actor in it and has an influence upon it; but his death is his own; and mean indeed must he be who would wish to meddle with that. I have often been told, "Your principles are very well to live by, but will they prepare you how to die?" They little know what a compliment they pay us by that admission. All we need is the right principles to live by, and the rest will take care of itself.

I desire not to speak lightly of an event which, in depriving us of those we love, brings desolation to our hearts, and sorrow to our homes; but I have sometimes asked them to point me out a single instance where a person has ever tried hard and failed at last; and we will set up a school to teach man how to die. This senseless talk of teaching man how to die while he is left utterly ignorant how to live—to make the world wiser, better, and happier for his living in it—is as ridiculous as it is pernicious, for it diverts man's attention from life and its duties, and prevents him from acquiring a knowledge of his being, the laws that govern him, and the relation he sustains to his fellow man. And if our ghostly teachers of death, who live in luxury and idleness, and pass indifferently by the vice, crime, and suffering which everywhere abound, without inquiring into the causes that plant pangs in the bosom, draw tears from the eye, and blood from the heart, would help to remove these causes—to do away forever with slavery, poverty, and superstition, and inculcate justice, charity, and love—they would do far more good than they can ever do with all their teaching and preaching about death. The beautiful lines of [Alexander] Pope—who must pardon me for slightly altering them—are very applicable to the subject:

"On modes of death
Let graceless bigots fight;
His can't be wrong
Whose life is in the right."

# LETTER TO THE EDITOR:
## "FAREWELL LETTER OF MRS. ROSE"
April 30, 1856
New York, New York

Ernestine and William Rose decided to travel to Europe in the spring of 1856. Ernestine Rose was, by then, a public person and wrote to her constituency to explain her absence and reflect on her contributions to date. She had been ill since the beginning of the year with "an inflammation of the lungs," probably a bronchial infection, and hoped that a vacation of six months abroad would provide rest and recovery (Kolmerten 1999, 181–82). She tells her readers that she hopes she will be excused for taking a furlough, "after twenty years as a volunteer soldier in the cause of Truth," and states her intention to return in November in time for the next national women's rights convention in New York City. This letter was published, with a brief introduction by the editor, in the *Boston Investigator* on May 5, 1856.

⋙

*Our readers will perceive by the following interesting letter from Mrs. Rose, that probably by this time she is at sea, on her passage to Europe. We trust that the voyage and the visit may effect her complete restoration to health; that herself and husband may be fortunate enough to escape all mishaps; enjoy a very pleasant entertainment wherever they may travel, and return in safety to the land of their adoption. These wishes, we are certain, will be sincerely responded to by the many friends of this worthy couple, who are deservedly esteemed by all who have the pleasure of their acquaintance. Therefore, we commend them to the kind attention of the English Liberals, who, we doubt not, will give them a cordial welcome and also warmly appreciate the ability and eloquence of Mrs. Rose as a lecturer, if the state of her health enables her to engage in that undertaking. We are much gratified to learn that during her absence she will correspond with the* Investigator; *and as her letters will be read with interest, we shall receive them with great satisfaction. And now, farewell to our good friends for a season. We would give them a "benediction," only that is not exactly in our line—but perhaps it will be just as profitable if we hope that their ship, the Northumberland, may have pleasant breezes and a quick passage.*

*Blow ye west winds, blandly hover*
*O'er the ship that bears them over.*

New York, April 30th, 1856

Mr. Editor:— I see, by the *Investigator*, that you are apprised of our intention to visit Europe, but before leaving America, I wish, though very much occupied with making necessary preparations for a long journey, to say a few parting words to our Liberal friends, many of whom I should much like to write personally—but as I am not able to do this for want of time, I will speak through the *Investigator*, and hope that they will appropriate as much to themselves as will be agreeable to their feelings and wishes.

It is customary, in the military world, that a soldier, particularly a volunteer, after serving some years, should be permitted a furlough, or leave of absence. In the religious world too, it has become a custom, or rather fashion, that ministers who have for a few years read a chapter in the Bible every Sunday, and delivered a sermon of half an hour's duration, (no matter who wrote it,) should go to Europe for their health. So I too may be pardoned, though not a minister, after twenty years as a volunteer soldier in the cause of Truth, for leaving my post, not as a deserter, but on furlough, to gather fresh strength for the glorious battle of freedom.

On the 14th of May it will be twenty years, since we arrived in this country. During that period, (and for some years previous,) I have endeavored to the best of my powers and ability to serve the cause of progress and humanity; to advocate what to me seemed the truth; to defend human nature from the libel cast upon it by superstition; to claim human rights irrespective of sex, country, or color—in fine, to devote and direct all my efforts to the elevation of the ignorant, the poor, and the oppressed. In the little I was able to do, I had no ulterior end to serve; no personal interest to gain, except the gratification that springs from the performance of duty; and if, in expressing my opinions, I have been severe alike on friend and foe, it is because in principle I know no compromise, I expect no reward, I fear no opposition—but with an earnest desire my aim has been steadily directed onward and upward; and if my labors have not been as successful as I could wish, they have, I hope, at least to some extent, had the effect to eradicate error, to inculcate truth, and to instill charity and. kindness for the failings and frailties of misdirected human nature.

But, finding that my health has been greatly impaired by too long continued exertions and exposure, it is advisable for me to visit Europe, in hopes that a sea voyage, change of climate, cessation from labor, and a few months' traveling, might to some extent at least renovate a once exceedingly strong and enduring constitution, so as to enable me to perform my part in the great drama of life a few years longer.

In taking a retrospective view of the period of my residence here, and in casting up accounts, it gives me pleasure to say, that although I have met with some severe reproach, slander, and persecution for daring to oppose the popular and fashionable superstition called religion, (for superstition in fashion is always called religion, till the religion becomes out of fashion—then it again changes back into superstition,) yet they were but isolated instances, while by the mass of the people I have always been treated with civility and kindness. It is worthy of notice that during twenty years, in all my travels and lectures more or less in twenty three States, and with my well known heresies on religion and society, I have *never* been disturbed in *any* of my meetings, except at the Hartford Bible Convention by some young clerical rowdies; at an Anti-Slavery Convention in Boston, when the Puritan spirit could not brook to have the "blue laws" of Massachusetts called to account in connection with the black laws of the South; and by a few silly boys at a Woman's Rights Convention in the city of New York. With these exceptions, I have always been treated by audiences with attention and respect.

The papers too, without soliciting their favors, have treated me wherever I been with courtesy and kindness, many of them with marked generosity, with the exception of the *Little-Griswold-Mercury* of Bangor, Me., and the pious *Courier and Enquirer* of New York, whose censure I would much rather deserve than its praise. Among the Liberals and Reformers I have met with many noble spirits and generous friends, who are doubly dear to me, not only on account of being engaged in the same cause that I am, but for their generous feelings and personal kindness towards me. I wish I could see them before I leave, but as this cannot be, let me assure them that I will carry with me a most grateful remembrance of their warm friendship which will make me anticipate with pleasure the time when we shall meet again.

We intend to visit England, France, Germany, and Italy. Whether I shall be able once more to see my own poor native land, I know not; nor could it be much gratification to me, except that I could find it in a happier condition, or could be instrumental in placing it in one. During my absence, I shall miss, every week, the friendly and welcome visit of the *Investigator*, but I will have the satisfaction of knowing that it is ever at its post, doing the good work of combating, error and promoting knowledge, justice, and truth, and I hope that our Liberal friends will continue to do their part to aid in the diffusion of "universal mental liberty." There is enough to do for all. In gratitude to the past we owe a duty to the future. Let every one, then, be true to his highest convictions, and faithful to the cause of human progress. Truth is the highest aim in principle, and goodness the noblest object in practice.

Should my health permit, I may occasionally send a letter to the

*Investigator*, as I doubt not that I shall meet with incidents that may interest your readers. I anticipate much pleasure in seeing once more our dear venerable friend Robert Owen, and regret we could not have left here in time to be in London on the 14th of May, his 86th birthday. I shall try to see some of the active Liberals in England and elsewhere, and consult with them about the World's Bible (or Anti-Bible) Convention, and other matters of progress and reform, and I hope that the friends here will correspond on the subject, and mature a plan so as to ensure a successful World's Convention to be held in May 1857, in the city of New York, that locality being the focus and centre of the Union.

We intend to sail the 6th of May in the ship Northumberland; and, if all is well, to return in November. In conclusion, I would ask the Liberals in general, and my dear friends among them in particular, to excuse the shortcomings, pardon the sins of commission and of omission, and remember that with the kindest feelings I bid them all an affectionate farewell.

Ernestine L. Rose

# TRAVEL LETTER NO. 2:
# VISITING ROBERT OWEN
July 6, 1856
London, England

In this second letter from abroad, Rose speaks of her visit with Robert Owen and describes his life of mental, physical, and political activity despite his advanced age of eighty-six. She reports that his efforts to convince her of his newfound embrace of spiritualism, and hers to convince him out of it, are equally futile. Yet there is a hint of fun in the contest. This would be their last visit, a fact that, in hindsight, lends poignancy to their continued comradeship and mutual fondness and respect, despite their differences. Rose goes on to describe her tour of London with William to such sites as the (then new) Tussaud Wax Museum, the British Museum, and the tunnels under the Thames. As a reformer, Rose is ever observant of social factors—the extremes of poverty and wealth, the British class system, and exclusion of women from government. Women were barred even from observation of Parliamentary debates—a challenge Rose deals with by simply walking in. This letter appeared in the *Boston Investigator* on August 6, 1856.

⤞

London, Stanhope Street, Park Place,
Regent's Park, (Eng.) July 6, 1856

Mr. Editor:—In my former letter, I spoke of our sea voyage with all the little disagreeables connected with it. In this, I promised to say something about the external and internal of this mighty metropolis. But what can I say in the space of a letter on a subject so vast, so immense, so teeming with glory and degradation, splendor and wretchedness, the highest cultivation and refinement, and the almost barbarian ignorance and rudeness, the immense wealth with all its pride, and the lowest depth of poverty with all its abjectness, and of the tyranny, oppression, apathy, indifference, and subservience and submission which the terrible misrule of such extremes must naturally engender? It would require more than the graphic pen of a "Trollope" to do it justice. I must therefore confine myself to a simple statement of our doings here.

After our arrival, and as soon as we got comfortably settled down for a few weeks, we went to Seven Oaks, 27 miles from London, to see our dear and venerable friend, Robert Owen. We found him in excellent health and spirits. He writes, walks, and rides every day, and at intervals

211

between his physical and mental exercise, he amuses himself with feeding the chickens which come at his call. He lives in a delightful place, and has most beautiful gardens and parks to walk in. The lady he boards with is very much attached to him, and exceedingly kind. She usually takes him out riding and accompanies him in his walks. He regretted that we had not come to London on the 14th of May, his 86th birth-day, on which he had a large meeting and made a long speech. In conversation, he exclaimed with much energy, "Since I saw you, nine years ago, I have not spent an hour without laboring for the cause of humanity." On Spiritualism he is as earnest and enthusiastic as his truthful and warm nature has ever been on any subject that he believed to be good and true. It is needless to say, that his endeavors to convince me *into* it, and mine to convince him *out* of it, met with equal success. He is very remarkable for his age; still we could see quite a change in him. He does not come to London often now, for it is too fatiguing to him. We hope to have the pleasure of seeing him on our return before we leave for home.

. . . . . . . .

The Parliament House is famous for its architectural beauty. It abounds in carvings both in the inside and out. By a permit from the Lord Chancellor, visitors of both sexes are admitted into the House of Lords when not in session, perhaps at all times to the House of Commons. Men are admitted to the debates if they bring a permit from a member, but women are not admitted unless a permit is obtained through a member from the Sergeant-at-Arms, which has to be applied for in writing, and after the lapse of ten or fourteen days a permit may or may not be obtained. The gallery for ladies is so small that hardly ten persons can stand there. It is enclosed in the front by a close metal wire-work, like that of a prison window, which allows you to look through only with one eye at a time. Of the whole English policy it seems to me the strangest why woman should so entirely be excluded from the House of Commons; but let silly men do all they can to keep woman out, she can always outwit them! If she only wished to enter into the Garden of Eden, not even the cherubim with fiery swords could keep her out; and as I had a desire to hear the debate in the House of Commons, I went in, and that without any permit. The subject under discussion was a bill for the improvement of the Irish dwellings. . . .

. . . . . . . .

The Tunnel under the Thames is a wonderful piece of workmanship. It is quite dry, lighted with gas, and contains stores the whole length. It does not pay, however. It is frequented only by strangers from motives of curiosity.

There are various other wonderful sights in London that I should like to speak of; but, as to describe them all at this time, would make my letter too long, I must defer a notice of them until I write you again, which will be shortly.

Yours, &c.,

Ernestine L. Rose

# TRAVEL LETTER NO. 3:
## THE TOWER OF LONDON, SYMBOL OF CRUELTY
July 13, 1856
London, England

At the Tower of London, Rose expresses her sadness and disgust at the inhumanity of rulers with absolute power over their subjects, even to the murder of children of their own families. In one of her rare references to her fellow Jews, Rose writes of the sufferings of hundreds of Jews crowded into a small space in the Tower's dungeon. As did her interest in the tunnel under the Thames in her previous letter, Rose's fascination with the structural details of the Crystal Palace reveal a keen interest in engineering feats. This letter was printed in the *Boston Investigator* on August 13, 1856.

⤳

London, Stanhope Street, Park Place,
Regent's Park, (Eng.,) July 13, 1856

. . . The Tower had very little interest for me, except a painful one. . . . In the White Tower, is the dungeon where the two children of Edward IV were stifled, and the dark cell where Sir Walter Raleigh was incarcerated for thirteen years, together with the block and axe that performed the cruel function of a cruel age and government. In the large room for State prisoners, the walls are covered with the names, dates, and last sentiments, engraven with the agony of death, as a legacy to and a protest from the spirit of humanity. In the underground dungeon 600 Jews were incarcerated at one time. The place is filled with reminiscences of barbarism, which sicken the heart and crush the spirit even to behold. . . .

. . . . . . . .

[T]he greatest attraction is the Crystal Palace at Sydenham. It contains all that is interesting and beautiful to be found in all other public establishments, and a great variety in addition. The Crystal Palace is a magnificent structure, composed of glass and iron; the framework seems very light, which gives it a very airy appearance. The name is very appropriate, for when the sun shines on it, it looks like an immense crystal reflecting the rainbow colors. The length is 1608 feet; the general width 384; the height of the centre transept, from the basement, is 197; the area, including the wings, 603,072; the area of galleries is 261,568. It represents all that is grand and beautiful in nature and in art, of ancient and modern times, of rude barbarity and the most refined civilization.

We have seen the painting of Rosa Bonheur. It is a representation of a horse fair, and is 20 feet by 9, and considered a great master-piece. [Rosa Bonheur, a French realist painter, was the most famous woman artist of her time. *The Horse Fair*, her best-known painting, was on display at the Crystal Palace when Ernestine and William Rose toured London.] A Mr. Wright from New York City bought it for 2200 pounds. So much for sight seeing, and now I must say something of a different nature, for time and space admonish me to draw my letter to a close. . . .

Yours, &c.,<br>Ernestine L. Rose

# TRAVEL LETTER NO. 10:
## MANNERS AND MORALS OF THE FRENCH
September 30, 1856
Berlin, Prussia

In this letter from her travels, Rose compares French manners, morals, and behaviors with those she has observed in the United States and England. Consistent with her lifelong affinity for the French, she admires their politics, and their wholesome public recreation across class and generation, which she contrasts to countries that pass "Blue Laws" limiting activity on Sundays, a practice which she regards as discriminatory to working people. She views the French practice of linking wine-drinking with dining as preferable to the Anglo culture of drinking alcohol alone, which contributes to public drunkenness. The letter, sent during a subsequent stop in Berlin, appeared in the *Boston Investigator* on December 3, 1856.

❧

Berlin, (Prussia,) September 30, 1856

. . . As to the character of the French, as a people, I have always liked them, and like them more now.—The English and Americans do not know them. The Frenchman has to be seen and studied at home, on his own soil. When he comes to England or America he cannot bend to the gloomy superstition of Puritanism. He is taken out of his element, and for want of the rational and refined recreation and amusements with which his own country abounds, he becomes noisy and at times dissipated. I wish our Maine temperance law and Blue Law people would come to Paris to learn their first lesson of temperance, sobriety, and good behavior. I have been fifteen months in Paris before, but I thought perhaps I was too young then to judge of such matters; but I found my ideas of the people were correct. They combine the finest elements in human nature. The Frenchman is frivolous on trifles, but he is the philosopher on any subject of importance. The mass of the people work hard and live still harder; but they have the arts, the sciences, the beautiful, the elevating. No country so abounds in these elements, and no people on earth enjoy them as much as the French.

Even the most ignorant man, he who cannot write his name, visits and examines the various museums and inquires into the nature and meaning of things; he looks with rapture at a beautiful piece of sculpture, or painting of a philosopher or a patriot, and listens with delight to the elevating strains of Beethoven, or Mozart. Take these elevating enjoyments from him, and you change his nature. In taste, natural grace, and a certain degree of refinement, all Frenchmen are alike. In other countries, there is an inseparable distinction and barrier between the educated and uneducated. The highly educated transcend so far in artificial refinement, that the mass of the people cannot reach them. There is no affinity, no sympathy between them. The high look with contempt at the low, and the low return it with envy, jealousy, and dislike. The rich Englishman or American is stultified by his pride; the poor by his poverty; both are rude and ill-mannered. This is the only equality between them. In Paris, (and Paris is France,) there is no overwhelming pride in the rich and the learned; no slavish humility in the poor and ignorant, for whatever his position or means, he is always natural, easy, affable, graceful, and generous, and therefore an equal. In the theatres, gardens, walks, museums, concerts, balls, they mix together, treat each other with becoming respect and fraternal civility.

We were four weeks in Paris, went into all parts of the city, and wherever we knew the largest number would assemble; and during the whole time we did not see one single drunken man, or any rudeness, or impropriety. We were in Versailles on a feast Sunday, where about thirty thousand people were collected, men and women, old and young, rich and poor, visiting the palace, the museums, the gardens, looking at the fountains, and listening to the music, and during the whole day, by that whole mass of people not a rudeness was committed, not a harsh word spoken, and I looked with greater admiration on the people than on all the objects of beauty to be seen—not that I deemed it strange that people should be so well behaved, but I could not help contrasting them with even small gatherings in England and America. Perhaps some one will say that they are so surrounded by gendarmes that they have to behave! Then let me reply, that we never saw the least interference nor the slightest necessity for any gendarmes in all Paris. In visiting the theatres, there is not only perfect decorum during the performance, but between the acts not a loud word is spoken. The people move in and out, walk about in the halls, take refreshments with the same order, politeness, and good breeding which is to be found in the best regulated families. There is a tacit understanding between the people wherever and whenever assembled, that they have come to enjoy themselves; that they have all a right to be there, and therefore no one interferes with the equal rights of another. If they have to wait, they wait quietly and enter gently; there is no pushing, squeezing, nor rudeness.

I have asked myself, over and over again, why it cannot be so with us too?—and the only solution I could come to was Puritanism. It has prohibited enjoyments; it has made public amusement and recreation low, because it has made it a crime. The arts and sciences, the great civilizers of men, were inaccessible to the mass of the people; music, the purifier of the sentiments, the refiner of thoughts; and dancing, the poetry of graceful motion, was proscribed by it, and as human nature will not entirely be stifled, it seeks excitement in other ways. Hence the amount of intemperance, lawlessness, and rudeness of the lower classes whenever they assemble, which has become such a habit that it is to be seen at all times and on all occasions. It is a curious fact that the French people never drink out of time; they drink wine as a part of their food, some only at dinner. The very poor, whose almost only food is bread, take it at every meal; the wine is light and pure, being tested by chemists to be free from adulteration; but they never drink any strong drinks between meals.

Lemonade, soda, liquorish and raspberry water are sold in all the streets, walks, and places of amusements; and even at evening parties, wine or liquor of any kind is never offered.

But enough. I have said too much, and not enough of what I wished to say, having had so little time to write, and so many times interrupted, that I have not been able to read what I have written, before sending it; but I trust that my observations, imperfect as they are, will give your readers some correct ideas of the manners and customs of the French people.

Yours, &c.,

Ernestine L. Rose

# TRAVEL LETTER NO. 11:
## ITALY AND THE CHURCH
October 20, 1856
Paris, France

In this, her last letter from abroad, Rose gives her impressions of Italy, especially instances of poverty and misery, which she attributes to the power and wealth of the Catholic Church. She takes the opportunity to compare a church-dominated country with the happy state she described in more secular France, to which she had returned. Her letter appeared in the *Boston Investigator* on December 10, 1856.

~&~

Paris, October 20, 1856

Mr. Editor:—Here we are once more, in the city of the gay, the emporium of elegance and politeness. But, methinks I hear you say you have already spoken to us of Paris, but not one word of any other place. Where have you been? What have you done since you left Paris? Is there no other place in your whole journey worth mentioning. . . . After leaving Paris, we went to Lyons, Geneva, and Chamberry in Switzerland, where we ascended a very high mountain near Mont Blanc;—thence we went to Basle, Strasborg, Badenbaden, (a terrible gambling place,) Heidelberg, Frankfort, and then on the Rhine to Coblentz, Cologne, Berlin, Dresden, Prague, Vienna, Trieste, Venice, Milan, Turin, Genoa, Leghorn, Florence, Rome, and Naples.

Though our limited time prevented us from remaining long in any of these places, we saw the principal objects of interest and curiosity. The most interesting places we have visited were Venice, Rome, and Naples. These cities are replete with interest and instruction; every stone speaks to you in an unmistakable language of the past, present, and future. But, alas! poor degraded Rome, it lives only on the decay of the past. So despicable is its condition, that the glory visible even through the ruins of its past greatness, proclaims louder and places in still bolder relief its present shame. The space once occupied by 500,000 inhabitants, evidently possessed of the highest culture, the arts, sciences, refinement, and also abundance, is now inhabited by 150,000, who with the exception of a small portion of the population, consist of priests, soldiers, and beggars. The first two classes of beggars are impudent, well dressed, and well fed; but the last unhappy class of beggars, equally large but not being licensed by church nor State to beg, rob and plunder, having no authority on their side except their own misery, are in such abject degradation, that were it not that the cause of it is but too visibly written in the bloated figures of the thousands of priests, in the churches filled with incalculable wealth, and the dark superstition which weighs the people down, one would almost despair of the race, and blush to belong to it. But as it is, humanity pleads more earnestly for aid, and calls for greater efforts, energy, and perseverance, to utterly destroy root and branch that cursed superstition that could sink a once noble people into so debased a condition as Rome, as Italy now is.

The roads from Florence to Rome, and from Rome to Naples, are infested by beggars, brigands, and priests. The priests are necessary to the other two classes; for the beggars, to direct them to some other life, otherwise they might not so willingly submit to their miserable condition in this; and for the brigands, to give them absolution (with a free license for their trade). While we were in Rome, a diligence [a public stagecoach] from Naples to Rome was attacked; eight balls were fired into it; fortunately, no one was injured, except a horse; the other horses from fright ran away with the wagon, and so saved it from being plundered. This took place in the morning, and only twenty miles from Rome, within hearing of the soldiers. The diligence had three thousand dollars in it, and the brigands seem to be well informed when much money is carried; but who can wonder at all this? A religion of falsehood, force, and fraud, can produce no other characters but just such as we there beheld.

Naples, though a large commercial city, surrounded by a country gifted with all the advantages of climate, fruitfulness, and scenery unequalled in the world, presents just as miserable an aspect of idleness, beggary, cruelty, and priests. Thousands of *lazzaroni* [idlers, beggars, or persons who subsist on odd jobs] are in the daily pay of a miserable pittance from the King, to be ready at his bidding to massacre and plunder the better portion of the people. We have visited Pompeii, and ascended Mount Vesuvius. These places are full of wonder and interest, but in this necessarily short letter I cannot even begin to speak on the subject.—From Naples, we went by steamer to Marseilles, and from there direct to Paris. In a day or two we shall start to London, thence to Liverpool, where we shall sail on the first of November by the steamer Europa for home.

I regret most exceedingly to be obliged to disappoint our friends in London, Liverpool, Glasgow, and other places, who wished me to speak before we leave. But we could not return any sooner to England, and the winter is too close at hand to delay the voyage any longer.

Yours, for human emancipation from all bondage,
Ernestine L. Rose

[The Europa, with Mr. And Mrs. Rose on board as passengers, arrived at New York on November 13.]

.

# SPEECHES AT THE SEVENTH NATIONAL
# WOMAN'S RIGHTS CONVENTION
November 26, 1856
New York, New York

Less than two weeks following her return from six months of traveling in Europe, Rose attended this convention held in downtown Manhattan with Lucy Stone presiding. Many of her remarks focus on the political aspirations of women in Europe. Rose spoke several times on the convention's second day, first in response to a resolution stating, "That the close of the Presidential election affords a peculiarly appropriate occasion to renew the demands of women for a consistent application of Democratic principles." In this statement, she makes a point of addressing the importance of the antislavery and women's rights issues to presidential politics. In response to another resolution, this one praising the efforts of women in England, Rose lauds the growing awareness of women's rights among English women and girls, who faced even greater obstacles than American women. She then offers a resolution in support of the women of France, condemning the suppression of free expression in that country, then under the despotic rule of Emperor Napoleon III, while praising the character and spirit of the people.

In her major speech, made on the evening of the second and final day, Rose presents a systematic analysis of women's rights in the United States. While covering some of the same ground as in her highly praised speech at the 1851 convention, here Rose omits the anecdotes, and looks again at the four realms of women's rights—education, occupation (which she here calls "industrial avocations"), legal rights, and political rights—and considers what the movement has accomplished by 1856. At the height of her powers as an orator, Rose even praises a heckler in the audience for his spirit of free inquiry. Recently returned from a trip abroad, Rose concludes with a reading of a Married Women's Property Bill proposed in England as a show of women's international solidarity, and ends with a ringing declaration that women everywhere must have their rights.

&

## HUMAN RIGHTS AND ELECTORAL POLITICS

Mrs. Ernestine L. Rose advanced from her seat on the platform and said:

. . . I would remark in reference to this last election here [the presidential election of 1856], though it was not my good fortune to be here during the time of that great excitement, being then on the continent of Europe; yet, even at that great distance, the fire of freedom that was kindled here spread itself across the Atlantic, and we felt its benign rays even there. The liberal, intelligent, and reformatory portion of the people of

Europe, as well as in England, have most warmly, most heartily sympathized with us in the last struggle of freedom against slavery. It is a most
glorious epoch. I will not enter into a political or anti-slavery lecture, but
simply state this fact—the time has come when the political parties are
entirely annihilated. They have ceased to exist. There is no longer Whig
and no longer Democrat—there is Freedom or Slavery. We have here an
equally great purpose to achieve. This, too, is not woman's rights or man's
rights, but it is human rights. It is based on precisely the same fundamental truths that the other question is based upon. In accordance with
the last election, the interest it created, and the general feeling that has
prevailed that woman ought to take a greater part and more interest in it,
and, in fact, with the noble work woman has done during the campaign,
it seems to me most extraordinary that the friends who have worked thus
nobly for freedom of one kind, should yet refuse freedom of the other
kind—both being based on the same principles.

Rose concludes this speech by reading changes to married women's
property rights proposed in England. Barbara Leigh Smith (Bodichon),
a founder of the woman's rights movement in England, was the guiding
spirit whose pamphlet in 1853 brought married women's property rights
to the attention of the British public, With a committee, Leigh-Smith
(Bodichon), circulated petitions in the following year, then in 1856 presented 26,000 signatures to the House of Lords. This was the first organized women's rights action in England. It was rejected, but in 1857, the
year following Rose's visit to England, the Married Women's Property
Bill passed its first and second readings in the House of Commons.


## WOMEN'S RIGHTS STRUGGLES IN EUROPE

Mrs. Rose wished to remark, in reference to the resolution offered by Mr.
Higginson [praising the achievements of women in England], that English women, to her knowledge, were very active in forwarding the Woman's Rights movement throughout Great Britain. And not only English
women, but young and noble English girls—girls, who were too timid to
take part publicly in the movement, but who were untiring and indefatigable in making converts and enlisting aid. There was Miss Smith, Miss
Fox, the daughter of the celebrated W. J. Fox, the eloquent lecturer and
Member of Parliament for Oldham, Miss Parkes, and others. They had
devoted themselves to the great work, which was more difficult in that
country than this. They had no Declaration of Independence to appeal to,
declaring that all men were created equal, and endowed with the incalculable right to life, liberty, and the pursuit of happiness. They had no

such standard to appeal to there, because men there were not recognized as free. Banking interests, manufacturing interests, land monopolism, and monopolism of every other kind were represented in England, but not men. The principle of universal suffrage had not yet obtained in England, and hence the greater difficulties that woman had to encounter there.

Another obstacle was the division of the people into classes and castes. No movement could make headway in England unless it was commenced among what are termed the higher classes. Every petition to Parliament must first have some names that have a title attached to them before it can obtain other signatures. The thinking portion of the middle classes were kept silent to a great extent, because of their utter inability to do anything unless it was taken up and supported by the higher classes. But this state of things would not continue long; there was "a good time coming" there as well as here. Signatures by thousands had been obtained to the Woman's Petition, and she presumed by the time it was presented to Parliament it would contain tens of thousands of names. . . . Mrs. Rose then offered the following resolution from the Committee:

*Resolved,* That we also present our assurances of respect and sympathy to the supporters of the cause of women in Paris, the worthy successors of Pauline Roland and Jeanne Deroine, who, in the face of imperial despotism, dare to tell the truth.

In commenting on this resolution, Mrs. Rose remarked that if the difficulties surrounding English women who advocated an amelioration of woman's condition were great, how much greater were those which surrounded the French women, owing to the blight of despotism in that country. They could write their thoughts, but their writings could not be published in France. They had to send their writings to the one State in Italy, which was not crushed by dark and bitter despotism. That bright spot is Sardinia. The works of the noble French women had to be sent to Turin, printed there, and sent back to Paris for private, secret distribution. And when these women met in consultation, they had to watch the doors and windows, to see that all was secure. She knew many of them, but dared not mention their names, for fear they might be borne across the Atlantic, and lead to their oppression and proscription. The noblest thoughts that had ever been uttered in France were uttered by women, not only in past times, before the Revolution, but down to the present day. Madame Roland was imprisoned for uttering the truth, in consequence of which imprisonment she lost her arm. Jeanne Deroine was exiled, and now resides in London, where she supports herself and her two daughters and son. She was educating them herself, because she had no means to pay for their education. She filled their minds with noble thoughts and feelings, even to the very sacrifice of themselves for the benefit of the race, and more especially for the elevation of woman, without which she feels convinced that the elevation of man can never be accomplished.

But while the names of a few such noble women were made public, hundreds, nay, thousands, who had done as much, and even more than these, were in obscurity. They were constantly watching to find what was done in America. And there was one thing which characterized these French women, and that was, the entire absence of jealousy and envy of the talents and virtues of others. Wherever they see a man or woman of intellect or virtue, they recognized them as a brother or sister; and they never ask from whom a great thought or a virtuous action comes, but, is it good, is it noble? It seemed to her that the character of the French women was the very essence of human nobility. They are ready to welcome, with heart and hand, every reformer, without stopping to inquire whether he is English, American, German, or Turk. But poor France was oppressed as she never was oppressed before. The usurper that now disgraces the throne, as well as the name he bears, does not allow the free utterance of a single free thought. Men and women are taken up privately and imprisoned, and no newspaper dared to publish any account of it. Women alone—and they at the risk of their lives—spoke and published their thoughts. They sent their thoughts to other countries and published and disseminated them there, whence their thoughts were wafted back into their own country, where they were privately circulated in pamphlets by thousands and tens of thousands, and connected with the subject of political, of social and religious freedom, the subject also of Woman's Rights was discussed in their publications.

## FOUR PARTS OF WOMEN'S RIGHTS

The President then introduced Mrs. Ernestine L. Rose as the next speaker, but before Mrs. R. took the platform, she wished to say to all self-respecting men, that this is the last place in which they should create a disturbance, especially in a matter which concerns their sisters, their wives, and their mothers.

Ernestine L. Rose said: At this stage of the proceedings, whatever branch of the subject connected with Woman's Rights I speak upon, I must necessarily repeat some of the ideas that already have been advanced during this Convention, and yet it is necessary to do so, as I doubt not that there are some here this evening who have not been here at the previous meetings. To make myself comprehensible to those who are unacquainted with what is meant by Woman's Rights, I will divide the subject into four parts, viz. Education, Industrial Avocations, and Legal and Political Rights.

But before I proceed to speak on any of these branches, I will lay down the basis upon which our claims are erected, and you will find it precisely the same foundation upon which the rights of men rest, viz., the principles of humanity. And do you ask me why we claim our rights? I answer, for precisely the same reason that you claim yours. Do you wish to know our authority? Then I again reply, the same authority that you bring in support of your claims, for humanity recognizes no sex, mind recognizes no sex, morals recognize no sex, virtue and vice, pleasure and pain, happiness and misery, life and death recognize no sex. Like man, woman possesses a physical, mental, and moral nature, upon the proper cultivation of which depends her highest health and happiness. Like him she is subject to all the vicissitudes of life. Like him, if she violates the laws of her being, she has to pay the penalty. When she breaks the laws of the land, she has to suffer the punishment. Like him she enjoys or suffers with her country; and as she is amenable to the laws, she has a right to have a voice in the formation of the laws. As her property is taxed in support of government, she has a right to be personally represented in the government.

Surely here these ideas ought not to be considered strange. The Declaration of Independence, based as it is upon the recognition of man's equality, which has given to the world the immutable truth, that "all men are created equal, and endowed with the inalienable right to life, liberty, and the pursuit of happiness," has already proclaimed (theoretically, at least) the equality of the sexes. But as theory alone is not sufficient for the practical purposes of life, we claim the practical fulfillment of that declaration.

Do you not yet understand the deep import of that glorious truth? Have you had it ever since the time of Jefferson, and cannot yet read its significance? Then it is high time you should learn it from a woman. It does not mean the oldest, biggest, strongest, wisest, or the most cunning only, is endowed with natural rights, but "all," and by all, "all" are meant.

This morning a young man made some remarks in opposition to our claims. We were glad to hear him, because he gave evidence of an earnest, sincere spirit of inquiry, which is always welcome in every true reform movement. And as we believe our cause to be based on truth, we know it can bear the test of reason, and like gold doubly refined, will come out purer and brighter from the fiery ordeal. The young man, who I hope is present, based his principal argument against us, "Because," said he, "you can bring no authority from revelation or from nature." I will not enter into an inquiry as to what he meant by these terms, but I will show him the revelation from which we derive our authority, and the nature in which it is written, in living characters. It is true we do not go to revelations written in books; but ours is older than all books, and whatever of good there is in any written revelations, must necessarily agree with ours, or it is not true, for ours only is the true revelation, based in nature and in life. That revelation is no less than the living, breathing, thinking, feeling, acting revelation manifested in the nature of woman. In her manifold powers, capacities, needs, hopes, and aspirations, lays her title-deed, and whether that revelation was written by nature or nature's God, matters not, for here it is. No one can disprove it. No one can bring an older, broader, higher, and more sacred basis for human rights. Do you tell me that the Bible is against our rights? Then I say that our claims do not rest upon a book written no one knows when, or by whom. Do you tell me what Paul or Peter says on the subject. Then again I reply that our claims do not rest on the opinions of any one, not even on those of Paul and Peter, for they are older than they. Books and opinions, no matter from whom they came, if they are in opposition to human rights, are nothing but dead letters.

I have shown you that we derive our claims from humanity, from revelation, from nature, and from your Declaration of Independence; all proclaim our right to life, liberty, and the pursuit of happiness; and having life, which fact I presume you do not question, then we demand all the rights and privileges society is capable of bestowing, to make life useful, virtuous, honorable, and happy. The first of our claims, then, is education, to develop all the powers and capacities of her nature; not a superficial literary education that shall attract for the moment, sparkle with a superficial luster for a little while, and then become extinct, and leave nothing but smoke and darkness behind; but an education which shall endure, and every day's experience shall expand her mind, increase her knowledge, and add freshness and vigor to her powers and abilities. This is necessary not only for her as a human being, but it is indispensable to the welfare of society, for woman in her fourfold capacities, namely, as companion, wife, mother, and, what is still more important, teacher of infancy and childhood, moulds and makes society what it is, and therefore if any difference ought to be made in the education of the sexes, woman ought to have the benefit; and yet what is her present education? Compare it with that of man—not indeed do I wish you to understand that his education is what it ought to be. Far from it: nor *can it ever be what it ought to be*, until woman's nature is developed and elevated in unison with his. But imperfect as his education now is, compare hers with it, and you will find how far, very far short it falls even to that.

When the young man returns from college, where he has graduated in all the schools limited by four walls, the unlimited school bound only by heaven and earth stands open to receive him; in it he can perfect himself in that most *important of all* educations, the knowledge of himself and of society. He may choose from the arts, sciences, professions, and various avocations, what would best suit his capacities, tastes, and means. He may ascend into the very heavens, or descend into the depth of the ocean, to gather from nature's rich stores the golden treasures of knowledge and of wealth, and all admire, and the many aid the young and noble aspirant after greatness.

But, oh, how different is it with woman? The girl, even in the most favorable position, when she comes from boarding-school, the mere child of sixteen, with her mind undeveloped, her powers uncultivated, without a knowledge of herself or society, imbued with the erroneous idea that her whole and only aim and end in life is to please man, in that imperfect and often worse than ignorant condition, her education is said to be finished, and all that is needed to complete her destiny, is to enter into fashionable life, place her name on the matrimonial list, and then, like a picture that has received the last finishing touch from the artist's hands, to which nothing more can be added, she is placed in a frame, perchance a gilded one, to grace the drawing-room, or a rude one for the use of the kitchen; but thenceforth there she is. Just at a period in life when his wider and more expanded education commences, hers is said to be finished, and even the little education she has received dwindles, for want of use, into nothing, the few accomplishments acquired, not for their intrinsic worth, but as a means to an end (namely, to get married); that end once obtained, they are cast aside as useless.

But I am told that woman needs not as extensive an education as man, as her place is only the domestic sphere; *only* the domestic sphere! Oh, how utterly ignorant is society of the true import of that term! Go to your legislative halls, and your Congress; behold those you have sent there to govern you, and as you find them high or low, great or small, noble or base, you can trace it directly or indirectly to the domestic sphere.

The wisest, in all ages, have acknowledged that the most important period in human education is in childhood—that period when the plastic mind may be moulded into such exquisite beauty, that no unfavorable influences shall be able entirely to destroy it—or into such hideous deformity, that it shall cling to it like a thick rust eaten into a highly polished surface, which no after scouring shall ever be able entirely to efface. This most important part of education is left entirely in the hands of the mother. She prepares the soil for future culture; she lays the foundation upon which a superstructure shall be erected that shall stand as firm as a rock, or shall pass away like the baseless fabric of a vision, and leave not a wreck behind. But the mother cannot give what she does not possess; weakness cannot impart strength. With an imperfect education—a dependent position—made, from the cradle to the grave, to look to man for strength, support, and protection; can she develop the powers, call out the energies, and impart a spirit of independence in her sons? Can a weak, timid, cowardly mother, call out in her sons courage, fortitude, and heroism? Brought up ever to look up to man as her only oracle of right, can she inspire her sons with a love of truth and an adherence to right, which not even the fear of death shall be able to shake? No; the stream cannot run higher than the source that feeds it. The mother must possess these high and noble qualities, or she never can impart them to her offspring.

Much more ought to be said on this all-important subject, of the education and influence of woman in every sphere of life; but I must leave this branch of our claims at present, and say something on her industrial avocation. On this alone evenings ought to be spent, to fathom the depth of the existing misery and wretchedness, the immediate result of the injustice done to woman, in depriving her of an industrial avocation, and almost of every means of an honorable independence.

Man, in addition to his enlarged education, receives also an industrial avocation, to fit him for all the purposes of life. He can study the professions, the arts, the sciences, or engage in mercantile pursuits, and if he finds one does not answer his purpose, he can change it for another. The shoemaker, tailor, or carpenter, if he finds that his trade is not in accordance with his taste or his abilities, or that it does not supply him with the necessary means, can change for any other; they are all open before him; the world is open to receive him, if he has abilities. He can become banker, lawyer, doctor, minister, or anything he pleases, to better his condition. How is it with woman? What are means given to her to enable her to obtain an honorable independence? Why, society have [sic] assigned her the kitchen, the needle, and the school-room!—and even here, on this narrow and contracted platform, man stands as her competitor, and, from the nature of the thing, her successful competitor. The female teacher gets three hundred dollars for the same amount of labor for which the male teacher gets five hundred. The male cook gets sixty dollars a month, and the woman cook gets for the same labor, from eight to twelve; for in the possession of a man, cooking assumes the dignity of a profession—in the hands of a woman it is considered a mere drudgery. The fact is, man has a choice—woman has not.

We all know that commerce regulates itself by the demand and supply;

and herein lays the secret why woman's labor is undervalued and underpaid. The market is overstocked with her labor. Having no choice of any other branch, she must take the pittance offered her, or starve; and when the girl who has no father or brother to look to for the necessaries and comforts of life, and she finds, by sad experience, that the kitchen, or the needle and the school-room cannot supply the demands of her physical, mental, and moral nature, what other resource has she to fly to except the last sad alternative: to sell herself in matrimony, or out of it?—and it would take the wisest heads, and the best hearts, to decide which is the worst. Both are evil, and productive of incalculable vice and misery in society.

My friends, time will not permit me to enter fully upon this important branch of our claims, to make you realize the dire results from the injustice done to woman; and as wrong always punishes itself, it recoils on society, and all suffer from it. Crippled in her education, dependent in her position—then talk to her about protection! Man protecting woman! Go into your streets at night—look at the wretched beings who wander them, in many cases the only home they possess—and you will have the practical evidence of his protection. What a bitter mockery it is, to make a being helpless—to tie hand, heart, and head, and tell him that it is from pure affection, so as to have the pleasure of protecting him! When our opponents ridicule the Woman's Rights movement—or even with their best feelings, tell us that if woman gets all her rights equal with man, particularly if she should come in contact with him in the forum, at the ballot-box, or in the legislative halls, that she might lose her modesty, innocence, and virtue; do they ever remember that these wretched victims of wrong are women too?—that they belong not only to the same sex, but to the same race?—beings like ourselves, with the same hopes and aspirations, and often endowed with a superior nature? Have you ever asked yourself what has brought them so low? If not, it is high time you should. Man's protection brought them there! He has brought her up so helpless as to be unable to protect herself—to look to him, her only assailant, as her natural protector; and then he has taken advantage of her ignorance, inexperience, and dependence, united to a warm, affectionate nature, a trusting and confiding spirit—to attract, ensnare, betray—to draw her from the summit of virtue and self-respect, and consign her to an abyss of vice, sin, shame and misery, from which nothing but death can release her! Say not the accusation is hard—the fact is harder; and yet I lay it not to man's willfulness, but to his ignorance; for he is as greatly the sufferer as woman is. But I state it as a fact, with an earnest hope and a sincere desire to point out the cause of the evil and facilitate its removal—to blot out this dark stain from our social and moral horizon.

But woman must help—those who are in a happier condition, must work for those who have been prostrated so low that they cannot help themselves; and dependent as woman now is, yet she can do much—she has done much. And although man, in his very becoming modesty (for modesty is as becoming in man as in woman), pronounced her his inferior, at times he acknowledges she can do something. The politician who requires her influence, knows it; the minister, in want of means to build churches, endow colleges to educate young men too lazy to work and ashamed to beg, know it; and it is high time that you, my sisters, should know it too. To all these things woman gives freely. Millions are sent out of the country for missionary purposes; much of that money is supplied by woman; and it is strange to me that rational, reflecting minds, can act so blindly, so inconsistently, as to leave ignorance, poverty, vice, and misery all around us, and send the means so indispensable at home, to foreign countries to convert the heathen. And what are they converted to?—to the civilized vices of the use of rum, tobacco, and gunpowder! It is high time that charity should begin at home—that the means so generously given, should be applied to the worse than heathen in our midst—the poor, helpless, degraded, vicious of our own sex; or, which is best of all— to prevent their becoming such.

Sisters! You have a duty to perform—and duty, like charity, begins at home. In the name of your poor, vicious, outcast, down-trodden sister!—in the name of her who once was as innocent and as pure as you are!—in the name of her who has been made the victim of wrong, injustice, and oppression!—in the name of man!—in the name of All, I ask you, I entreat you, if you have an hour to spare, a dollar to give, or a word to utter—spare it, give it, and utter it, for the elevation of woman! And when your minister asks you for money for Missionary purposes, tell him there are higher, and holier, and nobler missions to be performed at home. When he asks for colleges to educate ministers, tell him you must educate woman, that she may do away with the necessity of ministers, so that they may be able to go to some useful employment. If he asks you to give to the churches (which means to himself), then ask him what he has done for the salvation of woman. When he speaks to you of leading a virtuous life, ask him whether he understands the causes that have prevented so many of your sisters from being virtuous, and have driven them to degradation, sin, and wretchedness. When he speaks to you of a hereafter, tell him to help to educate woman, to enable her to live a life of intelligence, independence, virtue, and happiness here, as the best preparatory step for any other life. And if he has not told you from the pulpit of all these things; if he does not know them; it is high time you inform him of it, and teach him his duty here in this country and this life.

This subject is deep and vast enough for the wisest heads and purest hearts of the race; it underlies our whole social system. Look to your criminal records—look to your records of mortality, to your cemeteries, peopled by mothers before the age of thirty or forty, and children under the age of five; earnestly and impartially investigate the cause, and you can trace it directly or indirectly to woman's inefficient education; her helpless, dependent position; her inexperience; her want of confidence in her own noble nature, in her own principles and powers, and her blind reliance in man. We ask, then, for woman, an education that shall cultivate her powers, develop, elevate, and ennoble her being, physically, mentally, and morally; to enable her to take care of herself, and she will be taken care of; to protect herself, and she will be protected. But to give woman as full and extensive an education as man, we must perceive the same motives.

No one gathers keys without a prospect to have doors to unlock. Man does not acquire knowledge without the hope to make it useful and productive; the highest motives only can call out the greatest exertion. There is a vast field of action open to man, and therefore he is prepared to enter it; widen the field or sphere of action for woman, throw open to her all the avenues of industry, emolument, usefulness, moral ambition, and true greatness, and you will give her the same noble motives, the same incentives for exertion, application, and perseverance that man possesses, and this can be done only by giving her her legal and political rights; pronounce her the equal of man in all the rights and advantages society can bestow, and she will be prepared to receive and use them, and not before. It would be folly to cultivate her intellect like that of man without giving her the same chances to use it—to give her an industrial avocation without giving her the right to the proceeds of her industry, or to give her the right to the proceeds of her industry without giving her the power to protect the property she may acquire; she must therefore have the legal and political rights, or she has nothing.

The ballot-box is the focus of all other rights, it is the pivot upon which all others hang; the legal rights are embraced in it, for if once possessed of the right to the ballot-box, to self-representation, she will see to it that the laws shall be just, and protect her person and her property, as well as that of man. Until she has political rights she is not secure in any she may possess. One legislature may alter some oppressive law, and give her some right, and the next legislature may take it away, for as yet it is only given as an act of generosity, as a charity on the part of man, and not as her right, and therefore it cannot be lasting, nor productive of good.

I will not be able to enter fully upon the laws to show you how grievously unjust and oppressive they are to married woman, that at marriage she is legally annihilated, except when she has property to be taxed, or committed some crime to be punished for. It is true that she has now the right in several of the States—thanks to the persevering efforts of a few persons—to hold the real estate she brings at marriage, or that may fall to her subsequent to marriage; but how far does that extend? It is at best but for the favored few, but not for the laboring many. In this country there are comparatively few girls with fortunes. The vast majority commence married life with the united capital of head, hand, and heart. To the result of this best of all capital, the wife has no right. During the lifetime of her husband she cannot claim the value of one dollar as her own, no matter by whom the property is acquired, whether by the united efforts of both, or by the industry, perseverance, and economy of the wife alone: it still belongs to the husband. The law makes no distinction between man and man, only between man and woman; it has given the wife into his uncontrolled possession—her person, her talents, her time, her industry: all are his by right of law (which means by right of might). Even the husband who spends his time in idleness, dissipation, and vice; he who cannot feel the sacred tie of home and of family; he has the same power over his wife, and if she has to go out to daily labor to keep herself and children from starving, the worthless husband can come and claim his wife's earnings from the employer, or force it out of her hands; and if she remembers her starving children, and resists, he can use the means the law has provided him with, to enforce obedience, namely, give her a "wholesome chastisement," to make her sensible of the "husband's prerogative" over the wife.

For this deep degradation of subjecting her body, mind, and soul, unconditionally to the husband, the law makes amends, and allows the wife, at the husband's death, the widow's encumbrance—an encumbrance indeed it is. When the husband dies intestate she is entitled to a life interest in one-third of the real estate; not the third of the estate in fee simple, but only a life interest. She may have depending upon her an aged parent, a child by a former husband, or a helpless, unprotected brother or sister; yet, at her death, she cannot leave even the pittance the law allows her. Even where there are no children, it is taken from her and given to some of his relations, back, far back, to his fifty-ninth cousin, or some other relative, all the way down to Adam. Of the personal property the law gives her some things belonging to the household—a bed to lay on, a chair to sit on, and a table to eat on, after depriving her of the means to have something to eat; but it is too degrading even to talk about it. Truly, when we consider the outrageous injustice of the present laws to woman, we can hardly realize that they can be the emanations of men who could call themselves husbands, fathers, sons, and brothers; for not only have they robbed the married woman of her own identity, and her property, but they have robbed the mother of her children.

Mothers, women of America! When you hear the subject of Woman's Rights broached, laugh at it and us, ridicule it as much as you please; but never forget that, by the laws of your country, you have no right to your children—the law gives the father as uncontrolled power over the child as it gives the husband over the wife, only the child, when it comes to maturity, the father's control ceases, while the wife never comes to maturity. The father may bequeath, bestow or sell the child without the consent of the mother. But methinks I hear you say that no man deserving the name of man, or the title of husband and father, could commit such an outrage against the dearest principles of humanity; well, if there are no such men, then the law ought to be annulled, a law against which nature, justice, and humanity revolts, ought to be wiped off from the statute book as a disgrace; and if there are such—which unhappily we all know there are—then there is still greater reason why the laws ought to be changed, for bad laws encourage bad men and make them worse; good men cannot be benefited by the existence of bad laws; bad men ought not to be; laws are not made for him who is a law unto himself, but for the lawless. The legitimate object of law is to protect the innocent and inexperienced against the designing and the guilty; we, therefore, ask every one present to demand of the Legislatures of every State to alter these unjust laws; give the wife an equal right with the husband in the property acquired after marriage; give the mother an equal right with the father in the control of the children; let the wife at the death of the husband remain his heir to the same extent that he would be hers, at her death; let the laws be alike for both, and they are sure to be right; but to have them so, woman must help to make them.

I know there is great prejudice against our claim to political rights, childish fears and apprehensions are rife, but this is only from a mistaken idea or an utter ignorance on the subject; as soon as it is understood, all opposition is removed. It is true it is a Herculean task to make it known; it requires a great moral courage to stem the tide, to say to those who believed themselves the only lords of creation, Stand aside; give us space to grow. Our title-deed to life, and to all that belongs to it, to make it useful and happy, is as clear as yours; and woman, timid as she is, yet when it is necessary she has moral courage for any emergency.

We hear a great deal about the heroism of the battle-field, What is it? Compare it with the heroism of woman who stands up for the right, and it sinks into utter insignificance. To stand before the cannon's mouth, with death, before him and disgrace behind, excited to frenzy by physical fear, encouraged by his leader, stimulated by the sound of the trumpet, and sustained by the *still emptier sound of glory*, requires no great heroism; the merest coward could be a hero in such a position; but to face the fire of an unjust and prejudiced public opinion, to attack the adamantine walls of long-usurped power, to brave not only the enemy abroad, but often that severest of all enemies, your own friends at home, requires a heroism that the world has never yet recognized, that the battle-field cannot supply, but which woman possesses.

Even in this movement, who can tell the amount of moral courage and true heroism it required in her who first dared publicly to proclaim herself the coequal with the lords of creation, and demand back her birth-right they have so long unjustly usurped. To see *such* an audience before us, listening with evident interest to what we have to say in support of our claims, you cannot realize what it was twenty-five and twenty years ago to call public attention to these wrongs, and prepare the way for such conventions, and *such* audiences; and yet woman had the moral courage to do it, and do it as fearlessly as now; for though she had nothing else to support her, she had the consciousness of possessing the *might of right* to sustain her. Moral warfare has always to contend with greater difficulties than physical, but it has one glorious advantage which outweighs all others, and is sure to make it victorious at last.

When the Allied Powers endeavored to take Sebastopol they found that every incision and inroad they made in the fortress during the day, was filled out by the enemy during the night; and even now, after the terrible sacrifice of life to break it down, they are not safe, but the enemy may build it up again. But in a moral warfare, no matter how thick and impenetrable the fortress of prejudice may be, if you once make an inroad in it, that space can never be filled up again; every stone you remove is removed for aye and for good; and the very effort to replace it, tends only to loosen every other stone, until the whole foundation is undermined, and the superstructure crumbles at your feet.

This has been demonstrated in every moral reform, and probably in none more so than in the Woman's Rights movement. Since our first conventions, the change in public opinion is so immense, that the most sanguine friends of the cause look at it with wonder. Some changes in the laws have already begun to be made, and more will be made. until the whole is obtained. Its influence has been felt, not only here, but all over Europe. I wish I had time to tell you of the efforts that have already been made in England, France and Germany; but as there are other speakers to come after me, I will only mention that in England petitions, signed by

thousands of the most intellectual portion of society, have been presented to Parliament by Lord Brougham, and sustained by Lord Lyndhurst,
the Hon. G. W. Hastings, and others, demanding, among other things,
the right of married woman to her earnings. A committee appointed by
the "Law Amendment Society" sent in a most able and favorable report,
relating to the property of married women—Sir Erskine Perry, a member of that committee, is said to have been mainly instrumental in the
report—in it is given the conflict between law and equity, relating to the
property of married women. That committee recommended the adoption
of the following principles:

## HEADS OF NEW LAW OF PROPERTY AS TO MARRIED WOMEN

1. The Common Law rules, which make marriage a gift of all the
woman's personal property to the husband, to be repealed.

2. Power in married woman to hold separate property by law, as she
now may in equity.

3. A woman marrying without any ante-nuptial contract, to retain her
property and after acquisitions and earnings as if she were a *feme sole.*

4. A married woman having separate property to be liable on her separate contracts, whether made before or after marriage.

5. A husband not to be liable for the ante-nuptial debts of his wife,
any farther than any property brought to him under settlement by his
wife extends.

6. A married woman to have the power of making a will; and on her
death intestate, the principles of the Statute of Distributions, as to her husband's personality, *mutatis mutandis,* to apply to the property of the wife.

7. The rights of succession between husband and wife, whether as to
real or personal estate, to courtesy or dower, to be framed on principles of
equal justice to each party.

These just demands will have to be granted, and more made, and
obtained, too.

Here, in England, and everywhere, woman's just claims are becoming
the topic of the day, and will continue to be so, until she will be restored
to herself, with the *practical* right to life, liberty, and the pursuit of happiness. And do you think, my friends, that she will be any less woman?
that placing her on the proud eminence of equality with man, in all the
rights, duties, and enjoyments of life will detract from her virtues? that to
give her educational, social and political rights will deteriorate her nature?
Have these advantages debased man? If not, then they will not debase

woman. Human rights, based upon the true principle of equality, would have as beneficial, as elevating, as ennobling an effect on woman as on man; and then, and not till then, will she deserve the name of woman; then only will she be capable of being an intellectual companion, an affectionate wife, a tender mother, a wise teacher, a useful member of society, and, to sum up the whole, a true woman.

# LETTER TO THE EDITOR: "THE ENGLISH DIVORCE BILL"
October 3, 1857
New York, New York

Rose's trip abroad in the prior year brought renewed contact with women in Europe, allowing her to follow more closely the progress of women's rights in the countries where she had traveled. When this newly passed British legislation gave men rights in divorce and remarriage that were denied to women, Rose was outraged. In this letter, published in the October 21, 1857, edition of the *Boston Investigator*, she excoriates the "unblushing shamelessness" of male legislators and clergy who clothe themselves in sanctimony as they misuse their power to restrict the freedom of women to the advantage of men.

$\sim\!\!\!\!\!\!\Rightarrow$

Mr. Editor:—At a Woman's Rights Convention, held three years ago at Cleveland, (Ohio,) while speaking on the injustice and inequality of the laws in regard to woman, I stated that not only does the civil code bear testimony that it was formed by one sex only, as it seems to be made almost exclusively for the benefit of that sex, but that the moral code, from the same reason, is stamped with the same impress. And as laws tend to favor public opinion, therefore what public opinion considers a sufficient crime in woman; to cast her out not only from society, but almost from the pale of Humanity, is, when perpetrated by man, the law-maker, considered a mere peccadillo and not only tolerated, but perfectly pardoned by all classes of society; and hence, while the poor victims of vice are degraded and outcast, the perpetrators fill the most honorable positions in church and state. This but too evident truth, called out the righteous indignation of a Reverend present, who, though not willing to defend the State, stood up for the purity of the Church, of which I need hardly say, that very few present were convinced.

But if any doubt could possibly have existed on the subject, the long looked for, but recently passed English "Divorce Bill," (an extract of which I send you from the N.Y. *Tribune*,) must set that doubt aside for ever. I will not comment on it at present, having had a severe attack of sickness, from which I have not sufficiently recovered to be able to write without injury, nor do I think that it needs any comments, for it carries its own condemnation on its own face.

But I must say, that low as my estimate has ever been of men who rob woman of her identity, her property, and her offspring, of statesmen and legislators who enact laws in defiance of human rights which recognize no sex, it falls far short of the utter contempt if not abhorrence with which "The grounds of the dissolution of marriage," "on the part of the husband," have inspired me with.

The vitiated taste, the unblushing shamelessness exhibited by these civil and ecclesiastical law-givers, in thus shielding and fencing around the depravity and corruption of their own sex, to the detriment and destruction of ours, far outdoes in impudence the Mormons themselves, and is a disgrace alike to the age, the country, and the sex.

In giving this article and the enclosed one a place in the *Investigator*, you will oblige,

> Yours, for the Right,
> Ernestine L. Rose
> New York, Oct. 3, 1857

# LETTER TO THE EDITOR:
## "ENGLAND RULED BY A PRAYER BOOK"
December 29, 1857
New York, New York

In this letter, Rose skillfully addresses and weaves together two of her key issues—the double standard of sexual morality between women and men, and the separation of church and state. By giving free rein to her gifts of sarcastic wit and eloquent logic, she vents her outrage in a manner that shows how religion can be used for the subordination of women. In this letter to the *Boston Investigator*, published January 13, 1858, Rose expresses fury at attempts to enforce a seventeenth-century statute requiring that the *Book of Common Prayer* of the Anglican Church be taken as the standard for laws to govern all citizens, irrespective of their beliefs. Was it too much to hope, she asks, that "common sense, justice, or right" would prevail as the basis for legislation? As in her preceding letter, Rose takes particular aim at proposed limits set on remarriage after divorce, which were written to the disadvantage of women while allowing greater freedom for men. In an unusual move, she refers to the Bible and the practices of God's "chosen people," the Jews, noting that both are less restrictive on the subject of remarriage than is the English law.

❧

Mr. Editor:—Believing that with the rest of mankind, you may labor under the mistaken idea that England is governed by a Queen, by certain codes of law, by acts of Parliament, etc., I send you the following article, being a few items taken from the New York *Tribune*, of the doings of the English clergy, which will set you all straight and convince you of two facts: first, that England is really governed by a prayer book; for whatever Parliament may do, their acts are to be judged not by *common sense, justice,* or *right*, but by the *common prayer book*, and if found guilty, to be dealt with accordingly; and secondly, that the church neither sleeps nor slumbers, but is ever at work to keep the supremacy over the people.

The English Divorce Bill, recognizing the dissolubility of marriage, (the only rational thing in it,) has reawakened the clergy to renewed efforts against it. "The act was to go into effect about the first of January, by an order issued in Council for that purpose." To prevent this, a petition has been got up, praying the Queen not to issue any such order until the Act shall have been submitted again to Parliament for revision.

"The ground of this petition is, that those portions of the Divorce

Bill which recognize the absolute dissolubility of marriage by allowing the divorced parties to marry again, are in conflict, with certain portions of the 'Act of Uniformity,' (13 and 14 Charles 2d, ch. 4.) by which Act the book of common prayer is made the law of the land," every minister of the Established Church being required "To declare openly and publicly before the congregation his unfeigned assent and consent to the use of all things contained in it." That book of common prayer, thus made the law of the land, contains, as a part of the form of the solemnization of marriage, the following prayer:—

"Oh! God, who by thy mighty power hast made all things out of nothing; who also (after other things set in order) didst appoint that out of man (created after thy own image and similitude) woman should take her being; and knitting them together, didst teach that it should never be lawful to put asunder those whom thou by matrimony hast made one."

Such being the case, the petitioners expressed the apprehension that, in passing the Divorce Bill, "Parliament have inaugurated a most alarming precedent." "The Act of Uniformity is the legal constitutional basis of the public ministrations; and if the principle is once admitted, directly or indirectly, of repealing any portion of it, the plain meaning of the prayer book may be nullified, its express directions imperceptibly abrogated, fundamental alterations may be effected—in fact, by this process, the establishment may be all frittered away before anybody knows what is going on."

To avert this alarming danger to the *Establishment*, the petitioners wish the Act again submitted to Parliament, "that at least care may be taken that no violence be done to the plain language of the prayer book, to the consciences (pockets) of the clergy of the Church of England, and the law of the church."

Poor fellows! They are dreadfully alarmed for their holy religion; and, were it not for them, what would become of it all? But, sure enough, they are right, and we must give them credit at least for clear-sightedness enough to see that even the most minute fraction of reform contains in itself the germ to destroy their superstition and consequently their assumption of power and authority.

But the supremacy of the prayer book has recently been fully proclaimed by the Court of Equity. You are aware that the Church of England forbids a man to marry his deceased wife's sister, which has long caused a good deal of interesting agitation and controversy. But such marriages being considered lawful in all other Protestant countries, this prohibition of the English Ecclesiastical canons was disregarded, and up to 1835 such marriages were considered valid, and the children of such a marriage were legitimate, unless proceedings were instituted in the Ecclesiastical Court during the life-time of both parties, and then the marriage was pronounced void. The effect of this law was, not to prevent such marriages, but to give the husband the power, if he should choose to do so, to repudiate his wife and disinherit his children. To remedy this evil, "Parliament passed an Act in 1835, which declared that all such marriages already contracted to be valid and binding, but all future marriages of that sort to be absolutely void." But even this decision of the law did not prevent such marriages from being contracted; and in many cases, to give them a more binding character, the parties celebrated the marriage abroad in a country where such marriages were legal.

But in a recent case of Brook vs. Brook on this subject, the Court decided that all such marriages between English subjects are just as void when celebrated abroad as when at home.

In answer to the cases cited to show that by the law of nations the validity of a marriage depends on the law of the country where it was celebrated, 'The Court denied that any validity is given on the strength of foreign laws, to marriages deemed contrary to God's law and holy Scripture; as is the marriage of the sister of a deceased wife by the English prayer book."

By this decision a great number of marriages are null and void, and the children illegitimized and disinherited, all for the glory of "God's law and the holy Scripture!"

But the curiosity of it is, that their "God's laws," as given in their "holy Scripture," forbid no such marriages at all; on the contrary, the "chosen children of God" married near relatives, and the very oracles of God from among his "chosen people," the very patriarchs, Abraham, Isaac, and Jacob, married relations such as first cousins and nieces, and Jacob would not even wait until his wife should die, to marry her sister, but actually married live sisters; and we don't find that "God's law" or "holy Scripture" reproved them for it. The Jews now marry near relatives, first cousins, nieces, and of course can have no objection to marry the sister of a dead wife, which is no relation at all, particularly as this very law of God and holy Scripture enjoins it on them as a duty, that if a man dies without children, his brother shall marry the widow. Now whatever difference there may be between tweedledee and tweedledum, I can see no difference between a man marrying his dead wife's sister, and a woman her dead husband's brother. Well, perhaps I can't understand such heavenly wisdom.

But the richest part of it is, that the very prayer book which is cited as supreme authority against absolute divorce between husband and wife, (as in the divorce bill,) is the main cause for now actually divorcing so many marriages, and that too without the parties concerned wishing it, and dis-inheriting children, which would not be the case according to the divorce bill. But the prayer book says so, and so it must be right.

Thus, you see that "England, the civilizer," the country that boasts (and to some extent justly so) of ruling and governing the world, is ruled and governed by a prayer book! But it is useless to expect common sense or justice on the subject of marriage, until that most pernicious and unho-ly marriage of "Church and State" is divorced forever.

Yours, for the right,
Ernestine L. Rose
New York, Dec. 29, 1857

# LETTER TO THE EDITOR:
## "THE FREE LOVE QUESTION"
June 29, 1858
New York, New York

Rose wrote this letter to the *New York Times* rebutting its inaccurate coverage of her speech to the Free Convention held in Rutland, Vermont, on June 25–27, 1858. The convention was intended to offer cross-fertilization of ideas from various reform movements, with the platform open to all. The article on the convention published in the *New York Times* on June 29, 1858, is sensationally entitled "A Spicy Time on Free-Love—Broad Doctrines Freely Avowed," with the subheading "A Small Bit of Abolitionism, Touches of Spiritualism, and a great deal of Woman's Rights." The *Times* reported attendance by a diverse group of reformers characterized as free love advocates, spiritualists, radical abolitionists, and women's rights advocates. Apparently unable to distinguish between advocacy of free love, which often opposed marriage altogether, and advocacy of women's equal rights within marriage, it erroneously identified Rose as representing the free love movement. As she always did when falsely accused, Rose wrote to correct the record, and to distance herself from Mrs. Branch's position, stating that she was a woman's rights advocate and had "nothing to do with the marriage question, except as to have the laws so altered as to have them equal for husband and wife." Although Rose's letter was addressed "To the Editor of the *New York Times*," there is no record of it in their index, and no evidence that they chose to publish it. It was printed in the *Boston Investigator* on July 28, 1858, under the heading "The Free Love Question—Letter from Mrs. Rose."

❧

To The Editor Of The *New York Times*:—

New York, Tuesday, June 29, 1858

Dear Sir—I am perfectly willing, nay, desirous, that the sentiments and principles I advocate should be known and criticized by the public; but I am not willing to have imputed to me sentiments which do not belong to me, and, believing that you do not willfully misrepresent me, I take the liberty to correct some errors in regard to myself, in the account of the Rutland Convention, in your paper of this morning.

The report says: "Mrs. Ernestine L. Rose is active, so is Mrs. Julia Branch; both these ladies go for free love on principle."

This I most emphatically deny. I have never advocated these sentiments, from the simple reason that I do not believe in them. The facts are these:—

Mrs. Branch, in speaking to resolution No. 5, said:

"Mrs. Rose and others go down to the influence of the mothers. This is not enough. I go further."

I spoke in favor of the amendment moved by Mr. Foster, to the resolution, namely, to insert after the words "exclusive conjugal love" the words "perfect equality," so as to read thus: "*Resolved*, That the only true and natural marriage is an exclusive conjugal love based on perfect equality between one man and one woman; the only true home is the isolated home based on this exclusive love."

In referring to Mrs. Branch, I said:—"The lady is a stranger to me. I have never seen her. I do not know what she means on the subject of marriage. I did not understand her in the same way that Mr. Tiffany did, but if she meant what he made it out to be, then I most emphatically differ from her." In reference to her allusion to me, I said, "I go before, beyond, and above the influence of mothers, but I have nothing to do with the marriage question, except as to have the laws so altered as to have them equal for husband and wife," and in endeavoring to enforce the necessity of the equality of right, I showed that the "two halves of the pair of scissors," which Mr. Tiffany represented as belonging to the husband and wife, are given to him alone, and even when the whole pair belongs to her, the law still gives it to him, that Blackstone says "husband and wife are one," and the laws declared *that* one to be the husband, by giving *him* all the rights that belong to both.

This is all I said on the subject connected with marriage, except that when the laws proclaim woman civilly and politically equal with man, and she is educated to enable her to promote her own independence, then she will not be obliged to marry for a home and a protector, for she well knows that she can never be protected unless she protects herself, and matrimony (not a matter of money) will take place from pure affection.

Hoping you will do me the justice to give this a place in your paper, I am, very respectfully,

Ernestine L. Rose

# SPEECH AT THE THOMAS PAINE
## CELEBRATION: SEPARATION
## OF CHURCH AND STATE
January 31, 1859
New York, New York

In this speech at the annual Thomas Paine Celebration, Rose took as her subject threats to the separation of church and state. She decried violations of the Constitutional doctrine in the United States, ranging from Sunday "blue laws" to the use of the Bible in public schools. As an example of the dangers of combining the powers of church and state, Rose points to the Papal States, the region of central Italy where the Pope was civil as well as religious leader. Her reference to "the case of Mortara" would have been well-understood by her audience, for the kidnapping of Edgardo Mortara, a six-year-old Jewish child, had been reported in the press internationally. Agents of the Papal States had seized the child from his family home in Bologna so that he could be reared in the Catholic religion. The rationale for the kidnapping was that during a serious illness, a domestic servant, fearing the boy would die and go to hell, baptized him without his parents' permission. Despite numerous appeals to the papacy by the parents, and by international figures as Napoleon III and the European Jewish activist Sir Moses Montefiore, the child was never returned. As an adult, he chose to remain with the church and became a canon in Rome and professor of theology (Berenbaum and Skolnik 2007, [14] 513; see also Kerzer 1999). The speech was published as part of a report on the event in the *Boston Investigator*, February 16, 1859. The report referred to her talk as "a spicy exposé of the faith" and described the reverberations of the applause as causing the crockery to "fairly dance with approbation."

⤙

Mrs. Ernestine L. Rose, on being called to respond to the second toast— "The Rights of Man,"—arose and delivered the following address:—

Mr. President and Friends—Thanking you for the honor conferred upon me, in wishing me to speak on this interesting occasion, allow me to assure you that no public event inspires me with as heartfelt an interest as the annual assembly of Liberal friends to celebrate the natal day that gave to the world the noble champion of political and religious freedom, one who by his devotion to human rights, has proved himself indeed the "Friend of Man"—Thomas Paine. Were we to measure the talents, virtue and services of Paine by the extent, fierceness and duration of the slander, abuse and persecution that he suffered, not only during life, but from which even the grave has not been able to shield him, we would have to pronounce him the greatest man that probably ever lived. It is true some of the noble defenders of liberty had to pay for the prerogative of benefiting the race with a forfeiture of life; but, at least, they were permitted to rest in peace in the grave, and the people endeavored to make restitution by bestowing upon them that honor, after death, of which despotic and corrupt governments deprived them while living. Thomas Paine was allowed to die a natural death; the laws of the country sanctioned no actual decapitation; but religious intolerance, fiercer and more brutal than law, that hardly permitted him to die in peace, will not let him, even after the lapse of fifty years, rest in peace in his grave. This unrelenting persecution is not the work of a despotic government. No! Not of Rome, where in the name of religion and of God, bands of ecclesiastical marauders break in at the dead of night to rob parents of their children—as in the case of Mortara—where the "glad tidings of the gospel" are enforced by the light of the dungeon, the rack and the stake, but here, in Protestant republican America, where a Thomas Paine projected and a Thomas Jefferson perfected the immortal declaration that man has an inalienable right to "life, liberty and the pursuit of happiness."

Yet through the venomous shafts of slander, of a corrupt clergy, the sworn enemies of free thought and free speech, the warfare against Paine has not yet ceased. Hardly a week passes but you can see in some of the religious papers the same falsehoods that were long ago invented; and every one who has the good sense to appreciate, and the justice to honor his devotion to the rights of man, comes under the same stigma and shares the same fate. Freedom of conscience is guaranteed in theory and punished in practice. The Constitution has divorced that unnatural marriage—the union of Church and State—but by Government it is re-united. In Washington chaplains' pray[ers] open Congress, while the members prey upon the people; our State Governors issue out annual mandates for fasts, feasts and thanksgiving over roast turkeys, which is quite an improvement on the "Pope's bulls"; for it certainly is pleasanter to roast a turkey than to be roasted. Christian Jersey sold recently the furniture of a poor man to pay a fine for doing something to his garden on the "Sabbath"—the day that her patron saint, Christ, said was "made for man," and not man for it. In "free and enlightened" Massachusetts, within the shadow of Bunker Hill—on the steps of the "Cradle of Liberty"—if your conviction will not permit you to believe in the fashionable superstition called religion, your character may be unblemished, your reputation untarnished; you may be a kind husband, a tender father, or a good citizen; a zealous patriot, an honest, virtuous man; yet your evidence is not taken before a court of justice, and any believing scoundrel has but to prove you an Infidel to be set free. Even in the Empire City of the Empire State the same intolerance is visible. The Bible—a book utterly unfit to be placed in the hands of children—is forced on the public schools against the conscientious convictions of a great portion of the people. Sunday, the working man's holiday to renew his physical and mental strength by rational recreation and amusements, by moral and scientific lectures, music, dancing and the theatre, is forced upon him as a day of gloom, to be dozed away in church or at home.

. . . . . . . .

But the worst is, they are never satisfied; not content with the pulpit, where they are as safe as any coward in his castle . . . they must monopolize the forum also, and take every opportunity to decry Infidel lecturers as dangerous to the community. In a discourse recently given before the Historical Society, the clerical orator took pains to speak reproachfully of societies for accepting "lecturers who, under fine rhetoric, sowed the seed of Pantheism, materialism, and other sophistries," and, said he, "the fact of having their names associated with such as these caused many able lecturers to withdraw from the field." A great pity, truly—for, though the public don't suffer by the loss, I fear the pious souls, in their self-inflicted retirement must, as it is well known that the nerve leading to a clerical pocket is very largely developed. But the richest thing is for clergymen to be afraid of sophistry, when they stand at the very fountain head whence all sophistry flows. Materialism they might well fear. The difference between materialistic and spiritual lecturers is great indeed. The one is for life, the other for death; the one speaks about the universe with all it contains, the other about the man in the moon. Morality, the Infidel's textbook, teaches man how to live; superstition, the priest's weapon, teaches him how to die. Let us, then, my friends, be content, by reason, justice and truth, to secure a happy life, and they are welcome to the rest.

# LETTER TO THE EDITOR:
## "RISE, PROGRESS, AND FALL OF A FREE CHURCH"
December 14, 1859
New York, New York

Part of the freethought movement was made up of liberal Christians who wished to attend a church without a set creed, one that allowed free discussion of issues between a minister and parishioners. Rose chose to attend the initial meetings of one such "free church," under the leadership of a Rev. Noyes. As a radical freethinker opposed to all organized religion and clergy, Rose's purpose may have been to test just how free of creeds and dogma a church could be while still being a church. And indeed, after a promising beginning in which a wide range of belief and nonbelief was welcomed, Rose witnessed the rapid decline of freedom of thought at the free church. The letter was published in the *Boston Investigator* on December 28, 1859.

Mr. Editor: It was asked in former times, "Can any good come out of Nazareth?" I ask, can a church be free? In the following article you may find the solutions. On a subject of a purely secular nature, no one seems to be afraid to hear the opinions of another, and bring it to the test of reason and of truth, by it to stand or to fall. But the moment you touch on religion, the believer seems to shrink as if afraid that an exposure to the light might impair its beauty, in which he seems to have no great confidence, or to discover its deformity, which his very fear gives evidence to have been more than half suspected. Some weeks ago I gave you a little account of "The First Independent Society" at Hope Chapel. I will now give you my experience in connection with it and its present position.

Last September we heard that the Rev. Mr. Noyes held conference every Sunday morning. This being a novel thing for a church, we attended, and were very much pleased with the liberality of the sentiments advocated. Mr. N. stated that he wished to establish a free church; he did not desire to occupy the place as speaker alone. "The old church was dead; it had lost its vitality, for there is no freedom in it; ministers wish to be listened to, but are unwilling to hear others; my object in coming here is to establish what seems to me the great need of the age, a church where all who feel it their duty shall be able to express their opinions on subjects of importance."

He then spoke on the Sunday question, and in favor of more freedom on that day, but said, "Although I am against legal restraint, yet rather than have the day observed as it is in Paris, where the young men are let loose to license and intemperance, I would prefer the strictest Puritanical observance."

As the invitation was given for others to say something on the subject, I made some remarks to correct the false impression as to the Parisian Sunday, assuring them that not the slightest license or intemperance could be found in the streets or gardens or concerts or theatres or museums, galleries of paintings, or libraries, for the people of Paris had something more interesting to occupy their attention, and to impress the necessity of proper recreation and amusements, for the health of body and mind, as the surest means to keep the unemployed masses from license and intemperance. Several others spoke, and the meeting closed.

On the following Sunday, Mr. Noyes spoke on the necessity of setting apart one day in every week as a day of rest, and stated that "in Paris, during the Revolution, the seventh day as a day of rest was abolished and replaced by the tenth day; but they found it would not answer, and medical men declared that one day of rest out of every seven was absolutely necessary for the preservation of health." I fully coincided with that idea, but said, that in my opinion rest does not always consist in inaction, in sleeping at home or dozing at church, nor even in listening to three sermons in one day; but that change of occupation was rest; and as the employment during six days of the week differ, so also must the rest on the seventh differ, and it would be just as consistent to restrict and regulate the labor of the week, compelling all to do one kind of work, as to compel them to have one kind of rest. Some need rest of body, others of mind, some to exercise the voice in speaking or singing, others the limbs in walking, riding, gymnastics, or dancing, others in purely intellectual pursuits, and others still, as is the case with ministers, to work on that day for a living. Several gentlemen then spoke, and the meeting closed apparently to the satisfaction of all.

On the Sunday after that, Mr. Noyes spoke on the "irrepressible conflict." He regretted the Harper's Ferry insurrection, and after dwelling on the evils of slavery, cited, the Revolutionary heroes, Washington, Jefferson, and others, as being on the side of freedom. In my remarks, I reminded them that there was another Revolutionary hero devoted to freedom, particularly to American freedom, Thomas Paine, but owing to Puritanism he is seldom remembered except to be abused. In allusion to John Brown, I said that if the Harper's Ferry insurrection was to be regretted, the cause that produced it was infinitely more so, and I greatly feared we would have to regret many more unhappy results springing from the same miserable cause, for as long as the cause remains the effects in some shape or other must follow. It is the nature of right to be in opposition to wrong, of freedom eternally to war against oppression, hence the irrepressible conflict until one destroys the other, for freedom and slavery *can never exist together* in peace.

The following Sunday, Mr. Noyes spoke on a "free church," impressing the absolute necessity of a church where the members should be able to interchange opinions with the speaker and each other, as the great need of society. It was a very liberal and interesting discourse. I expressed my gratification, and said, that although the very term church is associated, in my mind, with superstition, intolerance, and an entire absence of freedom, yet I was very glad to see at least one church open its doors wide enough for freedom to enter. It was then proposed that in the evening, after the discourse, a society should be formed. Accordingly, in the evening it was stated that as expenses were incurred, it became necessary to form an organization for financial purposes. A committee of five gentlemen was then appointed to draw up a constitution and report on the following Sunday evening.

In the morning, the Rev. gentleman spoke on the question, "What is true religion?" He was very liberal, and treated the subject as well as could be expected, dwelling on all the good attributes of man, and called it God. In my remarks I said, if anything were wanting to show us the progress we have made; the interesting discourse we have just heard would prove it beyond a doubt; for as every age makes its own religion and its own God, we certainly must live in a more civilized and humane age, from the fact that religion is now made so much more civilized and humane. I am very happy to see it, and hail it as the beginning of a good time coming. But the definition just given of religion is simply morality, and that of God is of a good man governed by the law of justice and kindness; and my objection to call it by any other name is, that it robs man of the virtues and noble elements belonging to his nature and transfers them to some unknown power, and he is told to pray to the God he has made out of himself, to bestow upon him a portion of what was his own. Truth, justice, charity, kindness and love, combined, make the creed of morality and virtue belonging to man, and necessary to this life; for it teaches him his duty to his fellow man, while religion, being a mystery, belongs wholly to some other unknown life, hence we can make no use of it in this. It teaches faith, blind, implicit faith, in things unseen and unknown; morality has nothing to do with religion, for a man may be ever so virtuous and moral, yet if he does not profess faith, he is called an Infidel.

Others also spoke, and the remarks were listened to with great interest and attention. In conclusion, Mr. Noyes said, that as this question is of great importance, he would leave it for the next Sunday's conference, and "he would expect those who don't believe in the existence of a God to give a reason why people in all countries and all ages believed in God." So, of course, I felt myself in duty bound to prove at the next conference, first, that all nations do not believe; second, that if they did, why they did so; and third, that the belief of the whole world, that two and two makes five, would not make it any more than four, nor can any amount of belief transform falsehood into truth.

In the evening, after the discourse, the committee reported a short pre-amble and constitution, stating the desirability of a society "for moral and religious instruction, to teach man his duty to God and to his fellow man" and a proposition for several committees, one of them a Sunday School committee. Before it was put to vote, I asked the chairman, Dr. Warner, whether they would admit a member who, though willing to the utmost in her power to aid in the moral instruction of man, would not be willing to do anything for religious instruction, simply because she did not know any-thing about religion, and therefore could not know what kind of instruction was required? Dr. Warner said that they had no creed to subscribe to, and did not interfere with any one's belief. At this point, Mr. Potter, a member of the committee; arose, filled with pious indignation, and said, "The lady is out of order. I want to know what kind of society we are going to have? I wanted to have a Christian society, but the other members of the commit-tee thought fit to overrule me. The First Independent Society is based upon the fatherhood of God as well as the brotherhood of man, and I want to know whether we are going to have meetings here every Sunday morning to discuss the existence of a God and to advocate Infidelity? If that is to be the case, I will not belong to the society."—Several other gentlemen spoke, and said I was perfectly in order and did right to express my opinions freely on the subject of religion.

I then told them I liked the society for its liberality, and, in any prac-tical measure for the benefit of man, I should be very happy to co-oper-ate with them, but I did not wish to sail under false colors, not even to be admitted to this society or to any other. I therefore felt it my duty to define my position on a subject that appears to most people of the high-est importance, and I freely own that while I accept with pleasure the "brotherhood of man," I cannot accept the "fatherhood of God." I do not know whether it is father or mother, person or power or principle; and as I know nothing about it, I can give it no name, and can owe it no duty. I can understand from myself what duty I owe to man, but not being able to comprehend the nature of a God, I cannot understand what duty could be required of me, nor what service I could render him, and if as we are told, God is all-wise and all-powerful, he can need no services from us, while man does need them, and as long as there is so much poverty, ignorance, superstition, vice, crime, and its consequent suffering, we have neither time, nor talents, nor means nor love, nor devotion to spare—the race needs it all.

This caused quite a little commotion. Dr. Warner said, "By the term God we only mean supreme goodness." I told them that as I am unable to understand the term good except as an attribute applicable to man, and as a quality attached to an act, I could not personify it into a God. The constitution was then adopted, committees appointed, and the meeting dismissed.

A young Unitarian minister from Rochester, (I forget his name,) introduced himself, and expressed his gratification at my remarks. "You (said he) are the only person I have ever met who believes less than I do; I had no idea that any person entertained these views." I told him he could find many, some even in his own church, had they only the moral courage to express themselves, and I hoped, he would set them the good example to speak freely his opinions.

And now for the last act in the drama of the free church. You remember that the following Sunday morning we were to have the same question as on the last, viz., "What is true religion?" when, I was to give such formidable proofs. Well, I went to meeting, groaning under the weight of responsibility and argument. But, alas! it was not to be. Mr. Noyes spoke, "but a change had come over the spirit of his dream." The subject was "Modern Atheism."—His principal arguments were, "that it is no use for unbelievers to ask a definition of God: he cannot be demonstrated; the finite cannot comprehend the infinite." "But we feel him, we know we have a father." "Those who are not receptive cannot realize God, but there is no such thing as an Atheist in existence, for though a person may not believe in him, yet God the Father is in him." "His conscience tells him what is right, it makes him feel remorse, and condemns him when he does wrong." "Man needs sympathy, and in great affliction and sorrow the Father only can sustain him." "Do you think, seeing how the papers speak about me, that I could, although surrounded by my friends, and having their sympathy, speak here as I do without the sustaining help of God?"

In conclusion, after clearly demonstrating to my mind that, as God cannot be defined nor demonstrated, we can know nothing about him, and therefore all are Atheists, and endeavoring to prove that there was *no* Atheist, for although man cannot realize God, God realizes him, he exclaimed, "Show me the Atheist who has ever done any good to the race," and after insisting that "religion was natural to all men," he finished by saying, "Then let us have a Sunday School to develop the belief in God in our children."

These arguments being so conclusive, no discussion was needed; and so the conference was given up, and from what I heard, will not again be resumed. Thus ended the "Free Church," and I will have to bottle up and cork down my arguments to prevent explosion.

But now for the moral. The Rev. Mr. Noyes is one of the most liberal ministers I have ever met with: but whether his own belief, *little* as it is, made him afraid to have his religion analyzed, or whether he had not the moral courage to retain the independent position he assumed; and so had to succumb to some more Orthodox member, I leave for others to judge; but certain it is, that had all those who took part in the conference agreed in his religious opinions, or at all events not gone beyond them, the conference would have continued; but they found that, some not only differed, but entirely disbelieved, and were willing to give reasons for it, and therefore the doors had to be closed against free thought and free speech. They could do no otherwise. *Religion cannot bear the light of reason, and a church can never be free. "The flesh is willing, but the spirit is weak."*

My plea for the length of this article is, that I could not make it any shorter and give a connected account of my experience with the Independent Society; and as I don't often trespass in this manner, I beg the privilege to give it entire in the Investigator, and oblige,

Yours, for mental freedom,
Ernestine L. Rose
New York, Dec. 14, 1859

# LETTER TO THE EDITOR WITH
# TEXT OF THE NEW YORK STATE
# MARRIED WOMEN'S PROPERTY ACT

March 28, 1860
New York, New York

In 1860, after more than a decade of petitioning, agitation, passage, and rescission, Rose and her women's rights colleagues at last celebrated passage by the New York State Legislature of a stronger, more comprehensive Married Woman's Property Act. The new law included the long-sought equal guardianship rights over children, and came closer to Rose's ideal of laws that equalize the benefits and burdens of marriage between women and men.

Rose includes a copy of the act to be reproduced in its entirety in the press for the benefit of readers. In her comments, Rose is triumphant, expressing a sense of well-earned satisfaction. She revisits many of these points in her first speech at the following year's Women's Rights Convention. In concluding her letter, however, she makes it clear that she accepts incremental reform only as a stepping-stone toward the goal of "full equality for women in every area of personal and civic life." This letter appeared in the *Boston Investigator* on April 11, 1860, under the heading "Woman's Rights."

⁓❧

Mr. Editor:—As the above subject has at times been discussed in your paper, and the justice of its claims and utility of the movement, and particularly the Woman's Rights Conventions questioned by some of your readers, it may be interesting to them to learn what has been done in connection with that movement. The following is an "Act" just passed in our Legislature on the "Rights and Liberties of Husband and Wife.":—

**RIGHTS OF MARRIED WOMEN.**
**an act concerning the rights and liabilities of husband and wife.**
Section 1. The property, both real and personal, which any married woman now owns, as her sole and separate property; that which comes to her by descent, devise, bequest, gift, or grant.; that which she acquires by her trade, business, labor, or services, carried on or performed on her sole or separate account; that which a woman married in this State owns at the time of her marriage, and the rents, issues, and proceeds of all such property, shall, notwithstanding her marriage, be and remain her sole and

separate property, and may be used, collected, and invested by her in her own name, and shall not be subject to the interference or control of her husband, or liable for his debts, except such debts as may have been contracted for the support of herself or her children, by her as his agent.

Sec. 2. A married woman may bargain, sell, assign, and transfer her separate personal property, and carry on any trade or business, and perform any labor or services on her sole and separate account, and the earnings of any married woman, from her trade, business, labor, or services, shall be her sole and separate property, and may be used or invested by her in her own name.

Sec. 3. Any married woman possessed of real estate as her separate property, may bargain, sell, and convey such property, and enter into any contract in reference to the same, but no such conveyance or contract shall be valid without the assent in writing of her husband, except as hereinafter provided.

Sec. 4. In case any married woman possessed of separate real property, as aforesaid, may desire to sell or convey the same, or to make any contract in relation thereto, and shall be unable to procure the assent of her husband, as in the preceding section provided, in consequence of his refusal, absence, insanity, or other disability, such married woman may apply to the County Court; in the county where she shall at the time reside, for leave to make such sale, conveyance, or contract, without the assent of her husband.

Sec. 5. Such application may be made by petition, verified by her, and setting forth the grounds of such application. If the husband be a resident of the county, and not under disability, from insanity or other cause, a copy of said petition shall be served upon him, with a notice of the time when the same will be presented to the said Court, at least ten days before such application. In all other cases the County Court, to which such application shall be made, shall, in its discretion, determine whether any notice shall be given; and if any, the mode and manner of giving it,

Sec. 6. If it shall satisfactorily appear to such Court, upon such application, that the husband of such applicant has willfully abandoned his said wife and lives separate and apart from her, or that he is insane, or imprisoned as a convict in any State prison, or that he is a habitual drunkard, or that he is in any way disabled from making a contract, or that be refuses to give his consent, without good cause therefor, then such Court shall cause an order to be entered upon its records, authorizing such married woman to sell and convey her real estate, or contract in regard thereto, without the assent of her husband, with the same effect as though such conveyance or contract had been made with his assent.

Sec. 7. Any married woman may, while married, sue and be sued in matters having relation to her property, which may be her sole and separate property, or which may hereafter come to her by descent, devise, bequest, or the gift of any person except her husband, in the same manner as if she were sole.— And any married woman may bring and maintain an action in her own name for damages against any person or body corporate for any injury to her person or character, the same as if she were sole; and the money received upon the settlement of any such action, or recovered upon a judgment, shall be her sole and separate property.

Sec. 8. No bargain or contract made by any married woman; in respect to her sole and separate property, or any property which may hereafter come to her by descent, devise; bequest, or gift of any person except her husband, and no bargain or contract entered into by any married woman in or about the carrying on of any trade or business, under the statutes of this State, shall be binding upon her husband, or render him or his property in any way liable therefor.

Sec. 9. Every married woman is hereby constituted and declared to be the joint guardian of her children, with her husband, with equal powers, rights, and duties in regard to them, with the husband.

Sec. 10. At the decease of husband or wife, leaving no minor child or children, the survivor shall hold, possess, and enjoy a life estate in one-third of all the real estate of which the husband or wife died seized.

Sec. 11. At the decease of the husband or wife intestate, leaving minor child or children, the survivor shall hold, possess, and enjoy all the real estate of which the husband or wife died seized, and all the rents, issues, and profits thereof during the minority of the youngest child, and one-third thereof during his or her natural life.

But how has all this been accomplished? by what means was it brought about? The answer is, by agitation—conventions and public lectures to enlighten woman on the laws which oppressed her—to enlighten man on the injustice he perpetrated against her, and to convince all parties that wrong, sooner or later, reacts upon itself and punishes the perpetrator of it as well as his victims. By forming public opinion in favor of our claims, the Legislature was induced to make some concessions; and as history demonstrates that legislative bodies are not apt to do justice to any party, and particularly when they think it would infringe on their own cherished privileges, without the force of public opinion, agitation to enlighten and form that opinion is the only means to obtain the desired end. The rest of our claims must be obtained through the same means, but it will be much easier, for every step taken in the right direction prepares the way for every other. The first step in a reform is the most difficult, and those who undertake it, have a hard and thankless task to perform; and yet how rich is its reward, the reward springing from the consciousness of right, of endeavoring to benefit unborn generations, though the present like the future is ignorant of it!—and how delightful to see the gradual moulding of the minds around you, the infusing of your thoughts and aspirations into others, till one by one they stand by your side without knowing how they came there!

Frances Wright was the first woman in this country who lectured and wrote on the equality of the sexes. It was a Herculean task, the ground was wholly unprepared, all the elements were antagonistic, and consequently she received the reward of all noble reformers in the avant-guard of a good cause—slander, abuse, and persecution—yet her agitation shook the time-hardened crust of conservatism and prepared the soil for the plough. This was her work; it is her glory, and it will one day be fully recognized.

In 1837, another woman took up the work where she left off, and in addition to lecturing, took a more progressive step, and commenced sending petitions to our Legislature. It were vain to describe the obstacles that surrounded this first practical step to obtain signatures to the petitions. So gross was the ignorance of the laws, that the very mention of a change subjected you to ridicule, if not to a worse treatment. "I don't want any more rights—I have rights enough," was the answer of woman, and no better was that of man. It was indeed discouraging, for the most hopeless condition is that, when a patient loses all sensation of pain and suffering.

But by depicting their condition to themselves, by holding before them the mirror of facts, it had the wholesome effect of an irritant, and roused to some extent at least their dormant energies; and by perseveringly sending petitions to our Legislature year after year, we finally succeeded in the winter of 1848 and 1849 to have a law passed to give a married woman the right to hold the real estate she brought at marriage in her own name. This was not much, to be sure; for at best it was only for the favored few, and not for the suffering many. But it was a beginning, and an important step, for it proved that a law had to be altered, and some others might need it just as much.

It is a curious fact, that as soon as that law passed every one considered it not only perfectly right, but wondered how it ever could have been otherwise!—The field of labor then grew wider, and in 1850 commenced our conventions, which have been held ever since, and what was the result? It would make this article too long for publication to point out the change in public opinion—the constantly widening and increasing avenues of industry for woman, in the mercantile, mechanical, and professional avocations, and perhaps nowhere is the change more perceptible than in the press. In every reform the press has to pass three stages: 1st. Opposition and abuse, 2d. Slander and ridicule; 3d. Silence, standing on the fence—outgrown the former cowardly weapons, and still fearing to speak in favor except of what has already been achieved. In the Woman's Rights movement, the whole press (I mean in the free States) has passed the first two stages. They are now in the third, and when they next find their voices, it will be to advocate and to praise. Indeed, since the Legislature passed the above law, the papers speak of it as a very just movement, and it would not much surprise me if they claim the merit of it as their own achievement! Let them; they are welcome to it, as long as it is done.

But this is not the end. More, much more has to come. In 1855, while speaking before the Legislature, I told them we claimed perfect equality of rights; we ask for no more, we can be satisfied with no less; we will accept as much as you are prepared to accede, and then claim the rest; and now, having obtained this much, we can "wait a little longer" not in silence and inaction, but in the faith which springs from work. Agitate! agitate! ought to be the motto of every reformer. Agitation is the opposite of stagnation—the one is life, the other death.

Yours, for work,
Ernestine L. Rose
New York, March 28, 1860

# SPEECH AT THE TENTH NATIONAL WOMAN'S RIGHTS CONVENTION: POLITICAL ACTIVISM AND WOMEN'S RIGHTS

May 10, 1860
New York, New York

On the first day of this convention, Ernestine L. Rose spoke on the importance of "agitation" in the fight for women's rights, and the need for women's rights conventions, where thoughts and ideas could be presented, debated, and then turned into action. She praises Frances Wright as the first to bring women's rights to a public platform in the United States, and regrets that Wright had to suffer such outrageous treatment for her efforts, as she has mentioned in previous documents. Traveling lecturers in the days before radio and television, constantly reused their material. The unique aspect of this speech is that Rose goes on to present her own history of work for women's rights, and her philosophy of social change.

～❧

Mrs. President and Friends,—It is a well known fact, that stagnant atmosphere and stagnant waters can only be purified by agitation. This is no more true in the physical world than in the social and moral world. What, then, is to purify the social and moral atmosphere regarding the wrongs and the rights of woman? Agitation! Public lectures, conventions, and writings on the subject. Thus, by making the public mind acquainted with the wrongs we suffer and the rights we claim, by enlightening the mind of woman as to the injustice that oppresses her, by enlightening the mind of man on the injustice he perpetrates against her, by convincing all parties that wrong always reacts upon its perpetrator, and punishes him as much as the victim, we create a public opinion in favor of the right, and right has commenced to be done. To speak of the progress we have made would take too much time, and I presume it will be done during this Convention; but, however much *has* been done, much more is left yet to be accomplished. But whatever remains to be acquired will be easily obtained, compared with that which has been already secured. The first step in every great movement is the most difficult. Frances Wright (nicknamed "Fanny Wright," because the world has not grown up to the high standard on which she took her position here)—Frances Wright was the first woman in this country who spoke on the equality of the sexes. She had indeed a hard task before her. The elements were entirely unprepared. She had to break up the time-hardened soil of conservatism, and her reward was sure—the same reward that is always bestowed upon those who are in the vanguard of any great movement. She was subjected to public odium, slander, and persecution. But these were not the only things that she received. Oh! she had her reward!—that reward which no enemies could deprive her, which no slanders, could make less precious—the eternal reward of knowing that she had done her duty; the reward springing from the consciousness of right, of endeavoring to benefit unborn generations. How delightful to see the moulding of the minds around you, the infusing of your thoughts and aspirations into others, until one by one they stand by your side, without knowing how they came there! That reward she had. It has been her glory, it is the glory of her memory; and the time will come when society will have outgrown its old prejudices, and stepped, with one foot, at least, upon the elevated platform on which she took her position. But owing to the fact that the elements were unprepared, she naturally could not succeed to any great extent. After her, in 1837, the subject of woman's rights was again taken hold of—aye, taken hold of by woman; and, the soil having been already somewhat prepared, she began to sow the seeds for the future growth, the fruits of which we now begin to enjoy. Petitions were circulated and sent to our Legislature, and who can tell the hardships that then met those who undertook that great work? I went from house to house with a petition for signatures simply asking our Legislature to allow married women to hold real estate in their own name. What did I meet with? Why, the very name exposed one to ridicule, if not to worse treatment. The women said, "We have rights enough; we want no more;" and the men as a matter of course, echoed it, and said, "You have rights enough; nay, you have too many already." (Laughter.) But by perseverance—for we expected nothing better at that early day—by perseverance, and constantly sending petitions to the Legislature, and, at the same time enlightening the public mind on the subject, we at last accomplished our purpose. We had to adopt the method which physicians sometimes use, when they are called to a patient who is so hopelessly sick that he is unconscious of his pain and suffering. We had to describe to women their own position, to explain to them the burdens that rested so heavily upon them, and through these means, as a wholesome irritant, we roused up public opinion on the subject, and through public opinion, we acted upon the Legislature, and in 1848–'49, they gave us the great boon for which we asked, by enacting that a woman who possessed property previous to marriage, or obtained it after marriage, should be allowed to hold it in her own name.

Thus far, thus good; but it was only a beginning, and we went on.

In 1850, we had the first National Woman's Rights Convention, and then some of our papers thought that it was only a very small affair, called together by a few "strong-minded women," and would pass away like a nine-days' wonder. They little knew woman! They little knew that if woman takes anything earnestly in her hands, she will not lay it aside unaccomplished. (Applause.) We have continued our Conventions ever since. A few years ago, when we sent a petition to our Legislature, we obtained, with but very little effort, upwards of thirteen thousand signatures. What a contrast between this number and the five signatures attached to the first petition, in 1837! Since then, we might have had hundreds of thousands of signatures, but it is no longer necessary. Public opinion is too well known to require that a long array of names should grace our petitions. All we have now to do is to send them in, and ask for our rights, and in process of time, we shall obtain them.

A word more. We have been often asked, "What is the use of Conventions? Why talk? Why not go to work?" Just as if the thought does not precede the act! Those who can act without previously thinking, their actions are not good for much. Thought is first required, then the expression of it, and that leads to action; and action based upon thought is action that never needs to be reversed; it is lasting and profitable, and produces the desired effect.

Mention has been made here this morning of the fact that the effects of this movement are to be seen springing up here and there, yes, all over the world. It would be impossible to point out, in a short discourse, the actual progress that has been made, not only here in this country, but also in Europe—not directly, but indirectly—through the movement here. Our movement is cosmopolitan. It claims the rights of woman wherever woman exists, and this claim makes itself felt wherever woman is wronged. In England, great efforts have been made of late years, and great accessions have been made to the rights and liberties of women. The same thing is taking place in France and Germany, and, in fact, everywhere. In England, almost all the operators in the magnetic telegraph offices are women. And why, pray, should not woman have the avocation, if she chooses, and has the capacity for it? It takes but five hours to acquire it. Is not woman as well fitted for it as man? Nay, better; for if she is unoccupied for half an hour, she can knit or do some kind of needlework, and that is more than men can do. (Laughter.) I have from the very commencement advised women to adopt all such occupations, on utilitarian grounds, because, in reality, they could perform the duties better than men. Look at our grand and magnificent building in Washington, called the Patent Office. Go in there and walk from hall to hall, and what will you see? Why, young men, stalwart, strong, hearty young men, capable of tilling the ground which is waiting for them, sitting there, with their arms folded, or with the eternal newspaper before their eyes, or worse still, smoking a cigar. (Laughter.) Now, if the Patent Office were filled with women, they could not only sit there and have an eye to the whole hall, and see that nothing was deranged—for certainly women are quite as regular in housekeeping as men are (laughter)—but they could also perform some light work, either for their own use, for their children, or for the poor unhappy little ones who have no one to care for them. Would not that be preferable? I do not mean that women should be forced to go there—far from it; but I think it would be of great advantage if she were there. Nor is that the only place. She could do it in Congress, too. Go there and see how your representatives occupy their time, with their feet on the top of their desks, a paper before them, and a thing that ought to be exiled from civilized life (you know what I mean) at their side, but which must be there, if the floor is to be kept clean! (Laughter.) Now, if woman were there, she could keep head and hand occupied, and the one would keep the other in equilibrium; the heads would not get too hot, but would keep the hands from fighting with each other. (Applause.) Here would be another advantage. But the advantages are infinite that would result from having woman in every place she is capable of filling, not only to herself, but to society at large; I cannot enumerate them here.

But the work is going on. We have had some important rights acceded to by the Legislature, of which mention has been made this morning. They have commenced the good work, and we will induce them to go on with it, for much more is to be obtained than has yet been granted. I said some years ago, when laying our claims before the Legislature, "I know you are not prepared to give us all we ask, but we claim *all* our rights. We ask for no more; we can be satisfied with no less. Yet we will take what you are prepared to give us, and then claim the rest." That is the only position for a reformer to take. The Anti-Slavery Society, the Garrisonian Society, is consistent. It declares that principle does not admit of compromise. It asks all; or none. We ask all, but we differ from that Society in this, that we are ready to take as much as we can get, for we know that society is not prepared to give the whole at once. But we must enunciate the whole principle. The Abolitionists do it, and they are correct. They cover the whole ground, and ask that all shall be granted. There are always those who stand on intermediate ground; let them ask society to come half way, we ask that it shall come the whole distance.

I know that there are a great many who take advantage of this movement that we have worked out, and then say, "You are doing nothing;

only talking." Yes, doing nothing! We have only broken up the ground and sowed the seed; they are reaping the benefit, and yet they tell us we have done nothing! Mrs. Swisshelm, who has proclaimed herself to be "no woman's rights woman," has accepted a position as inspector of logs and lumber. (Laughter.) Well, I have no objection to her having that avocation, if she have the taste and capacity for it—far from it. But she has accepted still more, and I doubt not with a great deal more zest and satisfaction—the five hundred dollars salary; and I hope she will enjoy it. Then, having accepted both the office and the salary, she folds her arms and says, "I am none of your strong-minded women; I don't go for woman's rights." Well, she is still welcome to it. I have not the slightest objection that those who proclaim themselves not to be strong-minded, should still reap the benefit of a strong mind (applause and laughter); it is for them we work. So there are some ladies who think a great deal can be done in the Legislature without petitions, without conventions, without lectures, without public claim, in fact without anything, but a little lobbying. Well, if they have a taste for it, they are welcome to engage in it; I have not the slightest objection. Yes, I have. I, as a woman, being conscious of the evil that is done by these lobby loafers in our Legislature and in the halls of Congress, object to it. (Loud cheers.) I will wait five years longer to have a right given to me legitimately, from the sense of justice rather than buy it in an underhand way by lobbying. I am one who acts above-board. Whatever my sentiments may be, good, bad or indifferent, I express them, and they are known. Nevertheless, if any desire it, let them do that work. But what has induced them what has enabled them, to do that work? The Woman's Rights movement, although they are afraid or ashamed even of the name "woman's rights."

You have been told, as much more might be said on the subject, that already the Woman's Rights platform has upon it lawyers, ministers, and statesmen—men who are among the highest in the nation. I need not mention a Wm. Lloyd Garrison or a Wendell Phillips; but there are others, those even who are afraid of the name of reformer, who have stood upon our platform. Brady! Who would ever have expected it? Chapin! Beecher! Think of it for a moment! A minister advocating the rights of woman, even her right at the ballot-box! What has done it? Our agitation has thus much purified the atmosphere, and enabled them to see the injustice that is done to woman. Then there has been a great enlargement of the industrial sphere of woman. Hours might be spent in contrasting the present position of woman in this respect with what it has been. Many are now engaged in printing offices as type-setters, and they do the work to the satisfaction of their employers and with profit and credit to themselves. Dry good stores, fancy stores, and others, are kept by women, and why not? If man is fitted for stronger labors, let him leave the lighter to woman, until, by proper exertions to develop her own being, she shall become physically stronger. Let man plough the ground, instead of standing behind a counter, measuring off a yard of calico or tape. The soil is waiting his plough. And so it is waiting for women. Not only the physical, but the social soil is waiting the plough, wielded by woman's heart and head. Even a woman who has been all over Europe and all over America, and who feels it her duty to instruct women how to retain the color in their cheeks, by sandwiching them between two pieces of meat, disclaims being a woman's rights woman, and I am thankful for it. Of course she is not. Who would expect she would be? But I do not blame such women. I only speak of the fact, that when you hear others say, "Why hold these Conventions?—why not go to work?" you may tell them that these Conventions are not only working, but compelling all others to work for us. If we were not to break up the soil, it could not be ploughed; if we were not to sow the seed, the fruit would not grow. But I need not detain you longer upon that subject, or state the grounds of the opposition to woman's claim from the beginning until now; but while we are giving their due to those now living, let us not forget those no longer with us, who so nobly stood in the van [vanguard], and commenced the hard labor of the reform called the Woman's Rights movement. (Applause.)

# THE DIVORCE DEBATE

*By Elizabeth Cady Stanton,*
*Antoinette Brown Blackwell,*
*and Ernestine L. Rose*
May 11, 1860
New York, New York

The debate on divorce reform came at a time when this issue was in the news, especially in New York State where the convention was being held. Horace Greeley, editor of the *New York Tribune* had debated Robert Dale Owen, U.S. Senator from Indiana and divorce reform advocate, in the pages of Greeley's paper for over two months. Against the wishes of many of the women's rights reformers who preferred not to have the divisive issue of divorce raised at the convention, Elizabeth Cady Stanton introduced a series of resolutions arguing for liberalized divorce laws and followed with a speech demanding that women be free to leave marriages that were abusive or harmful. Furthermore, she argued, all individuals, women and men, had an inalienable right to be happy. Rev. Antoinette Brown Blackwell countered with a series of resolutions arguing that marriage is a sacrament and cannot be dissolved any more than a parent can sever a relationship with a child. She urged that women become strong within themselves so that they can withstand marriage to men who would otherwise degrade them. Ernestine L. Rose disagreed with Brown on the sacramental nature of marriage, arguing that marriage was a *human* institution contracted voluntarily and therefore not binding for life unless the parties continued to love and care for one another. For Rose voluntary choice was at the heart of her ideal of "true marriage." The right to divorce would free men and women to escape unhappy but legally binding marriages and prevent attendant crimes, ranging from adultery to murder. Rose noted that prison sentences for certain crimes, were already grounds for divorce and demanded that abusing or assaulting one's spouse be added to the list. Curiously, Stanton ended her radical appeal for liberalization of divorce with retrograde Christian images of maternal sacrifice. Rose's argument, terse and to the point, was unique in making a modern, feminist argument for the right to divorce.

⤙

Mrs. Elizabeth Cady Stanton then presented the following resolutions, in support of which she purposed to address the Convention:

1. Resolved, That, in the language (slightly varied) of John Milton, "Those who marry intend as little to conspire their own ruin, as those who swear allegiance, and as a whole people is *to an ill government*, so is one man or woman *to an ill marriage*. If a whole people, against any authority, covenant or statute, may, by the sovereign edict of charity, save

not only their lives, but honest liberties, from unworthy bondage, as well may a married party, against any private covenant, which he or she never entered, *to his or her mischief*, be redeemed from unsupportable disturbances, to honest peace, and just contentment."

2. Resolved, That all men are created equal, and all women, in their natural rights, are the equals of men; and endowed by their Creator with the same inalienable right to the pursuit of happiness.

3. Resolved, That any constitution, compact or covenant between human beings, that failed to produce or promote human happiness, could not, in the nature of things, be of any force or authority;—and it would be not only a right, but a duty, to abolish it.

4. Resolved, That though marriage be in itself divinely founded, and is fortified as an institution by innumerable analogies in the whole kingdom of universal nature, still, a true marriage is only known by its results; and, like the fountain, if pure, will reveal only pure manifestations. Nor need it ever be said, "What God hath joined together, let not man put asunder," for man could not put it asunder; nor can he any more unite what God and nature have not joined together.

5. Resolved, That of all insulting mockeries of heavenly truth and holy law, none can be greater than that *physical impotency* is cause sufficient for divorce, while no amount of mental or moral or spiritual *imbecility* is ever to be pleaded in support of such a demand.

6. Resolved, That such a law was worthy those dark periods when marriage was held by the greatest doctors and priests of the Church to be a *work of the flesh only*, and almost, if not altogether, a defilement; denied wholly to the clergy, and a second time, forbidden to all.

7. Resolved, That an unfortunate or ill-assorted marriage is ever a calamity, but not ever, perhaps never, a crime;—and when society or government, by its laws or customs, compels its continuance, always to the grief of one of the parties, and the actual loss and damage of both, it usurps an authority never delegated to man, nor exercised by God himself.

8. Resolved, That observation and experience daily show how incompetent are men, as individuals, or as governments, to select partners in business, teachers for their children, ministers of their religion, or makers, adjudicators or administrators of their laws; and as the same weakness and blindness must attend in the selection of matrimonial partners, the dictates of humanity and common sense alike show that the latter and most important contract should no more be perpetual than either or all of the former.

9. Resolved, That children born in these unhappy and unhallowed connections are, in the most solemn sense, of *unlawful birth*,—the fruit

of lust, but not of love;—and so not of God, divinely descended, but from beneath, whence proceed all manner of evil and uncleanness.

10. Resolved, That next to the calamity of such a birth to the child, is the misfortune of being trained in the atmosphere of a household where love is not the law, but where discord and bitterness abound; stamping their demoniac features on the moral nature, with all their odious peculiarities;—thus continuing the race in a weakness and depravity that must be a sure precursor of its ruin, as a just penalty of long-violated law.

## ADDRESS OF MRS. E. C. STANTON.

Mrs. President,—In our common law, in our whole system of jurisprudence, we find man's highest idea of right. The object of law is to secure justice. But inasmuch as fallible man is the maker and administrator of law, we must look for many and gross blunders in the application of its general principles to individual cases.

The science of theology, of civil, political, moral and social life, all teach the common idea, that man ever has been, and ever must be, sacrificed to the highest good of society; the one to the many—the poor to the rich—the weak to the powerful—and all to the institutions of his own creation.

. . . . . . . .

I repudiate this popular idea. I place man above all governments, all institutions—ecclesiastical and civil—all constitutions and laws. (Applause.) It is a mistaken idea, that the same law that oppresses the individual, can promote the highest good of society. The best interests of a community never can require the sacrifice of one innocent being—of one sacred right. In the settlement, then, of any question, we must simply consider the highest good of the individual. It is the inalienable right of all to be happy. It is the highest duty of all to seek those conditions in life, those surroundings, which may develop what is noblest and best, remembering that the lessons of these passing hours are not for time alone, but for the ages of eternity. They tell us, in that future home—the heavenly paradise—that the human family shall be sifted out, and the good and pure shall dwell together in peace. If that be the heavenly order, is it not our duty to render earth as near like heaven as we may?

For years, there has been before the Legislature of this State a variety of bills, asking for divorce in cases of drunkenness, insanity, desertion, cruel and brutal treatment, endangering life. My attention was called to this question very early in life, by the sufferings of a friend of my girlhood, a victim of one of those unfortunate unions, called marriage. What my great love for that young girl, and my holy intuitions, then decided to be right, has not been changed by years of experience, observation and reason. I have pondered well these things in my heart, and ever felt the deepest interest in all that has been written and said upon the subject, and the most profound respect and loving sympathy for those heroic women, who, in the face of law and public sentiment, have dared to sunder the unholy ties of a joyless, loveless union.

If marriage is a human institution, about which man may legislate, it seems but just that he should treat this branch of his legislation with the same common sense that he applies to all others. If it is a mere legal contract, then should it be subject to the restraints and privileges of all other contracts. A contract, to be valid in law, must be formed between parties of mature age, with an honest intention in said parties to do what they agree. The least concealment, fraud, or intention to deceive, if proved, annuls the contract. . . . But in marriage, no matter how much fraud and deception are practiced, nor how cruelly one or both parties have been misled; no matter how young, inexperienced or thoughtless the parties, nor how unequal their condition and position in life, the contract cannot be annulled.

Think of a husband telling a young and trusting girl, but one short month his wife, that he married her for her money; that those letters, so precious to her, that she had read and re-read, and kissed and cherished, were written by another; that their splendid home, of which, on their wedding day, her father gave to him the deed, is already in the hands of his creditors; that she must give up the elegance and luxury that now surround her, unless she can draw fresh supplies of money to meet their wants! When she told the story of her wrongs to me,—the abuse to which she was subject, and the dread in which she lived,—I impulsively urged her to fly from such a monster and villain, as she would before the hot breath of a ferocious beast of the wilderness. (Applause.) And she did fly; and it was well with her. Many times since, as I have felt her throbbing heart against my own, she has said, "Oh, but for your love and sympathy, your encouragement, I should never have escaped from that bondage. Before I could, of myself, have found courage to break those chains, my heart would have broken in the effort."

Marriage, as it now exists, must seem to all of you a mere human institution. Look through the universe of matter and mind,—all God's arrangements are perfect, harmonious and complete! There is no discord, friction, or failure in his eternal plans. Immutability, perfection, beauty, are stamped on all his laws. Love is the vital essence that pervades and permeates, from the centre to the circumference, the graduating circles of all thought and action. Love is the talisman of human weal and woe,—the *open sesame* to every human soul. Where two beings are drawn together, by the natural laws of likeness and affinity, union and happiness are the result. Such marriages might be Divine. But how is it now? You all know our marriage is, in many cases, a mere outward tie, impelled by custom, policy, interest, necessity; founded not even in friendship, to say nothing of love; with every possible inequality of condition and development. In these heterogeneous unions, we find youth and old age, beauty and deformity, refinement and vulgarity, virtue and vice, the educated and the ignorant, angels of grace and goodness, with devils of malice and malignity: and the sum of all this is human wretchedness and despair; cold fathers, sad mothers, and hapless children, who shiver at the hearthstone, where the fires of love have all gone out. The wide world, and the stranger's unsympathizing gaze, are not more to be dreaded for young hearts than homes like these. Now, who shall say that it is right to take two beings, so unlike, and anchor them right side by side fast bound—to stay all time, until God shall summon one away?

. . . . . . . .

Fathers, do you say, let your daughters pay a life-long penalty for one unfortunate step? How could they, on the threshold of life, full of joy and hope, believing all things to be as they seemed on the surface, judge of the dark windings of the human soul? How could they foresee that the young man, to-day so noble, so generous, would in a few short years be transformed into a cowardly, mean tyrant, or a foul-mouthed, bloated drunkard? What father could rest at his home by night, knowing that his lovely daughter was at the mercy of a strong man drunk with wine and passion, and that, do what he might, he was backed up by law and public sentiment? The best interests of the individual, the family, the State, the nation, cry out against these legalized marriages of force and endurance. There can be no heaven without love, and nothing is sacred in the family and home, but just so far as it is built up and anchored in love.

Our newspapers teem with startling accounts of husbands and wives having shot or poisoned each other, or committed suicide, choosing death rather than the indissoluble tie; and, still worse, the living death of faithless wives and daughters, from the first families in this State, dragged from the privacy of home into the public prints and courts, with all the painful details of sad, false lives. What say you to facts like these? Now, do you believe, men and women, that all these wretched matches are made in heaven? that all these sad, miserable people are bound together by God?

I know Horace Greeley has been most eloquent, for weeks past, on the holy sacrament of ill-assorted marriages; but let us hope that all wisdom does not live, and will not die, with Horace Greeley. I think, if he had been married to the *New York Herald*, instead of the Republican party, he would have found out some Scriptural arguments against life-long unions, where great incompatibility of temper existed between the parties. (Laughter and applause.)

Our law-makers have dug a pit, and the innocent have fallen into it; and now will you coolly cover them over with statute laws, *Tribunes*, and Weeds, and tell them to stay there, and pay the life-long penalty of having fallen in? Nero was thought the chief of tyrants, because he made laws and hung them up so high that his subjects could not read them, and then punished them for every act of disobedience. What better are our Republican legislators? The mass of the women of this nation know nothing about the laws, yet all their specially barbarous legislation is for woman. Where have they made any provision for her to learn the laws? Where is the Law School for our daughters?—where the law office, the bar, or the bench, now urging them to take part in the jurisprudence of the nation?

But, say you, does not separation cover all these difficulties? No one objects to separation when the parties are so disposed. Now, to separation there are two very serious objections. First, so long as you insist on marriage as a Divine institution, as an indissoluble tie, so long as you maintain your present laws against divorce, you make separation, even, so odious, that the most noble, virtuous and sensitive men and women choose a life of concealed misery, rather than a partial, disgraceful release. Secondly, those who, in their impetuosity and despair, do, in spite of public sentiment, separate, find themselves in their new position beset with many temptations to lead a false, unreal life. This isolation bears especially hard on woman.

Marriage is not all of life to man. His resources for amusement and occupation are boundless. He has the whole world for his home. His business, his politics, his club, his friendships with either sex, can help to fill up the void made by an unfortunate union or separation. But to woman, marriage is all and every thing; her sole object in life,—that for which she is educated, the subject of all her sleeping and her waking dreams. Now, if a noble, generous girl of eighteen marries, and is unfortunate, because the cruelty of her husband compels separation, in her dreary isolation, would you drive her to a nunnery; and shall she be a nun indeed? Her solitude is nothing less, as, in the present undeveloped condition of woman, it is only through our fathers, brothers, husbands, sons, that we feel the pulsations of the great outer world.

One unhappy, discordant man or woman in a neighborhood, may mar the happiness of all the rest. You cannot shut up discord, any more than you can small-pox. There can be no morality, where there is a settled discontent. A very wise father once remarked, that in the government of his children, he forbid as few things as possible; a wise legislation would do the same. It is folly to make laws on subjects beyond human prerogative, knowing that in the very nature of things they must be set aside. To make laws that man cannot and will not obey, serves to bring all law into contempt. It is very important in a republic, that the people should respect the laws, for if we throw them to the winds, what becomes of civil government? What do our present divorce laws amount to? Those who wish to evade them have only to go into another State to accomplish what they desire. If any of our citizens cannot secure their inalienable rights in New York State, they may in Connecticut and Indiana.

Why is it that all agreements, covenants, partnerships, are left wholly at the discretion of the parties, except the contract, which of all others is considered most holy and important, both for the individual and the race? This question of divorce, they tell us, is hedged about with difficulties; that it cannot be approached with the ordinary rules of logic and common sense. It is too holy, too sacred to be discussed, and few seem disposed to touch it. From man's stand-point, this may be all true,—as to him they say belong reason, and the power to ratiocinate. Fortunately, I belong to that class endowed with mere intuitions,—a kind of moral instinct, by which we feel out right and wrong. In presenting to you, therefore, my views of divorce, you will of course give to them the weight only of the woman's intuitions. But inasmuch as that is all God saw fit to give us, it is evident we need nothing more. Hence, what we do perceive of truth must be as reliable as what man grinds out by the longer process of reason, authority, and speculation.

Horace Greeley, in his recent discussion with Robert Dale Owen, said, this whole question has been tried, in all its varieties and conditions, from indissoluble monogamic marriage down to free love; that the ground has been all gone over and explored. Let me assure him that but just one-half of the ground has been surveyed, and that half but by one of the parties, and that party certainly *not* the most interested in the matter. Moreover, there is one kind of marriage that has not been tried, and that is, a contract made by equal parties to live an equal life, with equal restraints and privileges on either side. Thus far, we have had the man marriage, and nothing more. From the beginning, man has had the sole and whole regulation of the matter. He has spoken in Scripture, he has spoken in law. As an individual, he has decided the time and cause for putting away a wife, and as a judge and legislator, he still holds the entire control.

In all history, sacred and profane, the woman is regarded and spoken of simply as the toy of man,—made for his special use,—to meet his most gross and sensuous desires. She is taken or put away, given or received, bought or sold, just as the interest of the parties might dictate. But the woman has been no more recognized in all these transactions, through all the different periods and conditions of the race, than if she had had no part nor lot in the whole matter. The right of woman to put away a husband, be he ever so impure, is never hinted at in sacred history. Even Jesus himself failed to recognize the sacred rights of the holy mothers of the race. We cannot take our gauge of womanhood from the past, but from the solemn convictions of our own souls, in the higher development of the race.

No parchments, however venerable with the mould of ages, no human institutions, can bound the immortal wants of the royal sons and daughters of the glories of eternity.

If in marriage, either party claims the rights to stand supreme, to woman, the mother of the race, belongs the scepter and the crown. Her life is one long sacrifice for man. You tell us that among all womankind there are no Moses, Christs, or Pauls—no Michael Angelos, Beethovens, or Shakespeares,—no Columbuses or Galileos,—no Lockes or Bacons. Behold those mighty minds attuned to music and the arts, so great, so grand, so comprehensive,—these are our great works of which we boast! Which think you stands first, the man, or what he does? By just so far as Galileo is greater than his thought, is the mother far above the man. Into you, oh sons of earth, go all of us that is great and grand. In you centre our very life thoughts, our hopes, our intensest love, for you we gladly pour out our heart's blood and die. Willingly do we drink the cup in the holy sacrament of marriage in the same faith that the Son of Mary died on Calvary, knowing that from our suffering comes forth a new and more glorious resurrection of thought and life. (Loud applause.)


## SPEECH OF REV. ANTOINETTE BROWN BLACKWELL.

Mrs. President,—Ours has always been a free platform. We have believed in the fullest freedom of thought and in the free expression of individual opinion. I propose to speak upon the subject discussed by our friend, Mrs. Stanton. It is often said that there are two sides to every question; but there are three sides, many sides, to every question. Let Mrs. Stanton take hers; let Horace Greeley take his; I only ask the privilege of stating mine. (Applause.) I have embodied my thought, hastily, in a series of resolutions, and my remarks following them will be very brief.

Resolved, That marriage is the voluntary alliance of two persons of opposite sexes into one family, and that such an alliance, with its possible incidents of children, its common interests, &c., must be, from the nature of things, as permanent as the life of the parties.

Resolved, That if human law attempts to regulate marriage at all, it should aim to regulate it according to the fundamental principles of marriage; and that as the institution is inherently as continuous as the life of the parties, so all laws should look to its control and preservation as such.

Resolved, That as a parent can never annul his obligations towards even a profligate child, because of the inseparable relationship of the parties, so the married partner cannot annul his obligations towards the other, while both live, no matter how profligate that others conduct may be, because of their still closer and alike permanent relationship; and, therefore, that all divorce is naturally and morally impossible, even though we should succeed in annulling all legalities.

Resolved, That gross fraud and want of good faith in one of the parties contracting this alliance, such as would invalidate any other voluntary relation, are the only causes which can invalidate this, and this, too, solely upon the ground that the relation never virtually existed, and that there are, therefore, no resulting moral obligations.

Resolved, however, That both men and women have a first and inviolable right to themselves, physically, mentally and morally, and that it can never be the duty of either to surrender his personal freedom in any direction to his own hurt.

Resolved, That the great duty of every human being is to secure his own highest moral development, and that he cannot owe to society, or to an individual, any obligation which shall be degrading to himself.

Resolved, That self-devotion to the good of another, and especially to the good of the sinful and guilty, like all disinterestedness, must redound to the highest good of its author, and that the husband or wife who thus seeks the best interests of the other, is obedient to the highest law of benevolence.

Resolved, That this is a very different thing from the culpable weakness which allows itself to be immolated by the selfishness of another, to the hurt of both; and that the miserable practice, now so common among wives, of allowing themselves, their children and family interests, to be sacrificed to a degraded husband and father, is most reprehensible.

Resolved, That human law is imperatively obligated to give either party ample protection to himself, to their offspring, and to all other family interests, against wrong, injustice, and usurpation on the part of the other; and that, if it be necessary to this, it should grant a legal separation; and yet, that even such separation cannot invalidate any real marriage obligation.

Resolved, That every married person is imperatively obligated to do his utmost thus to protect himself and all family interests against injustice and wrong, let it arise from what source it may.

Resolved, That every woman is morally obligated to maintain her equality in human rights in all her relations in life, and that if she consents to her own subjugation, either in the family, Church or State, she is as guilty as the slave is in consenting to be a slave.

Resolved, That a perfect union cannot be expected to exist until we first have perfect units, and that every marriage of finite beings must be gradually perfected through the growth and assimilation of the parties.

Resolved, That the permanence and indissolubility of marriage tend more directly than any thing else towards this result.

I believe that all the laws which God has established are sacred and inviolable; that his laws are the best which exist; that they are all founded on the natures or relation of things, and that he has no laws which are not as eternal as the natures and relations to which he has given existence. (Applause.) I believe, therefore, that the highest laws of our being are those which we find written within our being; that the first moral laws which we are to obey are the laws which God's own finger has traced upon our own souls. Therefore, our first duty is to ourselves, and we may never, under any circumstances, yield this to any other. I say, we are first responsible for ourselves to ourselves, and to the God who has laid the obligation upon us to make ourselves the best, the grandest we may. Marriage grows out of the relations of parties. The law of our development, comes wholly from within; but the relation of marriage supposes two persons as being united to each other, and from this relation originates the law. Mrs. Stanton calls marriage a "tie." No, marriage is a *relation*; and, once formed, that relation continues as long as the parties continue with the natures which they now essentially have. Let, then, the two parties deliberately, voluntarily consent to enter into this relation. It is one which, from its very nature, must be permanent. Its interests are permanent. Can the mother ever destroy the relation which exists between herself and her child? Can the father annul the relation which exists between himself and his child? Then, can the father and mother annul the relation which exists between themselves, the parents of the child? It cannot be. The interests of marriage are such that they cannot be destroyed, and the only question must be, "Has there been a marriage in this case or not?" If there has, then the social law, the obligations out-growing from the relation, must be life-long.

But I assert that every woman, in the present state of society, is bound to maintain her own independence and her own integrity of character;

to assert herself, earnestly and firmly, as the equal of man, who is only her peer. This is her first right, her first duty; and if she lives in a country where the law supposes that she is to be subjected to her husband, and she consents to this subjection, I do insist that she consents to degradation; that this is sin, and it is, impossible to make it other than sin. True, in this State, and in nearly all the States, the idea of marriage is that of subjection, in all respects, of the wife to the husband—personal subjection, subjection in the rights over their children, and over their property; but this is a false relation. Marriage is a union of equals—equal interests being involved, equal duties at stake; and if any woman has been married to a man who chooses to take advantage of the laws as they now stand, who chooses to subject her, ignobly, to his will, against her own, to take from her the earnings which belong to the family, and to take from her the children which belong to the family, I hold that that woman, if she cannot, by her influence, change this state of things, is solemnly obligated to go to some State where she can be legally divorced; and then she would be as solemnly bound to return again, and, standing for herself and her children, regard herself, in the sight of God, as being bound still to the father of those children, to work for his best interests, while she still maintains her own sovereignty. Of course, she must be governed by the circumstances of the case. She may be obliged, for the protection of the family, to live on one continent while her husband is on the other; but she is never to forget that in, the sight of God and her own soul, she is his wife, and that she owes to him the wife's loyalty; that to work for his redemption is her highest social obligation, and that to teach her children to do the same is her first motherly duty.

Legal divorce may be necessary for personal and family protection; if so, let every woman obtain it. This, God helping me, is what I would certainly do; for under no circumstances will I ever give my consent to be subjected to the will of another, in any relation, for God has bidden me not to do it. But the idea of most women is, that they must be timid, weak, helpless, and full of ignoble submission. Only last week, a lady who has just been divorced from her husband said to me—"I used to be required to go into the field and do the hardest laborer's work, when I was not able to do it; and my husband would declare, that if I would not thus labor, I should not be allowed to eat, and I was obliged to submit." I say, the fault was as much with the woman as with the man; she should *never* have submitted. Our trouble is not with marriage as a relation between two; it is all individual. We have few men or women fit to be married. They neither fully respect themselves and their own rights and duties, nor yet those of another. They have no idea how noble, how godlike is the relation which ought to exist between the husband and wife.

Tell me, is marriage to be merely a contract—something entered into for a time, and then broken again—or is the true marriage permanent? One resolution read by Mrs. Stanton said that, as men are incompetent to select partners in business, teachers for their children, ministers of their religion, or makers, adjudicators or administrators of their laws, and as the same weakness and blindness must attend in the selection of matrimonial partners, the latter and most important contract should no more be perpetual than either or all of the former. I do not believe that, rightly understood, she quite holds to that position herself. Marriage must be either permanent, or capable of being any time dissolved. Which ground shall we take? I insist, that from the nature of things, marriage must be as permanent and indissoluble as the relation of parent and child. If so, let us legislate towards the right. Though evils must sometimes result, we are still to seek the highest law of the relation.

. . . . . . . .

Look at those who believe in thus easily dissolving the marriage obligation! In very many cases, they cannot be truly married, or truly happy in this relation, because there is something incompatible with it in their own natures. It is not always so; but when one feels that it is a relation easily to be dissolved, of course, incompatibility at once seems to arise in the other, and every difficulty that occurs, instead of being overlooked, as it ought to be, in a spirit of forgiveness, is magnified, and the evil naturally increased. . . .

So, let any married person take the idea that he may dissolve this relation, and enter into a new one, and how many faults he may discover that otherwise never would have been noticed! The marriage will become intolerable. The theory will work that result; it is in the nature of things, and that to me is every thing. Of course, I would not have man or woman sacrificed—by no means. First of all, let every human being maintain his own position as a self-protecting human being. At all hazards, let him never sin, or consent to be sacrificed to the hurt of himself or of another; and when he has taken this stand, let him act in harmony with it. Would I say to any woman, "You are bound, because you are legally married to one who is debased to the level of the brute, to be the mother of his children?" I say to her, "No! while the law of God continues, you are bound never to make one whom you do not honor and respect, as well as love, the father of any child of yours. It is your first and highest duty to be true to yourself, true to posterity, and true to society." (Applause.)

Thus, let each decide for himself and for herself what is right. But, I repeat, either marriage is in its very nature a relation which, once formed, never can be dissolved, and either the essential obligations growing out of it exist for ever, or the relation may at any time be dissolved, and at any time those obligations be annulled. And what are those obligations? Two persons, if I understand marriage, covenant to work together, to uphold each other in all excellence, and to mutually blend their lives and interests into a common harmony. I believe that God has so made man and woman, that it is not good for them to be alone, that they each need a co-worker. There is no work on God's footstool which man can do alone and do well, and there is no work which woman can do alone and do well. (Applause). . . .

What do you, the guides of our youth, say? You say to the young girl, "You ought to expect to be married before you are twenty, or about that time; you should intend to be; and from the time you are fifteen, it should be made your one life purpose; and in all human probability, you may expect to spend the next ten or twenty years in the nursery, and at forty or fifty, you will be an old woman, your life will be well-nigh worn out." I stand here to say that this is all false. Let the young girl be instructed that, above her personal interests, her home, and social life, she is to have a great life purpose, as broad as the rights and interests of humanity. I say, let every young girl feel this, as much as every young man does. We have no right, we, who expect to live for ever, to play about here as if we were mere flies, enjoying ourselves in the sunshine. We ought to have an earnest purpose outside of home, outside of our family relations. Then let the young girl fit herself for this. Let her be taught that she ought not to be married in her teens. Let her wait, as a young man does, if he is sensible, until she is twenty-five or thirty. (Applause.)

She will then know how to choose properly, and probably she will not be deceived in her estimate of character; she will have had a certain life-discipline, which will enable her to control her household matters with wise judgment, so that, while she is looking after her family, she may still keep her great life purpose, for which she was educated, and to which she has given her best energies, steadily in view. She need not absorb herself in her home, and God never intended that she should; and then, if she has lived according to the laws of physiology, and according to the laws of common sense, she ought to be, at the age of fifty years, just where man is, just where our great men are, in the very prime of life! When her young children have gone out of her home, then let her enter in earnest upon the great work of life outside of home and its relations. (Applause.)

It is a shame for our women to have no steady purpose or pursuit, and to make the mere fact of womanhood a valid plea for indolence; it is a greater shame that they should be instructed thus to throw all the responsibility of working for the general good upon the other sex. God has not intended it. But as long as you make women helpless, inefficient beings, who never expect to earn a farthing in their lives, who never expect to do any thing outside of the family, but to be cared for and protected by others throughout life, you cannot have true marriages; and if you try to break up the old ones, you will do it against the woman and in favor of the man. Last week, I went back to a town where I used to live, and was told that a woman, whose husband was notoriously the most miserable man in the town, had in despair taken her own life. I asked what had become of the husband, and the answer was, "Married again." And yet, every body there knows that he is the vilest and most contemptible man in the whole neighborhood.

Any man, no matter how wretched he may be, will find plenty of women to accept him, while they are rendered so helpless and weak by their whole education that they must be supported or starve. The advantage, if this theory of marriage is adopted, will not be on the side of woman, but altogether on the side of man. The cure for the evils that now exist is not in dissolving marriage, but it is in giving to the married woman her own natural independence and self-sovereignty, by which she can maintain herself. Yes, our women and our men are both degenerate; they are weak and ignoble. "Dear me!" said a pretty, indolent young lady, "I had a great deal rather my husband would take care of me, than to be obliged to do it for myself." "Of course you would," said a blunt old lady who was present; "and your brother would a great deal rather marry an heiress, and lie upon a sofa eating lollypops, bought by her money, than to do any thing manly or noble. The only difference is, that as heiresses are not very plenty, he may probably have to marry a poor girl, and then society will insist that he shall exert himself to earn a living for the family; but you, poor thing, will only have to open your mouth, all your life long, like a clam, and eat." (Applause and laughter.)

So long as society is constituted in such a way that woman is expected to do nothing if she have a father, brother, or husband, able to support her, there is no salvation for her, in or out of marriage. When you tie up your arm, it will become weak, and feeble; and when you tie up woman, she will become weak and helpless. Give her, then, some earnest purpose in life, hold up to her the true ideal of marriage, and it is enough—I am content! (Loud applause.)

## SPEECH OF MRS. E. L. ROSE.

Mrs. President,—The question of a Divorce law seems to me one of the greatest importance to all parties, but I presume that the very advocacy of divorce will be called "Free Love." For my part, (and I wish distinctly to define my position), I do not know what others understand by that term; to me, in its truest significance, love must be free, or it ceases to be love. In its low and degrading sense, it is not love at all, and I have as little to do with its name as its reality.

The Rev. Mrs. Blackwell gave us quite a sermon on what woman ought to be, what she ought to do, and what marriage ought to be; an excellent sermon in its proper place, but not when the important question of a Divorce law is under consideration. She treats woman as some ethereal being. It is very well to be ethereal to some extent, but I tell you, my friends, it is quite requisite to be a little material, also. At all events, we are so, and being so, it proves a law of our nature. (Applause.)

It were indeed well if woman could be what *she* ought to be, man what *he* ought to be, and marriage what it ought to be; and it is to be hoped that through the Woman's Rights movement—the equalizing of the laws, making them more just, and making woman more independent—we will hasten the coming of the millennium, when marriage shall indeed be a bond of union and affection. But, alas! it is not yet; and I fear that sermons, however well meant, will not produce that desirable end, and as long as the evil is here, we must look it in the face without shrinking, grapple with it manfully, and, the more complicated it is, the more courageously must it be analyzed, combated, and destroyed. (Applause.)

Mrs. Blackwell told us that, marriage being based on the perfect equality of husband and wife, it cannot be destroyed. But is it so? Where? Where and when have the sexes yet been equal in physical or mental education, in position, or in law? When and where have they yet been recognized by society, or by themselves, as equals? "Equal in rights," says Mrs. B. But are they equal in rights? If they were, we would need no conventions to claim our rights. "She can assert her equality," says she. Yes, she can assert it, but does that assertion constitute a true marriage? And when the husband holds the iron heel of legal oppression on the subjugated neck of the wife until every spark of womanhood is crushed out, will it heal the wounded heart, the lacerated spirit, the destroyed hope, to assert her equality? And shall she still continue the wife? Is that a marriage which must not be dissolved? (Applause.)

According to Mr. Greeley's definition, viz., that there is no marriage unless the ceremony is performed by a minister and in a church, the tens of thousands married according to the laws of this and most of the other

States, by a lawyer or justice of the peace, a Mayor or an Alderman, are not married at all. According to the definition of our Rev. sister, *no one has ever yet been married*, as woman has never yet been perfectly equal with man. I say to both, Take your position, and abide by the consequences. If the few only, or no one, is really married, why do you object to a law that shall acknowledge the fact? You certainly ought not to force people to live together who are not married. (Applause.)

Mr. Greeley tells us that marriage, being a Divine institution, nothing but death should ever separate the parties; but when he was asked, "Would you have a being who, innocent and inexperienced, in their youth and ardor of affection, in the fond hope that the sentiment was reciprocated, united herself to one she loved and cherished, and then found (no matter from what cause) that his profession was false, his heart hollow, his acts cruel, that she was degraded by his vice, despised for his crimes, cursed by his very presence, and treated with every conceivable ignominy—would you have her drag out a miserable existence as his wife?" "No, no," says he; "in that case, they ought to separate." Separate? But what becomes of the union divinely instituted, which death only should part? (Applause.)

The papers have of late been full with the heart-sickening accounts of wife poisoning. Whence come these terrible crimes? From the want of a Divorce law. Could the *Hardings* be legally separated, they would not be driven to the commission of murder to be free from each other; and which is preferable, a Divorce law, to dissolve an unholy union, which all parties agree is no true marriage, or a murder of one, and an execution (legal murder) of the other party? But had the unfortunate woman, just before the poisoned cup was presented to her lips, pleaded for a divorce, Mrs. Blackwell would have read her a sermon equal to St. Paul's "Wives, be obedient to your husbands," only she would have added, "You must assert your equality," but "you must keep with your husband and work for his redemption, *as I would do for my husband*;" and Mr. Greeley would say, "As you chose to marry him, it is your own fault; you must abide the consequences, for it is a 'divine institution, a union for life, which nothing but death can end.'" (Applause.)

The *Tribune* had recently a long sermon, almost equal to the one we had this morning from our Rev. sister, on "Fast Women." The evils it spoke of were terrible indeed, but like all other sermons, it was one-sided. Not one single word was said about fast men, except that the "poor victim had to spend so much money." The writer forgot that it is the demand which calls the supply into existence. But what was the primary cause of that tragic end? Echo answers, "what?" Ask the lifeless form of the murdered woman, and she may disclose the terrible secret, and show you that, could she have been legally divorced, she might not have been driven to the watery grave of a "fast woman." (Applause.)

But what is marriage? A human institution, called out by the needs of social, affectional human nature, for human purposes, its objects are, first, the happiness of the parties immediately concerned, and secondly, the welfare of society. Define it as you please, these only are its objects; and therefore if, from well ascertained facts, it is demonstrated that the real objects are frustrated, that instead of union and happiness, there are only discord and misery to themselves, and vice and crime to society, I ask, in the name of individual happiness and social morality and well-being, why such a marriage should be binding for life?—why one human being should be chained for life to the dead body of another? "But they may separate and still remain married." What a perversion of the very term! Is that the union which "death only should part"? It may be according to the definition of the Rev. Mrs. Blackwell's Theology and Mr. Greeley's Dictionary, but it certainly is not according to common sense or the dictates of morality. No, no! "it is not well for man to be alone," *before* nor *after* marriage. (Applause.)

I therefore ask for a Divorce law. Divorce is now granted for some crimes, I ask it for others also. It is granted for a State's Prison offence, I ask that personal cruelty to a wife, whom he swore to "love, cherish, and protect," may be made a heinous crime—a perjury and a State's Prison offence, for which divorce shall be granted. Willful desertion for one year should be a sufficient cause for divorce, for the willful deserter forfeits the sacred title of husband or wife. Habitual intemperance, or any other vice which makes the husband or wife intolerable and abhorrent to the other, ought to be sufficient cause for divorce. I ask for a law of Divorce, so as to secure the real objects and blessings of married life, to prevent the crimes and immoralities now practised, to prevent "Free Love," in its most hideous form, such as is now carried on but too often under the very name of marriage, where hypocrisy is added to the crime of legalized prostitution. "Free Love," in its degraded sense, asks for no Divorce law. It acknowledges no marriage, and therefore requires no divorce. I believe in true marriages, and therefore I ask for a law to free men and women from false ones. (Applause.)

But it is said that if divorce were easily granted, "men and women would marry to-day and unmarry to-morrow." Those who say that only prove that they have no confidence in themselves, and therefore can have no confidence in others. But the assertion is false; it is a libel on human nature. It is the indissoluble chain that corrodes the flesh. Remove the indissolubility, and there would be less separation than now, for it would place the parties on their good behavior, the same as during courtship. Human nature is not quite so changeable; give it more freedom, and it will be less so. We are a good deal the creatures of habit, but we will not be forced. We live (I speak from experience) in uncomfortable houses for years, rather than move, though we have the privilege to do so every year; but force any one to live for life in one house, and he would run away from it, though it were a palace.

But Mr. Greeley asks, "How could the mother look the child in the face, if she married a second time?" With infinitely better grace and better conscience than to live as some do now, and show their children the degrading example, how utterly father and mother despise and hate each other, and still live together as husband and wife. She could say to her child, "As, unfortunately, your father proved himself unworthy, your mother could not be so unworthy as to continue to live with him. As he failed to be a true father to you, I have endeavored to supply his place with one, who, though not entitled to the name, will, I hope, prove himself one in the performance of a father's duties. (Applause.)

Finally, educate woman, to enable her to promote her independence, and she will not be obliged to marry for a home and a subsistence. Give the wife an equal right with the husband in the property acquired after marriage, and it will be a bond of union between them. Diamond cement, applied on both sides of a fractured vase, reunites the parts, and prevents them from falling asunder. A gold band is more efficacious than an iron law. Until now, the gold has all been on one side, and the iron law on the other. Remove it; place the golden band of justice and mutual interest around both husband and wife, and it will hide the little fractures which may have occurred, even from their own perception, and allow them effectually to reunite. A union of interest helps to preserve a union of hearts. (Loud applause.)

# PETITION: APPEAL TO THE WOMEN OF NEW YORK

*By Elizabeth Cady Stanton, Lydia Mott, Ernestine L. Rose,*
*Martha C. Wright, and Susan B. Anthony*
November 1860
Albany, New York

This appeal, signed by many of the leading women's rights reformers in New York State—and indeed, in the country—celebrates the accomplishments of the women's rights movement over the prior decade, and sets forth an agenda for the immediate future. We can see Rose's influence in this jointly signed appeal—its pride in the "agitation" that has brought about so much change, for example, and the bold references to religion as a barrier to women's equality. Having won a major battle in New York State with the passage of the Married Women's Property Law, women's rights advocates set their sights on an upcoming revision of the State Constitution, which they are determined will include suffrage for women. In the meantime, they demand of male lawmakers that they begin to make laws that "bear equally on man and woman." They urge women to support these goals by collecting signatures to the petition and donating money.

❧

Women of New York:—Once more we appeal to you to make renewed efforts for the elevation of our sex. In our marital laws we are now in advance of every State in the Union. Twelve years ago New York took the initiative step, and secured to married women their property, received by gift or inheritance. Our last Legislature passed a most liberal act, giving to married women their rights, to sue for damages of person of property, to their separate earnings and their children; and to the widow, the possession and control of the entire estate during the minority of the youngest child. Women of New York! You can no longer be insulted in the first days of your widowed grief by the coarse minions of the law at your fireside, coolly taking an inventory of your household goods, or robbing your children of their natural guardian.

While we rejoice in this progress made in our laws, we see also a change in the employment of women. They are coming down from the garrets and up from the cellars to occupy more profitable posts in every department of industry, literature, science, and art. In the church, too, behold the spirit of freedom at work. Within the past year, the very altar has been the scene of well-fought battles; women claiming and exercising their right to vote in church matters, in defiance of precedent, priest, or Paul.

Another evidence of the importance of our cause is seen in the deep interest men of wealth are manifesting in it. Three great bequests have been given to us in the past year. Five thousand dollars from an unknown hand, a share in the munificent fund left by that noble man of Boston, Charles F. Hovey, and four hundred thousand dollars by Mr. Vassar, of Poughkeepsie, to found a college for girls, equal in all respects to Yale and Harvard. Is it not strange that women of wealth are constantly giving large sums of money to endow professorships and colleges for boys exclusively—to churches and to the education of the ministry, and yet give no thought to their own sex—crushed in ignorance, poverty, and prostitution—the hopeless victims of custom, law, and Gospel, with few to offer a helping hand, while the whole world combine to aid the boy and glorify the man?

Our movement is already felt in the Old World. The nobility of England, with Lord Brougham at their head, have recently formed a "Society for Promoting the Employments of Women."

All this is the result of the agitation, technically called "Woman's Rights," through conventions, lectures, circulation of tracts and petitions, and by the faithful word uttered in the privacy of home. The few who stand forth to meet the world's cold gaze, its ridicule, its contumely, and its scorn, are urged onward by the prayers and tears, crushed hopes and withered hearts of the sad daughters of the race. The wretched will not let them falter; and they who seem to do the work, ever and anon draw fresh courage and inspiration from the noblest women of the age, who, from behind the scene, send forth good words of cheer and heartfelt thanks.

Six years hence, the men of New York purpose to revise our State Constitution. Among other changes demanded, is the right of suffrage for women—which right will surely be granted, if through all the intervening years every woman does her duty. Again do we appeal to each and all—to every class and condition—to inform themselves on this question, that woman may no longer publish her degradation by declaring herself satisfied in her present position, nor her ignorance by asserting that she has "all the rights she wants."

Any person who ponders the startling fact that there are four millions of African slaves in this republic, will instantly put the question to himself, "Why do these people submit to the cruel tyranny that our government exercises over them?" The answer is apparent— "simply because they are ignorant of their power." Should they rise en masse, assert and demand their rights, their freedom would be secure. It is the same with woman. Why is it that one-half the people of this nation are held in abject dependence—civilly, politically, socially, the slaves of man? Simply because woman knows not her power. To find out her natural rights, she must travel through such labyrinths of falsehood, that most minds stand appalled before the dark mysteries of life—the seeming contradictions in all laws, both human and divine. But, because woman can not solve the whole problem to her satisfaction, because she can not prove to a demonstration the rottenness and falsehood of our present customs, shall she, without protest, supinely endure evils she cannot at once redress? The silkworm, in its many wrappings, knows not it yet shall fly. The woman, in her ignorance, her drapery, and her chains, knows not that in advancing civilization, she too must soon be free, to counsel with her conscience and her God.

The religion of our day teaches that in the most sacred relations of the race, the woman must ever be subject to the man; that in the husband centers all power and learning; that the difference in position between husband and wife is as vast as that between Christ and the church; and woman struggles to hold the noble impulses of her nature in abeyance to opinions uttered by a Jewish teacher, which, alas! the mass believe to be the will of God. Woman turns from what she is taught to believe are God's laws to the laws of man; and in his written codes she finds herself still a slave. No girl of fifteen could read the laws concerning woman, made, executed, and defended by those who are bound to her by every tie of affection, without a burst of righteous indignation. Few have ever read or heard of the barbarous laws that govern the mothers of this Christian republic, and fewer still care, until misfortune brings them into the iron grip of the law. It is the imperative duty of educated women to study the Constitution and statutes under which they live, that when they shall have a voice in the government, they may bring wisdom and not folly into its councils.

We now demand the ballot, trial by jury of our peers, and an equal right to the joint earnings of the marriage co-partnership. And, until the Constitution be so changed as to give us a voice in the government, we demand that man shall make all his laws on property, marriage, and divorce, to bear equally on man and woman.

*New York State*
*Woman's Rights Committe*
*November, 1860*

N. B.—Let every friend commence to get signatures to the petition without delay and send up to Albany early in January, either to your representative or to Lydia Mott.

How can any wife or mother who to-day rejoices in her legal right to the earnings of her hands, and the children of her love, withhold the small pittance of a few hours or days in getting signatures to the petition or a few shillings or dollars to carry the work onward and upward, to a final glorious consummation.

1861-1867

# SPEECH AT THE THOMAS PAINE
## CELEBRATION: "FREEDOM OR SLAVERY"
January 29, 1861
New York, New York

When the annual Thomas Paine Celebration took place in January 1861, Abraham Lincoln had been elected president, although he would not take office until March. South Carolina had begun the drive toward secession, and the United States was just months away from a full-scale civil war over the issue of slavery. Rose begins by addressing victories in the struggle for human rights in Europe, including the unification of Italy and the freeing of the serfs in Russia. She moves on to address the great human rights struggle facing her own adopted country: "[S]hall henceforth freedom or slavery be the ruling principle of this republic?"

Rose concluded her talk with opposition to Sunday laws, an important local issue to the predominantly immigrant constituency of New York's freethought movement. Her speech was printed in the *Boston Investigator* on February 20, 1861.

⚭

*Mr. President*—Friends, it has ever given me great pleasure . . . to welcome you on the natal day of the great apostle of liberty—Thomas Paine. There has never been a fitter time to honor the author of the "rights of man;" for freedom never more justly called on her champions, nor humanity more earnestly appealed to the devotion of her children, than at the present. The year just past has been full of interest. In that year a noble people, so long oppressed by temporal and spiritual despotism that her emancipation was almost beyond hope, has raised her prostrate form, and assumed a position among the nations of the earth. Italy, the favored garden of nature—the emporium of the arts—the home of poetry and song—the birthplace of the highest stars in the intellectual and moral constellation—reduced by foreign usurpers, hireling mercenaries, almost to beggary, inaction and helplessness, has, by the magic arm of Garibaldi, demonstrated that the spirit which once animated her children is not extinct. But this unparalleled struggle, crowned as it has been with a yet more unparalleled victory, is not complete. Her right arm is yet paralyzed. Venice, the bridge of the ocean, once the centre of commerce, as she stands like an enchanted isle, unique and alone in the world, is still in the despotic power of Austria. And Italy's noble head, Rome, the Eternal City—once the cradle of civilization—the great lawgiver of nations—now the tomb of her past glory—whose very ruins attest her former greatness—the theatre of the most desperate as the most sublime achievements, the wildest passions, the most glorious deeds, the highest hopes and noblest aspirations—to whose genius the very paving stones stand an undying monument, is still in the fiendish grasp of spiritual tyrants, more corrupt and implacable than all others, whose spare time from heavenly affairs is spent in stealing children from their parents. But let us hope that long before we again assemble to celebrate the birth-day of Thomas Paine, Garibaldi will break the chains of Venice and of Rome, like those of Sicily and of Naples, and give to the world a truly united and happy Italy.

But 1860 has done more: it has demonstrated that at times it may be the interest of tyrants to espouse a good cause. Russia, the sworn enemy of liberty, the plunderer of Poland, has stepped out of his time-hardened despotism to give freedom to the serfs. And Louis Napoleon, the republican President of '48, the usurper of an Emperor's throne of '52, the banisher of the noblest spirits of France, the executioner of her liberties, proclaimed himself the champion of freedom in Italy. We understand his motives, but let us accept the fact; this is only the beginning. The same reason that induced him to aid Italy against Austria has forced him to relax his iron grasp from the throat of subjugated France, and give her back a part of the rights he so basely deprived her of. But freedom is not satisfied with half measures. What he gave will soon make it indispensable for his own safety to return the rest, or lose all.

But I must leave the destiny of Europe to the present year, and note some of the events of 1860 in this country. Last summer we had the pleasure of . . . the visit from the amiable, modest Prince of Wales, who it is to be hoped, after getting over the affliction of being forced to dance with so many pious old ladies, and of being worshiped at Trinity Church, will look with satisfaction and pride on his visit to and reception from his American cousins. With these pleasing events passed the summer months, then came autumn with her ripe fruits, far more important and enduring, for of all the days of that year will stand in prominent and ineffaceable character the 6th of November [Election Day].

On that day, unlike similar occasions, when party men with party measures stood in antagonistic position, principles were brought face to face. The question was not one of Whig or democrat, high or low tariff, but shall henceforth freedom or slavery be the ruling principle of this republic? Shall the yet virgin soil, the broad acres stretched in the far West, waiting the magic hand of free labor to pour forth her golden treasures to the needy children of man, be consecrated to freedom or polluted by the unhallowed touch of slavery, which, like a destroying angel, blasts the fair works of nature and of man? And the 6th of November, burdened with the accumulated progress of 1860, answered to freedom. Then see to it, free men of America, that the battle so nobly fought in 1860 shall be brought to a happy termination in 1861, that those whom you have honored with your confidence betray not that voice, violate not the sacred pledge, and turn traitor to the present and future generations.

"These are the times that try men's souls." The question which now distracts the country is no longer one of color—it is freedom or slavery, life or death of the North—it is whether a vile mob, headed by corrupted and treacherous politicians, who would dissolve not only the Union but the universe to get themselves into office, shall be allowed to trample the dignity, the manhood and the liberties of the North in the dust—whether we shall barter away the rights, the progress and the civilization of the free States for the inestimable blessing to belong to South Carolina. But President Buchanan, by whose criminal contrivance the mob was let loose, being too cowardly and inefficient to weather the storm he helped to raise, took refuge in fasting and prayer; but while the North prayed, the South acted. Ask the national forts stolen, the flag trampled under foot, the laws violated, the ships fired into, the government disgraced, which of the prayers was most successful? Prayed! for what? One party for secession, the other for non-secession; . . . one side claims the Bible for and the other claims it against slavery, and they both are right. That book is so accommodating that it proves and disproves anything you choose. Chameleon like, it reflects the color of the glass you look through. But it strikes me if a wise and good Power really heard these praying machines, He would say, "Cease importuning me with your mad wailings; go to work, act like rational beings, be true to your highest conviction—to human rights and human freedom—and when these are in danger, take a lesson from Major Anderson, and 'keep your powder dry;' I only help those who help themselves."

"But cotton is king," and the Northern cowards whose souls are composed of that material tremble at His mandates. South Carolina dissolve the Union!—a Union with a vengeance; like that of husband and wife; with all the rights on one side and all the penalties on the other. There never yet was a true Union, for there was no equality between the free and the slave states. The slaveholder could come here and say what he pleased—expatiate on the beauties of "our peculiar institution;" but the free man could never go South and say his soul was his own, without the risk of being lynched. Ask those who have been tarred and feathered, whipped, expelled and imprisoned, for the crime of belonging to a free State, and you will learn the value of such a Union. No—Freedom and slavery cannot live in harmony; the one must destroy the other; the last feeble threads which gave it the appearance, reckless hands have snapped asunder. South Carolina set up an independent empire! For my part, I would give her a passport to Heaven to keep away from us. But whether the South is allowed to drift to her downward destiny, or forced into submission, let the watchword be, "No more compromise!" We expiate now the crime of having compromised so often, and even if we again tried to reconcile the irreconcilable, would the evil be cured? No; the disease would only gather strength and break out with increased virulence. The danger, therefore, is not the secession of the South from the North; but of the North from herself, from the self-evident truth of man's right to life, liberty and the pursuit of happiness. Let that danger only be averted, and all will be well. There may yet be hope even for the South, for

"While the lamp holds out to burn,
The vilest sinner may return."

In conclusion, allow me to glance at another danger we must guard against. The National Constitution guarantees perfect freedom of conscience, and yet through the influence of a bigoted and corrupt priesthood, infamous Sunday laws have been enacted to persecute and punish unoffending citizens for keeping that day according to their consciences, for preferring rational recreation and amusement to rioting and drunkenness; for preferring a good concert, a comedy or tragedy in a theatre to the priestly farce in the church. If the Sunday is to be kept apart from general business and labor, it is precisely for the purpose to enable the working classes, who cannot spare the time the rest of the week, to enjoy healthful recreation and amusement as a safeguard against physical and mental stagnation and moral corruption. And if that baneful influence is not speedily counteracted, where will it end? Who can say that it will not again draw chains across our streets, and lead to Salem witchcraft, the Blue laws, the whipping post and all the horrors of old Puritanism? Let us, then, my friends, do all that we can to wipe out those dark spots that obscure the light of freedom, impede progress, and prevent this country from becoming the free, enlightened and happy republic Thomas Paine spent his best energies and devotion to enable her to become; for only a republic without chains of slavery, craft of priests, and tricks of knavery can make man wise, great and free.

# SPEECH: "A DEFENCE OF ATHEISM"
## April 10, 1861
## Boston, Massachusetts

Although Rose had advocated for the radical freethought movement throughout her quarter-century in the United States, her personal views had sometimes been interpreted as Deistic—believing in the existence of a supreme being based upon reason and observation of nature, rather than received doctrine. In this public lecture, given at Boston's Mercantile Hall, she comes out proudly as an atheist. Ridicule was a favorite tool of freethinkers against biblical narrative. Rose is relentlessly caustic in her review of the Bible as the revealed word of an all-knowing and all-powerful God. In questioning the validity of the biblical God and religion, Rose seeks evidence of the existence of God in all the sciences of the time, and finds none. In this aspect of her talk, she shows herself to be knowledgeable about evolution well before these ideas had permeated even forward-thinking reform circles. After Darwin's *The Origin of Species* was published in 1859, a gradual change began to take place in public discourse. By the end of the 1860s, most liberal religious believers accepted the new science while reserving matters of faith to the clergy, their churches, and private conscience (Warren 1966). Rose consistently stayed abreast of new scientific knowledge, always firmly on the side of scientific rather than religion-based narratives of creation. Although she had so often in the past spoken out against the Bible and all religions texts as particularly oppressive to women, it is surprising that in this speech, Rose entirely neglects women's issues relative to biblical narrative (Anderson 2002).

The *Boston Investigator* reported on Rose's talk in its editions of April 17, 1861, and May 8, 1861, but did not print the text because Rose was working on a written version (Kolmerten 1999, 230–31). This version is excerpted from a pamphlet (1889) published by J. P. Mendum, publisher of the *Boston Investigator*, twenty years after Rose had left the United States to live in England.

❧

My Friends:—In undertaking the inquiry of the existence of a God, I am fully conscious of the difficulties I have to encounter. I am well aware that the very question produces in most minds a feeling of awe, as if stepping on forbidden ground, too holy and sacred for mortals to approach. The very question strikes them with horror, and it is owing to this prejudice so deeply implanted by education, and also strengthened by public sentiment, that so few are willing to give it a fair and impartial investigation, knowing but too well that it casts a stigma and reproach upon any person bold enough to undertake the task, unless his previously known opinions are a guarantee that his conclusions would be in accordance and harmony

with the popular demand. But believing as I do, that Truth only is beneficial, and Error, from whatever source, and under whatever name, is pernicious to man, I consider no place too holy, no subject too sacred, for man's
earnest investigation; for by so doing only can we arrive at Truth, learn to
discriminate it from Error, and be able to accept the one and reject the
other.

Nor is this the only impediment in the way of this inquiry. The question arises, Where shall we begin? We have been told, that "by searching none can find out God," which has so far proved true; for, as yet, no
one has ever been able to find him. The most strenuous believer has to
acknowledge that it is only a belief, but he *knows* nothing on the subject.
Where, then, shall we search for his existence? Enter the material world;
ask the Sciences whether they can disclose the mystery? Geology speaks
of the structure of the Earth, the formation of the different strata, of coal,
of granite, of the whole mineral kingdom. It reveals the remains and trac-
es of animals long extinct, but gives us no clue whereby we may prove the
existence of a God.

Natural history gives us a knowledge of the animal kingdom in general; the different organisms, structures, and powers of the various species.
Physiology teaches the nature of man, the laws that govern his being, the
functions of the vital organs, and the conditions upon which alone health
and life depend. Phrenology treats of the laws of mind, the different portions of the brain, the temperaments, the organs, how to develop some
and repress others to produce a well balanced and healthy condition. But
in the whole animal economy—though the brain is considered to be a
"microcosm," in which may be traced a resemblance or relationship with
everything in Nature—not a spot can be found to indicate the existence
of a God.

Mathematics lays the foundation of all the exact sciences. It teaches
the art of combining numbers, of calculating and measuring distances,
how to solve problems, to weigh mountains, to fathom the depths of the
ocean; but gives no directions how to ascertain the existence of a God.

Enter Nature's great laboratory—Chemistry. She will speak to you
of the various elements, their combinations and uses, of the gasses constantly evolving and combining in different proportions, producing all the
varied objects, the interesting and important phenomena we behold. She
proves the indestructibility of matter, and its inherent property—motion;
but in all her operations no demonstrable fact can be obtained to indicate
the existence of a God.

Astronomy tells us of the wonders of the Solar System—the eternally revolving planets, the rapidity and certainty of their motions, the

distance from planet to planet, from star to star. It predicts with astonishing and marvelous precision the phenomena of eclipses, the visibility
upon our Earth of comets, and proves the immutable law of gravitation,
but is entirely silent on the existence of a God.

In fine, descend into the bowels of the Earth, and you will learn what
it contains; into the depths of the ocean, and you will find the inhabitants
of the great deep; but neither in the Earth above, nor the waters below,
can you obtain any knowledge of his existence. Ascend into the heavens, and enter the "milky way," go from planet to planet to the remotest
star, and ask the eternally revolving systems, Where is God? and Echo
answers. Where?

The Universe of Matter gives us no record of his existence. Where
next shall we search? Enter the Universe of Mind, read the millions of
volumes written on the subject, and in all the speculations, the assertions,
the assumptions, the theories, and the creeds, you can only find Man
stamped in an indelible impress his own mind on every page. In describing his God, he delineated his own character: the picture he drew represents in living and ineffaceable colors the epoch of his existence—the
period he lived in.

It was a great mistake to say that God made man in his image. Man,
in all ages, made his God in his own image; and we find that just in accordance with his civilization, his knowledge, his experience, his taste, his
refinement, his sense of right, of justice, of freedom, and humanity, so has
he made his God. But whether coarse or refined; cruel and vindictive, or
kind and generous; an implacable tyrant, or a gentle and loving father; it
still was the emanation of his own mind—the picture of himself.

But, you ask, how came it that man thought or wrote about God at
all? The answer is very simple. Ignorance is the mother of Superstition.
In proportion to man's ignorance is he superstitious—does he believe in
the mysterious. The very name has a charm for him. Being unacquainted
with the nature and laws of things around him, with the true causes of
the effects he witnessed, he ascribed them to false ones—to supernatural
agencies. The savage, ignorant of the mechanism of a watch, attributes
the ticking to a spirit. The so-called civilized man, equally ignorant of
the mechanism of the Universe, and the laws which govern it, ascribes
it to the same erroneous cause. Before electricity was discovered, a thun-
der-storm was said to come from the wrath of an offended Deity. To this
fiction of man's uncultivated mind, has been attributed all of good and
of evil, of wisdom and of folly. Man has talked about him, written about
him, disputed about him, fought about him, sacrificed himself, and extir-
pated his fellow man. Rivers of blood and oceans of tears have been shed

to please him, yet no one has ever been able to demonstrate his existence.

But the Bible, we are told, reveals this great mystery. Where here Nature is dumb, and Man ignorant, Revelation speaks in the authoritative voice of prophecy. Then let us see whether that Revelation can stand the test of reason and of truth. God, we are told, is omnipotent, omniscient, omnipresent,—all wise, all just, and all good; that he is perfect. So far, so well; for less than perfection were unworthy of a God. The first act recorded of him is, that he created the world out of nothing; but unfortunately the revelation of Science—Chemistry—which is based not on written words, but demonstrable facts, says that Nothing has no existence, and therefore, out of Nothing, Nothing could be made. Revelation tells us that the world was created in six days. Here Geology steps in and says, that it requires thousands of ages to form the various strata of the earth. The Bible tells us that the earth was flat and stationary, and the sun moves around the earth. Copernicus and Galileo *flatly* deny this *flat* assertion, and demonstrate by Astronomy that the earth is spherical, and revolves around the sun. Revelation tells us that on the fourth day God created the sun, moon, and stars. This, Astronomy calls a moon story, and says that the first three days, before the great torchlight was manufactured and suspended in the great lantern above, must have been rather dark.

The division of the waters above from the waters below, and the creation of the minor objects, I pass by, and come at once to the sixth day.

Having finished, in five days, this stupendous production, with its mighty mountains, its vast seas, its fields and woods; supplied the waters with fishes—from the whale that swallowed Jonah to the little Dutch herring; peopled the woods with inhabitants—from the tiger, the lion, the bear, the elephant with his trunk, the dromedary with his hump, the deer with his antlers, the nightingale with her melodies, down to the serpent which tempted mother Eve; covered the fields with vegetation, decorated the gardens with flowers, hung the trees with fruits; and surveying this glorious world as it lay spread out like a map before him, the question naturally suggested itself. What is it all for, unless there were beings capable of admiring, of appreciating, and of enjoying the delights this beautiful world could afford? And suiting the action to the impulse, he said, "Let us make man." "So God created man in his own image; in the image of God created he him, male and female created he them."

I presume by the term "image," we are not to understand a near resemblance of face or form, but in the image or likeness of his knowledge, his power, his wisdom, and perfection. Having thus made man, he placed him (them) in the garden of Eden—the loveliest and most enchanting spot at the very head of creation, and bade them (with the single restriction not to eat of the tree of knowledge), to live, to love, and to be happy.

What a delightful picture, could we only rest here! But did these beings, fresh from the hand of omnipotent wisdom, in whose image they were made, answer the great object of their creation? Alas! no. No sooner were they installed in their Paradisean home, than they violated the first, the only injunction given them, and fell from their high estate; and not only they, but by a singular justice of that very merciful Creator, their innocent posterity to all coming generations, fell with them! Does that bespeak wisdom and perfection in the Creator, or in the creature? But what was the cause of this tremendous fall, which frustrated the whole design of the creation? The serpent tempted mother Eve, and she, like a good wife, tempted her husband. But did God not know when he created the Serpent, that it would tempt the woman, and that *she* was made out of such frail materials (the rib of Adam), as not to be able to resist the temptation? If he did not know, then his knowledge was at fault; if he did, but could not prevent the calamity, then his power was at fault; if he knew and could, but would not, then his goodness was at fault. Choose which you please, and it remains alike fatal to the rest.

Revelation tells us that God made man perfect, and found him imperfect; then he pronounced all things good, and found them most desperately bad. "And God saw that the wickedness of man was great in the earth, and that every imagination of the thought of his heart was evil continually. And it repented the Lord that he had made man on the earth, and it grieved him at his heart." "And the Lord said, I will destroy man whom I have created, from the face of the earth; both man and beast, and the creeping things, and the fowls of the air, for it repenteth me that I have made them." So he destroyed everything, except Noah with his family, and a few household pets. Why he saved *them* is hard to say, unless it was to reserve materials as stock in hand to commence a new world with; but really, judging of the character of those he saved, by their descendants, it strikes me it would have been much better, and given him far less trouble, to have let them slip also, and with his improved experience made a new world out of fresh and superior materials.

As it was, this wholesale destruction even, was a failure. The world was not one jot better after the flood than before. His chosen children were just as bad as ever, and he had to send his prophets, again and again, to threaten, to frighten, to coax, to cajole, and to flatter them into good behaviour. But all to no effect. They grew worse and worse: and having made a covenant with Noah after he had sacrificed of "every clean beast and of every clean fowl,"—"The Lord smelt the sweet savour; and the Lord said in his heart, I will not again curse the ground any more for

man's sake; for the imagination of man's heart is evil from his youth; neither will I again smite any more everything living, as I have done." And
so he was forced to resort to the last sad alternative of sending "his only
begotten son," his second self, to save them. But alas! "his own received
him not," and so he was obliged to adopt the Gentiles, and die to save
the world. Did he succeed, even then? Is the world saved? Saved! From
what? From ignorance? It is all around us. From poverty, vice, crime, sin,
misery, and shame? It abounds everywhere. Look into your poor-houses,
your prisons, your lunatic asylums; contemplate the whip, the instruments
of torture, and of death; ask the murderer, or his victim; listen to the rav-
ings of the maniac, the shrieks of distress, the groans of despair; mark
the cruel deeds of the tyrant, the crimes of slavery, and the suffering of
the oppressed; count the millions of lives lost by fire, by water, and by the
sword; measure the blood spilled, the tears shed, the sighs of agony drawn
from the expiring victims on the altar of fanaticism;—and tell me from
what the world was *saved*? And why was it not saved? Why does God still
permit these horrors to afflict the race? Does omniscience not know it?
Could omnipotence not do it? Would infinite wisdom, power, and goodness allow his children thus to live, to suffer, and to die? No! Humanity
revolts against such a supposition.

. . . . . . .

In conclusion, the Atheist says to the honest, conscientious believer,
Though I cannot believe in your God whom you have failed to demonstrate, I believe in man; if I have no faith in your religion, I have faith,
unbounded, unshaken faith in the principles of right, of justice, and
humanity. Whatever good you are willing to do for the sake of your God,
I am full as willing to do for the sake of man. But the monstrous crimes
the believer perpetrated in persecuting and exterminating his fellowman
on account of difference of belief, the Atheist, knowing that belief is not
voluntary, but depends on evidence, and therefore there can be no merit in
the belief of any religions, nor demerit in a disbelief in all of them, could
never be guilty of. Whatever good you would do out of fear of punishment, or hope of reward hereafter, the Atheist would do simply because
*it is* good; and, *being so*, he would receive the far surer and more certain
reward, springing from well-doing, which would constitute his pleasure,
and promote his happiness.

# LETTER AND TOAST FOR THE COMMITTEE OF THE PAINE CELEBRATION, BOSTON

January 27, 1862
New York, New York

The occasion of an invitation to the Paine Celebration in Boston provided an opportunity for Rose to make a freethinker's case for action on the abolition of slavery. The freethinkers and secularists who attended these annual events regarded belief in religion as *mental* enslavement, the underlying cause of all other oppression. Thus, for ideological reasons or simply due to indifference or racism, they tended not to take action on abolition, preferring to focus first on freeing minds from superstition. Rose never felt she had to choose between these two essential struggles. During the Civil War years, in particular, she spoke with great passion on the antislavery issue, viewing emancipation as the only meaningful goal of the war. At the end of her letter, Rose appended a toast, presumably to be read at the celebration—which began with a fervent statement of support for the Union in the war, and ended with a demand for an "Edict of Emancipation." Rose's letter and her toast were published in the *Boston Investigator* on February 5, 1862.

⤙

New York, Jan., 27, 1862

To the Committee of the Paine Celebration, Boston:

Dear Friends:—Your favor of the 23d came duly to hand. Please to accept our warmest thanks for your kind invitation. I need not dwell on the assurance that it would give us great pleasure could we avail ourselves of this favorable opportunity to enjoy with you the next annual festivity of the Paine Celebration, but, unfortunately, indisposition will not permit me to leave home at this inclement season of the year. Allow me, however, to assure you that though absent in person, we will be present with you in thought and feeling.

Who that has Freedom at heart can be indifferent to the natal day of the Author of the "Rights of Man"—of one of the purest and most devoted champions of civil and religious Liberty? "*These* are the times that try men's souls." When the nation groans under the desolating effect of a civil war—a war instigated by the fiendish desire to subvert our free institutions to the use of slavery, and to trample the immortal declaration of human equality under foot, can we help recalling the following glowing and soul-stirring words of Thomas Paine, on contemplating the sad event of a departure from the principles of Freedom upon which alone a Republic can be maintained? In comparing such an event with the fall of ancient empires, he said:—

"But when the Empire of America shall fall, the subject for contemplative sorrow will be infinitely greater than decaying brass or crumbling marble can inspire. It will not then be said, Here stood a temple of vast antiquity, here rose a Babel of Invisible height, or there a palace of sumptuous extravagance; but here, oh! painful to relate, the noblest work of human wisdom, the greatest scene of human glory, the fair cause of Freedom rose and fell!"

What Thomas Paine then deplored even in the distant possibility, was not the destruction of Fifth Avenue palaces, State Street mansions, the marble Capitol, or the White House, but the downfall of free institutions based upon the declaration of man's right to life, liberty, and the pursuit of happiness. Then let every friend of Thomas Paine resolve, like him, to devote himself to the promotion of human Freedom; and as the greater includes the lesser, remember that the first of rights is the right of man to himself, and in honoring the memory of Thomas Paine proclaim the rights of man without distinction of sex, country, or color. Permit me, with the above lines, to send to your celebration the following toast.

Yours, with affection,
Ernestine L. Rose

[Toast to] The President, Cabinet, and Commander-in-Chief—The captain, mates, and pilot of the National Ship Republic—May they soon awaken from the lethargy in which the opiate of slavery has so long kept them, to the consciousness of the facts—1st, that there is a war; 2d, that it cannot be brought to a successful termination by the sugar-plums fired from Sherman's pop-gun on the "hospitable shores" of South Carolina, but by bullets directed with a fearless and energetic hand; 3d, that no lasting peace and prosperity can be secured, until the primary cause of this civil war is removed, and as slavery like a curse has for years silently but steadily undermined the healthful action of the Republic, until it has broken out in the most wicked rebellion that ever disgraced the annals of human history—whose diabolical aim is to destroy human rights—to trample the declaration of human equality in the dust, and engulf the nation in irretrievable ruin, the voice of reason, justice, and humanity demand the eradication of the cause of this war, by directing against the Rebels the Battery of Freedom, and hurling at them the Edict of Emancipation.

# SPEECHES AT THE NATIONAL CONVENTION OF THE LOYAL WOMEN OF THE REPUBLIC

May 14, 1863

New York, New York

While National Woman's Rights Conventions were suspended during the Civil War years, women of the Union states formed local "Loyal Leagues" to contribute to the war effort and provide support to the soldiers at the front. In 1863, as hopes for a victory that would expand human freedom seemed at risk, women's rights advocates Elizabeth Cady Stanton, Susan B. Anthony, Lucy Stone, and Ernestine L. Rose called a National Convention of the Loyal Women of the Republic to be held in New York. The convention attracted one thousand women, including women primarily interested in patriotic activity to support the Union, abolitionists, and women's rights reformers. U.S. Senator Charles Sumner credited the work of the assembled women, who collected 400,000 signatures, with passage of the Thirteenth Amendment for emancipation of all enslaved people in the United States (DuBois 1978, 53).

The opening discussion included challenges by attendees who believed that a Loyal League convention should focus exclusively on supporting the Union troops and ending slavery, with no discussion of women's rights permitted. In the first of the speeches included here, Rose responds to the fifth proposed resolution, summarized by Susan B. Anthony as stating simply that in a democracy, every person should have the right to vote. After statements by a few more speakers, the resolution was passed by a majority, despite the vigorous opposition of those abolitionist women who did not wish to see suffrage for women tied explicitly to suffrage for African Americans, fearing that this would weaken support for the latter. At a later session, Rose presented a prepared speech calling for a Union worth supporting, one that lived up to the human rights values of its founding documents. She demands emancipation of all enslaved people as the only reasonable goal for which it would have been worth resorting to war. At the outset, preservation of the Union had been the declared reason for the war; only in January 1863 did Abraham Lincoln issue the Emancipation Proclamation, and even by May it enjoyed less than universal support in the North.

In this speech, Rose showed her familiarity with the political actions of Civil War generals, especially those who publicly and actively differed from the President. For example, Major General John C. Fremont issued a proclamation on August 10, 1861, declaring free all enslaved people owned in Missouri. President Lincoln, fearing that Fremont's order would lead the Border States to affiliate with the South, demanded that Fremont modify the order to apply only to those slave-owners actively aiding the Confederacy. This Fremont refused to do (Spartacus n.d.).

On May 9, 1862, General David Hunter declared free all enslaved persons in South Carolina, Georgia, and Florida. On May 19, President Lincoln nullified Hunter's emancipation edict and also urged the Border States to adopt gradual, compensated emancipation ("Chronology of Emancipation during the Civil War" 2007).

Union Army general George B. McClellan to whom Rose referred as "our little Napoleon" was known as "the Young Napoleon" for his study of European military strategy earlier in his career. Later he was dubbed by the media as "Mac the Unready" because of his dilatory tactics and perhaps for his inability to cooperate with other generals and his refusal of a Presidential order (Sifakis 2003).

Henry W. Halleck had retired from the U.S. Army in 1854, but joined the Union Army when Civil War broke out. He was appointed general-in-chief in Washington by Lincoln and specialized in defensive strategies. He was regarded as overly cautious and blamed for prolonging the war by those who wished to prosecute the war more vigorously.

∾

## HUMAN RIGHTS MUST INCLUDE WOMEN'S RIGHTS

Ernestine L. Rose :- . . . I for one, object to throw women out of the race for freedom. (Applause.) And do you know why? Because she needs freedom for the freedom of man. (Applause.) Our ancestors made a great mistake in not recognizing woman in the rights of man. It has been justly stated that the [N]egro at present suffers more than woman, but it can do him no injury to place woman in the same category with him. I, for one, object to having that term stricken out, for it can have no possible bearing against anything that we want to promote, for we desire to promote human rights and human freedom. It can do no injury, but must do good, for it is a painful fact that woman under the law, until very recently, has been entirely in the same category with the slave. Of late years she has had some small rights conceded to her. Now, mind, I say *conceded*; for publicly it has not yet been recognized by the laws of the land that she has a right to an equality with man. In that resolution it simply states a fact, that in a republic based on freedom, woman, as well as the [N]egro, should be recognized as an equal with the whole human race. (Applause)

[Following other speakers, Rose continued to speak on this issue].

It is exceedingly amusing to hear persons talk about throwing out Woman's Rights, when, if it had not been for Woman's Rights, that lady would not have had the courage to stand here and say what she did. (Applause.) Pray, what means "loyal?" Loyal means to be true to one's highest conviction. Justice, like charity, begins at home. It is because we are loyal to truth, loyal to justice, loyal to right, loyal to humanity, that woman is included in that resolution. Now, what does this discussion mean? The lady acknowledges that it is not against Woman's Rights itself; she is *for* Woman's Rights. We are here to endeavor to help the cause of human rights and human freedom. We ought not to be afraid. You may depend upon it, if there are any of those who are called copperheads—but

I don't like to call names, for even a copperhead is better than no head at all—(laughter)—if there are any copperheads [refers to Northerners, usually Democrats, who wanted the Union to conclude the war because of their pro-slavery sympathies.] here, I am perfectly sure that they will object to this whole Convention; and if we want to consult them, let us adjourn *sine die*. If we are loyal to our highest convictions, we need not care how far it may lead. For truth, like water, will find its own level. No, friends; in the name of consistency let us not wrangle here simply because we associate the name of woman with human justice and human rights. Although I always like to see opposition on any subject, for it elicits truth much better than any speech, still I think it will be exceedingly incon- sistent if, because some women out in the West [referring to the previ- ous speaker, a Mrs. Hoyt from Wisconsin] are opposed to the Woman's Rights movement—though at the same time they take advantage of it— that therefore we shall throw it out of this resolution.

## WAR FOR THE UTTER EXTINCTION OF SLAVERY

Mrs. Ernestine L. Rose, a native of Poland, was next introduced.

. . . . It is unnecessary to point out the cause of this war. It is writ- ten on every object we behold. It is but too well understood that the pri- mary cause is Slavery; and it is well to keep that in mind, for the purpose of gaining the knowledge how ultimately to be able to crush that ter- rible rebellion which now desolates the land. Slavery being the cause of the war, we must look to its utter extinction for the remedy. Without the entire and complete destruction of every vestige of slavery, we can have no peace. (Applause.)

We have listened this evening to an exceedingly instructive, kind and gentle address, particularly that part of it which tells how to deal with the South after we have brought them back. But I think it would be well, at first, to consider how to bring them back!

Abraham Lincoln has issued a Proclamation. He has emancipated all the slaves of the rebel States with his pen, but that is all. To set them really and thoroughly free, we will have to use some other instrument than the pen. (Applause.) The slave is not emancipated; he is not free. A gentleman once found himself of a sudden, without, so far as he knew, any cause, taken into prison. He sent for his lawyer, and told him. "They have taken me to prison." "What have you done?" said the lawyer. "I have done nothing," he replied. "Then, my friend, they can not put you in pris- on if you have done nothing." "But I am in prison." "Well, that may be; but I tell you, my dear friend, they can not put you in prison." "Well," said he. "I want you to come and take me out, for I tell you, in spite of all your lawyer logic, I am in prison, and I shall be until you take me out." (Great laughter.) Now the poor slave has to say, "Abraham Lincoln, you have pronounced me free; still I am a slave, bought and sold as such and I shall remain a slave till I am taken out of this horrible condition."

Then the question is. *How?* Have not already two long years passed over more than a quarter of a million of the graves of the noblest and bravest of the nation? Is that not enough? No; it has proved not to be enough. Let us look back for a moment. Had the Proclamation of John C. Fremont been allowed to have its effect; had the edict of [Union General David] Hunter been allowed to have its effect, the war would have been over. (Applause.) Had the people and the Government, from the very commencement of the struggle, said to the South, "You have openly thrown down the gauntlet to fight for Slavery; we will accept it, and fight for Freedom," the rebellion would long before now have been crushed. (Applause.)

You may blame Europe as much as you please, but the heart of Europe beats for freedom. Had they seen us here accept the terrible alternative of war for the sake of freedom, the whole heart of Europe would have been with us. But such has not been the case. Hence the destruction of over a quarter of a million of lives and ten millions of broken hearts that have already paid the penalty; and we know not how many more it needs to wipe out the stain of that recreancy that did not at once proclaim this war a war for freedom and humanity.

And now we have got here all around us Loyal Leagues. Loyal to what? What does it mean? I have read that term in the papers. A great many times I have heard that expression to-day. I know not what others mean by it, but I will give you my interpretation of what I am loyal to. I speak for myself. I do not wish any one else to be responsible for my opinions. I am loyal only to justice and humanity. Let the Administration give evidence that they too are for justice to all, without exception, without distinction, and I, for one, had I ten thousand lives, would gladly lay them down to secure this boon of freedom to humanity. (Applause.) But without this certainty, I am not unconditionally loyal to the Administration. We women need not be, for the law has never yet recognized us. (Laughter.) Then I say to Abraham Lincoln, "Give us security for the future, for really when I look at the past, without a guarantee, I can hardly trust you." And then I would say to him, "Let nothing stand in your way; let no man obstruct your path."

Much is said in the papers and in political speeches about the Constitution. Now, a good constitution is a very good thing; but even the best of constitutions need sometimes to be amended and improved, for after all there is but one constitution which is infallible, but one constitution that ought to be held sacred, and that is the human constitution. (Laughter.) Therefore, if written constitutions are in the way of human freedom, suspend them till they can be improved.

If generals are in the way of freedom, suspend them too; and more than that, suspend their money. We have got here a whole army of generals who have been actually dismissed from the service, but not from pay. Now, I say to Abraham Lincoln, if these generals are good for anything, if they are fit to take the lead, put them at the head of armies, and let them go South and free the slaves you have announced free. If they are good for nothing, dispose of them as of anything else that is useless. At all events, cut them loose from the pay. (Applause.) Why, my friends, from July, 1861, to October, 1862—for sixteen long months—we have been electrified with the name of our great little Napoleon! [referring to Union general George McClellan] And what has the great little Napoleon done? (Laughter.) Why, he has done just enough to prevent anybody else from doing anything. (Great applause.) But I have no quarrel with him. I don't know him. I presume none of you do.

But I ask Abraham Lincoln—I like to go to headquarters, for where the greatest power is assumed, there the greatest responsibility rests, and in accordance with that principle I have nothing to do with menials, even though they are styled Napoleons—but I ask the President why [General George] McClellan was kept in the army so long after it was known—for there never was a time when anything else was known—that he was both incapable and unwilling to do anything? I refer to this for the purpose of coming, by and by, to the question, "What ought to be done?" He was kept at the head of the army on the Potomac just long enough to prevent [General Ambrose] Burnside from doing anything, and not much has been done since that time. Now, McClellan may be a very nice young man—I haven't the slightest doubt of it—but I have read a little anecdote of him. Somebody asked the president of a Western railroad company, in which McClellan was an engineer, what he thought about his abilities. "Well," said the president, "he is a first-rate man to build bridges; he is very exact, very mathematical in measurement, very precise in adjusting the timber; he is the best man in the world to build a good, strong, sound bridge, but after he has finished it, he never wishes anybody to cross over it." (Great laughter.) Well, we have disposed of him partially, but we pay him yet, and you and I are taxed for it. But if we are to have a new general in his place, we may ask, what has become of Sigel? Why does that disinterested, noble-minded, freedom-loving man in vain ask of the Administration to give him an army to lead into the field?

A Voice: "Ask Halleck."

Halleck! If Halleck is in the way, dispose of him. (Applause.) Do you point me to the Cabinet? If the Cabinet is in the way of freedom, dispose of the Cabinet—(applause)—some of them, at least. The magnitude of this war has never yet been fully felt or acknowledged by the Cabinet. The man at its head—I mean [Secretary of State William H. Seward]—has hardly yet woke up to the reality that we have a war. He was going to crush the rebellion in sixty days. It was a mere *bagatelle*! Why, he could do it after dinner, any day, as easy as taking a bottle of wine! If Seward is in the way of crushing the rebellion and establishing freedom, dispose of him. From the cause of the war, learn the remedy, decide as to the object, lay down the policy, and place it in the hands of men capable and willing to carry it out. I am not unconditionally loyal until we know to what principle we are to be loyal. Promise justice and freedom, and all the rest will follow. Do you know, my friends, what will take place if something decisive is not soon done? It is high time to consider it.

I am not one of those who look on the darkest side of things, but yet my reason and reflection forbid me to hope against hope. It is only eighteen months more before another Presidential election—only one year before another President will be nominated. Let the present administration remain as indolent, as inactive, and, apparently, as indifferent as they have done; let them keep generals that are inferior to many of their private soldiers: let them keep the best generals there are in the country—Sigel and Fremont—unoccupied—(applause); let them keep the country in the same condition in which it has been the last two years, and is now, and what would be the result, if, at the next election, the Democrats succeed—I mean the sham Democrats? I am a democrat, and it is because I am a democrat that I go for human freedom. Human freedom and true democracy are identical. Let the Democrats, as they are now called, get into office, and what would be the consequence? Why, under this hue-and-cry for Union, *Union*, Union, which is like a bait held out to the mass of the people to lure them on, they will grant to the South the meanest and the most contemptible compromises that the worst slaveholders in the South can require. And if they really accept them and come back—my only hope is that they will not—but if the South should accept these compromises, and come back, slavery will be fastened, not only in the South, but it will be nationally fastened on the North.

Now, a good Union, like a good Constitution, is a most invaluable thing; but a false Union is infinitely more despicable than no Union at all; and for myself, I would vastly prefer to have the South remain independent, than to bring them back with that eternal curse nationalized in the country. It is not enough for Abraham Lincoln to proclaim the slaves in the South free, nor even to continue the war until they shall be really free. There is something to be done at home; for justice, like charity, must begin at home. It is a mockery to say that we emancipate the slaves we can not reach and pass by those we can reach. First, free the slaves that are under the flag of the Union. If that flag is the symbol of freedom, let it wave over free men only. The slaves must be freed in the Border States. Consistency is a great power. What are you afraid of? That the Border States will join with the now crippled rebel States? We have our army there, and the North can swell its armies.

But we can not afford to fight without an object. We can not afford to bring the South back with slavery We can not compromise with principle. What has brought on this war? Slavery, undoubtedly. Slavery was the primary cause of it. But the great secondary cause was the fact that the North, for the sake of the Union, has constantly compromised. Every demand that the South made of the North was acceded to, until the South came really to believe that they were the natural and legitimate masters, not only of the slaves, but of the North too.

Now, it is time to reverse all these things. This rebellion and this war have cost too dear. The money spent, the vast stores destroyed, the tears shed, the lives sacrificed, the hearts broken are too high a price to be paid for the mere *name* of Union. I never believed we had a Union. A true Union is based upon principles of mutual interest, of mutual respect and reciprocity, none of which ever existed between the North and South. They based their institutions on slavery; the North on freedom.

I care not by what measure you end the war, if you allow one single germ, one single seed of slavery to remain in the soil of America, whatever may be your object, depend upon it, as true as effect follows cause, that germ will spring up, that noxious weed will thrive, and again stifle the growth, wither the leaves, blast the flowers and poison the fair fruits of freedom. Slavery and freedom cannot exist together. Seward proclaimed a truism, but he did not appreciate its import. There is an eternal war conflict between freedom and slavery. . . . You might as well say that light and darkness can exist together as freedom and slavery. We, therefore, must urge the Government to do something, and that speedily to secure the boon of freedom, while they yet can, not only in the rebel States but in our own States too, and in the Border States. It is just as wrong for us to keep slaves in the Union States as it ever was in the South. Slavery is as great a curse to the slaveholder as it is a wrong to the slaves; and yet while we free the rebel slaveholder from the curse, we allow it to continue with our Union-loving men in the Border States. Free the slaves in the Border States, in Western Virginia, in Maryland, and wherever the Union flag floats, and then there will be a consistency in our actions that will enable us to go to work earnestly with heart and hand united, as we move to free all others and crush the rebellion. . . . We have had no energy yet in the war, for we have fought only for the purpose of reuniting, what has never been united, restoring the old Union—or rather the shadow as it was.

A small republic, a small nation, based upon the eternal principle of freedom, is great and powerful. A large empire based upon slavery, is weak and without foundation. The moment the light of freedom shines upon it, it discloses its defects, and unmasks its hideous deformities. As I said before, I would rather have a small republic without the taint and without the stain of slavery in it, than to have the South brought back by compromise. To avert such calamity, we must work. And our work must mainly be to watch and criticize and urge the Administration to do its whole duty to freedom and humanity.

# DEBATE ON THE JEWS IN THE
# *BOSTON INVESTIGATOR*
*By Ernestine L. Rose and Horace Seaver*
October 28, 1863 to April 13, 1864
New York and Boston

On October 28, 1863, Horace Seaver, editor of the freethought weekly, *The Boston Investigator*, published an editorial attacking "the Jews" as a people. The Civil War years, 1861–1864, were a time of rising anti-Semitism, and Seaver focused on two prevalent anti-Jewish prejudices: that Jews were more likely to buy their way out of the draft than non-Jews, and that they were war profiteers. Such prejudices had had real consequences. For example, General Ulysses S. Grant had barred Jews from certain war zones based on this canard. In his letter of February 17, Seaver combined these dual prejudices into one sentence, and further compounded the offense by mocking the accents of immigrant Jews in rendering percent as "per shent."

As the debate continued over months, it was clear that Rose and Seaver could not agree. Seaver doggedly reiterated his partiality toward the Universalists, while Rose departed from her commitment to infidelism to express a preference for the monotheism of the Jews compared to the Trinitarian views of most Christians. She makes it clear, however, that she is still an "infidel," and is defending the Jewish people, and not the religion. Seaver, on his part, claims to be attacking the religion and not the people, but his anti-Semitism is unmistakable. Rose's rhetoric is based on human rights and social justice for all irrespective of religion or ethnicity.

The debate between Rose and Seaver is published here in full. Seaver's original editorial is followed by Rose's responses, which with publication of her letter of January 29 extended through eight weekly issues of the *Boston Investigator*, from February 10 to April 13, 1864. Seaver, as editor, controlled the discourse by cutting Rose's letters in half and spreading them over two weeks of issues, with each half followed by Seaver's "Remarks," which were often longer than Rose's letters. In the interest of keeping this text to a reasonable length, I cut some of the most repetitious parts of his "Remarks." Seaver continued to respond as long as Rose continued to write, but the practice of following her letters with his remarks insured that he would have the last word. The letters appear here with their original headings and dates of publication; dates of composition also appear at the end of Rose's letters.

∾

## THE JEWS, ANCIENT AND MODERN [EDITORIAL BY HORACE SEAVER], OCTOBER 28

The ancient Jews were said to be the chosen people of God and we are further informed that he personally instructed and guided them. If this were the case, we should naturally expect to find them the best people who have ever lived, and a pattern for all nations through all time; instead of which, they were about the worst people of whom we have any account, and the poorest guides to follow. Their principal business or occupation, according to the Old Testament, seems to have been, to seize upon the lands of the surrounding communities and kill off the inhabitants. Such massacres as were committed or ordered by Moses and Joshua, destroying not only men, but women, children, sucklings and in a word, "everything that breathed," are unparalleled in all history; and if perpetrated by our armies in this present war would convulse the world with horror. Of course, the Lord never commanded these barbarities, and it is mere superstition to suppose so. They were the work of bad men, who covered up their designs and imposed upon their dupes with a pretended message from Heaven.

But the modern Jews appear much better in history than their ancient brethren. Perhaps this was owing to their loss of power and their being scattered among other nations, which has rendered them comparatively harmless. It was a lucky thing for their immediate neighbors that the Jews were scattered, for they were a troublesome people to live in proximity with, and all such persecuting people had better be scattered as much as possible, rather than kept intact to plague the peaceable and well-disposed. The Jews in these days, however, are quite an improvement upon their Israelitish ancestors, and the fact goes to show that scattering has been a decided benefit to them, though this does not appear to have been the object of "prophecy."

Yet it is somewhat singular that the Jews, notwithstanding their improvement in civilization, still cling with wonderful tenacity to the old religious superstition of Moses with all its absurd rites and ceremonies. Neither the Protestants nor Catholics can vie with them in this respect. The Jews have several churches in Boston as well as in New York and other cities, and a few weeks since they dedicated here in Warren Street, a large synagogue. It was a building formerly occupied by a Universalist Society which broke down, or gave up, or something of the kind. We were sorry to see the change, for though Universalism is not wholly to our taste, yet it is far better than Judaism. One is liberal, democratic, equal, and saves the entire race; the other is bigoted, narrow, exclusive, and totally unfit for a progressive people like the Americans, among whom we hope it may not spread, and probably it will not, its converts being those who came here from abroad. We would give some account of the above synagogue, if we were able, but this is not the case; for when we applied at the door for admission, we were informed by a police officer that we could not enter without a ticket from head-quarters, meaning the chief rabbi of the concern. But as we had no such credentials to exhibit, we left the premises with the impression that a Jewish synagogue, even if Mosaical, was not very liberal.

## THE JEWS—JUSTICE TO ALL [FIRST LETTER, PART 1], FEBRUARY 10

Mr. Editor:—Not long after we arrived here, nearly 28 years ago, we saw an advertisement for a meeting at Tammany Hall to discuss Robert Owen's Community principles. Being interested in the subject we attended the meeting, but to our surprise, and I must say regret, the various speakers, instead of debating Owen's Community, debated Owen. I told them that, according to the notice, principles and not persons were to be discussed. In every controversy it is well to keep the two distinct. The *Investigator*, with its noble motto, its advocacy of equal justice to all irrespective of sect, has always endeavored to keep that distinction in view. But at times it may be useful to analyze sects as well as religions, and as the Jews (modern) are really very little known, for as a sect they are the least intrusive on public attention, it may be well to give a cursory glance not only at their religion, but at them as a people.

The Jews' religion in itself is a belief in one God, Deism—true Unitarianism, in which Thomas Paine, Thomas Jefferson, Voltaire, Dr. Channing, Theodore Parker believed, and the Hicksite Quakers and more liberal Unitarians (for some of them still preach the Trinity) believe in now. Whether all of them have taken their God from the Bible or not, (and I don't see where else they could find him,) matters very little. The belief is the same; the only difference is, those who take him from the Bible accept him in the old garb. Thousands, perhaps millions of years are given to him, while those who profess to have found him out of that book, invest him in more fanciful and polished garments. But strip him of the new drapery, expose him to the light of truth, and you will find him just the same, made of the same incongruous and inconsistent materials.

The Jews have traditions and ceremonies which are inculcated more as a distinguishing characteristic of the sect than as a part of their religion, the same as the "thee" and "thou," the scuttle-bonnet and round-tailed coat of the Quakers. Formerly the Quakers disowned their members for the least deviation from their laid-down rules, or discipline; now they are (the Hicksites at least) more civilized and liberal in such matters, though they still adhere to their religion. The Jews, too, have formerly been much stricter in the performance of their ceremonies than they are now; in fact, if a man believes in a God, comes once or twice a year to his synagogue, and conforms to one particular ceremony, (which I will mention present-ly,) he is considered one of them.

You will say the belief in such a God as the Bible describes is bad enough; very true, but the Universalists believe in precisely the same God, with the addition of two more; and if the belief in one is bad, the belief in three is three times as bad. It is true the Universalists do not believe in future punishment; they have discarded damnation, the fruit, though they cling to religion, the tree upon which it grows—and hence not believing in the "*nether*" regions, they "generously offer heaven to all mankind." But even here the Jews have the best of them, for Judaism promises no future at all; the belief in it makes no part of their religion; the Old Testament deals only in this life; all the promised rewards and threatened punish-ments were predicated for here and not hereafter. The Jews don't believe in the blood of any Saviour; not even the "barbarian Moses" was so bar-barous as to impose that falsehood upon the credulity of mankind. This is a Christian branch grafted upon the Jewish stem. Both parties believe in the same angry, wrathful, jealous, revengeful God, only the Christians add the monstrosity of making one God sacrifice the other to appease his own vengeance; and if the Jewish religion is a poor article, what must the others be with such additions? I therefore see no great danger in the superstition[substitution] of a synagogue for a Universalist church.

Perhaps it may reconcile you to the change to know that more than 20 years ago a Universalist church in this city, the very church in which Abner Kneeland used to preach, was supplanted by a Catholic church, yet New York has survived it. Are the Jews more dangerous than the Catho-lics? The difference between the two is, that the synagogue is consecrated to one God, while the church, even Universalists, to three. In the first, they talk about Abraham, (not Lincoln) Isaac, Jacob, and all the other worthies; in the latter, in addition to "the patriarchs," they talk about Paul, Peter, the crucified Saviour, the blood of the Lamb, the Devil, and the rest of the fraternity. So much for the two religions; the best we can say is, that they are six of one and half a dozen of the other.

Now for the people! Mr. Editor, I almost smelt brimstone, genuine Christian brimstone, when I read in the *Investigator*— "Even the modern Jews are bigoted, narrow, exclusive, and totally unfit for progressive people like the Americans among whom we hope they may not spread." Indeed! That hope smacks too much of the Puritan spirit that whipped and hung the Quaker women, to be found in the liberty-promoting, freedom-loving *Investigator*. You "hope." Now suppose, as we always desire to promote what we hope for, you had the power as well as the inclination, would you prevent their spreading? How? Would drive them out of Boston—out of "progressive America," as they were driven out of Spain?

But where is the danger of their "spreading?" In this city, Philadelphia, Cincinnati, and other places, they have synagogues, and have no doubt spread as much as they could, and no calamity has yet befallen any place in consequence of that fact; and wherever they are, they act just about the same as other people. The nature of a Jew is governed by the same laws as human nature in general. In England, France, Germany, and in the rest of Europe, (except Spain,) in spite of the barbarous treatment and deadly persecution they suffered, they have lived and spread and outlived much of the poisonous rancor and prejudice against them, and Europe has been none the worse on their account. Of course, where they are still under the Christian lash, as in Rome, where for the glory of God, their children even are stolen from them, self-preservation forces them to be narrow and exclusive. In other countries more civilized and just, they are so too; they progress just as fast as the world they live in will permit them. In France, there is hardly any difference between Jew and Christian. The Jews occupy some of the highest positions in the Army, the State, in literature, the arts, and sciences; the same is the case more or less in Germany and other enlightened centuries [countries]. Are then the Jews in Boston so much worse, that their spread is to be dreaded even by Infidels? If so, it would prove the pernicious example and influence of Puritanism.

But, "they are not progressive." In their religion the Jews have not much to progress and remain such. The Christian can change, and change, and change again, and still remain a Christian. The Catholic may become Protestant, but he remains a Christian; the Protestant may pass through all the different phases from Calvinism, through Episcopacy, Methodism, Baptism, Congregationalism, Quakerism, Shakerism, Mormonism, Unitarianism, Universalism to Transcendentalism, (including all other isms) and still remain a Christian; while the Jew only can make one change. There is but one step between his religion and Atheism. The Christian can step out of the darkness of night into a kind of twilight, "which makes the darkness more visible," while if the Jew takes one step in advance, he is out of the darkness into the broad light of day.

[Remainder next week.]
Ernestine L. Rose
New York, Jan. 29, 1864

**REMARKS.**

We are always pleased to hear from our good friend, whether in approval or in disapprobation of our views. If the former, as we prize her favorable opinion, it helps largely to persuade us we are in the right; and if the latter, as seems to be the case now, it sets us to thinking whether we may not possibly be in the wrong. But we do not yet think this is the state of things, so far as concerns the matter in dispute, and hence we remain unconvinced by her mode of reasoning.

The real point at issue, and to which the above is given as an answer, is, whether the Jews are as progressive a class of religionists as the Universalists? Mrs. Rose seems to take the affirmative of this question, and begins by saying that the belief in the Jewish God is Deism—or the same as Paine, Jefferson, Voltaire, and Theodore Parker possessed, and the same as the Unitarians accept. Here we differ from her. The Gods or rather the idea of the Gods, improves from age to age, and thus it is that the God of Deism, Universalism, and Unitarianism, is far superior to the Jewish God, who was as barbarous and savage as the people who worshiped him. The ancient Jews, being a particularly bad people, formed a God accordingly; for we suspect the doctrine will be found true, that men make Gods instead of Gods making men, and that a rude and barbarous people will always have a rude and barbarous God as their highest conception of truth and goodness. The Universalists, therefore, being a much better people than the ancient Jews, have a much better God and more benevolent religion, neither of which, nor the Jewish religion either, seem to us to be fairly stated by our opponent.

But the modern Jews are superior to their ancient brethren; we admitted this much; but in our giving the preference to the Universalists, our sister appears to imagine that she smells "brimstone" issuing from the office of the Infidel *Investigator* as from the veritable Orthodox "pit" itself! And what is the great objection of which she complains? Simply this: We said the Jews are too bigoted, exclusive, in their religion, for a progressive people like the Americans, and we hoped they would not spread among us. Of course we were speaking of them as a religious sect. We have nothing against a Jew personally, and never persecuted one in any way, and do not think that we ever shall; but we do not like Judaism well enough to see it spreading in this country, and if Mrs. Rose does, she is more friendly to superstition than we supposed her to be. We shall not attempt, however, to drive the Jews out of Boston, (what could have put such an idea into her head?—we intimated nothing of the kind,) but we shall continue to hope that "the freedom-loving *Investigator*" will never advocate the doctrine that Judaism is fit for a liberal, intelligent, and progressive people.

We presume it does not necessarily follow that because we are opposed to any particular religion, we wish to murder its worshipers; if it does, then our too sensitive sister can hardly escape condemnation, for we do not know the person who has said bitterer things against sorts of religion than herself. But we would not do her the injustice to suppose, for a moment, that in thus acting, she wishes to persecute anyone for his opinions; we are sure that we do not—at the same time we are not disposed to flatter either Jews or Catholics with the idea that their religion is equal to that of the Universalists. We believe there is progression in religion as in other things, and that while New York city is not swallowed up because Catholics occupy the church in which Abner Kneeland worshiped when he was a Universalist preacher, we see in this transformation no evidence of free inquiry and religious improvement. He or she who considers Popery equally progressive with Universalism, (and by the way, the latter is condemned by the former as Infidelity,) must have a strange taste, and exhibits more partiality for "brimstone" than we think has been manifested by us.

. . . . . . . .

### THE JEWS—JUSTICE TO ALL [FIRST LETTER, PART 2], FEBRUARY 17

But John W. Cole [a reader who wrote to the *Investigator* supporting Seaver's position], in his pious zeal to abuse the Jews, of whom he knows no doubt a great deal, as "several families live in the same street" where he lives, gives as a reason for his ill feelings towards them, that "They are tied down to all eternity to the letter of Moses." Now, for his instruction, which he really needs, allow me to inform him, that human nature (Jewish included) cannot remain tied down to all eternity. In Paris, Berlin, Vienna, so little are they tied down by Moses, that very few keep the Sabbath at all. In this city are said to be 30,000; very few comparatively keep the Sabbath or go to the synagogue except once or twice a year. But not only have they progressed in their traditions and ceremonies, but they have made great innovations in some of their synagogues. In Paris, Berlin, and the "Temple," in this city, organs and singers have been introduced, and sometime ago I saw a statement in a paper that some of the Jews in Cincinnati proposed to transfer, like the Christians, the Sabbath day over to Sunday. These are some of the changes—more might be mentioned.

Now for the "barbarity"—circumcision. Well, the best that could be said on the subject is, it is ridiculous. As to the "barbarity" which "shocks" the nerves of some weak brothers, I don't know that it is more barbarous, if as much, than piercing the ears of girls. From the former we have never heard of any dangerous consequences; from the latter, I have known pain and suffering to follow for months. I was one of the victims of that irrational practice, and I suppose that the Universalists, and even John W.

Cole, if he has daughters, are no doubt guilty of the same barbarity, and yet they may be fit "for progressive America."—What "other" barbarities are the Jews guilty of? I should to like to know, and expose them. Speak out, gentlemen, or "forever after hold your peace."

In conclusion, allow me to say, let the subject be impartially investigated, and it will be found, that take them all in all, the Jews are as good as any other sect, the Universalists not excepted. As a people, they are sober, industrious, good citizens, husbands, and fathers, as any in the land. They interfere with no one, hunt after no proselytes, follow the even tenor of their ways, glad to be left alone. Their morals, too, are quite as good as other sects, and according to statistics the number of Jews found in the State prisons are not greater than Universalists. From their domestic virtues something even might be learned. They are as benevolent as any other class of people. Nay! they not only take care of their own poor and sick, but often give largely to Christian institutions, as exemplified by "Judah Thoro," of New Orleans, and others,—in fine, they are as intelligent, social, and friendly as others.

Will you tell me they are cunning, sharp traders? Then I will point you to the renowned "Yankee," who, it is admitted by all, excels the Jew in that art. Sometime ago I saw in a paper a statement of some exploits of a "Down Easter," and the writer concluded by saying the "Jew cannot hold a candle to the Yankee in the art of tricking and cheating." Truly, "the glory has departed from Israel," yet I know there are honest, honorable Yankees as well as Jews: the Editor of the *Investigator* is one of the very best, and I hope Mr. J. W. Cole is not far behind. Then let us, as Infidels, while promoting liberty and spreading useful knowledge, to prevent any sect from getting power, not add to the prejudice already existing towards the Jews, or any other sect.

Yours for Justice,
Ernestine L. Rose
New York, Jan. 29, 1864

## REMARKS.

We have said about all that we deem necessary, on our part, in reply to our sister's objection to our article on the Jews, and have not much more to offer. Mr. Cole will probably speak for himself, so far as he is concerned. We will only add, that while we have not a particle of prejudice against the Jews as human beings, and merely meant to speak of them as religionists, we are very glad to learn by the communication of our friend, who has had good opportunities for judging, that they are improving socially and theologically. We hope that this statement is true, for the ancient Jews were barbarous and miserable specimens of humanity; and if their descendants are as progressive as represented, we are gratified to hear it—though we strongly suspect that they still cling too closely to the rites and ceremonies of old Moses to be as rational worshipers as the Universalists. We have heard it said that if a Jew or Jewess forsake their religion, they are disinherited by the family and regarded as dead forever afterwards. If this be true, they are not equal, socially, maternally, and paternally, to the Universalists, for they are more forgiving than to act in this manner. However, in the days of old Moses there do not seem to have been any Infidels or Liberals about, to contradict the "Divine" afflatus, which, in its effect, was most disastrous on the heathen. But in these our days, Liberalism abounds, and is probably the outside pressure which is doing more to reform Judaism than any inherent merit which that kind of religion possesses. Hence the superiority of modern to ancient Jews.

Still, we must regard circumcision as a barbarity—worse, rather, than piercing the ears which is heathenish enough, no doubt; but then the Universalists do not make it obligatory as a religious duty, indispensable to heavenly salvation. The Jews do, so far as relates to the "ridiculous" rite of circumcision. Besides, do not Jewish girls wear ear-rings as well as Universalist ones? If so, then the Jews are doubly barbarians, for they not only circumcise the boys, but they punch the ears of the girls. So it would seem that the Universalists are still ahead; and if the Yankees, as a class, like money as well as the Jews we question whether so many of the former would now be found in the ranks of the Union Army. They would be more likely to stay at home to deal in "old clothes," at a profit of "fifteen per shent." But, says, our good sister, the Jew is not so much of a sharper as he has been represented—and in fact, "The glory has departed from Israel," she says. We hope so, for as the ancient glory of that people was a very poor article, we are glad to know that it has not been inherited so largely by their modern descendants as we had supposed, to whom we wish no more harm that they may outgrow the teachings and examples of the barbarian Moses.

Correction.—In Mrs. Rose's communication of last week, there were a couple of errors. The word "superstition" was printed for substitution, and "centuries" for countries. These mistakes were accidentally overlooked in the proof, but we are nonetheless sorry they occurred.—[Ed. Inv.]

## THE JEWS [SECOND LETTER, PART 1], FEBRUARY 24

Brother Seaver:— I could not help laughing while reading your reply. You almost made me out an advocate and supporter of Catholicism, Judaism, and all other isms. But don't be alarmed. "Sister Rose" is not one jot "more friendly to superstition" than you "supposed her to be." She likes Judaism not one bit better than you do, though she may like some other isms a little less, and be less prejudiced against the "modern Jews."

I most heartily join in the "hope that the Freedom-loving *Investigator* will never advocate the doctrine that Judaism is fit for a liberal, intelligent, and progressive people." No! nor any other ism, not even Universalism, nothing less than Rationalism. So we agree, as we always did on the rights of conscience for all sects, and for no sect.

You say, you "have nothing against them individually"; you "were speaking of Jews as a religious sect." So far so good. If you meant that they should not increase (spread) in power, then the alarm was quite unnecessary, as the Jews as a sect don't increase except in the natural course, for they never attempt to make proselytes, and we should endeavor to prevent any sect from getting power. I would no more trust the Universalists with power than any other sect, would you? and yet I would not prevent them from having a church; then why should the Jews not have a synagogue?

"The real point at issue was [*not*] whether the Jews as a class were as progressive as the Universalists," but simply on what appeared to me a great prejudice evinced in the expression, that the "modern Jews" (*not Judaism*) "are bigoted, narrow, and exclusive, and totally unfit for a progressive people like the Americans, among whom we hope they may not spread." It was to convince you of the injustice towards them, that I endeavored to compare them with the Universalists.

That I may have failed, is not to be wondered at, knowing but too well how difficult it is to convince, and how much more so to elicit an acknowledgment, particularly from editors; and the Editor of the Boston *Investigator*, though, "like the wife of Caesar" he should be above suspicion, he is only a man after all, and as I don't consider him any more immaculate than the Virgin Mary, I will look upon that little prejudice only as slip of the pen, which, like the prayers of some Christians, means nothing at all.

To judge the ancient Jews by the God they made, (and it is a good criterion,) they must have been bad enough; but the ancient Christians who accepted that very God could certainly have been no better, nor have the modern Christians, the Universalists, who still believe in the same God, from the same book, even with the Christian additions, much to boast of. Yes! "men always make their Gods in their image, and a barbarous people will always have rude and barbarous Gods as their highest conception of truth and goodness."

Very true, truer than Gospel. But, Brother Seaver, don't the Universalists believe in the Bible? if so, don't they believe in the Bible God? If they do, must they not be a "rude and barbarous people" to "have" such a rude and barbarous God? Wherein, then, are they a better people than even the ancient Jews? On the contrary, those who thousands of years ago undertook the unprofitable task to make Gods out of the raw materials—before the discovery of steam—the invention of the printing press—before the school master was abroad—before the *Boston Investigator* existed, are certainly more to be excused for the rude and barbarous God they made, than the Universalists in the 19th century, in "modern Athens," with all the other privileges, to accept and retain him.

[Remainder next week.]
Ernestine L. Rose
New York, Feb. 13, 1864

## REMARKS

We are glad to find that Sister Rose is not likely to leave us and go to Rome or Judea, though we did fear at one time—well, "the least said the soonest mended." She does not exactly understand us, however, in our views of the Jews and Universalists, or rather she seems to think too highly of the former, and not high enough of the latter. When people get so far along in, or perhaps we should say out of, theology, as to become Universalists, they often go farther after awhile, and become Infidels. This was our case, and many others whom we might name besides Abner Kneeland. The fact shows, we think, that Universalism is the stepping-stone in[to] Infidelity; and it may be on this account, and also because we always like to speak a good word for "the bridge that brought us over," that we give this ism the preference over the other. Are there as many converts from Judaism to our side? Probably not, and herein is one reason why we do not expect much from it.

But we are told that we need not have said anything against the Jews, as they make no proselytes &e. We are not sure that they are not as active in this business as the Universalists; and besides, in attacking the lesser superstition, what consistency is there in sparing the greater? We have assailed Universalism first and last, a great many times, and our sister found no fault with us, but our first objections to Judaism have so touched her sensitiveness, that she thinks it necessary to reply to us at considerable length. Yet in our judgment, (for we must still adhere to it,) Universalism is the better religion of the two, and for this reason we prefer one of their churches to a Jewish synagogue.—But this is not saying that we wish to prevent the Jews from having such buildings; and in answer to the question, whether we would trust the Universalists with power? We say No, nor Jews either, but of the two sects, we prefer the Universalists. The question in dispute, therefore, as we regard it, has reference merely to the relative merits of these two kinds of religion.—nothing more; and if our sister supposed for a moment that our object has been to persecute in the slightest degree the Jews on account of their opinions, she either entirely misunderstood us, or else, which is not unlikely, we failed to express our meaning with sufficient clearness.—We certainly are not "immaculate," whether the Virgin Mary was or not, or whether the wife of Caesar ought to have been above suspicion; but we will venture the assertion, that an attack on the superstitious humbug of Judaism, does not necessarily imply a disposition to persecute its believers, and we marvel how this could have been imagined.

Respecting the Gods, (if we must talk about incomprehensible matters) we still keep to the Universalist conception, as being far preferable to that of the Jewish. The God whom Universalists profess to worship is represented as merciful, loving, and forgiving; while the God of the Old Testament or the Jewish God is described as cruel, vindictive, hateful, and unrelenting. He is a terrible God, of no compassion whatever, and whose anger and vengeance "burn to the lowest hell." This is a dreadful God, sure enough. "But Brother Seaver, don't the Universalists believe in the Bible God?" Why no Sister Rose, not in the Old Testament wing as the Jews do, and herein consists the difference between these worshipers in their conceptions of God. We say *conceptions* of him, because we do not presume to go any further on this mysterious subject. Now, then, as the idea of God improves from age to age with the progress of mankind, and as the Universalists of today are a superior people to the ancient Jews, not being so rude and barbarous, they have a better God, or a better conception of a God. We read in the Old Testament that when those Jewish barbarians, Moses and Joshua, burnt towns and cities, stole lands and treasures, and sometimes destroyed "every living thing that breathed," it was done by a command of "thus saith the Lord God of Israel." But we never read nor heard that John Murray or Hosea Ballou (Universalist pioneers) ever recommended such villainies under the plea of "Thus saith the Lord God of Universalism." So we must needs believe that there is considerable difference in these Gods, or in the conceptions entertained of them, and that when our sister says they are identical or similar, she does not appear to manifest her usual correct judgment. Nor can we understand the pertinence of the question, wherein are the Universalists better people than the ancient Jews? It seems to us that there is as much difference between these two classes of religionists, as there is between liberal, intelligent, well behaved people on the other hand, and a bigoted, ignorant, cruel, and semi-barbarous horde on the other. We grant that the Universalists are not perfect, nor have we said so, nor do we wish to become one; — but of all the people we ever read of, who pretended to be anything, we do not know of any so completely vile, worthless, miserable, contemptible, and abominable as the ancient Jews.

*Boston Investigator*, Feb. 24, 1864, p.331. cols. 1&2

### THE JEWS [SECOND LETTER, PART 2], MARCH 2

You say that "the Universalists, being a better people than the ancient Jews, have a much better God and a more benevolent religion." Have they? Where was the "better God" during that terrible catastrophe in Chili? [On December 14, 1863, a cathedral in Santiago, Chile, caught fire during a crowded service, and an estimated 2,500 worshipers inside were incinerated.] Would he not save those 2500 human beings because they were not Universalists? What would you call such a God, that could but would not save them, though they were there to worship him? It is no use to say they were Catholics. I ask, where was that "better God," that "more benevolent religion" of the Universalists? It may do for believers to talk about a "better God," but I cannot understand it in an Infidel. But why compare the Universalists with the ancient Jews? Why not with the present? Perhaps you don't know much about the "modern Jews." If so, then why mention them at all? But in what is the Universalist's God better, and their religion more benevolent? The difference between them and other Christian sects is that they have discarded Hell. So far they are more humane than the sects who still cling to that *divine* institution; but the Jews don't believe in that place at all. It is not a part of their religion, and is not taught in the Bible, that is purely a Christian addition. Then why do you overlook or ignore it, for the benefit of the Universalists?

There is no need "to flatter the Jews or Catholics"; no, nor any other sect, not even the Universalists. I am sure I don't desire it, nor do I flatter any of them, though personally I have not the past prejudice against the Universalists as a sect. I like them much better than any other Christian sect. Some years ago there was a controversy here between them and the Orthodox; the far-famed Barnum was their Secretary at the time; I took part in the discussion, and of course on the side of the Universalists, and I would do so again. But theirs, like all other religions, is based on "blind faith in things unseen and unknown;" one has more roots and branches, another less. The Catholics have most; their "name is legion." The Universalists have only three Gods; the Jews have only one. Now which is best, or rather which is worst?

"We believe there is progress in religion." All the progress I can see in religion is the getting out of it, not in it. In the discovery and invention of the arts and sciences, no matter how crude and imperfect the first representation or theory may be, in as far as they contain a truth, a principle, by application and steady progress can be made to develop, improve, and make them applicable to the necessities and comforts of man. Is that the case with religion? A chimera or false principle, erroneous in theory, pernicious in practice, where is the "progress" and the "benevolence" in religion? No! The only progress is to leave it behind and get out of it entirely. Have the Universalists got so far? Still you have a perfect right to prefer Universalism to Judaism. I don't wish either. Should I ever be placed in the unfortunate dilemma, as to be compelled to choose between a "Synagogue and a Universalist Church," between one God and three Gods, "or fare worse," if I did not rather accept the "worse," I would no doubt choose what to me at one time would appear "the least of the two evils." But as one is two less than three, it strikes me it would be rather difficult to convince me that the larger number is the lesser evil. But is Brother Seaver in that interesting dilemma already, to have "to choose," "or fare worse?"

I don't feel that I have any condemnation to escape from, for however warmly and earnestly (for whatever I do, I do it earnestly,) I have denounced superstitions, Jewish or Christian, I have ever refrained from singling out any sect for condemnation more than any other; and however severe I may have been on the religions, I have felt no "bitterness" even against them, much less against the victims of ignorance, the innocent dupes of a corrupt priesthood. No! only religionists when they denounce each other, or Infidels, for the glory of God, feel "bitterness" against them for the crime of not believing as they do. Those who advocate perfect freedom of conscience, and human rights without distinction of sect, sex, country, or color, only feel pity and commiseration. Perhaps the very endeavor to defend the more "benevolent religion," "the better God," may be the cause of the "bitterness" mentioned in your last article, and the prejudice evinced against an inoffensive sect who suffer quite enough from Christian prejudice without the help of Infidels. But as you "will not attempt to drive them out of Boston," nor do anything else very naughty, I hope you will live to see all the synagogues and churches, Universalists included, turned into Halls of science and rational recreation for the instruction and moral improvement of the people.

Yours as ever,
Ernestine L. Rose
New York, Feb. 19, 1864

## REMARKS.

"Amen" and "amen"! to that last wish; and that we could only live long enough to see its fulfillment, we don't know but that in the ecstasy of the hour we should be tempted to exclaim, like Simeon of old—"Lord, let thy servant depart in peace for my eyes have seen thy great salvation." But we must continue to doubt whether the course we are pursuing has a tendency to prevent this desired consummation; for that some religions are better than others, we consider self-evident, and our partiality is for the least objectionable, provided we must choose some particular kind which at present we are in no haste to do. However, we need not dwell on that point, as our good sister acted in the same manner as we would have done, when in the Barnum controversy to which she alludes, she "took the side of the Universalists." Of course, she did. What else could be expected from Ernestine L. Rose? And so for doing the same thing, "Brother Seaver is in the interesting dilemma already" of having to choose some sort of religion, is he?—he begs leave to say that he "does not see it in that light," and that the probabilities at present are, that he shall not become a Universalist until his sister has returned to Judaism—if indeed the transition takes place so soon!!

We shall keep, however, to the idea that the Universalists have "a better God and a more benevolent religion" than the Jews. . . . [Ed. Inv.]

## THE JEWS [THIRD LETTER, PART 1], MARCH 9
## (1864 MARCH 9, V. 33, #44, P. 347)

Mr. Editor:—Is it possible that even the mere preference and defense of the "more benevolent religion" and the "better God" has already the effect to make the Editor so mean as to give the following insinuation?

"We are glad to find that sister Rose is not likely to leave us and go to Rome or Judea, though we did fear at one time." Did you? When was that "one time?" Was it when I endeavored to convince you of a great injustice towards the modern Jews? What other time was that "one time?" Is it not mean and cowardly to insinuate where there is not even a shadow of a shade to base the insinuation upon? There is not one sentence in all I have said on the subject to warrant that insinuation. When had you that "fear?" If you really had, then I pity your head. If you had not and made the statement, I pity your heart and your candor. To save you such other fears allow me to assure you that the above insinuation of "fear" was just as silly as it was groundless. No! "she is not yet disposed to give up the ship." "She" has held fast to it long before she knew you, and as you did not at all help her to get on board of it, nor depend on your piloting, she is not likely to slip off, however unsteady you may navigate the "ship." But one error always leads to another. Having been unjust to the Jews, and not having the moral courage to acknowledge it, you must now be unjust to those who defend them. *You know* it is *not* true, that your "objection to Judaism" "has so touched her sensitiveness that she thinks it necessary to reply to us at considerable length." But your false insinuations, your false issues, and the evidence of your continued intolerance made me reply, and I will do so again.

Now how much nobler it would have been had you acknowledged the first error, and said yes, I was too hasty, it was wrong for me to make the sweeping denunciation against the modern Jews; for remember, your attack was not against Judaism, but the modern Jews. But your replies have not placed you in a very favorable light for fairness and candor, and I am most truly sorry for the fact. I am sure the adoption of the motto, "The least said the soonest mended," would have done you much more good then all you have said.

You are perfectly welcome to use all the invectives you can find, and in the conclusion of your article of the 24th, which I advise you to read over, you give evidence of possessing a much larger stock than I ever thought you possessed; but perhaps it has grown after your finding the "more benevolent religion" and the "better God."

Universalism may be a stepping stone out of the darkness into some twilight, (so are many other isms;) and some, as the Editor of the *Investigator* and Mr. Kneeland, have stepped out altogether. Wonderful to relate! "Are there as many converts from Judaism to our side?"

You answered your question by "probably not," and add, "herein is our reason why we don't expect much from it." That is the reason, is it?—Now we have something tangible to go upon. There are two Universalist converts to "our side." Well, that is promising. Are there as many "from Judaism?" Why, "Thomas," the "doubter," was one, and if we search very hard we may find another. But this is not the question; if it were, perhaps we might find two and a half on our side.—Would it alter your opinion?

[Remainder next week.]
Ernestine L. Rose
New York, Feb. 29, 1864


**REMARKS.**

We always desire to express ourselves with sufficient clearness, so that we may not be misunderstood;—hence if we say that the tone of the above appears slightly acrimonious we only mean that it seems to us—though it is possible that when our sister denounces us as "mean and coward-ly," and also applies to us other complimentary epithets, she uses them merely "in a Pickwickian sense," and not as intentional reproaches sug-gested by her usual tranquility and customary politeness. Whether it is owing to our "more benevolent religion and better God," this deponent saith not; but this much we will say, that when our good friend joked us about becoming a Universalist, we went not into convulsions, nor even indicated by any word of ours the remotest acerbity of feeling. But mark the difference! When we follow her example, and intimate in the same jocular manner that perhaps she may be thinking of turning Jew, she gives us a scolding as we have no recollection of ever receiving from any man, and we know we never did from any woman. We might enlarge upon the striking contrast here presented. But the advice of an ancient philosopher on the subject, being full of wisdom, we substitute his words in place of any of our own;—"If you cannot take a joke, don't give one."

Here we might rest the case and retire from the field. . . .

But, we are asked, whether it would alter our opinion of the Jews if as many of them came to us as we receive of Universalists? It would, for we should be convinced thereby that Judaism as well as Universalism is the stepping-stone to Infidelity. At present, however, we do not believe it; but if we ever should, we trust we shall be as willing to give due credit to Jews for their liberality as we are now to Universalists for theirs.

P.S.—We have known Universalist churches to invite Infidels to speak in their meetings and we have been present and heard them. Is this done, or was it ever done, or can it be done, in a Jewish synagogue? We know a noto-rious Infidel who for six consecutive Sunday evenings spoke in a Universal-ist vestry, and was listened to with the most respectful attention. Would such favor be shown him in any Jewish synagogue? If it would, Mrs. Rose will please communicate where that rare tabernacle is located. He might like to visit it some time, if only to have the gratification of seeing how Isra-el has progressed since the barbarian Moses issued his blood-thirsty edicts against all those who differed from him in religion.—[Ed. Inv.]

## THE JEWS [THIRD LETTER, PART 2], MARCH 16

Mr. Editor:—To my question, "Don't the Universalists believe in the Bible God?" you say, "Why no, Sister Rose, not in the Old Testament wing, as the Jews do." Did you express yourself "with sufficient clearness?" Pray what does that mean? Do they believe in the Old Testament or do they not? If they do not believe, they are Infidels, and you ought to have said so. If they do believe, they believe, and your qualification "not as the Jews do," means nothing. It is a mystery; does it belong to the "more benevolent religion" and "better God?"

"Not as the Jews do." How do you know how the Jews do now believe, or interpret the Old Testament wing? I have heard the Universalists speak. I have never heard any of them say they don't believe in the Old Testament. I have not heard them combat the Orthodox belief in a "hell" by proving that the Old Testament did not inculcate that belief at all. Do you mean they dress up the Bible God in more civilized human garments? Then how do you know that the "modern" Jews don't do the same? Please to keep the modern Jews and Judaism distinct.

Do you know that the modern Jews "conception of God" is not quite as modernized as that of the Universalists?

"I cannot understand the pertinacity" in constantly comparing the present Universalists, as they are only of a recent growth, as if it were since yesterday, with the ancient Jews, a people thousands of years old. It manifests a bad judgment, or which is worse, a bad temper. You say, it seems to you, "there is as much difference between these two classes of religionists as there is between liberal, intelligent, and well behaved people on the one hand, and bigoted, ignorant, cruel, and semi-barbarous horde on the other." Again I ask, how do you know that the modern Jews are what you here describe them to be in comparison with the Universalists? What ignorance, what bigotry, what rudeness, what barbarity are the present Jews guilty of more than any other religious sect, even the Universalists? You make unwarrantable assertions which convict you out of your own mouth of as much folly as bigotry, for you have not had the candor fairly to answer one question; but without giving a simple reason continue your, to say the least, unwarrantable tirade against them.

"John Murray and Hosea Ballou never recommended such villainies under the plea of Thus saith the Lord." Really, it was very kind of them not to do so, particularly as they never had the power. This is a knock down argument against all the Jews present and to come, but it is too silly an argument for me to try and knock it down.

But to enable you to make anything like a fair comparison, suppose you place the Christian John Murray and Hosea Ballou six thousand years back, and give them all the power the Jews then had, to see how much better they would have acted than the barbarian Moses. Whether they would not have said to you and me if we were there, "Thus saith the Lord." Or if that is too much trouble, suppose you take the Jews, Spinoza and Mendelsohn, and thousands of others and see whether they say so now any more than the Universalists.

Now whatever you may say on the subject, pray keep Judaism and the

Jews distinct, and don't compare January with May, but January with January, and May with May; for whatever you may know of the ancient, you evidently know nothing of the modern Jews, and don't accuse me of going to the moon or to some other wonderful thing simply because I don't like your prejudice against the Jews, nor against any other people; and above all, keep your temper in an argument.

Ernestine L. Rose
New York, March 15 [*sic*], 1864

**REMARKS.**

It is amusing to be told that we must "keep our temper," especially when the advice comes from one, who, with her other smart qualities, shows by her abusive personalities that she can scold bravely, if she cannot use convincing arguments. Such language as she has applied to us during this controversy may be in accordance with a pleasant temper, as she understands it, but if so, then tastes differ, for even if we cannot agree about Jews and Universalists, we are not obliged to quarrel with each other on that account. Perhaps a little of that influence of the "better God" and "more benevolent religion" might serve to make her rather better natured and less disposed to hit us quite so hard.

We have endeavored several times to explain our idea of progress in religion, and wherein we thought the Universalists superior in this respect to the Jews. . . . "Like priest, like people." Judaism has been tried and found wanting—do not therefore stop it on its march to oblivion. "Would you have a serpent sting you twice?"—[Ed. Inv.]

**THE JEWS [FOURTH LETTER, PART ONE], APRIL 6**

Mr. Editor:—Yes, with all my "usual tranquillity," which I feel on the present occasion, and "customary politeness," which I hope I will always retain, I assure you I did not mean it in a "Pickwickian sense," but what I said was in sober seriousness, which the insinuations, the evasions, and absence of a fair and candid reply to fair and candid questions, fully justified. It is not true that "our good friend joked us about becoming a Universalist." No. Your defense of the "better God" made her simply ask the question, in what was he better than the Jewish God, being taken from the same Bible? or, in what the Universalists, as a sect, were so superior to the modern Jews? Had you followed my "example," you would have answered these questions as impartially as they were asked; but you did not—hence what follows.

But, "she gives us such a scolding," &c. Well, "There is a point where patience, like forbearance, ceases to be a virtue," and I hoped, and do still hope, that it may be a benefit to you, . . . and perhaps if you had received a little more scolding from woman, the right kind I mean, you might deserve it less now. As it is, it may be better late than never.

I am quite willing to leave it to the readers of the *Investigator* to judge who used the most "invectives," who possessed the most "equanimity," and whether you fairly answered my questions. In reply to the question— where was the "better God" during the terrible calamity at Chili you talk about the Catholic God, the Jewish God, Moses, the barbarians, and everything else foreign from the subject, and then you say, "But he was not the Universalists' God." "He"—who? who was not "the Universalists' God"? The one who was in the church? Was the Universalists' God not there? Why not? Because it was a Catholic church? Would the "better God" not save the shrieking, burning, dying creatures because they were not Universalists?

Is this answer from an Editor of an Infidel paper? But when we defend a wrong, we cannot be right. The very espousal and defense of an inconsistensy makes us inconsistent. Again, to my question—whether the Universalists did not believe in three Gods? you say:—

"We were not before aware that they believed in three Gods."

Don't they believe in God the Father, God the Son, and God the Holy Ghost? Don't they believe in the Saviour, and that Christ by his death saved them? I have heard them use that as an argument against other Christians, that the blood of Christ has already saved them, and how could that be the case, if he were only a man? Now, should you see fit to reply again, try to answer plainly without prevaricating. Again, you say:—

"Whenever our Sister can point to as many converts from Judaism to our side as we can from Universalism, we will echo her expression of 'wonderful to relate!'"

Is it possible that you "know of no other Jew who has left the barbarism of Moses for the philosophy of the *Investigator*?" Better think again before you repeat the assertion. Did you never have a subscriber, or correspondent to the paper, from that "barbarous people"? Try, you may find one besides "the Rose that all are praising," if it were only to match the *two* Universalists who have come on our side.—But should you not be able to remember one, then it gives me great pleasure to inform you that you have several besides "the Rose" who have come from Judaism "on our side"—that she has plenty, and good company, and though personally acquainted with comparatively few, there are tens of thousands of Atheists in Europe, some of whom are at the very head and front in every reform. Then, are you convinced that Judaism, as well as Universalism, is the "stepping stone to Infidelity"?

[Concluded next week]
Ernestine L Rose
New York, March 22, 1864

## REMARKS.

We are very glad to find that from some cause (of course not from anything we have said) that our sister is better natured with us than she has been, and scolds considerably less. This is a decided improvement, and now that she is progressing toward her usual tranquillity and customary politeness, the storm will soon blow over and brighter skies succeed, making the slight "passage at arms" a benefit to us, for as Gen. Dumas says in the play, "It is strange how much better I like a man after having fought with him!" and we suspect that this is the case in a fight with a woman.

With the pleasant exception to which we have referred, we discover nothing new in the present response, and so we shall be brief in response to it. [After promising brevity, Seaver then goes on in a similar vein for several pages more.] . . . Ed. Inv.]

## THE JEWS [FOURTH LETTER, PART 2], APRIL 14

I am glad that Universalists have so far improved that they allow Infidels to speak in their meetings. I know the time when we would get even Baptist churches, but not a single Universalist. When the Jews have meetings for debate, they too "allow others to speak;"—they have no "vestry," so "he" cannot be invited to speak. Perhaps if the Jews were as anxious for converts and proselytes as Christian sects are, then "he" might be invited to come among them to speak as among the Universalists, but "he" has not the chance to speak in the synagogue. What then? Should they on that account be prevented from having a synagogue?

"Perhaps a little more of the influence of the better God and the more benevolent religion might serve to make her rather better natured, and less disposed to hit us quite so hard." Indeed! For example, she might borrow the good natured language of your replies, which abound in such epithets as "vile," "worthless," "miserable," "contemptible," "abominable," &c., &c., &c. I had thought these gentle terms must be the result of the defense of the newly found "better God and the more benevolent religion." But if that is the result, I beg to be excused from borrowing either the "religion" or the example.

In conclusion, allow me to inform you that Mrs. Rose has read "Lydia Maria Child's excellent and instructive work on the Progress of Religious Ideas," and was very much pleased with it, and it goes to prove just what I said in one of my articles, that the only progress in religion is to get out of it and leave it behind. Mrs. Rose has not the least desire to "scold you out of certain, positive, unmistakable truth," but she has a strong desire to reason you into it; yet if she fails in her good intentions, it may be owing to the "better God" whom she "presumes" to consider as bad as any other God you can mention: for if he is a God, he must be both powerful and good, (to be good for anything.) If he were good, he would have prevented the conflagration in the Catholic Church at Chili [Chile] and saved the lives of the two thousand victims. But he did not, and therefore he is as bad, as cruel, as barbarous as the God of the Jews.

But, as you say, I have "hit" you hard enough, and unless forced by further quibbles, insinuations, new issues, and prevarications, I am quite content to let the subject rest, satisfied in having done my duty in defense of justice.

I am as ever,
Ernestine L. Rose
New York, March 29, 1864


**REMARKS.**

We are not sorry that this dispute has come to an end, for of late it has been hardly anything more than a repetition on both sides. This response, therefore, is probably the last we shall make provided that the Jewish champion is willing to retire upon her laurels—such as they are.

It is true, what she says, that the Universalists sometimes allow Infidels to speak in their vestry meetings, and the fact shows that they are liberally inclined, "He" has frequently been allowed this indulgence and has always been treated kindly;—nor was "he" tried to be made a proselyte of—so far from it, "he" labored to make proselytes of them! Now if the Jews are as liberal, perhaps she has spoken in their meetings. We wonder much if she has; and if she will only say so, "he" would be much better treated, perhaps, in a New York synagogue than "he" was in a Boston one: for in the latter "he" was not only not allowed to speak, but "he" was not allowed to even enter into the building! Very liberal and progressive, was it not? "He" was never treated in such an exclusive and bigoted manner by Universalists, and the reason is, most likely, because they have "a better God and a more benevolent religion." Universalism takes the whole human race into the kingdom according to John Murray—while Judaism keeps them all out except a mere moiety, according to Moses.—There is, therefore, just the difference in these two kinds of religion, that there is between a broad and expanded liberality and a narrow and contracted bigotry. Yet we have not intimated that the Jews should be "prevented from having a synagogue," and perhaps she said that because she had nothing better to say.

But we are given to understand that our preference for Universalism has not improved our language—that we use reproachful epithets, &c. Very likely we do against the Jewish superstition for we think it deserves all we have said of it and more; but we have not made a single disrespectful allusion to Mrs. Rose; uttered not a word that a gentleman may not say with propriety to a lady, though we have had considerable provocation to retort in kind. Let us see. She has charged us with being "uncandid, silly, with having a weak head and a bad heart, making false insinuations and false issues, navigating the ship in an unsteady manner, being unjust, mean, cowardly," &c., &c. in a similar scolding tirade to the end of the chapter. Now as we have used no such language as this toward our sister, but have endeavored to be civil and good natured, we are willing to leave it to our readers to decide which of the twain has preserved the best temper.

. . . . . . .

As for our friend's desire to reason us into the truth, we are certainly obliged to her; doubtless we have much to learn before we get our education;—but the next time she assumes to instruct, let her be a little less sparing of her *compliments*. "Molasses catches more flies than vinegar."

With the respect to the idea of a God, there is probably no difference of opinion between us. We view it, as we have said before, as a mere *conception*, depending for its character upon the intelligence and progress of those who believe it; and as for the two thousand victims in the Catholic Church at Chili, we do not believe (nor does Mrs. Rose) that God had any agency in the affair, though if he had, it was not so cruel and barbarous as the butchery by Moses of the Midianites, according to the Jewish religion. The burning of the church was an accident—the massacre of the Midianites was premeditated, even as "the Lord God of Israel commanded." Hence the need of "a better God and a more benevolent religion."

Our sister seems to intimate, in closing, that it will depend upon our good behavior whether she will give us another "hit" or not. We have only to add that we shall always be happy to receive her communications, and though we rather prefer peace and harmony in the family, yet if she must have a little breeze once in a while—why, if it pleases her, it don't hurt us.—[Ed. Inv.]

# SPEECH AT THE FIRST ANNIVERSARY OF THE AMERICAN EQUAL RIGHTS ASSOCIATION: VOICES FOR VOTES
May 10, 1867
New York, New York

The Equal Rights Association was formed to advocate for votes for both African American men and all women on the basis of a belief in universal suffrage. Women's rights advocates had expected that they, too, would benefit from the drive toward expanding suffrage. When the universal rights strategy faltered in the Reconstruction era, women's rights reformers began to speak of themselves as a Women's Suffrage Movement.

Emancipation of four million formerly enslaved African Americans completely changed the political dynamic of the nation, and the relationships between abolitionists and women's rights reformers. African American men and their allies from the abolitionist movement and in the Republican Party saw this time as "the Negro's hour," and did not want to risk the opportunity for enfranchisement of African American men by advocating at the same time for votes for women. The Republican Party was the progressive party of its time. It had been more supportive of abolition of slavery and was then more supportive of reconstruction and enfranchising African American men, but not of voting rights for women.

At this First Anniversary of the American Equal Rights Association, Rose spoke in a spirited manner, demonstrating a modern awareness of the role of money in American politics. She urged both women and men to raise their voices for women's right to vote and called upon men to exercise the moral courage to share voting rights with women. Rose quotes Abraham Lincoln's famous statement, "A house divided against itself cannot stand" to argue that the nation should be "reconstructed" on a "sound foundation" that included equal rights for all people—blacks and whites, women and men.

Rose's discussion of "a social evil" refers to the dramatic rise that year of "preventing societies" to control prostitution in New York (Gilfoyle 1986). She raises important questions of sexual politics, asking, "Is this the only social evil there is? Are there not many kinds?" She addresses head on the issue of men who hold social power attempting to regulate the behavior of women who remain disenfranchised and asks that woman be given the vote so that she can protect herself.

❧

After all, we come down to the root of all evil— to money. It is rather humiliating, after the discourse that we have just heard, that told us of the rise and progress and destruction of nations, of empires and of republics, that we have to come down to dollars and cents. We live in an entirely practical age. I can show you in a few words that if we only had sufficient of that root of all evil in our hands, there would be no need of holding these meetings. We could obtain the elective franchise without making a single speech. Give us one million of dollars, and we will have the elective franchise at the very next session of our Legislature. (Laughter and applause.) But as we have not got a million of dollars, we want a million of voices. There are always two ways of obtaining an object. If we had had the money, we could have bought the Legislature and the elective franchise long before now. But as we have not, we must create a public opinion, and for that we must have voices.

I have always thought I was convinced not only of the necessity but of the great importance of obtaining the elective franchise for woman; but recently I have become convinced that I never felt sufficiently that importance until now. Just read your public papers and see how our Senators and our members of the House are running round through the Southern States to hold meetings, and to deliver public addresses. To whom? To the freedmen. And why now, and why not ten, fifteen, or twenty years ago? Why do they get up meetings for the colored men, and call them fellow-men, brothers, and gentlemen? Because the freedman has that talisman in his hands which the politician is looking after. Don't you perceive, then, the importance of the elective franchise? Perhaps when we have the elective franchise in our hands, these great senators will condescend to inform us too of the importance of obtaining our rights.

You need not be afraid that when woman has the franchise, men will ever disturb her. I presume there are present, as there always are such people, those of timid minds, chicken-hearted, who so admire and respect woman that they are dreadfully afraid lest, when she comes to the ballot-box, rude, uncouth and vulgar men will say something to disturb her. You may set your hearts all at rest. If we once have the elective franchise, upon the first indication that any man will endeavor to disturb a woman in her duty at the polls, Congress will enact another Freedman's Bureau—I beg pardon, a Freedwoman's Bureau—to protect women against men, and to guard the purity of the ballot-box at the same time.

I have sometimes been asked, even by sensible men, "If woman had the elective franchise, would she go to the polls to mix with rude men?" Well, would I go to the church to mix with rude men? And should not the ballot-box be as respectable, and as respected, and as sacred as the church? Aye, infinitely more so, because it is of greater importance. Men can pray in secret, but must vote in public. (Applause.) Hence the ballot, of the two, ought to be the most respected; and it would be if women were once there; but it never will be until they are there.

We have been told this evening that it is not good for man to be alone. No; if it was not well for him to be alone in the garden of Eden, it surely cannot be well for him to be alone at the ballot-box.

Our rights are so old as humanity itself. Yet we are obliged to ask man to give us the ballot, because he has it in his own hands. It is ours, and at the same time we ask for it; and we have sent on petitions to Congress. We have been told that the Republic is not destroyed. It has been destroyed, root and branch, because, if it were not destroyed, there would be no need to reconstruct it. And we have asked Congress, in the reconstruction of the Republic, to place it upon a sound foundation. Why have all former republics vanished out of existence? Simply because they were built upon the sand. In the erection of a building, in proportion to the height of the walls must be the depth and soundness of the foundation. If the foundation is shallow or unsound, the higher you raise your superstructure the surer its downfall. That is the reason a republic has not existed as long as a monarchy, because it embraced principles of human rights in its superstructure which it denied in its foundation. Hence, before this Republic could count a hundred years, it has had one of the mightiest revolutions that ever occurred in any country or in any period of human existence. Its foundation was laid wrong. It made a republic for white men alone. It discriminated against color; it discriminated against woman; and at the same time it pronounced that all men are created free and equal, and endowed with certain inalienable rights, among which are life, liberty, and the pursuit of happiness. It raised its superstructure to the clouds; and it has fallen as low as any empire could fall. It is divided. A house divided against itself cannot stand. A wrong always operates against itself, and falls back on the wrong-doer. We have proclaimed to the world universal suffrage; but it is universal suffrage with a vengeance attached to it—universal suffrage excluding the negro and the woman, who are by far the largest majority in this country. It is not the majority that rules here, but the minority. White men are in the minority in this nation. White women, black men, and black women compose the large majority of the nation. Yet, in spite of this fact, in spite of common sense, in spite of justice, while our members of Congress can prate so long about justice, and human rights, and the rights of the negro, they have not the moral courage to say anything for the rights of woman.

In proportion to power is responsibility. Our Republican senators and members of Congress have taken unto themselves great power. They have made great professions. There is a very good maxim, "Of him to whom much is given, much shall be required." In proportion to their claims to be friends of human freedom, lovers of human rights, do we demand of them our rights and justice. When Chase, Summer [Sumner], Stevens, and Wilson talk to the negro of the importance of having the franchise, and stop short of giving the franchise to woman, I proclaim them hypocrites—I proclaim them politicians. They speak so to the newly freed slave, because he has already the ballot in his hands, and they want him to vote for them. We have not that right, and hence they do not speak one word in favor of our attaining the elective franchise. I make no difference between one party and another. All parties are alike to me so far as they are right; and all parties are alike to me so far as they are wrong. For one, I would not be bound by party if I had the franchise in my hand to-day. I would go for my own highest convictions of right, irrespective of party. Perhaps our Senators know that woman would not be such a docile tool in their hands as the newly freed slave, and hence they will not give the ballot to us. If they do think so, they do us justice, because we would not be, you may depend on that.

There are a great many objections urged against the enfranchisement of women; and one that I have recently heard is that women would not go to war. Perhaps, if women had the franchise, men would not need to go to war neither. (Applause.) And this is one great reason why I demand the franchise. War is only a relic of the old barbarisms. So long as woman is deprived of her right, man is only next door to a barbarian. If he were not, he never would go to war. When woman has the franchise she will not want to go to war, and she will not want her husband to go to war, she will not want to have her son or her brother go to war; and none of them will need to go to war. Is war necessary? Are rowdies necessary? Is it necessary for man to be vulgar and corrupt? Is it necessary to disgrace the ballot-box by rows and fightings, so that a woman dare not go within its precincts? Are these things inalienable rights in a republic? Do they belong to the ballot-box? Do they belong to this country? Do they belong to the nineteenth century? For my part, I say, No!

The ballot is a teacher. Henry Ward Beecher, in a discourse on the subject last winter, said, in regard to woman's franchise, that the ballot is a teacher. I am glad to be able to agree with a minister, which is not often the case. Yes, it is a teacher. Yet, when a man alone has the ballot, it fails to be his teacher. It has not taught him the great lesson that the ballot is useless, that it becomes perverted and corrupt, when woman is kept from it.

One of the greatest Grecian philosophers has proclaimed that no one ought to be amenable to the laws of the land that has not voice in enacting the laws. Woman is amenable to our laws. She is punished; she is imprisoned; she is hung; but she has no voice in making the law that imprisons her or hangs her. She is taxed, but she has no voice in the laws that levy the tax. She is judged, but she has no voice in the laws, or in saying who shall judge her. Woman ought to be wherever her duty calls her—at the ballot-box, on the judge's bench, in the jury-box; the lawyer at the bar to plead her own case. Millions of money have been spent, many thousand lives have been lost, to obtain for man the great boon of being judged by his peers. Who are our peers? Are we the same that man is? Then we have the same rights that he has. Are we not the same that he is? Then what right has he to judge us? How can he plead for us? How can he understand the motives of a being so entirely different from himself? There is no justice in it. But it is an old error, and it is very difficult to eradicate it; it cannot be done except by money or by voices.

We have lately read in the papers, to the shame and disgrace of this civilized Republic in the nineteenth century, that the Legislature of New York took into consideration the enactment of laws against a "social evil." For my part, I never knew a social evil to be removed by force of law. Is there only one kind of social evil? Are there not many kinds? Is there not defalcation, deception, intrigue, swindling, defrauding—the government defrauding the people, and the people defrauding the government and each other? Why, then, not enact laws against these kinds of "social evil?" After you have stopped them, then you may talk about enacting laws to prevent another social evil. The prevention of that social evil must commence in the nursery. If you will bring up woman as you ought to bring up men—not as you do bring up men—acknowledging her right to live the same as men, giving her the same advantages and the same rights that men have, there will be no need to enact laws against a "social evil." It is a shame to talk about licensing a social evil. It is a shame to this Republic. It is a violation of woman's nature. It is an insult to womanhood; and if woman has one drop of pure blood stirring in her heart, she must revolt against it.

At the same time, I say to the Legislature that, if you enact laws against social evils, whatever those laws are, let them be alike for man and for woman. (Applause.) If you want to derive a revenue from the corruption of the community, let it be drawn alike from both sexes. The social evil belongs to both; the social remedy must belong to both. Do not degrade woman more than she is already degraded. Perchance she is driven, through your injustice, to that step to maintain her wretched existence, because every avenue of emolument is barred against her; and yet he that commits the injustice and takes advantage of her feebleness, her confiding nature, her helpless poverty, and her ignorance, enacts laws against woman and against the social evil! I would rather give the stray lamb into the power of the wolf for protection. (Applause.) Let woman have the franchise; let all the avenues of society be thrown open before her, according to her powers and her capacities, and there will be no need to talk about social evils. Depend upon it that she will not only take care of herself, but will help to take care of man, which is more than he has ever done for himself.

# FINAL LETTERS 1869-1880

# LETTER TO THE NATIONAL WOMAN SUFFRAGE CONVENTION IN WASHINGTON, D.C.

January 14, 1869
Washington, D.C.

Rose was invited to speak at a National Woman Suffrage Convention held in the nation's capital on January 19 and 20, 1869, and sponsored by a group called the Universal Franchise Association. This meeting was called The National Woman Suffrage Convention because there was no National Woman Suffrage Association until its founding in May of 1869. Its primary objective was universal suffrage, including votes for women. Rose declined, pleading "indisposition." She had not been well and was preparing to retire to England with her husband William. In her letter which she asked to have read at the convention, she demands votes for women and takes issue with the Fourteenth Amendment for its introduction of the word "male" into the U.S. Constitution.

Rose's letter was printed in full, along with extracts from other letters to the convention from those who could not attend, in the January 28, 1869, issue of *The Revolution*, a weekly newspaper devoted to women's rights.

⁓❦

Mrs. Josephine S. Griffing,—*Dear Madam*: Your favor of the 6th inst. is received. Permit me to assure you it would give me great pleasure to be present at your important convention of the 19th, but indisposition will not allow me that gratification.

Looking at all the circumstances; the position, the epoch, and the efforts now being made to extend the right to the ballot, your Convention is perhaps the most important that was ever held. It is a true maxim, that it is easier to do justice than injustice; to do right than wrong; and to do it at once, than by small degrees. How much better and easier it would have been for Congress, when they enfranchised all the men of the District of Columbia, had they included the women also; but better late than never. Let the national government, to which the states have a right to look for good example, do justice to woman now, and all the states will follow.

. . . . . . .

It was a terrible mistake and a fundamental error, based upon ignorance and injustice, ever to have introduced the word "male" into the Federal Constitution. The terms "male "and "female "simply designate

343

the physical or animal distinction between the sexes, and ought to be used only in speaking of the lower animals. Human beings are men and women, possessed of human faculties and understanding, which we call mind; and mind recognizes no sex, therefore the term "male," as applied to human beings—to citizens—ought to be expunged from the constitution and laws as a last remniscence of barbarism—when the animal, not mind, when might, not right, governed the world.

Let your Convention, then, urge Congress to wipe out that purely animal distinction from the national constitution. That noble instrument was destined to govern intelligent, responsible human beings—men and women—not sex.

The childish argument that all women don't ask for the franchise would hardly deserve notice were it not sometimes used by men of sense. To all such I would say, examine ancient and modern history, yes, even of your own times, and you will find there never has been a time when all men of any country—white or black—have ever asked for a reform. Reforms have to be claimed and obtained by the few, who are in advance, for the benefit of the many who lag behind. And when once obtained and almost forced upon them, the mass of the people accept and enjoy their benefits as a matter of course.

Look at the petitions now pouring into Congress for the franchise for women, and compare their thousands of signatures with the few isolated names that graced our first petitions to the Legislature of New York to secure to the married woman the right to hold in her own name the property that belonged to her, to secure to the poor, forsaken wife the right to her earnings, and to the mother the right to her children. "All" the women did not ask for those rights, but all accepted them with joy and gladness when they were obtained; and so it will be with the franchise.

But woman's claim for the ballot does not depend upon the numbers that demand it, or would exercise the right; but upon precisely the same principles that man claims it for himself. Chase, Sumner, Stevens, and many others of both Houses of Congress have, time after time, declared that the franchise means "Security, Education, Responsibility, Self-respect. Prosperity, and Independence." Taking all these assertions for granted and fully appreciating all their benefits, in the name of security, of education, of responsibility, of self-respect, of liberty, of prosperity and independence we demand the franchise for woman.

Please present this hastily-written contribution to your Convention with best wishes.

Yours, dear madam, very truly,
Ernestine L. Rose

# LETTER TO SUSAN B. ANTHONY:
## REFLECTIONS ON THE
## UNITED STATES CENTENNIAL
July 4, 1876
London, England

By 1876, Rose had been living in England for seven years. Missing her women's rights friends and colleagues, especially during the centennial celebrations of the Declaration of Independence and the founding of the United States, Rose was moved, on the Fourth of July, to write to Susan B. Anthony, asking that her letter be read to the Convention at Philadelphia on July 19 so that she could continue to contribute to women's rights. She urged the women to keep up the fight to "reassert in 1876 what 1776 so gloriously proclaimed . . . by giving woman the right of representation in the government which she helps to maintain."

To mark the U.S. centennial, Elizabeth Cady Stanton and Matilda Joslin Gage wrote the "Declaration of Rights of the Women of the United States," a strong protest against the establishment of an "aristocracy of sex" through women's lack of representation in government. It was signed by prominent women's rights activists, including Ernestine L. Rose, and circulated to the public by the National Woman Suffrage Association. The declaration was also meant to be read at the centennial celebration on July 4 in Philadelphia's Independence Square. When requests to present it were denied, Susan B. Anthony and several other women made their way to the stage to hand the document to the vice-president, handed out copies to the crowd, and read it aloud themselves (for an account of the event, and the full text of the declaration, see Stanton 1971 [1898], Chapter 19: "The Spirit of '76").

&

London, Eng., July 4, 1876

My Dear Susan: I sincerely thank you for your kind letter. Many times I have thought of writing to you, but I knew your time was too much taken up with the good cause to have any to spare for private correspondence. Occasionally I am pleased to see a good account of you and your doings in the *Boston Investigator*. Oh, I wish I could be with you on this more than ordinarily interesting and important occasion; or that I could at least send my sentiments and views on human rights, which I have advocated for over forty years, to the convention.

This being the centenary day of the proclamation of American independence, I must write a few lines, if but to let the friends know that though absent in body I am with you in the cause for which, in common with you, I have labored so long, and I hope not labored in vain.

The glorious day upon which human equality was first proclaimed ought to be commemorated, not only every hundred years or every year, but it ought to be constantly held before the public mind until its grand principles are carried into practice. The declaration that "All men [which means all human beings irrespective of sex] have an equal right to life, liberty, and the pursuit of happiness," is enough for woman as for man. We need no other; but we must, reassert in 1876 what 1776 so gloriously proclaimed and call upon the law-makers and the law-breakers to carry that declaration to its logical consistency by giving woman the right of representation in the government which she helps to maintain; a voice in the laws by which she is governed, and all the rights and privileges society can bestow, the same as to man, or disprove its validity. We need no other declaration. All we ask is to have the laws based on the same foundation upon which that declaration rests, viz.: upon equal justice, and not upon sex. Whenever the rights of man are claimed, moral consistency points to the equal rights of woman.

I hope these few lines will fill a little space in the convention at Philadelphia, where my voice has so often been raised in behalf of the principles of humanity. I am glad to see my name among the vice-presidents of the National Association. Keep a warm place for me with the American people. I hope some day to be there yet. Give my love to Mrs. Mott and Sarah Pugh. With kind regards from Mr. Rose,

Yours affectionately,
Ernestine L. Rose

# LETTER TO SUSAN B. ANTHONY:
## A LIFE OF ACTIVISM
January 9, 1877
London, England

Ernestine L. Rose wrote from London, a few days before her sixty-seventh birthday, in reply to a request from Susan B. Anthony for a summary of her participation in the women's rights movement in the United States. Anthony's request apparently came as part of her research for what was to become the six-volume *History of Woman Suffrage* (1881–1888), which she coauthored with Elizabeth Cady Stanton and Matilda Joslin Gage. Despite Rose's disclaimer that she lacked documentation, she manages to list, from memory, the many towns and states in which she had lectured. She also mentions that between 1850 and 1869 she had spoken at every national, and numerous state and local, women's rights convention; and had addressed the U.S. Congress and many state legislatures, including eleven appearances before the New York State Legislature often in the course of bringing petitions and advocating for passage of Married Women's Property Laws. Rose's letter is published in the first volume of the *History of Woman Suffrage*. The editors supplemented Rose's words with some appreciative commentary of their own, and added another short biography of Rose by L. E. Barnard.

⤳

London, January 9, 1877

My Dear Miss Anthony: — Sincerely do I thank you for your kind letter. Believe me it would give me great pleasure to comply with your request, to tell you all about myself and my past labors; but I suffer so much from neuralgia in my head and general debility, that I could not undertake the task, especially as I have nothing to refer to. I have never spoken from notes; and as I did not intend to publish anything about myself, for I had no other ambition except to work for the cause of humanity, irrespective of sex, sect, country, or color, and did not expect that a Susan B. Anthony would wish to do it for me, I made no memorandum of places, dates or names; and thirty or forty years ago, the press was not sufficiently educated in the rights of women, even to notice, much less to report speeches as it does now; and therefore I have not anything to assist me or you.

All that I can tell you is, that I used my humble powers to the uttermost, and raised my voice in behalf of Human Rights in general, and the elevation and Rights of Woman in particular, nearly all my life. And so little have I spared myself, or studied my comfort in summer or winter, rain or shine, day or night, when I had an opportunity to work for the cause to which I had devoted myself, that I can hardly wonder at my present state of health.

Yet in spite of hardships, for it was not as easy to travel at that time as now, and the expense, as I never made a charge or took up a collection, I look back to that time when a stranger and alone, I went from place to place, in high-ways and by-ways, did the work and paid my bills with great pleasure and satisfaction; for the cause gained ground and in spite of my heresies I had always good audiences, attentive listeners, and was well received wherever I went.

But I can mention from memory the chief places where I have spoken. In the winter of 1836 and '37 I spoke in New York and for some years after I lectured in almost every city in the State; Hudson and Poughkeepsie, Albany, Schenectady, Saratoga, Utica, Syracuse, Rochester, Buffalo, Elmira, and other places. In New Jersey, in Newark and Burlington; in 1837, in Philadelphia, Bristol, Chester, Pittsburg, and other places in Pennsylvania, and at Wilmington in Delaware; in 1842, in Boston, Charlestown, Beverly, Florence, Springfield, and other points in Massachusetts and in Hartford, Connecticut; in 1844 in Cincinnati, Dayton, Zanesville, Springfield, Cleveland, Toledo, and several settlements in the backwoods of Ohio and also in Richmond, Indiana; in 1845 and '46, I lectured three times in the Legislative Hall in Detroit, and at Ann Arbor and other places in Michigan; and in 1847 and '48, I spoke in Charleston and Columbia in South Carolina.

In 1850, I attended the first National Woman's Rights Convention in Worcester, and nearly all the National and State Conventions since until I went to Europe in 1869. Returning to New York in 1874, I was present at the Convention in Irving Hall, the only one held during my visit to America.

I sent the first petition to the New York Legislature to give a married woman the right to hold real estate in her own name, in the winter of 1836 and '37, to which after a good deal of trouble I obtained five signatures. Some of the ladies said the gentlemen would laugh at them; others that they had too many rights already. Woman at that time had not learned to know that she had any rights except those that man in his generosity allowed her; both have learned something since that time which they will never forget. I continued sending petitions with increased numbers of signatures until 1848 and '49 when the Legislature enacted the law which granted to woman the right to keep what was her own. But no sooner did it become legal than all the women said, "Oh! That is right! We ought always to have had that."

During the eleven years from 1837 to 1848, I addressed the New York Legislature five times, and since 1848 I can not say positively, but a good many times; you know all that better than any one else.

Your affectionate friend,<br>
Ernestine L. Rose

# LETTER TO THE NATIONAL
# WOMAN SUFFRAGE ASSOCIATION
# CONVENTION IN ROCHESTER, NEW YORK
July 19, 1878
Rochester, New York

In one of her last letters from England, Rose wrote to salute a celebration "at the close of the third decade of organized agitation in the United States." The call to the 1878 convention explained that the Seneca Falls Convention of July 19, 1848, was adjourned to meet again on August 2 in Rochester. Rose acknowledged the aptness of the celebration site in her nostalgic recollection of that second lesser-known convention of 1848. Rose was not present at the Seneca Falls Convention, and we do not know whether she attended the second convention of 1848 in Rochester. This letter hints she might have been there. She also mentions her own labors over forty years, taking credit for her earlier start on women's rights agitation, and looks to the future, urging her colleagues onward toward suffrage, "the magic key . . . the insignia of citizenship in a republic." Hers was one of a number of letters read at the thirtieth anniversary celebration. The following excerpt, including the asterisks indicating omitted text, was printed in volume three of *History of Woman Suffrage*; there is no record of the full text or exact date of the letter.

❦

Ernestine L. Rose, a native of Poland, and, next to Frances Wright, the earliest advocate of woman's enfranchisement in America, wrote from England:

How I should like to be with you at the anniversary—it reminds me of the delightful convention we had at Rochester, long, long ago—and speak of the wonderful change that has taken place in regard to woman. Compare her present position in society with the one she occupied *forty* years ago, when I undertook to emancipate her from not only barbarous laws, but from what was even worse, a barbarous public opinion. No one can appreciate the wonderful change in the social and moral condition of woman, except by looking back and comparing the past with the present.

* * * Say to the friends. Go on, go on, halt not and rest not. Remember that "eternal vigilance is the price of liberty" and of right. Much has been achieved; but the main, the vital thing, has yet to come. The suffrage is the magic key to the statute—the insignia of citizenship in a republic.

# LETTER TO ELIZABETH CADY STANTON
# FOR THE NATIONAL WOMAN SUFFRAGE
# ASSOCIATION CONVENTION OF 1880
## May 15, 1880
## London, England

Rose wrote from England to Stanton in the spirit of their shared decades-long experience as founding members of the early women's rights movement. She devotes her letter to the significance of suffrage as a human right, one that will serve as a "moral elevator" to bolster self-respect in women, and encourage higher aims in the improvement of society.

∽◆

London, May 15, 1880

Dear Mrs. Stanton,

You know me too well to require my assurance that it would give me great pleasure to be with you at your meeting on the second of June. But as that is impossible, I send my voice across the Atlantic to plead for Human rights without distinction of sex and to swell the grand chorus in the demand of Justice to Woman by declaring her right to the suffrage and proclaim her a citizen.

But the suffrage is not only a badge of citizenship but a mental and moral elevator that prepares the possessor of it to self-respect and dignity and prepares him for greater usefulness and higher and nobler aims in the progress of Humanity.

Success to our cause and love to the Friends devoted to it.

Yours affectionately,
Ernestine L. Rose

p.p.s. I would have written more but was too ill and could hardly write what I did.

My address is, in care of Mrs. A. Biggs, 19 Notting Hill Square, London

# OBITUARIES AND TRIBUTES

# OBITUARY FOR WILLIAM E. ROSE

*By J. P. Mendum*
February 22, 1882
Boston, Massachusetts

William E. Rose, husband of Ernestine L. Rose for forty-six years, was known to be unreservedly supportive of her work, personally as well as financially. In the women's movement he was known primarily by reputation, as a sympathetic and devoted husband (Kolmerten 1999, 173). In the freethought movement, William was an active and highly esteemed member in his own right. His portrait was one of four chosen to grace Paine Memorial Hall, the "Temple of Freethought" in Boston, along with those of Ernestine L. Rose, Thomas Paine, and Robert Owen. Though William rarely spoke in public except for offering toasts at the annual Paine Celebrations, he was active in fund-raising and organizational tasks. It is perhaps not surprising that he died while out doing an errand, for he preferred the role of behind-the-scenes supporter. His obituary notice is included here in recognition of his position as a rare early model of the supportive partner of an activist woman.

William E. Rose died on January 25, 1882. His obituary, published in the *Boston Investigator* on February 22, begins with notes sent by Philip S. Justice, the Roses' attorney in London, and by the prominent British freethinker Charles Bradlaugh, a close friend of the Roses, followed by a tribute from the editor, J. P. Mendum.

⤙

We deeply regret the sad occasion which requires us to publish the following note received a few days since:—

London, (England,) Jan. 26, 1882
J. P. Mendum, Esq.—It is my painful duty to inform you of the sudden death of our mutual friend, Mr. William E. Rose, whose demise occurred yesterday, of heart disease. He had gone into the city on some little business when he fell in the street, and although carried immediately to St. Bartholomew's Hospital, he died ere he reached it. -Mrs. Ernestine L. Rose, his dear wife, is terribly affected by this sad loss; but desires me to write for her to say that she would have written you some time since had her feeble state of health permitted her to do so.

I am, Sir, very respectfully yours,
Phillip S. Justice

In a few lines on the same subject from our friend Bradlaugh he says:—

"As soon as the sad, news reached me I hurried to the residence of Mrs. Rose and found the good old lady very brave but very heart-broken at the loss of her faithful partner."

Mr. and Mrs. Rose were formerly located in New York, but for a number of years past they have resided in London. Our acquaintance with them has extended over a period of forty years, and in all that time they have been amongst our best friends and the most devoted workers in the cause of Liberalism. Mr. Rose was a very worthy man in all the relations of life. Pleasant in his manners, prompt in all his duties, and remarkably kind and benevolent in his disposition, he was greatly esteemed by all who enjoyed the pleasure of his acquaintance. He was a genuine and an intelligent Liberal, made so by reading and reflection, and, although quiet and unassuming, yet his upright example and kind deeds spoke louder than words of the purity and goodness of his mind and heart.

We bid him farewell with deep regret, but with satisfaction that his life was useful and blameless, and that he leaves after him the memory of a good name and the influence of that noblest work of Nature or of God, a thoroughly honest man.

To our highly esteemed and afflicted sister, upon whom this heavy blow has fallen at her advanced age, we offer our sincerest sympathy, and hope it may be some mitigation of her grief to know that Mr. Rose was greatly respected by all who knew him, and that the intelligence of his sudden death was received by his friends here with unfeigned sorrow and regret.

# EULOGY FOR ERNESTINE L. ROSE

*By George Jacob Holyoake*
August 8, 1892
London, England

Ernestine L. Rose died in London on August 4, 1892. George Jacob Holyoake, successor to Robert Owen as leader of the British cooperative socialist movement, spoke
at a graveside ceremony attended by Rose's friends and a niece. Oddly, Holyoake's
eulogy focuses almost exclusively on Rose's antislavery advocacy and completely overlooks her work for women's rights and freethought. One of the participants listed in
the paper as Mrs. Bradlaugh Bonner, was the daughter of Charles Bradlaugh. After
the deaths of William Rose and Charles Bradlaugh, Hypatia Bradlaugh Bonner took
up her father's pledge to protect Rose from religious fanatics seeking the deathbed
conversion of well-known atheists. Bradlaugh Bonner was among the first British
women to graduate from university, and served as a Family and Children's Court
Judge through the early twentieth century.

   This account of the graveside ceremony, which includes Holyoake's eulogy, was
published in the *Boston Investigator* on August 24 under the heading "Funeral of Mrs.
Ernestine L. Rose," and apparently taken from an article in the *London Daily News*,
published on August 9, 1892.

～❧

Yesterday, at Highgate Cemetery, Mrs. Rose was interred in the grave of
William Ella Rose. Among the assembly were Mrs. Allison, a niece of the
deceased, Mr. Washington Epps, her medical attendant, Messrs. Justice,
Senior and Junior, her solicitors, Mr. Edward Truelove, Mr. Alfred Marsh,
Mrs. Bradlaugh Bonner, Miss E.A. Holyoake, Mrs. G. W. Foote, Mrs. J.
M. Robertson, Mrs. Wheeler, Mr. Mazzini Wheeler, Mr. And Mrs. M.
Q. Holyoake, Mrs. Taylor, Miss Trevillon, Miss Byrne, Mrs. Rose's atten-
dant, and many others.

   Mr. G. J. Holyoake, who spoke by the desire of Mrs. Rose, said, "The
grave at which we assemble is that of Mrs. Ernestine L. Rose, who has
lived until her eighty-third year, notwithstanding the stress and storm of
agitation through which she'd passed in perilous days. She was Polish by
birth, Jewish by race, German by education, American by adoption, and
English by affection. Her husband, a jeweler of New York, died in London ten years ago. His regard for his wife exceeded anything of the kind
I have ever known, and her affection for him was such that though she

had numerous personal friends in every great city of America, she would never leave England, where her husband lay buried. Her desire was to be in the same grave, and today, in this spot, her desire is fulfilled.

Mrs. Rose was the first woman who presented herself on a public platform in America as a speaker against Negro slavery. It was perilous in a man to do it when she did it. She even went into the slave states pleading for [N]egro freedom. She was threatened with tar and feathers. She answered that "for the sake of humanity she would risk the tar." More than comely in features which had the dignity of contour, Mrs. Rose had a voice which at once arrested attention by its strength and melody. She spoke with easy accuracy and with eloquence and reason. Robert Owen, on his visits to America, paid her great respect. From being an opponent she became the most influential advocate of his views in that country. There was genius in her sympathy with social improvement. In the words of a recent poetess, Mrs. Rose could say: -

"I said it in the meadow path,
I said it on the mountain stairs —
The best things any mortal hath
Are those which every mortal shares."

Her German education gave her intellectual intrepidity. In her youth her dark hair and gleaming eyes showed she had the fire of Judith in her; and her passion was to see women possess civil and social equality, and to inspire women and men with self-helping sense, not taking religion, politics, or social ideas secondhand from their "pastors and masters" but choosing principles of belief, government, and conduct for themselves. Like her great co-worker in the anti-slavery movement, Lucretia Mott, Mrs. Rose took truth for authority, not authority for truth.

After forty years of agitation—the period of her public activity—her end was painless peace. In her closing days she would often say, "It is no longer necessary for me to live. I can do nothing now. But I have lived." The slave she had helped to free from bondage of ownership, and the minds she had set free from the bondage of authority, were the glad and proud remembrance of her last days. If any around her grave shall provide memories of good done to brighten the end of life, it will be equally well with them and better for all who have passed within their influence.

*London Daily News*, Aug. 9

# TRIBUTE TO ERNESTINE L. ROSE
## AT THE 25TH ANNUAL CONVENTION
## OF THE NATIONAL AMERICAN
## WOMAN SUFFRAGE ASSOCIATION

*By Elizabeth Cady Stanton*
January 16–19, 1893
Washington, D.C.

This moving final tribute by Elizabeth Cady Stanton demonstrates her admiration and regard for Ernestine L. Rose as "the woman who could reason with logic and wisdom." Stanton acknowledged Rose's pioneering work on the Married Women's Property Act petition in the 1830s and continuing through the 1850s. She was pleased and grateful when Rose supported her controversial resolution on divorce reform at the Tenth National Women's Rights Convention in 1860. Stanton's tribute, which followed a resolution mourning the death of Rose, was read at the 1893 convention of the National American Woman Suffrage Association. This group was founded in 1890 when the National Woman Suffrage Association and the American Woman Suffrage Association united as a single national organization devoted to women's rights and suffrage, healing the rift of 1869.

∽℘

"Mlle. Siismund Potoski [*sic*], best known to us as Ernestine L. Rose, was born in Poland and belonged to a Jewish family. She was sincere in her faith and conscientious in the observance of all its ceremonies. She was a faithful student of the Scriptures and of the ritual and dogmas of her faith until the persecutions of the Jews in Poland and Russia led her to investigate the theologies of both Jews and Christians and to reject alike their creeds and ceremonies. This involved much suffering—all her life persecuted by Christians as well as those of her own faith. She was a liberal alike in religion and government and sympathized with France in her struggle for a Republic and rejoiced in its establishment in the United States. Traveling extensively on the continent, by her eloquent appeals to those in authority she relieved many cases of injustice and oppression, bringing peace and happiness to many an humble home. She married in England, where she spent several years, and in 1836 came to America and resided a long time in New York. She lectured extensively in this country, on religion, government, and many of the popular reforms, especially on the rights of women. She addressed the legislatures of several States on this question. In company with Paulina Wright, she circulated petitions for the property rights of married women in 1836 and presented them in person to the committee that had such matters in charge. Probably this was the seesawing for the bill which passed in 1848.

During the years of 1855 to 1860 Mrs. Rose traveled with Miss Anthony all over the State of New York, speaking to large audiences in fifty different counties. The result of their united labors was the passage of a bill securing to married women the right to their wages and guardianship of their children. For half a century, as a public speaker, her eloquent voice was heard on both continents, she having taken an active part in all the great progressive movements of our day, associated with the most influential classes of reformers in both Europe and America. All through those eventual years, Mrs. Rose fought a double battle, not only for the political rights of her sex, but for their religious rights as individual souls, to do their own thinking and believing. How much of the freedom we now enjoy may be due to this noble Polish woman cannot be estimated, for moral influences are too subtle for measurement. They who sat with her in bygone days on the platform will remember her matchless powers as a speaker, and how safe we all felt when she had the floor that neither in manner, sentiment, argument, nor repartee would she in any way compromise the dignity of the occasion. She had the advantage of rare grace and beauty, which in a measure heightened the effect of all she said. She had a rich musical voice and a ready flow of choice language. In style she was clear, logical, and at times impassioned. I visited her during her last sad days in London, after the death of her husband, when she was stricken with the disease that terminated her life. She talked with deep feeling of her eventful life and with a lively interest in what was still passing, familiar as she was with every step of progress in our movement, both in England and America. "I am happy," she said at parting, "that I have helped to usher in the dawn of a new day for woman . . ." Of death and the future life she said nothing. I had often heard her say in former days that of the future [life after death] she knew nothing, and seldom thought of that subject, as she had always found enough in this life to occupy her time and thoughts. She had no fears of death and passed away calmly, sustained in her last days by the same philosophy that inspired her noble, unselfish life.

# WORKS CITED

Anderson, Bonnie. 2000. *Joyous Greetings: The First International Women's Rights Movement, 1832–60*. New York: Oxford University Press.

———. 2002. "Ernestine Rose as International Citizen." The Life and Legacy of Ernestine L. Rose: Secular Jew; Women's Rights and Human Rights Activist; International Socialist. Panel. Berkshire Conference on the History of Women. University of Connecticut, Storrs. June 9.

Baxandall, Rosalyn Fraad. 2002. "Rebel With a Cause" (comment). The Life and Legacy of Ernestine L. Rose: Secular Jew; Women's Rights and Human Rights Activist; International Socialist. Panel. Berkshire Conference on the History of Women. University of Connecticut, Storrs. June 9.

Berenbaum, Michael and Fred Skolnik, eds. 2007. *Encyclopaedia Judaica*. 2nd edition. Detroit: Macmillan Reference USA.

Berkowitz, Sandra J., and Amy C. Lewis. 1998. "Debating Anti-Semitism: Ernestine Rose vs. Horace Seaver in the *Boston Investigator*, 1863–1864." *Communication Quarterly* 46(4):457–71.

Bodensteiner, Keri. 2000. *The Rhetoric of Ernestine L. Rose: Collected Speeches and Letters*. 3 volumes. Dissertation University of Kansas.

Boston Women's Health Book Collective. 1973. *Our Bodies Ourselves*. New York: Simon & Schuster.

Chevigny, Bell Gale. 1976. *The Woman and the Myth: Margaret Fuller's Life and Writings*. Old Westbury, NY: Tht Feminist Press.

"Chronology of Emancipation during the war." 2007. (last updated February 15). www.history.umd.edu/Freedmen/chronol.htm

Davis, Paulina Wright. 1871. *A History of the National Women's Rights Movement for Twenty Years*. New York: Journeymen Printers' Cooperative.

d'Héricourt, Jenny P. 1856. "Madame Rose." *Revue Philosophique et Religieuse* 5(2):129–39. Trans. Jane Pincus, Mei Mei Ellerman, Ingrid Kisliuk, Erica Harth, and Allen J. Worters, with Karen Offen.

Doress-Worters, Paula, ed. 2003. *Journal of Women's History* 15(1): 183–201.

DuBois, Ellen Carol. 1978. *Feminism and Suffrage: The Emergence of an Independent Women's Movement in America: 1848–1869*. Ithaca, N.Y.: Cornell University Press.

———. 1981. Elizabeth Cady Stanton, Susan B. Anthony, Correspondence, Writings, Speeches. New York: Schocken Books.

———. 1998. *Woman Suffrage, Women's Rights*. New York: New York University Press.

———. 2001. "Ernestine Rose's Judaism and the Varieties of Euro-American Emancipation of 1848." Presented at Sisterhood and Slavery, a Conference at the Gilder Lehrman Center for the Study of Slavery, Yale University, New Haven, Conn. October 25–28.

Ehrenreich, Barbara, and Deidre English. 2005. *For Her Own Good*. 2nd ed. New York: Anchor Books.

Everrett, Glenn. 1987. "Chartism or the Chartist Movement." (last updated 1999). www.victorianweb.org/history/hist3.html.

Flexner, Eleanor. 1973 [1959]. *Century of Struggle*. New York: Atheneum.

Gadon, Elinor. 2006. Personal communication. March 19.

Giladi, Ben. 1991. *A Tale of One City: Piotrków Trybunalski*. New York: Shengold Publishers.

Gilfoyle, Timothy J. 1986. "The Moral Origins of Political Surveillance: The Preventive Society in New York City, 1867–1918." *American Quarterly* 38(4)Autumn:637–52.

Goldsmith, Barbara. 1999. *Other Powers*. New York: HarperPerennial.

Gordon, Ann D. 1997. *The Selected Papers of Elizabeth Cady Stanton and Susan B. Anthony*. New Brunswick: Rutgers University Press.

Heine, Heinrich. 1995. "A Ticket of Admission to European Culture (1823, c. 1854)." Document No. 6. *The Jew in the Modern World: A Documentary History*. 2nd ed. Ed. Paul Mendes-Flohr and Jehuda Reinharz. New York: Oxford University Press.

Hertz, Deborah. 1986. "Inside Assimilation: Rebecca Friedlander's Rahel Varnhagen." *German Women in the Eighteenth and Nineteenth Centuries: A Social and Literary History*. Eds. Ruth-Ellen B. Joeres and Mary Jo Maynes. Bloomington: Indiana University Press.

————. 1995. "Emancipation Through Intermarriage in Old Berlin." *Jewish Women in Historical Perspective*. Ed. Judith R. Baskin. Detroit: Wayne State University Press.

Holyoake, George Jacob. 1904. "Unpublished Correspondence of the Robert Owen Family Part II" (35)25:733, April 23 and "Part VII" (35)17:465, June 18. *The Cooperative News*. Held at the National Co-operative Archive at the Co-operative College, Manchester, UK.

Infidel Convention. 1860. October 7. Reported in *Boston Investigator*, November 7, 1860, "Minutes of Infidel Convention." (30)29:226–27.

Jacoby, Susan. 2004. *Freethinkers: A History of American Secularism*. New York: Henry Holt and Company.

Jewish Reconstructionist Federation Board and Staff. "Follow the Leader" 2(2):24. *Jewish Record*. 1864. February 19.

Kanter, Rosabeth. 1972. *Community and Commitment*. Cambridge: Harvard University Press.

Kellman, Ellie. 1997. "Women as Readers of Sacred and Secular (Yiddish) Literature: An Historical Overview." *Proceedings of the Conference of the National Council of Jewish Women*, New York Section, 18–21.

Kerzer, David I. 1999. *The Kidnapping of Edgardo Mortara*. New York: Vintage Books.

Kolmerten, Carol A. 1999. *The American Life of Ernestine L. Rose*. Syracuse, N.Y.: Syracuse University Press.

Kraditor, Aileen S. 1981. *The Ideas of the Woman Suffrage Movement: 1890–1920*. New York: W.W. Norton.

Lerner, Gerda. 1971. *The Grimké Sisters from South Carolina*: Pioneers for Women's Rights and Abolition. New York: Schocken.

————. 1998. *The Feminist Thought of Sarah Grimké*. New York: Oxford University Press.

Lohmann, Christoph, ed. 1999. *Radical Passion: Ottilie Assing's Reports from America and Letters to Frederick Douglass*. New York: Peter Lang Publishing.

Morris, Celia. 1992. *Fanny Wright: Rebel in America*. Urbana: University of Illinois Press.

Midgley, Clare. 1992. *Women Against Slavery: The British Campaigns, 1780–1830*. London: Routledge.

National American Woman Suffrage Association. 1940. *Victory: How Women Won It*. New York: H.W. Wilson Co.

Offen, Karen. 2000. *European Feminisms, 1700–1950: A Political History*. Palo Alto, Calif.: Stanford University Press.

Paine, Thomas. 1794. *The Age of Reason*. New York: T. & J. Swords for J. Fellows.

Parush, Iris. 1994. "Readers in Cameo: Women Readers in Jewish Society of Nineteenth-Century Eastern Europe." *Prooftexts: A Journal of Jewish Literary History* 14(1):1–23.

Post, Albert. 1943. *Popular Freethought in America, 1825–1850.* New York: Columbia University Press.

Post, Tim. 2002. "A Woman of Contradiction." Minnesota Public Radio. September 26. Online: http://news.minnesota.publicradio.org/features/200209/23_steilm_1862-m/swisshelm.shtml.

Robertson, John M. 1957. *A Short History of Freethought.* New York: Russell & Russell.

Rose, Mrs. E. L. 1851. *An Address on Woman's Rights Delivered Before the People's Sunday Meeting, on Oct. 19th, 1851 in Cochituate Hall.* Boston: J. P. Mendum.

Rose, Ernestine. 1860. Speech on First Day of Infidel Convention. *Boston Investigator.* November 7.

Royle, Edward. 2003. Personal communication with author. November 6.

Sartre, Jean Paul. 1995 [1946]. *Anti-Semite and Jew.* New York: Schocken Books.

Schappes, Maurice U. 1949. "Ernestine L. Rose: Her Address on the Anniversary of West Indian Emancipation." *Journal of Negro History* 34(July):344–55.

————, ed. 1971. *A Documentary History of the Jews in the United States: 1654–1875.* 3rd ed. New York: Schocken Books.

Schneir, Miriam. 1994 [1972]. *Feminism: The Essential Historical Writings.* New York: Vintage Books.

Sifakis, Stewart. 2003. "Who Was Who in the Civil War." (last updated November 22, 2003). www.civilwarhome.com/macbio.htm.

Sklar, Kathryn Kish. 2000. *Women's Rights Emerges Within the Antislavery Movement, 1830-1870.* New York: Bedford/ St. Martin's.

Soeffing, Donald. 1999. Personal communication with author. September 25. Daniel Soeffing, expert on 19th-century Silversmiths. PO Box 411, Stuyvesant Station, New York, NY.

Spartacus. n.d. "John Fremont." (last accessed October 10, 2007). www.spartacus.schoolnet.co.uk/USAfremont.htm.

Standage, Tom. 1998. *The Victorian Internet.* New York: Berkley Books.

Stanton, Elizabeth Cady. 1971 [1898]. *Eighty Years and More: Reminiscences, 1815–1897.* New York: Schocken Books.

Stanton, Elizabeth Cady, Susan B. Anthony, and Matilda Joslin Gage, eds. 1881–1886. *History of Woman Suffrage.* 6 vols. New York: Fowler and Wells.

Sterling, Dorothy. 1991. *Ahead of Her Time: Abby Kelley Foster and the Politics of Antislavery.* New York: W.W. Norton.

Suhl, Yuri. 1959. *Ernestine Rose and the Battle for Human Rights.* New York: Reynal & Company.

————. 1990. *Ernestine L. Rose: Women's Rights Pioneer.* 2nd ed. Introduction by Francoise Basch and Preface by Rosalyn Fraad Baxandall. New York: Biblio Press.

Taylor, Barbara. 1993. *Eve and the New Jerusalem.* Cambridge: Harvard University Press.

Von Mering, Sabine. 2000. Personal communication with author. Spring.

Voorsanger, Catherine Hoover, and John K. Howat, eds. 2000. *Art and the Empire City: New York, 1825-1861.* New York: Metropolitan Museum of Art/New Haven: Yale University Press.

Walker, Alice. 1983. "Looking for Zora." *In Search of Our Mothers' Gardens.* New York: Harcourt, Brace, Jovanovich, 93–116.

Warren, Sidney. 1966. *American Freethought, 1860–1914.* New York: Gordian Press.

*Women in the Life and Times of Abraham Lincoln.* 1963. Reissued of the Proceedings of the Meeting of the Loyal Women of the Republic by Emma Lazarus Federation.

New York: May 14, 1863, with a foreword by Daisy Bates. New York: Emma Lazarus Federation of Jewish Women's Clubs.

Worcester Women's History Project. 30 Elm St. Worcester, Mass., 01609. wwhp.org/Resources/WomansRights/members.html.

Yale, Caroline A. 1931. *Years of Building: Memories of a Pioneer in a Special Field of Education.* New York: Dial Press.

# SOURCES

1840 January 29: Toasts at the Thomas Paine Celebration. Published in the *Boston Investigator* February 19, 1840. *This and all issues of the* Boston Investigator *from the collection of The American Antiquation Society in Worcester, MA.* www.historylearningsite. co.uk/Chartism.htm.

1844 May 30: Speech at the New England Social Reform Society Convention: "A Word to My Sisters." Published in John A. Collins, *The Social Pioneer, and Herald of Progress* (Boston: J. P. Mendum, 1844), 73–74. From the collection of the Syracuse University Library.

1844 December: Letter to Robert Owen. From Robert Owen Correspondence, item no. 1344, National Co-operative Archive at the Co-operative College, Manchester, UK. Reprinted with the kind permission of the National Co-operative Archive.

1845 April 14: Letter to Robert Owen. From Robert Owen Correspondence, item no. 1362, National Co-operative Archive at the Co-operative College, Manchester, UK. Reprinted with the kind permission of the National Co-operative Archive.

1845 May 4: Speech at the Infidel Convention. Convention proceedings published in the *Boston Investigator*, May 14, 1845; continued on May 28, 1845.

1845 September 31 [*sic*]: Letter to Robert Owen. From Robert Owen Correspondence, item no. 1389, National Co-operative Archive at the Co-operative College, Manchester, UK. Reprinted with the kind permission of the National Co-operative Archive.

1849 January 29: Speech at the Thomas Paine Celebration: The 1848 Revolutions in Europe. Published in the *Boston Investigator*, February 21, 1849.

1850 January 29: Speech at the Thomas Paine Celebration: Women in International Freedom Fights. Published in the *Boston Investigator*, March 6, 1850; first reported on February 13, 1850, but reprinted at Rose's request in order to correct errors.

1850 October 23: Resolution and Speech at the First National Woman's Rights Convention: "Woman's Sphere." Published in the *New York Tribune* 10 (2972), October 25, 1850.

1851 September 4: Letter to the Editor: Sketches of Lecturing. Published in the *Boston Investigator*, October 1, 1851.

1851 June 15: Letter from Two French Women's Rights Reformers. Read to the Convention on October 15. Published in the *Proceedings of the Woman's Rights Convention, held at Worcester, October 15th and 16th, 1851* (New York: Fowler and Wells, 1852), 32–35 (Letter from Imprisoned French Feminists).

1851 October 15 and 16: Speeches at the Second National Woman's Rights Convention. Published in the *Proceedings of the Woman's Rights Convention, held at Worcester, October 15th and 16th, 1851* (New York: Fowler and Wells, 1852), 36–47 ("Unsurpassed" Speech), and 104 (Closing Remarks). From the National American Woman Suffrage Association Collection, Rare Book and Special Collections Division, Library of Congress. Online at Votes for Women: Selections from the National American Woman Suffrage Association Collection, 1848–1921, American Memory project, Library of Congress: http://memory.loc.gov/ammem/naw/nawshome.html.

1851 November 29: Letter to the Editor: "The *Tribune* and the Great Accident." Published in the *Boston Investigator*, December 10, 1851.

1852 February–March: Reviews of Horace Mann's Two Lectures. Published as Ernestine Rose, *Review of Horace Mann's Two Lectures, Delivered in New York, February 17 and 29th, 1852.* From the collection of the Houghton Library, Harvard University, shelfmark Tract 2205, no. 16.

1852 September 8–10: Speech and Debates at the Third National Woman's Rights Convention. Published in the *Proceedings of the Woman's Rights Convention held at Syracuse, September 8th, 9th & 10th, 1852* (Syracuse: J.E. Masters, 1852), 63–64 ("A Child of Israel" Speech); 66–74 (Debate on Biblical Authority). From the collection of the Arthur and Elizabeth Schlesinger Library on the History of Women in America, Radcliffe Institute for Advanced Study, Harvard University. Online at Votes for Women: Selections from the National American Woman Suffrage Association Collection, 1848–1921, American Memory project, Library of Congress: http://memory.loc.gov/ ammem/naw/nawshome.html. Most of Rose's speech concluding the first day of Bible Debate and resulting in the passing of her resolution was also published as one of a series of Woman's Rights Tracts (no. 9) that were widely circulated at the time, and are available at many public and university libraries.

1853 May 13: Speech at Robert Owen's Birthday Celebration. Published in the *Boston Investigator,* June 1, 1853.

1853 June 4 and 14: Speech at the Hartford Bible Convention and Letter Describing the Convention. Speech published in the *Proceedings of the Hartford Bible Convention* (New York: Partridge & Brittan, 1854). From the collection of the Yale University Divinity School Library. Letter published in the *Boston Investigator,* June 29, 1853.

1853 August 4: Speech at the Anniversary of West Indian Emancipation. Published in the *Liberator* 23 (33), August 19, 1853. Also reported in the *National Anti-slavery Standard* 14 (12), August 13, 1853. Both publications are from the microfilm collection of the Boston Public Library.

1853 September 9: Speeches at the New York State Woman's Rights Convention ("Mob Convention"). Published in the *Proceedings of the Woman's Rights Convention, held at The Broadway Tabernacle in the City of New York, on Sept. 6th and 7th, 1853* (New York: Fowler and Wells, 1853). From the collection of the Arthur and Elizabeth Schlesinger Library on the History of Women in America, Radcliffe Institute for Advanced Study, Harvard University (microfilm reel 942, no. 8506). Online at Votes for Women: Selections from the National American Woman Suffrage Association Collection, 1848–1921, American Memory project, Library of Congress: http://memory.loc.gov/ ammem/naw/nawshome.html.

1853 October 7: Speech at the Fourth National Woman's Rights Convention: "The Double Standard of Sexual Morality." Published in the *Proceedings of the National Woman's Rights Convention held at Cleveland, Ohio, on Wednesday, Thursday, and Friday, October 5th, 6th, and 7th, 1853* (Cleveland: Gray, Beardsley, Spear, & Co., 1854), 74–82. From the collection of the Arthur and Elizabeth Schlesinger Library on the History of Women in America, Radcliffe Institute for Advanced Study, Harvard University. Online at Votes for Women: Selections from the National American Woman Suffrage Association Collection, 1848–1921, American Memory project, Library of Congress: http://memory.loc.gov/ammem/naw/nawshome.html.

1854 March 3: Testimony Before Select Committee of the New York State Assembly. Published in the *Albany Argus,* March 4, 1854, reprinted in Stanton, Anthony, and Gage, *History of Woman Suffrage* (1881–1886), Vol. 1, 607–08.

1854 March 6 and 7: Attack in the *Albany Register* and Erntstine L. Rose's Response. Article published in the *Albany Register,* March 6, 1854; article and letter reprinted in Stanton, Anthony, and Gage, *History of Woman Suffrage* (1881–1886), Vol. 1, 608–10.

1854 March 24–April 14: Diary of Lecture Tour to the Border South with Ernestine L. Rose. From the Susan B. Anthony Papers, Arthur and Elizabeth Schlesinger Library on the History of Women in America, Radcliffe Institute for Advanced Study, Harvard University (microfilm reel 42, 8–29, 35–39).

1854 April 14: Letter to the Editor: "Slavery and Reform," by Susan B. Anthony, Lecture Tour to the Border South with Ernestine L. Rose. Published in the *Liberator* 24 (15), April 14, 1854. From the microfilm collection of the Boston Public Library.

1854 October 18: Speech at the Fifth National Woman's Rights Convention: "A Great and Immutable Truth." Published in Stanton, Anthony, and Gage, *History of Woman Suffrage* (1881–1886), Vol. 1, 375–77.

1855 January 29: Speech at the Thomas Paine Celebration: "The Rights of Woman." Published in the *Boston Investigator* 24 (42), February 14, 1855.

1855 February 18: Testimony Before Select Committee of the New York State Assembly. Report from the *Albany Register* reprinted in the *Boston Investigator* 24 (46), March 14, 1855.

1855 May 30: Speech at the New England Anti-Slavery Convention: "All Free or All Slave." Published in the *Liberator* 25 (23), June 8, 1855. From the microfilm collection of the Boston Public Library. Thanks to Carol A. Kolmerten for citing this little-known speech in her biography of Rose.

1855 November 20: Letters to the Editor: Lecture Tour of "the West" and the Legacy of Frances Wright. Published in the *Boston Investigator*, December 5, 1855.

1855 December: Letter to the Editor: "Mrs. Rose and the *Bangor Mercury*." Published in the *Boston Investigator*, December 26, 1855.

1856 January 28: Speech at the Thomas Paine Celebration: Defending Herself, Thomas Paine, and Freethinkers. Published in the *Boston Investigator* 25 (35), February 13, 1856.

1856 April 30: Letter to the Editor: "Farewell Letter of Mrs. Rose." Published in the *Boston Investigator* 26 (2), May 5, 1856.

1856 July 6: Travel Letter No. 2: Visiting Robert Owen. Published in the *Boston Investigator*, August 6, 1856.

1856 July 13: Travel Letter No. 3: The Tower of London, Symbol of Cruelty. Published in the *Boston Investigator*, August 13, 1856.

1856 September 30: Travel Letter No. 10: Manners and Morals of the French. Published in the *Boston Investigator*, December 3, 1856.

1856 October 20: Travel Letter No. 11: Italy and the Church. Published in the *Boston Investigator*, December 10, 1856.

1856 November 26: Speeches at the Seventh National Woman's Rights Convention. Published in the *Proceedings of the Seventh National Woman's Rights Convention, held in New York City, at the Broadway Tabernacle, on Tuesday and Wednesday, Nov. 25th and 26th 1856* (New York: Edward O. Jenkins, 1856), (Human Rights and Electoral Politics) and 34–35 (Women's Rights Struggles in Europe). From the collection of the New-York Historical Society.

1857 October 3: Letter to the Editor: "The English Divorce Bill." Published in the *Boston Investigator*, October 21, 1857.

1857 December 29: Letter to the Editor: "England Ruled by a Prayer Book." Published in the *Boston Investigator*, January 13, 1858.

1858 June 29: Letter to the Editor: "The Free Love Question." Published in the *Boston Investigator* 28 (14), July 28, 1858.

1859 January 31: Speech at the Thomas Paine Celebration: Separation of Church and State. Published in the *Boston Investigator* 28 (43), February 16, 1859.

1859 December 14: Letter to the Editor: "Rise, Progress, and Fall of a Free Church." Published in the *Boston Investigator* 29 (36), December 28, 1859.

1860 March 28: Letter to the Editor with Text of the New York State Married Women's Property Act. Published in the *Boston Investigator* 29 (51), April 11, 1860. Thanks to Carol A. Kolmerten for calling this document to my attention and for providing an early copy.

1860 May 10: Speech at the Tenth National Woman's Right Convention: Political Activism and Women's Rights. Published in the *Proceedings of the Tenth National Woman's Rights Convention, held at the Cooper Institute, New York City, May 10th and 11th, 1860* (Boston: Yerrinton & Garrison, 1860), 7–12 (Political Activism and Women's Rights). From the collection of the Houghton Library, Harvard University, shelfmark AL2954.7.11*, no. 21.

1860 May 11: The Divorce Debate. Published in the *Proceedings of the Tenth National Woman's Rights Convention, held at the Cooper Institute, New York City, May 10th and 11th, 1860* (Boston: Yerrinton & Garrison, 1860), 65–84 (Divorce Debate). From the collection of the Houghton Library, Harvard University, shelfmark AL2954.7.11*, no. 21.

1860 November: Petition: Appeal to the Women of New York. Published in Stanton, Anthony, and Gage, *History of Woman Suffrage* (1881–1886), Vol. 1, 742–44.

1861 January 29: Speech at the Thomas Paine Celebration: "Freedom or Slavery." Published in the *Boston Investigator* 30 (44), February 20, 1861.

1861 April 10: Speech: "A Defence of Atheism." Published as a reissue of an earlier publication, as Ernestine L. Rose, *A Defence of Atheism: Being a Lecture Delivered in Mercantile Hall, Boston, April 10, 1861* (Boston: J. P. Mendum, 1889). Available at many libraries, including the Yale University Divinity School Library and the Boston Public Library.

1862 January 27: Letter and Toast for the Committee of the Paine Celebration, Boston. Published in the *Boston Investigator* 31 (42), February 5, 1862.

1863 May 14: Speeches at the National Convention of the Loyal Women of the Republic. Published in *Women in the Life and Time of Abraham Lincoln* (New York: Emma Lazarus Federation of Jewish Women's Clubs, 1963), a facsimile reproduction of the *Proceedings of the Meeting of the Loyal Women of the Republic, held in New York, May 14, 1863*, with a preface by Daisy Bates. This reissued pamphlet was produced one hundred years after the original. Thanks to Sarah Hutcheon of the Schlesinger Library at Harvard University for finding this document under its new title. The Emma Lazarus Federation was a group dedicated to interracial activism, and Daisy Bates, a civil rights activist and mentor to the Little Rock Nine, referred to this important event of the Civil War period—one thousand white women coming together to demand freedom for enslaved people—as counter-evidence that she or "any Negro mother" could cite whenever her child asked her, "Do all white people hate us?"

1863 October 28–1864 April 13: Debate on the Jews in the *Boston Investigator*. Published in the *Boston Investigator* 33 (25), October 28, 1863 (Mann's editorial); 33 (40), February 10, 1864 (Rose's first letter—part 1); 33 (41), February 17, 1864 (first letter—part 2); 33 (42), February 24, 1864 (second letter—part 1); 33 (43), March 2, 1864 (second letter, part 2); 33 (44), March 9, 1864 (third letter, part 1); 33 (45), March 16, 1864 (third letter, part 2); 33 (48), April 6, 1864 (fourth letter, part 1); 33 (49), April 13, 1864 (fourth letter, part 2).

1867 May 10: Speech at the First Anniversary of the American Equal Rights Association: Voices for Votes. Published in the *Proceedings of the First Anniversary of the American Equal Rights Association held at the Church of the Puritans, New York, May 9 and 10, 1867* (New York: Robert J. Johnston, 1867), 43–47. From the National American Woman Suffrage Association Collection, Rare Book and Special Collections Division, Library of Congress. Online at Votes for Women: Selections from the National American Woman Suffrage Association Collection, 1848–1921, American Memory project, Library of Congress: http://memory.loc.gov/ammem/naw/nawshome.html.

1869 January 14: Letter to the National Woman Suffrage Convention in Washington, D.C. Published in the *Revolution* 4 (59), January 28, 1869, 356–57; reprinted in Stanton, Anthony, and Gage, *History of Woman Suffrage* (1881–1886), Vol. 2, 356–57.

1869 June 12: *The Champions of Woman's Suffrage*. Published in *Harper's Bazar*, 381.

1876 July 4: Letter to Susan B. Anthony: Reflections on the United States Centennial. Published in Stanton, Anthony, and Gage, *History of Woman Suffrage* (1881–1886), Vol. 2, 50–51. The Declaration of Rights of the Women of the United States appears in the same volume, 31–34.

1877 January 9: Letter to Susan B. Anthony: A Life of Activism. Published in Stanton, Anthony, and Gage, *History of Woman Suffrage* (1881–1886), Vol. 1, 98–100. The editors supplemented Rose's words with some commentary of their own, and added another short biography of Rose by L. E. Barnard.

1878 July 19: Letter to the National Woman Suffrage Association Convention in Rochester, New York. Published in Stanton, Anthony, and Gage, *History of Woman Suffrage* (1881–1886), Vol. 3, 120. Asterisks indicating omitted text appeared in this version; there is no known record of the full text of the letter.

1880 May 15: Letter to Elizabeth Cady Stanton for the National Woman Suffrage Association Convention of 1880. From Chicago History Museum. Chicago Historical Society/Chicago History Museum from the National Woman Suffrage Association. Thanks to Deborah Vaughan at the Chicago History Museum.

1882 February 22: Obituary for William E. Rose by J.P. Mendum. Published in the *Boston Investigator* 51 (45), February 22, 1882.

1892 August 8: Eulogy for Ernestine L. Rose by George Jacob Holyoake. Published in the *Boston Investigator* 62 (21), August 24, 1892, reprinted from the *London Daily News*, August 9, 1892.

1893 January 16–19: Tribute to Ernestine L. Rose at the 25th Annual Convention of the National American Woman Suffrage Association held in Washington, D.C., 22–23. By Elizabeth Cody Stanton. Proceedings from Schlesinger Library, Harvard University. Thanks to Sarah Hutcheon, Reference Librarian.

# INDEX